The Economics
of Equal Opportunities

**Edited by
Jane Humphries
and Jill Rubery**

EQUAL OPPORTUNITIES COMMISSION

The Economics
of Equal Opportunities

Edited by
Jane Humphries
University of Cambridge

Jill Rubery
UMIST

Learning Resources
Centre

The research on which this study is based was supported
by the Equal Opportunities Commission. The views
expressed are those of the authors and do not necessarily
represent the views of the Commission.

Equal Opportunities Commission
Overseas House, Quay Street,
Manchester M3 3HN

Also in London, Cardiff and Glasgow

CONTENTS

TABLES AND FIGURES

Abbreviations

ABS	Australian Bureau of Statistics
ACAS	Advisory, Conciliation and Arbitration Service
ACTU	Australian Council of Trade Unions
AMB	Area Manpower Board
CBI	Confederation of British Industry
CBS	Central Bureau of Statistics
CCT	compulsory competitive tendering
CDL	Career Development Loan
CEDEFOP	European Centre for the Development of Vocational Training
CERE	Centre d'Etudes des Revenus et des Couts
COB/SER	Commissie Ontwikkeling Bedrijven/ Sociaal Economische Raad
DSS	Department of Social Security
EC	European Community
ED	Employment Department
ELM	external labour market
EOC	Equal Opportunities Commission
ESRC	Economic and Social Research Council
ET	Employment Training
EU	European Union
FC	Family Credit
FES	Family Expenditure Survey
FNV	Dutch Federation of Trade Unions
FT	Financial Times
GCSE	General Certificate of Secondary Education
GDP	gross domestic product
IAP	individual action plan
IDS	Incomes Data Services
ILM	internal labour market
ILO	International Labour Organisation
IMS	Institute of Manpower Studies
IPPR	Institute of Public Policy Research
IRC	Industrial Relations Commission
ISCO	International Standard Classification for Occupations
JAM	job classification, adversarial relations and minimal training
LAP	labour adjustment package
LEC	Local Enterprise Company
LEL	lower earnings limit
LFS	Labour Force Survey
LTD	Loontechnische Dienst
MCTA	married couple's tax allowance
MSC	Manpower Services Commission
NACETT	National Advisory Council for Education and Training Targets
NATFHE	National Association of Teachers in Further and Higher Education
NBER	National Bureau of Economic Research
NCDS	National Child Development Study
NES	New Earnings Survey
NHS	National Health Service
NI	National Insurance
NIACE	National Institute of Adult Continuing Education
NIESR	National Institute of Economic and Social Research
NIMMO	Netherlands Institute for Market Research
NTETs	National Training and Education Targets
NVQ	National Vocational Qualification

OECD	Organisation for Economic Co-operation and Development		WRR	Wetenschappelijke Raad voor het Regeringsbeleid
OPCS	Office of Population Censuses and Surveys			
ORF	output-related funding		YC	Youth Credit
			YT	Youth Training
			YTS	Youth Training Scheme
PRF	performance-related funding			
PSI	Policy Studies Institute			
RAAF	Royal Australian Air Force			
SDA	Sex Discrimination Act, 1975			
SERPS	State Earnings-related Pension Scheme			
SET	security of employment, employee involvement and training			
SIAU	Survey and Information Analysis Unit, Sheffield Hallam University			
SOC	standard occupational classification			
STNs	special training needs			
TC	training credit			
TCF	textiles, clothing and footwear			
TEC	Training and Enterprise Council			
TfW	Training for Work			
TOA	TEC operating agreement			
TOPS	Training Opportunities Programme			
TP	training plan			
TUC	Trades Union Congress			
UEL	upper earnings limit			
USDAW	Union of Shop, Distributive and Allied Workers			
VAT	value added tax			
VET	vocational education and training			
WES	Women and Employment Survey			
WIRS	Workplace Industrial Relations Survey			

List of Contributors

Irene Bruegel

School of Land Management and Urban Policy
South Bank University

Hugh Davies

Department of Economics
Birbeck College, University of London

Shirley Dex

ESRC Research Centre on Micro-Social Change
University of Essex

Alan Felstead

Centre for Labour Market Studies
University of Leicester

Paul Gregg

Centre for Economic Performance
London School of Economics and Political Science/
National Institute of Economic and Social Research

Damian Grimshaw

Manchester School of Management
UMIST

Sally Holtermann

Independent Research Economist

Jane Humphries

Faculty of Economics and Politics
University of Cambridge

Laurie Hunter

Department of Social and Economic Research
University of Glasgow

Heather Joshi

Social Statistics Research Unit
City University

Friederike Maier

Fachhochschule fur Wirtschaft
Germany

Gerry Makepeace

Department of Economics
University of Hull

Eithne McLaughlin

Department of Sociology and Social Policy
The Queen's University of Belfast

Neil Millward

Centre for Economic Performance
London School of Economics and Political Science/
Policy Studies Institute

Pierella Paci

Social Statistics Research Unit
City University

Diane Perrons

Department of Economics
London Guildhall

Janneke Plantenga

Economisch Instituut/CIAV
Universiteit Utrecht, Netherlands

Sheila Rimmer

Ormond College
University of Melbourne, Australia

Jill Rubery

Manchester School of Management
UMIST

Malcolm Sawyer

School of Business and Economics Studies
University of Leeds

Roger Sewell

Sangar Centre
University of Cambridge

Jonathan Wadsworth

Centre for Economic Performance
London School of Economics and Political Science/
National Institute of Economic and Social Research

Stephen Woodland

Centre for Economic Performance
London School of Economics and Political Science

ACKNOWLEDGEMENTS

This book is the outcome of a seminar organised by the Equal Opportunities Commission in October 1994 with additional financial support from the Economic and Social Research School. However, the responsibility for the views expressed lies with the authors concerned and not with the EOC or ESRC.

The project was developed with the aid of an Advisory Group consisting of: Kate Barker (Confederation of British Industry), Bill Callaghan (Trades Union Congress), Ira Chalphin, Zmira Hornstein (Employment Department), Pamela Meadows (Policy Studies Institute), Bill Solesbury (Economic and Social Research Council), Michael Taylor (Institute of Directors) and Stephen Ward (Institute of Personnel and Development). We are grateful to these individuals, and organisations which they represent, for their support and advice. EOC Chairwoman Kamlesh Bahl and EOC Commissioners Mary Berg and Clive Mather also played an active role in the Advisory Group and we thank them for their help. We would especially like to thank those members of the Advisory Group who took time out of their busy schedules to chair sessions: Kate Barker, Mary Berg, Ira Chalphin, Bill Solesbury and Pamela Meadows. Peter Naish, Susan Atkins and Frank Spencer, all of the EOC, also kindly chaired sessions.

The seminar was enriched by a number of discussants who led the responses to the papers in each session: Irene Bruegel, Paul Edwards, Diane Elson, Colette Fagan, Malcolm Sawyer and Holly Sutherland. We also thank other participants in the seminar for their useful contributions. Domestic arrangements were facilitated by White Rose Conferences to which we express our thanks.

We are also grateful to Damian Grimshaw and Eloise Turner at UMIST and to Peter Humphreys, Ed Puttick and Claire Faichnie of the EOC Research Unit for their help in the administration of the project and especially to Claire who also helped in the production of the final manuscript. Cherry Ekins copy edited and proof read each chapter.

Our biggest debt, of course, is to the contributors who made this book possible.

CHAPTER 1 # Introduction

Jane Humphries and Jill Rubery

Although the desirability of equality of opportunities between men and women is now widely accepted on ethical grounds, the perceived costs of equal opportunities policies act as barriers to change. Economic calculations appear to drive a wedge between morally desirable outcomes and the practical pursuit of efficiency. Policy interventions are held to threaten competitiveness. If they are to challenge this verdict, equal opportunity activists must engage with the theory and practice of economics, or risk equal opportunities policies being 'priced out of the market'. This collection of papers initiates such a project.

The first task is to consider the treatment of gender within economic theory and take stock of recent developments in the analysis of discrimination. Contributors to this volume perceive deep inadequacies in the treatment of gender differences, relating these to the narrow, static and ahistorical perspective of orthodox economics. This critique provides a theoretical framework within which to consider the costs and benefits of equal opportunities policies, understand these costs and benefits broadly, pursue the analysis at several different economic levels (for example, macro as well as micro, dynamic as well as static, and social as well as private), and compare and contrast policy impacts in terms of the structure and distribution of the gains and losses.

An economic perspective which embodies a deeper treatment of gender demands that social and economic institutions be recognised as significant. Three areas where institutional structures play a crucial role in the persistence of unequal opportunities are analysed by contributors: the acquisition of skills and access to employment; occupational segregation; and the maintenance of workers, raising of children and care of the elderly, summarised here as social reproduction.

Gendered skill formation and women's differential access to employment and careers is shown to be heavily dependent on the institutional organisation of training and education. Occupational segregation is a pervasive feature of all labour markets, but its implications for the economics of equal opportunities flow through its interaction with industrial organisation and systems of pay determination.

Social reproduction involves considerable labour input, much of it unpaid in the home but some of it paid in the form of services sold on the market. Women perform a disproportionate amount of this labour, which in turn conditions the extent and pattern of their participation in paid work. Their position and status is directly and indirectly affected by the institutional structures within which social reproduction takes place. The division of responsibilities for social reproduction has developed historically and untidily, and is reflected in complex interrelationships between the state, households and the labour market. These interrelationships may not appear logical, but partial adjustments which occur autonomously or as a result of policy initiatives may have knock-on effects creating intolerable pressures elsewhere or leaving individuals and families exposed to new economic conditions without customary social supports. Equal opportunities policies must be orchestrated around these interrelationships.

Gender and economic analysis: one step forward, two steps back?

Definition of discrimination

Positions taken in policy discussions in economics are always based on specific theoretical perspectives, though as Malcolm Sawyer points out in Chapter 2 these are seldom made explicit. The evaluation of equal opportunities policies is no exception. Views on how markets operate, and specifically how the labour market works, emerge as crucial. The overriding importance of the theoretical perspective taken is demonstrated in Chapter 2. Sawyer contrasts the dominant (and often implicit) neo-classical theory of a deregulated labour market with that associated with an alternative eclectic approach, and draws out their contrasting implications for the evaluation of equal opportunities policies.

Many objections to the way in which the economic analysis of gender proceeds derive from the unsatisfactory definition of discrimination embedded in the neo-classical theory of the labour market. Economists do not identify discrimination with labour market outcomes. As one orthodox economist recently put it, 'even if women were treated equally to men in terms of labour market opportunities, there is the distinct prospect that labour market outcomes would continue to be unequal' (Main, 1993: 22). Market outcomes reflect many differences among individuals and between men and women. These include tastes and endowments which affect productivity both directly and indirectly, for example by influencing occupational choice or work continuity, as well as pre-market behaviour in the acquisition of characteristics which enhance productivity, such as education and training. The systematic variation of such wage-generating characteristics with gender is cited as a defence of the use of sex, a readily-observable characteristic, as a proxy for productivity, a much less easily observed characteristic, in promotion and hiring decisions.

Discrimination, as defined in neo-classical economics, relates only to that portion of the gender wage gap which cannot be attributed to differences in productivity-enhancing characteristics. At the empirical level there is now a standard procedure for decomposing an observed average male–female wage gap into two parts: a component which is attributable to differences in wage-generating characteristics; and an otherwise unexplained residual which is identified with discrimination. One interpretation of the residual is that it represents differences in returns that males and females get for the same human capital.

Once discrimination is defined in this way, the structural incompatibility between neo-classical economics and discrimination becomes apparent. Discriminatory outcomes are not easily deduced from the standard axioms and usual behavioural assumptions. Theories of discrimination, as Jane Humphries shows in her survey in Chapter 3, do not seem adequate to explain what is a pervasive real-world phenomenon. Taste-based models of discrimination dominate the literature, but are inherently tautological (see Humphries, this volume, Chapter 3). Economists have generally agreed that customer discrimination could only play a minor part in the differences observed in earnings. The intuitively more realistic case where groups of employees dislike working with each other has attracted less attention, probably because it is not readily subjected to formal testing. Significantly it plays a key role in many feminist accounts of labour market inequality. But on its own it is not entirely consistent with empirical reality. Employer discrimination is again intuitively attractive as a source of discrimination, but the problem here is that with free entry in the product market, competition among firms is supposed to ensure that discriminating employers are eventually driven out of business.

Statistical theories of discrimination, too, though able to show how high-quality women may earn less than their male counterparts, which is a kind of discrimination, are not able to generate the type of empirical phenomenon observed (group differences in earnings unrelated to measured attributes) unless extended in various ways or accompanied by assumptions which seem incompatible with robust competition; for example, that employers make systematic mistakes. Thus:

> persistent discrimination remains somewhat of a puzzle to economists... because [the] competitive mechanism [would] lead to competition for any labour that is paid less than its true market worth or that is used in ways that do not bring out its full productivity. But this very competition, of course, drives wages up towards their full market value and discrimination is eliminated. (Main, 1993: 24.)

All this creates a dilemma for equal opportunity activists. Tolerating the definition of discrimination as a residual unexplained by differences in human capital secures a powerful alliance with orthodox economics: discrimination is identified with inefficiency as well as inequity, and both economists and advocates of equal opportunities seek its elimination. But economists and equal opportunity activists may not agree about policy solutions. For economists the way out is much more likely to be through wage flexibility than through intervention. Indeed, it is commonly argued that by outlawing differential wage payments by gender, sex discrimination legislation blunts the efficacious workings of the market mechanism and, ironically, prevents the very change that it seeks to foster: greater equality. Intervention has the unintended consequence of preserving discrimination (see Polachek and Siebert, 1993; Main, 1993).

Feminists prefer 'error discrimination' as an explanation of the empirical evidence. Here employers wrongly believe that women are less productive than men, and so mistakenly underpay women. But while this can explain observed differences in men's and women's pay seemingly unrelated to their human capital, it sits uneasily with neo-classical economics. Mistaken behaviour should not persist in competitive markets. More fundamentally, feminists balk at economists' basic approach. They doubt that the existing differences between male and female workers explain as much of the earnings gap as alleged and, most importantly, challenge economists' interpretation of these differences as the products of free choice or essential differences between men and women.

For feminists the differences themselves are socially constructed: the products of a history of subordination. In this way new realism is injected into some otherwise weak scenarios. Take the case of error discrimination, rejected because of its corollary – the persistence of systematic mistakes. Suppose that employers, wrongly in the first instance, perceive women as less productive than men. But suppose that they act on that perception not only in terms of their pay offers but in their assignment of women to specific jobs and their extension of training to women. Differences in the treatment of male and female workers create cumulative differences in the relative productivity of inherently similar men and women. The employers' perception was a self-fulfilling prophecy; it discriminated against women, but this discrimination was buried in the processes of job allocation and training and would not show up as an unexplained residual in a wage equation. Alternatively, then, unequal labour market outcomes are seen as *prima-facie* evidence of inequality, albeit often originating outside the labour market and perhaps even conveyed through gendered differences in behaviour.

In contrast, the tension between the existence of discrimination and the neo-classical view of the world pulls economists in the opposite direction: to reduce the part of observed wage differences which is ascribed to discrimination. Within the human capital model it is possible to argue that even different rewards for the same measured characteristics do not necessarily imply discrimination; they could be explained by bad measurement and/or unobserved characteristics. Employers may well have a clearer view of the worth of employees than do economists judging from afar and on the basis of selected inadequately-measured variables.

Gone now is the basis for an alliance between feminists and economists. Policy interventions aimed at equalising labour market outcomes, which fail to recognise that if men and women on average are different an efficient allocation of resources will reward them differently, run the risk of distorting the working of the market system and pushing employers away from their cost-minimising positions.

Empirical analyses serve to identify the proximate determinants of gendered differences in wages. But econometrics is no substitute for thought. These analyses do not resolve the debate about discrimination, which in this context simply becomes focused on the meaning of the independent variables. Do the regressors used to explain wage differences in the decomposition of an observed pay gap represent free choice by women and/or optimisation by families, or discrimination? To take an important example from the literature, women do participate less continuously than men and this is significantly correlated with relative pay. But this does not demonstrate that discontinuous participation really does adversely affect productivity. It could simply be an excuse used by employers to justify underpaying women. Even if discontinuous participation does reduce women's relative productivity, is it correct to see it as the product of free choice, or of social norms which benefit dominant males?

Even within orthodox economics there is debate about what variables can legitimately be included as non-discriminatory explanations of women's relatively low pay and what variables are inadmissible. Human capital theorists implicitly assume that labour is mobile across firms and occupations, and argue that only those variables which reflect the characteristics of individuals are admissible (see Paci *et al.*, this volume, Chapter 4). Other systematic differences between men and women, such as the occupation and type of firm in which they work, which appear correlated with pay differences are held to pick up discriminatory structures which channel men and women into different segments of the labour market. But it could be that occupation and job characteristics reflect gendered differences in preferences and so should be included in the decomposition of the wage gap, as otherwise discrimination will be overestimated.

As Pierella Paci and her co-authors warn in Chapter 4 (93):

> In reality any gender differences in occupational distribution and in other job characteristics are likely to reflect both employment discrimination and different preferences between the two groups. This means that the human capital specification, by treating all job-related differences as discriminatory, will overestimate the extent of discrimination. On the other hand, the more extensive model with job-related controls may underestimate the full magnitude of gender discrimination to the extent that there are discriminatory processes in the gendering of occupational and job-related outcomes.

But if statistical analyses do not answer the difficult question of where discrimination starts and legitimate market response to free choice ends, they still have important uses. The revelation that occupational and job-related variables are systematically related to differences in pay can be read as introducing the role of gendered choice, or as showing the way in which discrimination occurs. Paci *et al.*'s study, while itself adopting a conventional definition of discrimination as the residual portion of the gender wage gap left unexplained after controlling for a variety of differences between men and women, openly acknowledges that other interpretations of the statistical correlations are possible. By studying the determination of the relative earnings of part-time women separately, and by going beyond personal characteristics to include other labour market characteristics as independent variables (particularly size and sector of firm, and occupation and its degree of segregation) the results can be interpreted as showing the ways in which discrimination occurs.

For example, Paci *et al.* find that as employment in a small firm is associated with relatively low pay, and as women, especially part-timers, are more likely to work in small firms, controlling for firm size increases the 'explained' component of the pay gap, especially the full-time/part-time gap. The lower pay associated with small firms, in turn, is explained by the extent of monopoly power in the product and labour markets and employees' access to an internal market, which is more commonly found in larger firms where more complete information on individual productivity is more likely.

But why is it that women, particularly part-timers, are more likely to work in small firms given this context? Many reasons can be suggested, but most involve not some exogenous preference for small firms on women's part but rather the operation of constraints associated with gender differences in domestic and childcare responsibilities. Whether these aspects of what Irene Bruegel and Diane Perrons in Chapter 7 call 'the gender order' are taken as reflecting (optimal) specialisation within families or social conventions constructed to benefit dominant males remains undecided.

Take another important finding: that the most powerful explanatory factor accounting for the wage gap between full-time men and women is the segregation of the occupation. Does this demonstrate that women are prepared to sacrifice higher pay for their preferences for working in certain (feminised) occupations? If so, women's relatively low pay represents a compensating differential and is not discriminatory. Alternatively, it can be read as showing that discrimination operates through sex segregation rather than unequal pay for the same work: a hypothesis confirmed by other studies (Gunderson, 1989). As Paci *et al.* remark in Chapter 4, in motivating their choice of independent variables occupational segregation inhibits the effectiveness of equal pay legislation. It follows that equal opportunities policies must go beyond equal pay legislation to policies which allow comparisons of 'like work', and which emphasise equal access to employment and break down institutional and cultural barriers to entry (see also Millward and Woodland, this volume, Chapter 10). But note that even in the context of equal pay for equal value, it is more difficult to claim equal pay when male comparators are hard to find (Paci *et al.*, this volume, Chapter 4).

The broader the definition of discrimination, the wider the range of policy initiatives suggested. Here again the conflict with orthodox economics becomes almost inevitable. Studies have pointed to the importance of differences in cultural norms and education, for example, in influencing choice of jobs: an important determinant of gendered differences in labour market outcomes. Feminists want to examine the source of gendered preferences. Economists take preferences as given. But the feminist case is bolstered by the interaction between what happens in the 'market' and what happens 'pre-market'. The market is, after all, embedded in the society, as several contributors in Part 1 of this volume emphasise. Women's preferences are not autonomous but moulded by their experience and expectations, and so in part at least are responses to the *status quo*, including discrimination.

It has been noted that orthodox economists believe that, by and large, unequal market outcomes are not discriminatory but originate in gendered preferences and family optimisation. Why? It is argued that if they were discriminatory they imply inefficiency, and inefficiency simply cannot persist. The argument is circular, as feminists have long contended. It also derives from a specific theoretical perspective on the deregulated labour market, namely that it operates efficiently and effectively (see Sawyer, this volume, Chapter 2). But does it mean that equal opportunity activists must mount their case only on grounds of justice, accepting that equal opportunities interventions will impose costs in the first instance on employers, who may then pass them on to consumers via higher prices or back to employees via reduced employment? Do equal opportunity policies distort the necessarily efficient (market) allocation of resources?

Perhaps it is important to try to measure these costs at least insofar as they fall on employers, as Sally Holtermann does in Chapter 6. Perhaps even efficient market outcomes may be considered socially sub-optimal if distribution (across individuals and groups) is taken into account. In this case total social welfare can be increased by policy measures which redistribute well-being. But this argument has to be conducted at the level of high theory and involves the comparison of gains and losses experienced by individuals through a social welfare function. Fortunately there is no need to retreat to this rarefied if higher ground; it is enough to contest the theoretical framework as Sawyer (Chapter 2) does through his eclectic alternative to the neo-classical interpretation of the labour market.

On one level it is easy to challenge the theoretical framework which reads labour market outcomes as necessarily efficient. Economists themselves acknowledge that market solutions are not efficient in many contexts, suitably summarised as 'market failures'. Markets fail, *inter alia*, if private costs and benefits do not capture social costs and benefits, if static costs and benefits do not capture dynamic costs and benefits, if there are asymmetries of information, and if changes impose transition costs on agents who are not then able to capture the benefits which accrue. Most economists believe that market failures justify intervention which, by shifting behaviour, produces a superior allocation of resources, though many recognise that intervention itself imposes costs of various kinds which have to be set against the purported benefits. Some argue that intervention usually (always), by interfering with competition, imposes more costs than it provides benefits in the form of improved allocation. This leads back to the opposition of economists to equal opportunities policies.

Nonetheless, the way forward is clear. Equal opportunity activists must show that market failures characterise labour markets and contribute to unequal outcomes for men and women, and that therefore equal opportunities policies can provide benefits although they may impose costs. The eclectic model of the labour market, because it admits a variety of market failures, suggests that competition does not necessarily work to eliminate discrimination. Indeed, Sawyer shows how it is likely to reinforce discrimination through feedbacks, cumulative causation and interlinkages between market allocations and pre-market decisions; mechanisms which echo the feminists' critique of the neo-classical approach to discrimination. In consequence, not only are equal opportunity policies needed to mitigate market tendencies, but they may do so without damaging efficiency. Damian Grimshaw and Jill Rubery (this volume, Chapter 5) also contest the neo-classical perspective and explore the implications of an important example of market failure in the existence of internal markets. The chapters by Holtermann and Bruegel and Perrons in Part 2 initiate the cost-benefit analysis of equal opportunities policies.

Impact of new neo-classical institutionalism: progress and problems

Traditional approaches to gendered pay differentials assume that market failures are exceptional. In general, pay reflects human capital and productivity differences. But recently orthodox economics has undergone a silent revolution (see Humphries, this volume, Chapter 3). The new neo-classical institutionalism recognises the ubiquity of market failure and drives a variety of wedges between pay and productivity distributions. To what extent do these new approaches provide the basis for deeper understanding of gendered differences in labour market outcomes?

Humphries, in Chapter 3, suggests that insofar as neo-classical institutionalism sees institutions as continuously (if glacially) rationalised and replaced as agents seize new opportunities to achieve their aims at minimum cost, it merely replicates orthodox neo-classical economics' celebration of the *status quo*. Institutional efficiency is assured by individuals' rational pursuit of their self-interest. But even authors who earlier promulgated such a Panglossian view have come to recognise the possibility of institutional inertia associated with the development of vested interests and the entrenchment of power relations. Thus Douglas North writes:

> The resultant path of institutional change is shaped by (1) the lock-in that comes from the symbiotic relationship between institutions and the organisations that have evolved as a consequence of the incentive structure provided by those institutions, and (2) the feedback process by which human beings perceive and react to changes in the opportunity set. (North, 1990: 7.)

There may be scope here to develop a more satisfactory analysis of gender inequality. Neo-classical institutionalism highlights the possibility of enduring sub-optimality; transactions and transition costs associated with path dependencies (where equilibria are not uniquely determined but affected by the sequence of previous choices); the prevalence of bounded rationality (limits on individuals' abilities to acquire, process and act on information), and x-inefficiency (failure to minimise costs within the internal organisation of the firm); and the significance of power relationships and their importance in implicit contracts extending over time. Contributions to this volume show how these characteristics of economies help to explain gender discrimination and offer scope for effective and efficient policy interventions.

Research increasingly points to the significance of industrial and organisational factors in explaining wage differentials (Paci *et al.*, this volume, Chapter 4; Millward and Woodland, this volume, Chapter 10). But this has not led to systematic exploration of the links between employers' pay determination and employment policies and gender discrimination. Grimshaw and Rubery (this volume, Chapter 5) provide such an analysis in the important case of internal labour markets.

New institutional theories of internal labour markets represent a significant development of the orthodox neo-classical model of the labour market. Internal labour market theorists do not assume price-taking firms in which the wage paid matches the worker's contribution – the marginal productivity of labour. Economists with this approach highlight the institutional construction of the labour market and suggest that it influences labour market outcomes. For example, some models of the internal labour market formalise the impact of custom and fairness on the employment contract. Another set of models explores the implications of efficiency wages – wages which do not simply reflect workers' productivity, but which induce effort. Internal labour market theorists also focus on problems created by firm-specific skills.

By introducing a new indeterminacy into the relation between wages and productivity, internal labour market theory appears to offer scope for greater understanding of unequal labour market outcomes. But as Grimshaw and Rubery (this volume, Chapter 5) demonstrate, as a framework within which to analyse gender inequality, models of internal labour markets as currently understood have important limitations. Introducing a gender perspective reveals the diversity of forms that internal labour markets can take. The implications of internal labour markets for gender inequality essentially depend on the form of the internal market, which Grimshaw and Rubery relate to the interplay between internal and external factors. Internal labour markets may provide women with some protection from the exigencies of the external market, or may codify and reinforce discrimination generally. Again, the costs and benefits need to be investigated empirically.

One important implication of Grimshaw and Rubery's analysis of internal labour markets, which is characteristic of approaches based on the new institutional economics more generally, is that there appears to be considerable potential for economic organisations and structures to persist even when characterised by inefficiency. Attempts to move towards wage equity may impose substantial transactions and transition costs associated with institutional change. In the longer term the costs of mitigating discrimination may be outweighed by efficiency gains which flow from a superior allocation and development of labour. But these notional gains may not be apparent to individual employers, both because they may only materialise in the future and because they may be contingent on changes being made by several employers in concert. Moreover, individual employers may doubt their ability to capture the benefits produced by less inequality in the labour market, but are convinced that they will have to shoulder some of the costs.

The difficulties involved in making transitions from one kind of labour market to another when the transition requires decentralised individual action, and when the costs and benefits of the changes are uncertain and variable in their distribution over time and across employers, were introduced by Sawyer in Chapter 2. They are picked up and further developed in Chapter 7 by Bruegel and Perrons.

Recognition that not all firms will be cost-minimising at all times provides employers with some degrees of freedom. In turn this casts new light on discrimination. Slack in the system enables employers with prejudice to discriminate without necessarily or immediately being driven out of business by competition.

Another important implication of the application of the new institutional economics to the analysis of gender inequality, which goes hand in hand with the possibility of persisting inefficiency, is the possibility for employers to benefit in different ways and to differing extents from inequality embedded in labour market structures. Some employers may compete via cheap labour, and be able to do so because of their position in the labour market. It follows that not all employers have the same interests in dismantling inequality of opportunity in the labour market. Some employers may see equal opportunities legislation as in their interests, since it may well validate their existing good employment practices and prevent 'unfair' competition. Other employers may be opposed, because such intervention may seem incompatible with their way of competing. This heterogeneity implies the possibility of alliances between equal opportunities activists and some employers, as well as of opposition to intervention. Again, this implication is developed.

Levels of analysis

This critique of the neo-classical view of the labour market, and the definition of discrimination embedded in it, implies that a broader definition of discrimination and its effects is needed. Analysis of the costs and benefits of equal opportunities must be consistent with this broader perspective. The perspective of the individual and the firm is important, and the credibility of the case for equal opportunities policies must include an analysis of costs and benefits at this level (see Holtermann, this volume, Chapter 6). But it should not crowd out the relevance of economy-wide, social and dynamic perspectives. Focusing on these levels of analysis might seem to break with tradition, but in many other areas (for example the theory of comparative advantage in international trade, and choice of technique in development economics) it has long been recognised that market solutions may be socially and dynamically inefficient. These results extend to the labour market in ways which have significance for gender inequality.

The conventional analysis of a deregulated labour market suggests that it would demonstrate static efficiency, that is an efficient allocation of existing resources. In fact, as Sawyer points out in Chapter 2, many of the challenges to neo-classical theory contained in the eclectic approach question even this conclusion. But over and above these doubts, it is widely recognised even within the conventional paradigm that the deregulated labour market may not demonstrate dynamic efficiency. The market fails to secure the optimal level of investment in skills and training because the benefits of training may not be captured in full by those incurring the costs. Similarly, the deregulated labour market may not demonstrate social efficiency; again readily illustrated by investment in skills and training. Not only the individuals involved in the training decision but society more generally benefit from better educated and trained citizens. Private provision of training is therefore likely to be sub-optimal. The gender implications of this classic case of market failure are developed further by Felstead in Chapter 8.

The distinction between micro- and macro-efficiency is also relevant. Micro-efficiency refers to the result of each economic agent operating as best they can in the face of the constraints they face, including those arising from the behaviour of others. Macro-efficiency is the efficiency of the global outcome. Again there is a strong presumption in much neo-classical economic analysis that micro-efficiency will lead to macro-efficiency, mirrored within neo-classical institutionalism by the theme that if there are possibilities for improvement they will be taken, and so at a minimum there will be movement towards the best global outcome. Such Panglossian economics are seen by Humphries (this volume, Chapter 3) as ultimately blunting the usefulness of the paradigm by replicating the support for the market outcome embedded in conventional neo-classical economics only in a dynamic context and in a world where institutions are important but ultimately malleable.

There are well-known objections to these ideas. In terms of conventional economic theory, 'the prisoner's dilemma' (see Sawyer, this volume, Chapter 2) is the best-known expression of the case in which the pursuit of self-interest in a non-co-operative framework can lead to the worst outcome rather than the best. Several contributors, notably Bruegel and Perrons (this volume, Chapter 7), express individuals' difficulties in breaking out of the gender order in terms of a 'prisoner's dilemma'. Economic agents remain locked into an inherited set of gendered roles and behaviours, even though an alternative organisation involving concerted changes in economic, social and familial roles might be preferred. This raises the question of how social reproduction, and particularly the privatisation of most of its costs in the family, relates to the analysis of economic efficiency.

Modifications of the conventional vision of the deregulated labour market and the derived interpretation of market outcomes, some suggested within mainstream theory, some highlighted by the new institutional economics and some prompted by the deliberate consideration of different levels of analysis, mean that the analysis of equal opportunity policies becomes a whole new ball game. There is no necessary clash with efficiency. There may be losses and there may be gains. The balance is an empirical issue. But there is at least the possibility that these policies, far from imposing heavy costs, actually have positive effects on economic growth and performance.

Costs and benefits of equal opportunities

Developing a cost-benefit analysis of equal opportunities

To what extent can the costs of equal opportunities policies be measured at the level of the employer/firm? Holtermann in Chapter 6 surveys the quantitative evidence available on the costs to employers of providing conditions of employment which make it easier to combine work and family responsibilities. Holtermann begins with the working conditions and employment rights legally required according to the Sex Discrimination and Equal Pay Acts, and then considers recent and mooted changes in these statutory minima under the headings of maternity provisions, paternity leave, parental leave, leave for family reasons, assistance with childcare, reductions in hours, terms of employment for part-time workers, flexible working arrangements and in-work training.

Several of the recent and potential changes derive from EC directives. Since, by and large, women are mainly responsible for childcare and housework, such 'family-friendly' policies ease the pressures on women workers even if in the first instance the policies benefit men (paternity leave, for example). Estimates of the costs of such policies inevitably involve making assumptions about the take-up of benefits as well as about their specific terms; for example, the duration of the various family leave entitlements and whether they are paid or unpaid. A big problem is to estimate the indirect costs in terms of the disruption entailed by a worker's absence or the introduction of a temporary replacement for a worker on leave.

Even at the level of the individual employer, equal opportunities policies are not wholly negative, as Holtermann's chapter shows. Some benefits accrue to employers who offer family-friendly employment, in terms of greater worker loyalty, a less distracted labour force, reduced turnover and reduced absenteeism. But it is very difficult to establish the extent to which any specific policy will affect employees' behaviour, and even more difficult to quantify the effects and so value the benefits which an employer may capture. Holtermann surveys and annotates the evidence available.

Three points emerge from this important study. Firstly, many of the existing cost-benefit analyses of equal opportunities policies are incomplete in their coverage and inaccurate in their conceptualisation. With current levels of knowledge the narrow economic case against equal opportunities policies is not proven, and more empirical work is needed.

But secondly, Holtermann does show that costs may be high. It is easy to get figures in the billions. And although there may be offsetting benefits for individual employers, the effects in terms of reduced turnover and unofficial absence are more difficult to trace and measure. Other potential positive effects (for example, increased worker loyalty) are even more elusive. It is because the costs to firms seem immediate and palpable while the benefits are more distant and less easy to capture that individual initiatives may produce only slow and patchy changes. But how true is the proposition that prices equal marginal costs, and so firms face bankruptcy if costs rise? The new neo-classical economic theory recognises a significant likelihood of x-inefficiency. Slack in firms could be used to absorb any costs of equal opportunities policies in the short term, perhaps before benefits come on-stream. In pursuing these questions at the empirical level it might be useful to ask how other employment overheads which have recently been levied on firms (redundancy pay and sick pay) have affected their competitiveness. How is business expected to cope with the new standards of practice towards the handicapped, which have also been estimated to cost over a billion pounds?

Finally, Holtermann raises the important point of priorities. Given the costs of these policies, a practical equal opportunities strategy involves ranking policies. Again, this requires firmer evidence than is available to date on the relative contributions each policy can make to the objective of equal opportunities.

While it is important to start at this level, it is clear from the earlier discussion that the conceptualisation and measurement of the costs and benefits of particular policies will change if the perspective is shifted from the private to the social, from the micro to the macro and from the static to the dynamic. Although usually presented as new costs which an equal opportunities stance imposes on employers, if this broader perspective is taken (as used, for example, by Bruegel and Perrons in Chapter 7) it becomes apparent that in the pre-policy situation combining work and family life still involves costs. But in these circumstances the costs take a different form and are borne by different people.

For example, if a working mother has to cope with a sick child, in the absence of family leave she might simply absent herself from work, which would impose many of the same costs on the employer as the family-friendly stance. Indeed, such costs may be greater if the employer had not planned for this eventuality. Alternatively the mother might cobble together some childcare arrangements. The mother then bears the costs, in terms of money and organisational effort, though she may displace some of these on to other family members or back on to her employer if her performance on the job is adversely affected by the domestic disturbance. In the absence of equal opportunities policies, the costs are privatised and borne by women and their families.

Read through the gender order these arrangements seem natural and standard, rather than one way of organising the real resource costs of a particular aspect of social reproduction. Alternative arrangements, whereby the state and/or employers finance family leave in these circumstances, simply shift costs from some individuals (women and families) to others (taxpayers and firms). In the absence of alternative arrangements, some of the costs of the child's illness may well be born by the child itself, which might be thought to constitute a *prima-facie* case for state intervention. Mothers facing the prospect of these difficulties may simply decide not to do paid work; it might be the best they can do given the constraints they face, though they may prefer an alternative overall set of arrangements.

Although approaching greater equality through the kinds of policies surveyed by Holtermann (this volume, Chapter 6) appears to create new costs, perhaps new net costs, this is because the costs of existing arrangements are buried in the privatised family economy and mainly in the first instance born by women and children. Discussion of equal opportunities reconstructs mothering and housework as work which imposes costs, in terms of effort and forgone leisure, as well as benefits – private benefits associated with family life and social benefits in terms of the maintenance and development of existing and future workers and citizens. There are costs in introducing equal opportunity policies, but there are also costs in not doing so. This is the starting point of Bruegel and Perrons' analysis in Chapter 7.

The distribution of the costs and benefits of equal opportunities

Economists acknowledge that distribution of welfare matters, and in particular that some situations may be socially preferred to others if the associated distribution is 'better'. Generally, more equal distributions of welfare are considered 'better'. How do equal opportunities policies relate to this argument? Equal opportunity policies can be thought of as shifting some of the costs of social reproduction from individuals, usually women, within the family to employers and the state, and ultimately perhaps to consumers and taxpayers, as suggested earlier. Here, as elsewhere in economic analysis, the issues of organisation and distribution are deeply entangled. In the absence of lump-sum taxes and subsidies it is problematic to think of approaching efficient organisation and then seeking equity through redistribution. Cost-benefit analyses of equal opportunities policies have to extend beyond the measurement of the costs and benefits of the policies as they figure at each level of analysis to trace the effects on distribution.

Economists usually conceptualise equality and redistribution in terms of families and individuals located in a distribution of income. Here the implied redistribution may well be from men to women, but note that men may bear a significant share of the privatised cost of social reproduction through their support for families, as Davies and Joshi show in Chapter 14, and women, of course, are citizens and taxpayers. It may not be the case that all women benefit from the redistributory implications of the policies, especially if they are introduced piecemeal by individual employers. Several authors emphasise that as employers are driven by the most evident and pressing circumstances, they are likely to extend family-friendly terms and conditions of employment selectively to those employees they most fear losing. While neo-classical institutionalism might construct this pattern of adoption as efficient, the terms and conditions of employment being changed as and when benefits exceed costs, the market solution will be bound by the private individual perspective. Change may proceed at a sub-optimal pace and have regressive implications.

Nor need all firms face the same level of costs and benefits. Indeed, the perception that they gain, whether directly or indirectly, has driven some firms to introduce various family-friendly conditions of employment well in advance of statutory requirements, while others drag their heels. Many factors influence the structure and time horizon of the costs and benefits faced by individual firms, including their position in the product and labour markets, the kinds of skills they need, the extent of firm-specific skills, and the expense of in-firm training. As already noted, differences among firms afford possibilities for equal opportunity activists to form alliances as well as face opposition. Once firms have partially and patchily introduced elements of family-friendly policies, legal requirements will have widely different effects. Firms which have improved their terms and conditions ahead of the statutory requirement will have no difficulties complying. Laggards face transition costs, and so may be at a competitive disadvantage.

Left to private initiative, not only will different firms proceed at different paces, but different policies will be adopted at different rates. Several contributors note that employers have been swift to introduce flexible working and there is widespread part-time employment, presumably because these modifications to traditional working arrangements offered clear and immediate benefits to many employers. Significantly, several contributors to this volume, as well as other commentators, question whether these practices benefit women. They may provide ways to reconcile work and family life, but only by accepting disadvantageous terms and conditions. Neo-classical economics, both old and new, would perceive the adoption of these forms of employment as driven by mutual benefit to employers and employees. But, for example, the price that British women pay for part-time employment is hard to construe as a compensating differential.

Equal opportunities and competitiveness

Bruegel and Perrons in Chapter 7 pull many of these themes together. They ask how a broad analysis of the costs and benefits of equal opportunities policies relates to the charge that they erode competitiveness. They see the British economy as locked into a specific 'gender order', reinforced through interactions between labour market processes, household decisions and state policies. It has detrimental effects on women and imposes costs on firms and the economy at large. Comparisons with other advanced industrial economies (see also Plantenga, this volume, Chapter 12) suggest that though gender inequality is universal, its form and rigidity varies cross-nationally. It is not immutable. Bruegel and Perrons share much of Sawyer's (this volume, Chapter 2) eclectic view of the labour market, and consequently deduce a similar policy perspective. Given the sexual division of labour in the family, competitive market processes exacerbate inequality between men and women in the labour market, which then feeds back to rationalise family members' behaviour. From the point of view of equal opportunities this is a vicious circle, though not inescapable. Bruegel and Perrons suggest how certain policy measures could initiate a more egalitarian set of cumulative changes.

Bruegel and Perrons take up some of the issues raised by Holtermann in Chapter 6, arguing that employers face both short- and long-term costs associated with the way in which women's labour is utilised. But, in opposition to the neo-classical view, they emphasise the sub-optimality of an employer-driven pace and pattern of change. Most innovative of all, they link ways in which women's labour is utilised to the inability of firms to innovate and introduce technical change. Market forces have pushed the British economy along a trajectory where competition has been through low wages. Socially and dynamically the results are sub-optimal. There are other ways to compete, other equilibria, but interlocking structures, 'prisoner's dilemmas' and cumulative causation block individual initiative for change. At this level of analysis, equal opportunity policies serve not only to unlock the gender order but can contribute to improved macro-economic performance and actually enhance competitiveness.

Gendered skill formation and access to employment: the influence of the institutions of training and education

The economics of the training market and equal opportunities

Markets for training provide the classic example of market failure. Firms cannot secure the returns on their investments in training because the ownership of training remains with the individual, who is effectively free to leave the organisation. Attempts to overcome this failure by contracts requiring employees to reimburse their training costs if they leave are at best partially successful. The financial gains may be offset by low morale among those employees who would like to leave but feel unable to do so, and financial penalties may deter employees from taking training courses where they are uncertain of their value. Thus, as Felstead points out (this volume, Chapter 8), the 'market for training' is not equivalent to a consumer goods market, despite attempts to create a training market for individuals. Employers still bear risks of loss of investment and thus still act as gatekeepers for training, even when individuals have training vouchers or credits with which in principle they can purchase training like any other consumer commodity.

The result of market failure in training is that economic theory would predict that efficient provision of training requires institutional organisation and state intervention. In assessing the equal opportunities implications of training provision, the interactions between institutional organisation, employer policy and employee behaviour must be charted. The studies by Maier (Chapter 9) and Felstead (Chapter 8) in this volume provide an opportunity for comparative analysis of the equal opportunities implications of different institutional arrangements; Maier by comparing across countries and Felstead by comparing the training system in the UK in different time periods.

In Chapter 9 Maier compares the education and training system in Germany to that in the UK and other major European countries. The picture clearly emerging from this analysis is that it is not possible to identify a simple hierarchy of 'good' and 'bad' systems of training from the point of equal opportunities. The German training system perhaps facilitates women's entry into wage work compared with other European systems, where employers are not involved in the main vocational training system carried out in schools. In these countries there are perhaps more difficulties in securing first jobs, and women tend to lose out in this competition. However, the German system is highly stratified, which restricts job opportunities for those without training and may be disadvantageous to women. In this sense the informal systems of training and qualification prevalent in the UK provide more scope for individuals to be allocated to jobs according to competence instead of qualifications, but it may be the case that those German women who obtain qualifications through the dual training system may enjoy better protection against occupational downgrading when they return to the labour market after caring for children.

Felstead's analysis in Chapter 8 of the evolution of the training system in Britain highlights how the equal opportunities aspects of training reflect the influence of the method of funding, the eligibility conditions for access to training, and the influence of employers versus training providers in determining access to and the form of training. As funding has been increasingly linked to performance criteria by funding providers (both the TECs and the intermediary training managers), so the scope for implementing equal opportunities policies has declined. Performance criteria have favoured training which fits the existing system of allocating types of persons to jobs, by rewarding trainers not according to the success of the trainees on the course itself but according to their subsequent success in securing employment. Eligibility criteria, which restrict access to those formally unemployed instead of the more general criteria of being without a job or substantial recent work experience, also inhibit women's access to training. Finally, the move away from providing some training outside the workplace and employment towards training located in the workplace has enhanced the influence of employers in acting as gatekeepers to training opportunities. This status has been strengthened by the linking of funding to securing training places within firms, and to ensuring the trainees also subsequently achieve employment.

Training and education systems: agents of equal opportunities or agents of discrimination and segregation?

These two chapters also raise some important questions about the potential role for training and education systems as agents of equal opportunities. To what extent is it possible for these systems to provide an opportunity for overcoming gender segregation and gender inequality in the labour market? At an empirical level, results from both the UK (Felstead, this volume, Chapter 8) and Germany (Maier, this volume, Chapter 9) have found that in fact the level of segregation by occupation between men and women in training programmes is even higher than that found in the labour market as a whole. This reinforcement of gender segregation through training programmes which have an explicit equal opportunities objective has also been found at a European level (Rees, 1995). These findings certainly suggest that equal opportunities may not be achieved simply through action on the supply side, that is in offering more training to women. Action may need to be taken to improve access to employment before training systems can be a major engine of change in gendered patterns of segregation.

It may in fact be implausible and inadvisable to suggest that training systems could operate independently of the preferences of employers and the choices of trainees, as an advance engine of equal opportunity promotion. The choices of trainees are highly likely to be shaped by their own perceptions of employment opportunities. If these opportunities are seen as gendered, then training choices are also likely to reflect these patterns. Thus preferences are at least in part endogenous to the employment system, and changing the training system alone may be insufficient to establish a move away from traditional divisions of labour.

Evidence from both the UK and Germany suggests that women themselves tend to opt for training in traditional female areas, in response to their assessments of likely employment opportunities. It is in any case a high-risk strategy, both for the trainers and for the women themselves, to encourage women to acquire skills which may not help them to find a job because of employer discrimination and prejudice. Here the extra costs faced by those who first bring about changes in the field of equal opportunities are encountered (Bruegel and Perrons, this volume, Chapter 7). This has already been found to be the case with women taking equal opportunities cases to tribunals (Leonard, 1987); most of the benefits may accrue to other women employed in firms which may be more wary of breaking the law in the future as a result of the court case.

Similarly, with training there may need to be a critical mass of women already employed in an occupation before it becomes a relatively safe bet to acquire the skills in advance of securing employment. Moreover, until that critical mass is achieved, women find it difficult to adjust to the prevailing male-dominated job culture. But if no one takes the risk – neither the employers nor the women trainees themselves – then there will be little prospect of change.

Trade-offs clearly do exist between linking training to the labour market to ensure the skills are valued by employers, and providing training under a non-market environment where trainees can opt for non-traditional subjects and non-traditional methods of instruction (including, for example, women-only training). Non-traditional methods of training may help women acquire skills, but will only break down barriers if they subsequently find employment in that area.

One possible route out of the dilemma may be to emphasise training to improve women's vertical mobility within job areas where they are already established, in contrast to traditional equal opportunities polices which have concentrated mainly on using training to break down horizontal segregation. A breakthrough into new areas of employment is not very plausible in jobs where even male employment prospects are declining, so training to change gender segregation should perhaps be centred on areas of employment which are expanding and on training programmes for upward mobility within existing job areas.

Gendered skill formation and educational and training qualifications

One problem in the labour market has been that women's jobs have less of a tradition of formal training than is the case for men's jobs. This lack of established training schemes lies in part behind the tendency for women in training in Britain to achieve on average a lower NVQ level than men (Felstead, this volume, Chapter 8). Similar problems exist in Germany, where some women's jobs (such as nursing) fall outside the dual training scheme and where clerical workers are sometimes trained in colleges instead of through the dual training system. Skills acquired outside the dual system tend to have an ambiguous status in German labour market hierarchies. For example, these job areas are less well integrated into the system of further training in Germany (Maier, this volume, Chapter 9).

However, while the absence of formal training is a source of disadvantage to women, reducing the visibility of their skills, costs as well as benefits may arise if women's jobs and skills are integrated within the formal education and training system. For example, it is important to consider whether the development of qualifications in jobs where women are concentrated acts to exclude or to protect women. And does it provide better access for some women at the expense of other less well-qualified women, who were previously well able to undertake the work in the lower tiers of the hierarchy? Women are not a homogeneous group, and qualification requirements may restrict opportunities for the least skilled.

Indeed McLaughlin (this volume, Chapter 13) and Gregg and Wadsworth (this volume, Chapter 15) show that exclusion from employment has been an increasing problem for both low-skilled women and low-skilled men.

The formalisation of training also raises the question of how skills learned within the domestic sphere should be treated within the labour market. Recognition of these skills would do something to raise the status of domestic and caring work, but such recognition brings with it the danger that women's jobs may again be excluded from the formal training system and thereby accorded a lower status. It is also interesting to consider the role of women's interrupted career patterns and participation in part-time work in their construction as a less-skilled workforce. Are the problems women face in avoiding occupational downgrading into lower skilled work when they return to the labour market related to supply side constraints, such as working-time preferences and out-of-date skills, or to employer policies which restrict opportunities for re-entry into higher level jobs? Whatever the causes, the current system under-utilises both the actual and the potential skills of women returners. This is part of the low-skill gender order discussed by Bruegel and Perrons (this volume, Chapter 7), and imposes costs not only on the women themselves but also on the potential productivity level of the whole economy.

Pay structures, regulations and the consequences of employment segregation

Employment segregation and industrial organisation

Most discussion of employment segregation by gender has focused on occupational segregation at the labour market level. Segregation is of concern for equal opportunities because of its association with unfavourable economic outcomes, especially lower pay, worse conditions and fewer promotion prospects. However, recent trends towards decentralised pay determination have highlighted the importance of the establishment as the location of pay decisions. If establishments are increasingly free to set their own pay levels, segregation by establishment may have a major impact on the gender pay gap. Occupational segregation within establishments may still be important, as a negative wage premium may only be found in occupations where women are concentrated.

Millward and Woodland (this volume, Chapter 10) use data from the 1990 Workplace Industrial Relations Survey to show that a significant negative premium is attached to working in a female-dominated establishment and in female-dominated occupations within an establishment. These findings suggest that the almost exclusive attention paid to personal characteristics in explaining the gender pay gap is misplaced, and that more attention needs to be paid to the structural characteristics of the organisations and establishments in which women and men are employed.

This chapter also shows that the negative premium associated with working in a female-dominated establishment is much greater than the negative premium associated with working in a non-union environment. The so-called union wage mark-up has been the subject of extensive research, but no one previously has examined the issue of the gender wage premium. Indeed, the size and significance of the coefficients used to control for gender in the union mark-up literature appear to have gone unnoticed. In other WIRS-based studies cited by Millward and Woodland, for example, the coefficient on a dummy variable indicating that the observation was for a majority-male case is substantially greater than the premium associated with working in an establishment with recognised trade unions.

These findings reveal a great deal about the gender bias of existing research. By exploring the gender effect directly, Millward and Woodland also discover as a spin-off from their research that the influence of unions on wages varies between men and women. This demonstrates that exploring gender effects directly tends to increase the accuracy of the analysis of labour market processes considerably.

Employment segregation, systems of pay determination and regulation

In Chapter 11 Hunter and Rimmer provide further evidence that different systems of pay determination influence the economic costs of employment segregation, adding an Australian/British comparison to other comparative research which has emphasised both the system of pay determination and the spread of wage differentials as important factors in explaining the gender gap (Blau and Kahn, 1992; Whitehouse, 1992; Bettio, 1988; Rubery, 1992; Rubery and Fagan, 1994). This new study confirms the tendency found in other research for centralised systems of pay determination to be more effective in reducing the gender pay gap than decentralised systems.

The Australian system has been highly centralised until recently, and has delivered a relatively high female-to-male earnings ratio combined with strong female employment growth. The move to more decentralised pay bargaining is now threatening to widen the gender pay gap, not least because women tend to be concentrated in industries and occupations where there is either little scope or little pressure for enterprise productivity-related bargaining. Moreover, female-dominated occupations within plants using enterprise bargaining are more often excluded from such schemes.

In Britain the pay determination system has always been fairly decentralised and the gender pay gap relatively large. Current trends to decentralisation have tended to widen gender pay ratios if part-timers are taken into account. Dispersion of earnings among women has risen as well as among men, offsetting some of the negative effects of decentralisation on average wages for full-timers.

In Australia the moves to decentralisation are still very much in their early stage, such that women still benefit from some of the changes taking place in the central wage determination systems. In the early 1980s the Australian Accord to limit wage increases did provide for an expansion of non-wage benefits, such as pensions, which proved of considerable benefit to women. Moreover, women have gained in some areas, such as nursing, from attempts to modernise the structure of wage awards and provide a stronger career structure. These benefits, however, arise more out of the continuing centralised or co-ordinated elements of the wage and employment regulatory system in Australia.

Both Chapter 10 and Chapter 11 thus highlight the significance of mainstream pay determination policies in influencing trends in the gender pay gap, and Millward and Woodland (this volume, Chapter 10) point to the inadequacy of current equal value legislation for countering the effects of pay differentials between establishments related to gender segregation. Equal pay regulations have always limited action to a single employer, but this deficiency is even more evident in an economy where most systems of co-ordinated pay determination have disappeared.

The state, the family and the labour market

Equality of opportunity in the welfare state and in the household as well as the labour market

Men and women will never be able to compete on equal terms in the labour market so long as women continue to bear most of the responsibilities for childcare, housework and other caring work within the family. In terms of the standard neo-classical metaphor, the playing field is far from level. Feminists have made this point, illustrating the conflicting demands on women by the correlation between women's family circumstances and the distinctive kinds of jobs they take and hours they work, the significant costs they bear when interrupting their labour force participation to have and raise children, and the apparently greater ability of women who have no children to pursue careers.

Neo-classical economists, as Humphries shows (Chapter 3), do not disagree with the empirical evidence. The difference is in interpretation, with neo-classical economics seeing the privatisation of social reproduction in the family, and women's responsibility for most of the related work, as an efficient solution to the problem of co-ordinating production and social reproduction. The new institutionalism would point to the emergence of new institutions and the transformation of old as individuals search for more efficient ways of producing the goods and services associated with social reproduction in the face of shifts in relative prices. Changes in the relative responsibilities of different institutions for social reproduction, and particularly the emergence of the welfare state, can be interpreted along these lines. Feminists are suspicious of these arguments, and more attracted to analyses which emphasise the way in which differences in power in one sphere translate into disadvantage in another, and which suggest that autonomous changes are more likely to reproduce disadvantage than to represent optimisation at the institutional level.

These conflicting views colour interpretations of labour market innovations which facilitate women's participation by accommodating their domestic responsibilities. Part-time work provides one solution to the conflicting demands of work and family, as several contributors to this volume note. But as with other routes to reconciliation, ultimate outcomes depend on the particular institutional forms. Part-time work can play a positive role, enabling men and women to share responsibilities and compete more equally in the market. It can be a way to have the best of all worlds: a flourishing family life with time for children and a continuous and developing career. It can also serve employers' interests in flexibility, and is attractive to policy-makers because it offers a solution to rising unemployment. But if part-time work is not remunerated at the same rate as full-time work and not subject to the same employment protection, it can become a ghetto within the labour market where mothers or others with constraining family responsibilities are employed on poor terms and conditions.

Part-time work in Britain has developed along these lines as a result of the attitude of successive governments to part-time employment and employers' exploitation of this captive pool of labour. It is a key characteristic of the British gender order and heavily implicated in the low-skills equilibrium (see Grimshaw and Rubery, this volume, Chapter 5; Bruegel and Perrons, this volume. Chapter 7). But part-time work need not take this negative form, as studies of other advanced industrial economies suggest.

Janneke Plantenga's case study of part-time work in the Netherlands (Chapter 12) shows how such employment has both progressive and regressive potential. Plantenga describes the attractive features of part-time work in the Netherlands, but notes the potential for it to degenerate from a form of employment which reconciles work with the demands of family life, and so enhances welfare, into an institution through which vulnerable workers can be exploited by employers who compete through cheap labour. In particular, Plantenga argues that relatively short hours within part-time work are undesirable and jobs involving short hours are held reluctantly.

Different constituencies seek different things from part-time work: governments see it as a solution to rising unemployment; employers see it as a way to secure flexibility, and perhaps cheap labour; and employees see it as a way to combine paid and unpaid work. This pulls part-time work in different directions. Perhaps the lesson for equal opportunity activists is to struggle against the potential for degeneration. Significantly, policies which would transform the nature of part-time work in Britain are a cornerstone of the strategy for a more egalitarian society proposed by Eithne McLaughlin in Chapter 13.

As Bruegel and Perrons describe in Chapter 7, the gender order is reinforced by the effects of inequality in the labour market on the family and the welfare state. Women's relatively low earnings serve to rationalise and reinforce their specialisation in the home. The family, and in particular its income-sharing activities, can also be seen in both a negative and a positive light. Wives' access to the wage might be understood and legitimised as a just reward for the personal services performed for the wage-earner(s), just as transfers from the state might be thought of as a reward for social labour in raising children, reproducing workers and caring for the elderly. But instead both are deprecated alongside the work they reciprocate, partly because it is women who do the work and partly because the work takes place outside the dominant wage form and so appears as not work at all. Women appear to themselves and to others as dependants, and their status and claim on resources suffer.

In addition, income sharing subsidises women workers, facilitating their unequal treatment in paid work. As McLaughlin notes in Chapter 13, it allows employers who do not pay their workers a wage which is adequate for their maintenance to ride free on others, who pay the partners of these workers a wage which allows cross-subsidisation in the family. In turn, these arrangements can be cited to legitimise the underpaying of women workers through the 'pin money' argument.

On another level it can be argued that these women do not choose to be unwaged in the home from a wide range of feasible alternatives; their choices are constrained by their specific family circumstances and more broadly by the gender order. On the other hand, income pooling does allow married women and their children a standard of living which would be unavailable to them as single mothers. The innovative study by Hugh Davies and Heather Joshi (Chapter 14) provides vivid evidence here. Davies and Joshi construct lifetime income profiles for illustrative couples which are used to chart, *inter alia*, how much of a married women's lifetime income is derived from her partnership in comparison with the labour market and the state. The results are dramatic. Unless a married women is committed to a full-time career, approximately half her lifetime income is likely to be derived from her partnership.

These simulations suggest:

> that the rise in the labour market participation of married women, and the increase in labour market equality, have not yet wholly (or nearly) brought about the demise of intra-family transfers as a potentially major source of economic welfare for married women. (Davies and Joshi, this volume, Chapter 14: 327.)

Sceptics may point to the assumption that all income is pooled as unrealistic in the case of a male-breadwinner family. But Davies and Joshi are not arguing that all income is likely to be pooled in all circumstances. Nor do they wish to imply that spousal transfers are mere grants unrequited by a reciprocal flow of services. Their objective is to show the potential of the transfer in the context of likely earnings and welfare benefits.

Just as the labour market and the family have developed a symbiotic relationship which mutually determines women's position, so the welfare state has developed along specific lines. Several contributors to this volume suggest that the development of the welfare state was conditional on the existence of families supported by at least one adult full-time earner. This raises the question of how changes at one of the sites of social reproduction, say the labour market, affect the efficiency of social reproduction performed in the family and the welfare state. The problems for families and individuals of partial changes in these structures are pursued in the next section.

Social reproduction and institutional articulation

Social reproduction takes place within the family, the state and the labour market. Institutional efficiency at one location is contingent upon division of responsibilities and efficient performance at each of the others. Institutional interlock makes isolated changes potentially inefficient, or leaves groups and individuals vulnerable to exploitation in other areas. On the other hand, concerted action is more difficult to bring about and orchestrate. The implied major changes are in contrast to the usual piecemeal approach, and perhaps in conflict with the prudent recommendation to establish priorities made by Holtermann in Chapter 6.

McLaughlin, in Chapter 13, shows how changes at one of the sites of social reproduction, the labour market, can in the absence of any government response have serious negative consequences. But she also shows how articulated policies can work to build a more egalitarian welfare state and society.

McLaughlin argues that the current balance of responsibilities for welfare between employers and the state and between the state and individuals, especially parents, is out of kilter with changes in the labour market, specifically the rise in non-standard forms of work and falling wage rates at the bottom end of the pay distribution. Unless there is a coherent rethinking of welfare policies to integrate developments in family, labour market and welfare state, McLaughlin fears Britain will become a deeply polarised and rigid society. People with low earnings power will find themselves squeezed between an inability to meet the costs of parenthood through earnings and a government which takes a *laissez-faire* approach to wage determination and the familial costs of parenthood, relying instead on a social security approach which exacerbates rather than alleviates the pressures. The only option of the low paid as parents is to remain unemployed and accept welfare benefits.

McLaughlin gives specific content to her strategy for change in the labour market and welfare state. A minimum wage is needed to set a floor expressing the minimum obligations an employer has towards his/her workforce. These obligations relate to the costs of maintaining the labour upon which he/she draws, otherwise some employers will be subsidised by others through the wages paid to their workers, the partners of the underpaid, and/or by citizens generally through the taxes paid to finance the social security system of benefits (income support, housing benefits and Family Credit). A national minimum hourly wage rate, equally applicable to full-time, part-time and casual employees, should be set to cover an individual's basic needs when employed for, say, half the week. It should not be set to include the costs which some individuals have and others do not. Thus redistribution between those with and without children should be secured by the tax/benefit system.

Changes to the benefit system should both individuate men and women and recognise the parental and other caring responsibilities, which some people shoulder. This implies substantial changes to the social insurance system, both in contributions and in benefits, and a move towards greater insurance coverage and away from the means-tested approach of recent governments. Fiscal policy towards parents should address their extra costs by increasing tax/benefit assistance for parents, and the costs of pre-school children through public assistance with childcare and nursery education.

Employment legislation should apply equally to all workers, regardless of their hours of work; otherwise there are obvious incentives for some employers to evade basic obligations by manipulating employees' hours of work. In addition, McLaughlin favours legislation which would permit all employees at any occupational level to request less than full-time hours, a request adjudicated by an industrial tribunal and eventually supplemented by lengthier leave provisions than are at present embodied in maternity provisions.

Davies and Joshi's demonstration (this volume, Chapter 14) of the continuing importance of spousal transfers to the well-being of most married women also highlights the dangers when there are significant changes in one of the sites of social reproduction which are not accommodated by changes elsewhere. The important increases in women's labour market participation rates have provided many women with access to income and independence. But the simulations of women's lifetime incomes put these gains in sharp perspective. In the context of inequality within the labour market, and given the level of state benefits, the family remains a crucial source of economic support, especially at certain stages in the life cycle, namely when children are dependent and in old age. Increasing marital instability means that more women find themselves denied this source of support, and perhaps denied it at a time of life when it is desperately needed.

Davies and Joshi also highlight the value to women of access to their husbands' pensions. In this case the individuation of benefits available through the welfare state would prove injurious to one group of women, and any move in this direction must recognise the potentially adverse effects through escape clauses for groups and individuals whose expectations were based on different rules.

The family and the individual

Economic theory postulates the individual as the basic unit of analysis, but individuals live in families and their behaviour is often conditional on and determining of the behaviour of other family members. Much of traditional economics proceeds as if each household has only one member, but there are other possibilities (see Humphries, this volume, Chapter 3). At one extreme are models which, emphasising the cohesion of the family, typically proceed as though the behaviour of the entire household was guided by the pursuit of one uniform and integrated objective, namely the maximisation of a well-defined 'family welfare'. At the other extreme there is the model of family behaviour based on the individual pursuit of personal welfare, but admitting concern for others. Becker has called this 'the economic approach' (Becker, 1981: ix).

Feminists are rightly suspicious of approaches which present family relations as unproblematical, and so are uncomfortable with the first approach. But the second approach also has its drawbacks.

> This approach oversimplifies the problem of perception in a truly ambitious way, admitting no ambiguity about individual objectives. It underestimates the extent to which behaviour in family matters is governed by (non-market) rules, conventions and sense of propriety. (Kynch and Sen, 1983: 365.)

Problems of perception bias are particularly chronic as far as intra-family allocations are concerned, hence the difficulties in reading welfare from choice. It is the fact that various patterns of systematic discrimination may well be built into the sense of propriety as to who should do what which causes feminists to reject the neo-classical interpretation of gender divisions in the home, and their mirror image of unequal outcomes in the labour market.

The practical problem is how to combine the fact that as social beings most people live in families and are interdependent with equality of opportunity for each individual. Several authors have suggested partial or complete strategies to this end. But there are dangers that autonomous developments, and even policies which equalise opportunities between men and women, would be of great benefit to some women but would leave others vulnerable and exposed. There is a danger that equal opportunities policies will selectively benefit women who are in a position to take advantage of the opening doors while removing customary protection from those who are not.

Significantly, Dex and Sewell's analysis of the effects of policies (Chapter 16) suggests that equal pay and employment legislation helps (presumably educated) women break into 'top jobs' but has little impact on the proportion of women in low-paid jobs. Employer-led changes are even more likely to be selectively beneficial, as argued earlier. But the price of more equal opportunities does not have to be a widening gap between women. Several authors suggest a coherent package of policies specifically aimed at diffusing benefits and preventing the growth of new inequalities, though the idea of packages has to be reconciled with the need to establish priorities identified by Holtermann in Chapter 6.

In the enthusiasm for equality of opportunity it is easy to want to destroy institutions and practices which appear to have been instrumental in constraining women. But it must be remembered that many women, in making the best of their feasible options, have spent years sheltered under such constraints. Thus Davies and Joshi rehabilitate familial transfers of income by noting that:

> As long as there is unequal treatment in the labour market or division of unpaid and paid work between spouses, the family will be needed to act as a source of income security. That it has become superfluous in this respect for a privileged vanguard does not mean that it is dispensable for all. (Davies and Joshi, this volume, Chapter 14: 342.)

Reconciling work and family life

How does equality of opportunity between men and women fit into the pursuit of a balance between work and family life? As has been seen many times, traditional neo-classical economic analysis subordinates the organisation of the family to the efficiency of the market. The former is simply taken as given, or assumed itself to be an efficient institution or approaching efficiency. Beginning from a different economic perspective, it has been argued that welfare gains may be possible from co-ordinated changes in labour market and family organisation, and indeed that these need not threaten economic efficiency. In contrast, and in contradiction to the predictions of neo-classical economists, autonomous changes led by the market may not be welfare improving.

Gregg and Wadsworth illustrate this point in Chapter 15. They show how developments in the labour market, and in particular the fact that most jobs created in recent years have been part-time, have polarised households. One group of households has both adults in work, while the other group has both adults out of work. Gregg and Wadsworth shake feminists out of any complaisant belief that the rise in women's employment has led to a more equal society, though the household income distribution across working married couples has equalised (Machin and Waldfogel, 1994). But when all households are considered, including those with no earners, rising female employment has generated greater inequality. Women without a working partner, including those with no partner at all, are less likely to be in work than those with a working partner. Thus there has been a polarisation of households, with some increasingly starved of time for family life as both members work long hours while others, with both partners unemployed, have time but low incomes.

Gregg and Wadsworth examine a variety of explanations for this hollowing-out of the distribution of paid work. Their focus is on the decline in employment entry rates for non-working single women or women with partners who are not in work. Is it that women in workless households have characteristics which employers find undesirable? Or is it that the jobs on offer are not attractive to the women? Gregg and Wadsworth find that job characteristics are particularly important, especially in interaction with the benefit system (see McLaughlin, this volume, Chapter 13). The substantial shift towards part-time work, which now represents over 40 per cent of available vacancies, in conjunction with the means-testing of benefits, traps women in households where men are not working into worklessness, explaining around a third of the relative deterioration in the position of women in these families. A part-time job is not enough to lift a family off benefit. The remaining deterioration is probably explained by unobserved characteristics of the jobs, the individuals and the operation of the benefit system.

How to combine work in the modern economy with the space and time for a rich and satisfying family life is one of the most pressing problems of modern living. Its importance is independent of the issue of gender equality, though the focus in this volume has exposed the way in which developments in the labour market have created mounting pressures in the family and underscored the need for coherent policy in this area. Contributors to this volume have suggested partial solutions in terms of part-time work, shorter hours, job sharing, and more high-quality childcare, while warning of the need for a broad perspective and the articulation of policies. Solutions here will help not just women but men and children to lead better lives. Initiatives towards equalising opportunities might bring in their train social changes which have broader benefits.

Implications for policy

A major objective of exploring the economics of equal opportunities is to consider the implications of the analysis for equal opportunities policy. Is policy to improve equal opportunities always at odds with the search for economic efficiency? Can there be a justification for policy intervention within economic theory, or does economic theory suggest that discrimination in the long term is incompatible with competition? Do equal opportunities policies have any effect on the actual status of women in the labour market, or have the improvements which have occurred over recent years in women's position been primarily market-driven?

The problem for all policy-related analysis is to determine the counter factual – what might have happened in the absence of policy. Any method of isolating the effects of policy is fraught with difficulty, because of the problems of disentangling the effects of simultaneous changes in other variables. These problems increase if it is plausible that, for example, changes in pay determination systems have as much impact as actual targeted equal pay policies on gender pay gaps. Introducing an international comparative dimension to policy analysis can provide an alternative method of assessing policy impacts, as it provides a means of examining a wider range of policy effects than would be possible in a single country. On the other hand it also increases the complexity of the analysis, as it is not only the form of equal opportunities policies that varies but also the range of other policy variables, all of which may be implicated in influencing women's position on the labour market.

Dex and Sewell's study (Chapter 16) grapples with these analytical problems, drawing upon some European-funded research into the impact of equal opportunities policies on women's position in the labour market. This research immediately encountered yet further problems – namely a deficiency of data, particularly disaggregated by gender. To overcome these problems and maintain the twin objectives of including a wide range of countries and a wide range of policy variables to capture the different institutional arrangements of the labour market, Dex and Sewell adopt a Bayesian statistical method which allows for missing variables to estimate the impact of various policy measures on various indicators of women's labour market position. The results may be regarded as preliminary, subject to confirmation with better data, but do provide support for the notion that institutional arrangements have an impact on women's position in the labour market, and that specific equal opportunities policies are correlated with higher status for women in that market.

The final chapter by Humphries and Rubery comes back to the lessons this volume may have for those concerned in formulating policies to promote equal opportunities. The overriding message is that while the case for equal opportunities is first and foremost an ethical issue, the implementation of equal opportunities policies is not by any means necessarily incompatible with economic efficiency. Calculations of economic costs and benefits need to go beyond the short-term costs to firms; and the assumption which lies behind many economic arguments, that the market-based *status quo* is efficient, needs to be interrogated.

References

Becker, G. S. (1981). *A Treatise on the Family*. Cambridge, Mass: Harvard University Press.

Bettio, F. (1988). *The Sexual Division of Labour: The Italian Case*. Oxford: Clarendon.

Blau, F. D. and Kahn, L. M. (1992). *The Gender Earnings Gap: Some International Evidence*. NBER Working Paper 4224.

Gunderson, M. (1989). 'Male–female wage differentials and policy responses' in *Journal of Economic Literature*, 27 (1).

Kynch, J. and Sen, A. (1983). 'Indian women: well-being and survival' in *Cambridge Journal of Economics*, 7 (3/4).

Leonard, A. (1987). *Pyrrhic Victories: Winning Sex Discrimination Equal Pay Cases in the Industrial Tribunals, 1980–84*. London: Equal Opportunities Commission, HMSO.

Machin, S. and Waldfogel, J. (1994). *The Decline of the Male Breadwinner*. Centre for Economic Performance, Working Paper 601.

Main, B. (1993). 'Where "equal" equals "not equal": women in the labour market' in *Sex Equality: Law and Economics*. Hume Papers on Public Policy, 1 (1). Edinburgh University Press.

North, D. (1990). *Institutions, Institutional Change and Economic Performance*. Cambridge: Cambridge University Press.

Polachek, S. W. and Siebert, W. S. (1993). *The Economics of Earnings*. Cambridge: Cambridge University Press.

Rees, T. (1995). 'Policy update: women and training policy in the European Union' in *Gender, Work and Organisation*, 2 (1).

Rubery, J. (1992). 'Pay, gender and the social dimension to Europe' in *British Journal of Industrial Relations*, 30 (4).

Rubery, J. and Fagan, C. (1994). 'Equal pay policy and wage regulation systems in Europe' in *Industrial Relations Journal*, 25 (4).

Whitehouse, G. (1992). 'Legislation and labour market gender inequality: an analysis of OECD countries' in *Work, Employment and Society*, 6 (1).

Part I

Gender and Economic Analysis:
One Step Forward, Two Steps Back?

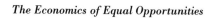

CHAPTER 2 **The Operation of Labour Markets and the Economics of Equal Opportunities**

Malcolm Sawyer

This chapter considers the effects of equal opportunities policies on the economy, with particular regard to the workings of the labour market. It pursues two themes in exploring the question of whether a deregulated labour market promotes or holds back the cause of equal opportunities.

The first theme is obvious, if seldom recognised: any evaluation, whether conducted theoretically or empirically, of the effects of equal opportunities policies (taken to include measures to reduce or eliminate differences in pay, access to particular jobs, promotion, training and so on which are based on gender and/or race, and promotion of family-friendly policies) is based on some theoretical perspective. Since the theoretical perspective used is generally not spelled out, there is often a degree of ambiguity over the framework. The (often implicit) theoretical framework used is constraining in at least two ways. It provides the background against which any empirical results are interpreted;[1] also, and of particular relevance to this chapter, it places limits on what are considered to be feasible policy interventions. To illustrate, a theoretical framework which permits only a negative relationship between wages and the amount of employment offered (a downward-sloping demand-for-labour curve) places constraints on the pursuit of, for example, minimum wage policies.

The second theme is related: the alternative theoretical frameworks which can be used for the analysis of deregulated labour markets and equal opportunities policies. Two frameworks are considered in this discussion: the orthodox neo-classical analysis, and an eclectic approach which draws on a range of ideas. It may be useful to draw here on the distinction between the exchange paradigm and the production paradigm (a distinction used particularly by Baranzini and Scazzieri, 1986, amongst others). The former paradigm is concerned only with exchange, and its representation of production is as an exchange of inputs for outputs as dictated by a production function. The latter paradigm encompasses the study of production (the labour process), and is concerned with questions such as the distribution of economic benefits, the creation and use of surplus, and the growth of productive forces.

A fully deregulated labour market is taken to be a situation in which there is minimal government involvement in influencing or determining rates of pay and conditions of work (other than the application of laws of contract). Although not of direct concern here, it would presumably involve no laws governing health and safety at work. More relevantly, a

---

[1] See Humphries, this volume, Chapter 3, for examples of the way in which the interpretation of figures of differences in male and female earnings is influenced by the theoretical framework used.

deregulated market would not involve any requirements concerning equal opportunities and equal pay, however defined.[2] The notion of a deregulated labour market is not unambiguous, and in effect seeks to replicate what would exist in the absence of government activities. But since government is not absent and there are laws regulaing, for example, contracts and formation of organisations (firms), there is no 'neutral' non-government labour market.

In particular, there is always some tension between creating a market along perfectly competitive lines and along *laissez-faire* lines. The latter would permit economic agents to pursue their own interests, including actions – such as mergers – which may lead away from some competitive norm. This becomes of some significance where adoption by firms of payment by efficiency wages (and hence setting their own wage), use of long-term employment contracts (even if implicit rather than explicit), and so on, run counter to the competitive norm, even though it is argued that the firm takes these actions because it perceives it to be in its interests to do so.

A neo-classical (perfect competition) analysis of the labour market would tend to point in the direction of short-term employment contracts, though recognition of hiring and firing costs would indicate a reluctance by firms to hire and fire (though not necessarily to issue, whether explicitly or implicitly, long-term contracts). In its strictest form, the neo-classical market analysis would involve all economic agents (employers and employees) having to accept the going market wage. There is a degree of anonymity in the sense that, for example, an employer decides to employ, say, ten employees but is indifferent to which ten are employed. Further, there is no market power involved, and each economic agent is small relatively to the overall market. Shifts in demand or supply lead to variations in wages and employment.

It is a moot point, then, how far a deregulated labour market would be akin to a spot market. Simply, in a deregulated labour market firms may find it in their interests, for example, to offer long-term employment contracts and a degree of wage stability. If that happened on an extensive scale, a deregulated labour market would not exhibit employment and wage flexibility.

There is much talk of the advantages of flexibility in the labour market and elsewhere. At one level, it is as easy to be against inflexibility as it is to be against sin; but, perhaps like sin, inflexibility has its uses. The term 'flexibility' is capable of many meanings: it may be flexibility of wages, employment levels, tasks undertaken by an individual, or work organisation. When defined in terms of the perfectly competitive norm, flexibility implies rapid adjustment of wages and employment levels in

---

[2] There is the question of how trade unions would be regarded in a deregulated labour market. They could be seen as a potential monopoly and subject to the competition and monopoly legislation. However, a *laissez-faire* approach would allow them to emerge if workers wished to form them and firms to recognise them, but would advocate a 'neutral' legal position towards them. Many would see trade unions as interfering with the operation of a deregulated market.

response to changes in the economic environment (such as a shift in demand from one product to another).

Although flexibility is considered beneficial against the benchmark of the perfectly competitive norm, against other criteria it may not be judged so positively. Clearly, this type of flexibility may result in fluctuating wages and employment, with consequent harmful effects on individuals and incentives for the provision of training. Fluctuating wages can confuse effective long-term decision-making: calculations on the profitability of an investment programme or the benefits of entry into a particular occupation are made more difficult if relevant wages and prices fluctuate in a volatile manner. But flexibility within an organisation may also mean its ability to change and adapt, or workers' willingness to retrain and be redeployed within the same organisation. Internal flexibility may be aided by a degree of external inflexibility, since internal responses have to be planned and managed, which is made more difficult if the external environment is continually changing.

A successful economy will be characterised by efficient use of existing resources and the development and growth of new resources; corresponding to the distinction between static and dynamic efficiency. In a different context, Schumpeter (1954) suggested that dynamic efficiency (in the creation and development of new processes and products) may require a degree of static inefficiency (in terms of a temporary monopoly position). The conventional analysis of a deregulated labour market suggests it would demonstrate static efficiency, though some arguments would question that conclusion.

Static efficiency is usually taken to mean allocative efficiency: the efficiency with which workers are allocated between different lines of production, and so on. However, static efficiency has two other important aspects: technical efficiency (the achievement of maximum output from given inputs); and utilisation efficiency, describing the extent to which workers' existing skills and talents are fully utilised. For example, employees working on a production line may be allocatively and technically efficient (in that the appropriate number of workers are employed and output is at a maximum given the capital equipment used and, more significantly, the nature of the jobs performed), but the full range of talents of the workers involved may not be used in these jobs.

Further, the deregulated labour market may not demonstrate dynamic efficiency,[3] particularly as a result of the tendency of a deregulated market to under-invest in skills and training simply because the benefits would not be fully captured by those incurring the costs of that training.

---

[3] The definition of dynamic efficiency is not straightforward. One aspect would be that since the creation of new resources (investment) may require some sacrifice of current consumption, the transformation in effect of current consumption into future consumption should reflect the society's rate of time preference. The phrase 'may require' is used since in a less than fully-employed economy there may be 'crowding in' (whereby higher levels of investment stimulate demand and consumer expenditure) rather than 'crowding out'. Problems of short-termism arise: the possible systematic tendency of market economies in effect to overweight the present relative to the future.

Another useful distinction can be drawn between micro- and macro-efficiency. Micro-efficiency refers to each person (or firm) operating as well as they can in the light of their own objectives and the constraints they face (including those arising from the behaviour of others). Macro-efficiency refers to the efficiency of the overall outcome. There is a strong presumption in much economic analysis, and more generally, that micro-efficiency for all will lead to macro-efficiency overall. The neo-classical approach would typically argue that the best overall outcome is actually achieved, and hence the observed outcome cannot be improved upon.[4] Some would argue further that if there are possibilities for improvement, they will be taken, hence at a minimum there will be movement towards the best outcome.[5]

However, this line of argument must be doubted in at least two respects. First, the pursuit of individual self-interest by each individual does not necessarily lead to the best overall outcome. The 'prisoners' dilemma' is a well-known expression of the case, in which the pursuit of self-interest in a non-co-operative framework can lead to the worst rather than the best outcome.[6] Second, there may be numerous alternative outcomes, in each of which everyone is doing as well as they can in the circumstances: technically there may be multiple equilibria rather than a unique equilibrium.

As an example, one outcome could involve a disadvantaged group receiving low wages, little training and being recruited into low-productivity jobs. These jobs would 'justify' low wages, which in turn would 'justify' low training. Another outcome could involve this group no longer being disadvantaged and receiving high wages, high-productivity jobs and high levels of training; correspondingly, high training generates high productivity which underpins high wages. How this group actually fared would depend on previous history: clearly the present position of women in the workforce and elsewhere cannot be understood without reference to centuries of patriarchy and exclusion from positions of status. In this case of multiple equilibria, there is no reason to think that the actual equilibrium reached (if indeed it is an equilibrium) is in any sense the best (though probably some people are better off and others worse off in one equilibrium as compared with another).

Coase (1937) drew attention to the fact that, in economies usually described as market economies, there are at least two alternative modes of resource allocation and co-ordination of economic activity: the price mechanism and the firm. The firm, as the market, to a more or less

---

[4] A perfectly competitive equilibrium is said to be Pareto optimal, which means that in achieving such an equilibrium no one can be made better off without someone else becoming worse off.

[5] This argument is encapsulated in the story of two economists walking down the street. One sees a £10 note lying in the road, and points it out to the other with a view to picking it up. The second economist responds that there cannot be a £10 note lying there, because if there was someone would already have picked it up.

[6] In its original formulation, two partners in burglary, kept in separate cells, face a range of sentences. If neither confesses, each will get one year for possession of stolen goods; if one confesses but not the other, the confessor will be given a reduced sentence of six months but the non-confessor will get five years. If both confess, each will receive two years. For each the calculation is that whether the other confesses or not, their interests would be served by confessing. Yet if both confess they receive two years each, whereas if neither confesses the sentence is only one year.

successful degree allocates the resources at its disposal and co-ordinates their use. In the hands of authors such as Williamson (1986), the boundary between the firm and the market (the determination of which activities are undertaken by the firm itself and which are purchased in the market from other firms) is influenced by the relative transaction costs involved. The use of the market involves transaction costs: finding potential sellers, negotiating a contract, and monitoring observance of the contract terms. Internal production by the firm avoids these costs but incurs costs of its own, such as those of administering and managing the internal production.

However, there are other important differences between the firm and the market. In crude terms, it could be said that the market relies on competition between firms for its successful operation,[7] whereas the firm requires co-operation for its success:[8] what Galbraith (1967) called the approved contradiction. In a similar vein, the successful operation of the firm requires a degree of stability, whereas the market can involve change, if not instability.[9] The stability (which is not the same as rigidity) within the firm has a number of dimensions, but the particularly relevant one here concerns the stability of the employment contract. There are obvious gains, including incentives to provide and undertake training, gains from 'learning by doing', and so on.

The neo-classical analysis of the 'free' labour market

Evaluation of the effects of the pursuit of equal opportunities policies (whether through legislation or not) cannot be separated from some theoretical perspective on how wages are set, employment conditions determined, and the effect of each of these on productivity and production. The theoretical perspective may not be fully articulated, but it is nevertheless there.

The terminology of the labour market is unfortunate in that it may suggest that the ways in which wages are actually set, employment determined, and so on, conform to some specific theoretical articulation of the labour market. But as argued elsewhere (Sawyer, 1992), the notion of a market and a market economy is ill-defined, and this applies *a fortiori* to the case of employment and wages. In particular, it should be noted that the ways in which wages are set and employment levels determined follow many patterns, only one of which is the pattern indicated by the market metaphor, even in economies which can reasonably be labelled market economies.

The perspective mostly closely associated with the terminology of the market is the neo-classical perception, which has a number of key features.

---

[7] This should be said in theory (or in some theories). In the neo-classical and Austrian approaches, competition is clearly viewed as integral to the beneficial operation of a market economy (see Sawyer, 1989).

[8] Some would dispute that – for example, Alchian and Demsetz (1972) would see the elimination of shirking through discipline and monitoring as the key ingredient for success.

[9] The degree of change involved in a particular market obviously depends on the extent to which demand and supply conditions are changing: a market may involve a considerable degree of stability of wages and employment.

- Wages and employment (including relative wages and the allocation of employment) are determined by the interaction of demand and supply. In any particular labour market (which may be for a particular skill level in a specific geographical area), there is a demand curve with employment demanded being negatively related to the wage, and a supply curve with employment offered often seen as positively related to the wage.

- The output produced by the labour employed is determined by the prevailing technology and co-operating factors of production (notably capital equipment). Hence labour can be treated like any other factor of production, and work intensity, efficiency and productivity are not affected by factors such as pay or morale.

- Each particular type of labour is viewed as homogeneous. Thus the employer does not care which particular people are hired for a specific task, and hence there are no grounds for screening people for employment. There is an essential anonymity in this modelling of the labour market.

- The relationship between employer and employee is mediated through price: labour time is bought and sold at the prevailing market wage. There is an essential parity of 'esteem' involved and no imbalance of economic power.

- This provides an analysis of a 'spot' market. The usual analysis does not specify the time period over which demand and supply relate (an hour, a week, a year?). But demand and supply can fluctuate on, say, a day-to-day basis, leading to corresponding fluctuations in wages and employment. However, it has long been recognised that there are 'hiring and firing' costs and that labour may be a quasi-fixed factor of production (Oi, 1962).

- In equilibrium each labour market clears with a balance between demand and supply, and hence in aggregate full employment will be attained in equilibrium. Unemployment is then viewed in terms of 'imperfections' which inhibit the market-clearing equilibrium being reached.

- There is a sense in which the analysis is gender- and race-blind. Labour is hired for its contribution to production, and insofar as different types of labour are differentiated it is in terms of their characteristics relevant to productivity. It should be noted that this remark could be made about much of the analysis in the next section.

This model of a labour market dominates economics textbooks. Many economists of an orthodox persuasion treat it at least as their starting point of analysis, although acknowledging that it is only a starting point and many refinements are proposed. Indeed, a number of recent ideas have been developed as refinements to this approach. However, these ideas by themselves do not change the substance of the neo-classical argument, though they take on a different significance when interpreted within a different paradigm.

The model has three important implications for equal opportunities policies. First, an employer faced with two (or more) types of labour which are productivity-identical but have some distinguishing characteristic (such as sex or race) would hire the cheaper type of labour, thereby helping to bid up the price of that cheaper labour and providing more employment for that type. Second, when there are competitive pressures on profits firms will have to hire the cheaper labour, strongly implying that discrimination can only flourish in the presence of monopoly power and profits. In effect, monopoly profits can be used to 'pay' for indulging in discrimination.[10] Third, any changes in the external environment which raise the effective cost of labour (such as raising wages, increasing employers' National Insurance contributions, or implementing health and safety regulations) lead to a reduction in the demand for labour and hence employment. Because firms are assumed to be already operating in a technically efficient manner, there is no scope for them to find ways of reorganisation to offset the increase in labour costs.

Although this model may have considerable influence over the thinking of economists, a more pertinent question is whether and how it influences thinking more generally. Politicians and others do not normally spell out their theoretical framework, but it is not difficult to believe that this broad neo-classical model has been extremely influential on the thinking of the current government over the past 15 years, and also in the policy prescriptions of a range of international organisations such as the OECD. The abolition of Wages Councils, changes in trade union legislation to reduce the economic influence of trade unions, and talk of 'workers pricing themselves back into work' are certainly consistent with this framework.

An eclectic view of the labour market

The neo-classical framework provides a coherent, if simplistic, model of the operations of the labour sector (for example, Becker, 1957; and see Lord, 1979, for a critique of this position). While there is probably no fully coherent alternative model, there are plenty of ideas, some of which may in the future be fused together to provide one or more coherent alternatives. Many of these ideas (and the implied critique of the neo-classical model) have a long pedigree.

---

[10] This discussion implicitly indicates many shortcomings in the neo-classical model. It should also be noted that there are considerable difficulties in applying the neo-classical model. For example, can the market for a particular type of labour ever be defined? There are well-known difficulties in defining a specific market, such as whether it extends over a locality, a region, a nation, the world? The boundaries of a specific market are constructed in terms of a uniformity of price, which itself is a equilibrium phenomenon. Thus the definition of the scope of a particular market cannot comprehend price adjustment in disequilibrium. Hence, in practice, the definition of a particular market is undertaken on pragmatic grounds, with an inevitable gap between the theoretical and empirical definitions. There must be considerable doubt as to whether there are or can be real world markets which correspond to the theoretical model.

The neo-classical model can be viewed not so much as an illustration of how labour markets do operate, but how they could and should operate. Thus the portrayed equilibrium between demand and supply may not be reached quickly because of various frictions, such as lack of information and barriers to mobility. But these frictions are seen as 'imperfections' which prevent the labour market from working as well as it could. In a similar vein, institutions such as trade unions and employers organisations, agreements amongst employers over the provision of training on an industry-wide basis, and legislation on minimum wages, health and safety and equal pay are also seen as 'imperfections'. However, 'imperfections' in one framework can be seen to have a rationale in another.

Various other recent (and not so recent) ideas from the analysis of labour markets are felt to be relevant to a consideration of equal opportunities policies.

Efficiency wages

The idea that the wage influences productivity can be traced back a long way. The Webbs (1911) and others argued in the first decade of this century that the imposition of minimum wages through Wages Councils would force employers to adopt more efficient and capital-intensive production methods, leading to higher levels of labour productivity. The general idea of efficiency wages has become particularly influential in macro-economic analysis in the past 15 years or so (see, for example, Weiss, 1990) to provide an explanation for unemployment. In effect, it is argued that many firms find it in their interests to pay a wage above the 'going' market rate, since by doing so they secure higher work effort and productivity which more than compensate for the higher wages which they pay.

The payment of higher wages than strictly necessary can benefit the employer through a physically stronger workforce, the ability to be more selective in hiring, and effects on morale and work commitment. An early and frequently-quoted example is Henry Ford paying $5 a day (roughly twice the going rate) fairly soon after the introduction of production line techniques. Ford allegedly suffered from high rates of turnover with consequent hiring costs and disruption to production when paying the market rate, but paying the higher wage rate reduced those costs.

The general line of argument is appealing at first sight, in that it suggests paying higher wages is beneficial in raising productivity rather than adversely affecting employment. Thus the imposition of a minimum wage or of equal pay which effectively raises the pay of a previously-disadvantaged group may lead to higher productivity and not to a reduction in employment. Indeed, the reduction in the pay differential between men and women which occurred in the UK in the mid-1970s does not (at least superficially) appear to have harmed the employment prospects of women differentially, which may suggest some 'efficiency wage' influences at work.

But 'efficiency wage' arguments are not as comforting as they initially appear. Efficiency wage considerations are most likely to apply in jobs where work cannot be closely monitored, when employers use a variety of devices to try to ensure high levels of work intensity and commitment, including payment of relative high wages (which increase the cost to the employee if their work effort is found inadequate and job loss results). But where work can be closely monitored, employers can 'crack the whip' rather than resort to the indirect means of paying higher wages. In some parts of the economy, relatively high pay is justified by resulting high productivity, but in other parts relatively low pay survives.

What is more, if a significant number of firms pay an efficiency wage above the going market rate, that market rate will itself be influenced; if all firms were to pay efficiency wages and there was full employment, the going market rate would become the lowest efficiency wage paid. (This argument is often attributed to Shapiro and Stiglitz, 1984; see also Bowles, 1985.) The significant inclusion here is full employment. When there is unemployment, workers losing their jobs would not be able to find alternative employment and hence would suffer consequent loss of income. The presence of unemployment means there is a pool of labour available at a going market wage rate below that which the employer is currently paying. On the other hand, the loss of a job imposes significant costs on the worker, thereby providing strong reasons for retaining a current job.

Screening

As anyone involved in making hiring decisions knows, it is not practical to investigate thoroughly the qualities and attributes of all applicants (at least not with present levels of unemployment, when numbers of applicants can easily run into three figures). It is thus inevitably the case that at least preliminary screening is undertaken in terms of a few readily observable characteristics, whether it be the neatness of the handwriting or the level and standard of qualifications. There is usually little way of knowing what the individual's productivity contribution will be, but a variety of more or less reliable and more or less observable[11] 'characteristics' are used to forecast this contribution.

The obvious point is that perceptions of some observable characteristics, such as sex or race, as being related to some performance characteristics will be used to screen out those deemed to have the 'wrong' attributes. These applicants will have little opportunity to demonstrate that perceptions are incorrect. But since productivity and performance are themselves difficult to measure, and since some of those with the 'wrong' characteristics will indeed perform poorly (as will some of those with the 'right' characteristics), any mechanism to correct false perceptions may be rather weak.

---

[11] In interviews it is often thought that characteristics are observed, but it is probably doubtful if this can be done at all accurately.

Internal labour markets

The idea of the internal labour market is as

> an administrative unit, such as a manufacturing plant, within which the pricing and allocation of labor is governed by a set of administrative rules and procedures. The internal labor market, governed by administrative rules, is to be distinguished from the external labor market of conventional economic theory where pricing, allocating, and training decisions are controlled directly by economic variables. (Doeringer and Piore, 1971: 1–2.)

(For a recent overview of internal and external labour markets, see Rubery, 1994.)

Further, much recruitment will be through internal promotion, with limited 'ports of entry' into the firm. This also suggests that the employment contract will (implicitly) be long term. The term 'internal labour market' is something of a misnomer, since an important feature of internal labour markets is that workers are allocated by conscious decision and wages are set to conform to the internal requirements of the organisation. This contrasts with the workings of the market, in which allocation is by the 'invisible hand' and wages are seen as set by 'market forces'.

The idea of the internal labour market strongly suggests that firms have a range of discretion in their employment practices, wage structures and so on, as the internal labour market represents some insulation from the pressures of external market forces – which could be seen, for example, to dictate wages. (For further discussion of internal labour markets in this regard, see Grimshaw and Rubery, this volume, Chapter 5.) Clearly, the range of discretion can be used in different ways. The literature on internal labour markets suggests that the discretion will be used to provide relatively good and stable working conditions. On the other hand, discretion can permit the continuation of, for example, segregation of pay and job structures by gender and/or race.

The significance of this idea is taken to be simply that, for various reasons, firms find it more effective to utilise internal rather than external labour markets. In effect, firms seek to forgo the flexibility of the external labour market for the stability of the internal labour market. A stable workforce would, for example, enable a firm to reap the benefits from training.

Cumulative causation

The general idea of cumulative causation is basically that there are significant economic, social and political forces which generate and reinforce disparities and inequalities, whether between individuals, regions, countries, or whatever. This is an application of the notion that 'success breeds success' and the corollary 'failure breeds failure'. In the economic sphere, the operation of market forces generates cumulative causation (Myrdal, 1957) and centrapetalism (Cowling, 1987, 1990). An economically successful region generates profits which enable further investment; such a region can attract mobile, often highly skilled, labour from other regions, and can benefit from static and dynamic economies of scale.

Other forces also arise: for example, local government revenue depends on local prosperity, thus more prosperous areas enjoy better public services. Firms and others in relatively poor areas and regions are likely to find it difficult to borrow money to finance expansion and growth. Whilst prosperous regions and groups benefit from growth and prestige, the less prosperous do not and their resources are under-utilised (for further discussion see Sawyer, 1989, 1991). Unemployment and low wages are both characteristics of relatively less prosperous regions. Even when more prosperous regions enjoy full employment, there is still unemployment in the less prosperous regions.

Myrdal (1944) first applied the idea of cumulative causation in the context of discrimination against Negroes in the USA. He argued that:

> white prejudice and discrimination keep the Negro low in standards of living, health, education, manners and morals. This, in turn, gives support to white prejudice. White prejudice and Negro standards thus mutually 'cause' each other. (Myrdal, 1944: 75.)

In the context of labour markets, it is relatively easily to see how the cumulative causation mechanism can work. The predominance of one group in a low-paying job conveys low esteem to that group, and as members of that group expect low pay there is little incentive for them to acquire training or for employers and others to provide it. The low training of the group provides a sort of justification for low pay and low status.

Segmented labour markets

There is extensive debate about the conceptualisation of, and indeed the existence of, segmented (or in their simpler form, dual) labour markets. (see, for example, Fine, 1990, 1994; for a recent brief overview of the critiques see Rubery and Wilkinson, 1994). Four particular ideas can be seen in this literature.

First, there are significant differences in the ways in which wages are determined, employment allocated and production organised in different parts of the economy. There may not be the sharp boundaries suggested by phrases such as 'primary' and 'secondary' labour markets, though there is only limited mobility of workers between sectors. Further, a single firm may operate in a range of different labour markets: for example, the way in which a university hires its professors and their conditions of employment is probably rather different from the way it hires its cleaners.

While the nature and competitive structure of the industry in which a firm operates may have some influence on its employment policies, this is not a determining factor.[12]

Second, it may be more relevant to think of firms offering jobs rather than demanding workers. This relatively minor semantic change conceals some significant differences of 'vision', suggesting that jobs are in short supply (relative to the potential workers available). More significantly, it suggests that jobs are first defined and then workers with at least the minimum qualifications sought; in general there will be a mismatch between the job requirements and the qualifications held by the worker, with over-qualification being the norm.

Third, jobs in primary sectors are viewed as preferable to those in secondary sectors (whether in terms of pay levels, employment stability, working conditions, or whatever). Movement by workers between sectors may be difficult, since employment in secondary sectors is not regarded as providing relevant experience and training for employment in the primary sector. Favourable employment conditions in primary sectors create an excess supply of labour available to those sectors, enabling employers to be selective in hiring decisions. Discrimination can be (and often has been) exercised in this way, so disadvantaged groups are concentrated in secondary sectors.

Fourth, secondary sectors are viewed as operating in ways akin to the 'spot' labour market, in which changes in demand and supply conditions are quickly reflected in variations in employment, hours of work and wages. Conversely, primary sectors are seen to involve stable employment conditions and wages.

Achieving high levels of productivity

This orthodox approach assumes, in the simple form outlined here, that securing the maximum output from given inputs is unproblematic. The recognition that this is not so (often linked with Leibenstein, 1966) has provoked a large literature, and an overview of this may be useful.

One distinction is made in terms of the nature of human behaviour. Authors such as Alchian and Demsetz (1972) take a 'pessimistic' view that workers seek to minimise work effort: their language is suggestive when they talk of 'shirking'. Others take a more 'optimistic' view of human behaviour: under the right conditions (often seen to include an opportunity to participate in decision-making and take decisions and initiatives over a range) people will produce high levels of work effort and commitment without close monitoring (which indeed generates its own difficulties).

---

[12] Primary labour markets are often associated with firms operating in concentrated industries using relatively capital-intensive high technology production techniques, whilst firms operating in secondary labour markets have the opposite characteristics. A firm may, of course, operate in a number of industries with different characteristics. The line adopted here is that a firm's employment policies will be influenced by the industry or industries in which it operates, but will also vary between different types of jobs and other factors.

The 'pessimistic' view of human behaviour suggests that high levels of technical efficiency[13] will result from competition, and a heavy reliance on the market and on hierarchy within the firm. Competition does not permit inefficient firms to survive. Reliance on the market enforces a strong budget constraint ('high-powered incentives', in Williamson's 1986 terms) in a way which does not always happen inside the firm. Hierarchy and a residual claimant provide incentives to an individual to 'crack the whip'.

The general push in favour of 'macho-management' in recent years is clearly consistent with this view (though leaving open the question of who manages the managers). This raises the question of whether a deregulated labour market would require significant levels of unemployment, despite the prediction from the neo-classical approach that such a labour market would exhibit full employment. Simply stated, there is little pressure on workers to obey orders in the presence of full employment, since the sanction of the sack has little impact when there is another job at much the same wage available down the road.

The 'optimistic' view suggests, in some contrast, that a framework of co-operation and participation within the firm, which is itself operating in a stable environment, will be conducive to high levels of static, and more particularly dynamic, efficiency. In such an environment training and skill acquisition is encouraged and rewarded, and workers are more likely to be able to utilise their own expertise and knowledge.

A variety of distinctions on how work may be organised have been made, including that between the 'commitment' approach and the 'control' approach (Walton, 1989).[14] Two separate issues are involved: the degree to which current work organisation can be characterised by one of these approaches (specifically the commitment approach);[15] and the potential for developing the commitment approach. In a similar vein, Brown *et al.* (1991) distinguish between SET (Security of employment, Employee involvement and Training) and JAM (Job classification, Adversarial relations and Minimal training). These distinctions refer to differences in employment practices which already occur, although casual observation would suggest that there has been a broad shift from SET policies towards JAM.

The important consideration is the extent to which there is an association between the control (or JAM) approach and deregulated markets on the one hand, and between the commitment (or SET) approach and a regulated market on the other.[16] In a deregulated market some employers

---

[13] A high level of technical efficiency is necessarily not the same as a high level of (labour) productivity, since the latter depends on the skills and training of the workforce, and the use of co-operating factors of production such as capital equipment.

[14] Any particular firm is likely to combine some elements of both approaches, and indeed, in an economy characterised by unemployment the commitment approach is in effect backed up by the control coming from fears of dismissal and unemployment.

[15] A related distinction could be seen in that between flexible specialisation and Taylorist modes of production.

[16] In this context it is envisaged that legislation supporting a regulated labour market would include provisions governing dismissal of workers, minimum training requirements, health and safety laws, workers' rights on consultation, trade union rights, and so on.

may choose, for example, to provide training for workers, but many would not; in a regulated labour market all may be compelled to do so. The argument can be readily advanced that firms using the control approach will welcome ways of enhancing control over the workforce. This can be seen to lead to the de-skilling of (some of) the workforce (Braverman, 1974), with increased polarisation between the more skilled and the less skilled. Divisions within the workforce, whatever their origins, can enhance control: at a minimum there would be little incentive for the firm to reduce divisions through the promotion of equal opportunities.

Implications for equal opportunities policies

There is a substantial overlap between the implications for equal opportunities policies and for a high-productivity economic strategy, simply because both involve making better use of the skills and talents of significant parts of the labour force – including some 'discouraged workers' not currently measured as in the labour force (for a discussion on a high-productivity and high-wage strategy see Sawyer, 1994).

Equal opportunities policies are defined here as including government measures to encourage or compel firms and others to reduce or remove pay differences which cannot be accounted for by differences in productivity, and/or to eliminate differential barriers to access into and advancement within jobs, careers and training.[17] Equal opportunities policies would thus encompass family-friendly policies providing for both maternity and paternity leave, childcare, and leave to care for sick children. This places equal opportunities policies as interventions in the operation of the labour market, in the sense of altering the decisions which firms would have otherwise made.

It comes as no surprise to say that the implications for equal opportunities policies (and also for a high-productivity economic strategy) of a deregulated labour market are heavily conditioned by the theoretical perspective adopted. There seems little doubt that the neo-classical analysis of 'free' labour markets suggests that deregulation, assuming thereby the creation of a 'free' labour market, would be beneficial for the promotion of equal opportunities (even if the opportunities are equalised at a relatively low level).[18]

In addition, within that framework any attempt to impose equal pay for work of seemingly equal value would be at best of little consequence and at worst counter-productive. Simply, if the work were perceived by firms to be of equal value, then equal pay would emerge through pressures of competition.

---

[17] There are at least two difficulties with this definition. Firstly, the productivity of any individual or group of workers is very hard to measure in most cases. Secondly, as the 'efficiency wage' arguments suggest, low pay may generate low productivity. Differences in pay between two groups may appear to be justified on grounds of productivity, but those differences may reflect different strategies adopted by the employers.

[18] The neo-classical approach says little about the type of jobs which are available, but training tends to be under-provided, which would suggest relatively low levels of skill requirements.

The final implication is that any equal opportunities policies should be restricted to reducing or removing pre-market discrimination over entry into particular careers, subjects, and so on. Particular careers and jobs may, for example, be stereotyped as male or female, which influences entrants into the labour force as to which careers and jobs to pursue and what training to seek. The effective supply of labour into different jobs and careers is thereby affected, with a consequent impact on wages.

However, matters look rather different when viewed from the eclectic approach, which has at least three relevant considerations. First, production cannot be assumed always to be undertaken in an efficient manner, and labour productivity emerges as a variable depending not only on capital equipment and management but also on training and worker commitment (see also Bowles and Gintis, 1993). Second, the 'flexibility' of the deregulated labour market (especially as a spot market) relates to wages and employment variations, and comes at the expense of insecurity for workers. There are gains from long-term relationships between employers and employees which would appear as inflexibilities. Third, the market forces which operate to reduce inequalities and disparities (such as incentives for firms to hire low-wage labour) are relatively weak, and other forces (those of cumulative causation) are also present.

When considering the implications of the eclectic view, it is necessary to distinguish between those relevant to what would happen if there were a deregulated labour market, and what could be achieved with relevant institutional arrangements (including a degree of labour market regulation).[19]

It could be argued that a deregulated labour market would not include any equal opportunities policies, since such policies would involve forms of regulation of the labour market. A deregulated labour market will contain forces which maintain and perhaps reinforce existing discrimination, including perceptions that low levels of training are suitable for low-paying jobs and low-paying jobs only require low levels of training. As already suggested, the reinforcement of discrimination is an important aspect of the forces of cumulative causation. Low pay confers low status and esteem, which produces low skills and low productivity, which 'justifies' the low pay. No individual firm would find it worthwhile to break out of that vicious circle, and hence market forces will not operate to correct the situation.

Further, as argued earlier, the association between a deregulated labour market and the use of the control approach would lead firms to draw upon existing divisions within the workforce. In contrast with the implications of the neo-classical analysis, the eclectic approach would not see a deregulated labour market as reducing and removing discrimination without external pressures from legislation.

---

[19] There is the argument that a deregulated labour market as envisaged by neo-classical analysis could not exist. For the general argument that 'free' markets could not exist, see Richardson (1960) and Hodgson (1988).

Low pay is associated with low productivity, but the direction of causation is as much from pay to productivity as the reverse. There are, of course, limits on how far the productivity of individuals can be raised, and these in effect place the upper limit on their pay. But there is no similar limit on equal opportunities policies, in that they have been defined to include the removal of pay differences not associated with differences in productivity. It can be readily observed that for many jobs the skills required to undertake the job fall far short of the skills possessed by the individual doing the work, and equally short of the skills used by the individual in private life. There is thus untapped potential for increasing productivity which can be utilised to underpin higher rates of pay. It is argued here that the degree to which potential is untapped will be greater amongst members who are discriminated against and for whom opportunities are more restricted, and hence more room for improvements in pay and productivity.

In deregulated labour markets, equal opportunities policies will be seen by employers as raising the cost of some types of labour (above what it would have otherwise been), with the almost inevitable consequence that employment of that labour will be reduced.[20] The eclectic view suggests this is not necessarily the case. But employers would have to adopt a strategy rather like that described as SET, involving employment security, employee involvement and training. That security, involvement and training may have to be imposed, which implies a regulated rather than a deregulated labour market. The key element is whether employers respond to higher wages by reducing employment levels or by adopting strategies to raise productivity.

Equal opportunities policies are often seen as involving significant costs, especially for employers, and hence resisted on these grounds. Extra costs for employers may include higher wages, provision of nursery facilities, maternity leave, and so on. The cost calculus of equal opportunities policies is rather complex, however, and initial appearances may be deceptive.

First, even when employers appear to bear the cost they may not do so, in that they can shift the costs on to others. There is, for example, extensive literature suggesting that employers' social security contributions are not ultimately borne by the employers but passed on to consumers or back to employees. In a similar vein, any costs of equal opportunities policies may be shifted on to employees and consumers.

Second, what appear as costs to one party (such as wages to the employer) are benefits to another party (wages to the employee). If higher wages stimulate higher productivity (as suggested by efficiency wage arguments, and by retraining workers to facilitate higher productivity matching the higher wages) then no extra costs would be involved. However, it may take some time before the higher productivity comes through. If the higher

---

[20] There are models involving the market power of employers (monopsony) whereby an imposed increase in the wage of labour need not lead to a reduction in employment.

wages represent a correction of previous under-payment, then in effect the costs of non-equal opportunities are borne by the disadvantaged.[21]

Third, (and not unrelated to earlier points), equal opportunities policies can represent a redistribution of costs rather than the creation of new costs. As an example, take a policy which permitted a parent to take paid absence from work to care for a sick child. At present the costs of such care are borne by the parents and to an extent by the child; a policy as outlined would shift some of those costs on to the employer (in the first instance).

Conclusions

Much of this chapter has been taken up with outlining two alternative frameworks for the analysis of labour markets, and hence for the implications of equal opportunities policies. It is argued that the neo-classical approach portrays deregulated labour markets as operating efficiently and effectively, such that equal opportunities policies should be limited to addressing pre-market discrimination. In contrast, the eclectic approach sees discrimination as often reinforced by the operation of market forces, thus equal opportunities policies are required to redress these tendencies. Further, it is argued that equal opportunities policies which release and utilise the talents of currently disadvantaged groups may come at low or zero costs.

Acknowledgements

The author is grateful to Philip Arestis, Paul Edwards, Diane Elson, Francis Green, Jane Humphries, Peter Nolan, Jill Rubery and the participants at the Economics of Equal Opportunities Expert Seminar for comments on earlier drafts of this chapter.

References

Alchian, A. and Demsetz, H. (1972). 'Production, information costs, and economic organizations' in *American Economic Review*, 62.

Baranzini, M. and Scazzieri, R. (eds.) (1986). *Foundations of Economics: Structure of Inquiry and Economic Theory*. Oxford: Blackwell.

Becker, G. (1957). *The Economics of Discrimination*. Chicago: University of Chicago Press.

Bowles, S. (1985). 'The production process in a competitive economy: Walrasian, neo-Hobbesian and Marxian models' in *American Economic Review*, 75.

---

[21] In conventional economic analysis terms, if an employer has market power in the labour market (acts as a monopsonist) then wages will typically be below the (marginal) productivity of labour. It is often argued that employers possess more market power when hiring the relatively disadvantaged group than the relatively advantaged group, and hence the ratio of wage to productivity is lower for the disadvantaged group.

Bowles, S. and Gintis, H. (1993). 'The revenge of homo economicus: contested exchange and the revival of political economy' in *Journal of Economic Perspectives*, 7.

Braverman, H. (1974). *Labor and Monopoly Capitalism: The Degradation of Work in the Twentieth Century*. New York: Monthly Review Press.

Brown, C., Reich, M. and Stern, D. (1991). 'Innovative labor-management practices: the role of security, employee involvement and training' in *Report for the US Department of Labor*. Berkeley: Institute of Industrial Relations, University of California.

Coase, R. (1937). 'The nature of the firm' in *Economica*, 4.

Cowling, K. (1987). 'An industrial strategy for Britain' in *International Review of Applied Economics*, 1.

Cowling, K. (1990). 'The strategic approach to economic and industrial policy' in Cowling, K. and Sugden, R. (eds.) *A New Economic Policy for Britain*. Manchester: Manchester University Press.

Doeringer, P. B. and Piore, M. J. (1971). *Internal Labor Markets and Manpower Analysis*. Heath Lexington Books.

Fine, B. (1990). 'Segmented labour market theory: a critical assessment' in *Thames Papers in Political Economy*, Spring.

Fine, B. (1994). 'Segmented labour market theory' in Arestis, P. and Sawyer, M. (eds.) *The Elgar Companion to Radical Political Economy*. Aldershot: Edward Elgar.

Galbraith, J. K. (1967). *The New Industrial State*. Harmondsworth: Penguin Books.

Grimshaw, D. and Rubery, J. (1995). 'Gender and internal labour markets' in this volume.

Hodgson, G. (1988). *Economics and Institutions*. Oxford: Polity Press.

Humphries, J. (1995). 'Economics, gender and equal opportunities' in this volume.

Leibenstein, H. (1966). 'Allocative efficiency vs X-efficiency' in *American Economic Review*, 56.

Lord, S. (1979). 'Neo-classical theories of discrimination: a critique' in Green, F. and Nore, P. (eds.) *Issues in Political Economy*. London: Macmillan.

Myrdal, G. (1944). *The American Dilemma: The Negro Problem and Modern Democracy*. New York: Harper & Row.

Myrdal, G. (1957). *Economic Theory and Underdeveloped Regions*. London: Duckworth.

Oi, W. (1962). 'Labor as a quasi-fixed factor' in *Journal of Political Economy*, 70.

Richardson, G. B. (1960). *Information and Investment*. Oxford: Oxford University Press.

Rubery, J. (1994). 'Internal and external labour markets: towards an integrated analysis' in Rubery, J. and Wilkinson, F. (eds.) *Employer Strategy and the Labour Market*. Oxford: Oxford University Press.

Rubery, J. and Wilkinson, F. (1994). 'Introduction' in Rubery, J. and Wilkinson, F. (eds.) *Employer Strategy and the Labour Market*. (*Op. cit.*)

Sawyer, M. (1989). *The Challenge of Radical Political Economy*. Hemel Hempstead: Harvester-Wheatsheaf.

Sawyer, M. (1991). 'Analysing the operation of market economies in the spirit of Kaldor and Kalecki' in Michie, J. (ed.) *The Economics of Restructuring and Intervention*. Aldershot: Edward Elgar.

Sawyer, M. (1992). 'The nature and role of the market' in *Social Concept*, 6 (2). (A slightly revised version appeared in Pitelis, C. (ed.) *Transaction Costs, Markets and Hierarchies*. Oxford: Blackwell, 1993.)

Sawyer, M. (1994). 'Industrial strategy and employment in Europe' in Grieve Smith, J. and Michie, J. (eds.) *Unemployment in Europe – Policies for Growth*. London: Academic Press.

Schumpeter, J. (1954). *Capitalism, Socialism and Democracy* (4th edition). London: Allen and Unwin.

Shapiro, C. and Stiglitz, J. E. (1984). 'Involuntary unemployment as a worker discipline device' in *American Economic Review*, 74.

Spence, A. M. (1973). *Market Signalling: Information Transfer in Hiring and Related Processes*. Cambridge, Mass: Harvard University Press.

Streeck, W. (1991). 'On the institutional conditions of diversified quality production' in Matzner, E. and Streeck, W. (eds.) *Beyond Keynesianism: The Socio-Economics of Production and Full Employment*. Aldershot: Edward Elgar.

Walton, R. (1989). *Up and Running: Integrating Information Technology and the Organization*. Boston: Harvard Business School Press.

Webb, S. and Webb, B. (1911). *The Prevention of Destitution*. Longmans.

Weiss, A. (1990). *Efficiency Wages*. Princeton: Princeton University Press.

Williamson, O. E. (1986). *Economic Organisation: Firms, Markets and Policy Control*. Brighton: Wheatsheaf Books.

CHAPTER 3   # Economics, Gender and Equal Opportunities

Jane Humphries

Feminism and economics

Economics has been socially constructed. The agents involved have been mainly men. Women have been notably absent as researchers, and issues to do with women have been neglected as the subject matter of research.

Most economists agree with the liberal feminist charge that there are not enough women in economics and endorse an affirmative action response. But the problem is the under-representation of women and not necessarily anything connected with the way economics is done. The policy prescription is for a professional pressure group to monitor gender proportions and encourage women to become economists. The majority of economists might also favour a broadening of the empirical domain of economics to include more topics relevant to women, though they might at the same time defend their discipline by citing the topicality of the family, female labour supply and male–female wage differentials. Anyway, it would be reasonable to argue that these sins of omission do not demand an explicit policy response; increased numbers of women economists imply a broadening of the content of research as new recruits work on issues which they see as important.

Yet from the outset feminists expressed reservations about the work of neo-classical economists when their attention did turn to issues to do with women; notably the family, women's labour supply and male–female wage differentials. All too often this work seemed to rationalise traditional gender stereotypes and justify the *status quo*, despite the latter's palpable association with inequality of various kinds between men and women (for surveys see Amsden, 1980; Blau and Ferber, 1986; Ferber and Nelson, 1993). Through their rationalisation of gendered outcomes in family and labour market, economists have themselves contributed to differences in men's and women's expectations and self-perceptions, and so reinforced existing gender standards. Economics has contributed to the cultural production of gender.

Drawing on feminist criticism of other disciplines, particularly the natural sciences (Harding, 1986), critics of economics detected male bias in the way topics were approached and the interpretation of results. They began to question the neutrality and objectivity of researchers.

Feminists traced their dissatisfaction to economists' neglect of both the sources of women's preferences (Sawhill, 1977; Woolley, 1993) and the particular constraints which women faced (Bergmann, 1987; Boserup,

1987), to economists' deployment of a gendered concept of rationality (England, 1989; Nelson, 1992; Feiner and Roberts, 1990), and their disregard for the ways in which current outcomes through feedback effects into preferences could produce self-fulfilling prophesies (Humphries and Rubery, 1984; Folbre, 1994).

Of course, the problems are more general than the feminist representations. It is not just the sources of women's preferences which economists neglect; their methodology has long been criticised for its naive failure to problematise the relationship between structure and agency (Granovetter, 1985). More generally, the notion of rational economic man, shorthand for what feminists find objectionable within economics, has been widely criticised within other social sciences.

> When it is not a transparent caricature (the text-book consumer who cares only about consumption of goods and services), it is often an obscure tautology (with no definite limits set on what may affect 'utility' and hence choice). (Winter, 1987: 616.)

The interesting issues are the extent to which economists cling to the concept of rational economic man and why.

Feminists propose several remedial strategies. The first involves the self-conscious introduction and highlighting of women's experience: a feminist standpoint. Feminist-standpoint epistemology is not simply intended to reach a better understanding of 'marginal lives', but to use this perspective to explain the whole social order (Harding, 1992). It readjusts the content and practice of economics but is not intrinsically in opposition to mainstream methodology, though it may prove hard to analyse 'marginal lives' using the standard axioms of economic theory, let alone direct such analysis to reassess other economic phenomena.

The second remedial strategy involves an ever-more-determined pursuit of neutrality and objectivity as traditionally understood: a feminist empiricism. The biases of the discipline can be eliminated by an even stricter adherence to the alleged methodological norms of scientific inquiry. More dispassion, less involvement and a purer scientific approach will purge andocentrism. At fault is the actual practice of economics, which falls short of its idealised and gender-neutral counterpart.

But some critics have gone so far as to charge that gender bias is not incidental to economics, caused by flawed objectivity and bad practice, but that it is embedded in what has been embraced as good practice and 'scientific detachment'. These deeper feminist critiques branch off in different directions, but they share common ground. Post-modernism has had a heavy influence through its exposure of the artifice inherent in categories such as 'nature' and 'gender', through its understanding of the multiple determinants that figure in a person's identity, and through its dismantling of binary thinking (Poovey, 1988). In other fields feminist criticism at this level has long been acknowledged and solutions to gender bias sought – not so in economics. Why?

The answer lies in the uncompromising attachment mainstream neo-classical economists have to their methodology. Their economics is peculiar among the empirical sciences in being defined by an approach, a way of looking at the world, rather than by a subject matter. Neo-classical economists practise by applying constrained maximisation in models peopled by rational, calculating, self-interested individuals.

> The combined assumptions of maximising behaviour, market equilibrium, and stable preferences, used relentlessly and unflinchingly, form the heart of the economic approach. (Becker, 1976: 4.)

This approach has given economics its muscle, and has powered economics' imperialist expansion into the traditional domains of sociology, political science, anthropology, law and sociobiology, where at first it has been rewarded by easy gains (Hirshleifer, 1985).

The methodological definition of economics has significant implications for the development of feminist and other criticisms. On the one hand, it makes economists particularly reluctant to admit dissent which challenges their approach, for this threatens a methodological unravelling that would leave them naked in the world. The feminist bugbears listed earlier are not incidental to neo-classical economics but essential aspects of mainstream methodology. To respond properly to these criticisms would transform economics as it is known. On the other hand, although some economists are critical of neo-classical methodology, their stance is enough to sever them from the mainstream. There is no way of challenging from within the discipline. Dissidents are pushed to the periphery or frozen out altogether: if you do not want to do economics in the neo-classical way then you are not really doing economics at all.

Moreover, economics remains doggedly (though usually implicitly) Popperian. The idea of data representing an independent reality unrelated to the theories is still widely accepted. Feminist critiques which focus on the role of language and gender metaphor, and seek progress through the deconstruction of hierarchical dualisms which structure the discipline and the world, seem exotic and irrelevant.

Without going hell for leather down the post-modernist road and cutting off communication with the mainstream, is it possible to use the feminist critique to deconstruct existing methodology and rebuild a richer and more useful discipline? Feminists disagree about the viability of a strategy which seeks to patch up neo-classical economics. Some see nothing left once the objectionable assumptions and practices have been cleared away (Sap *et al.*, 1993), while eclectics believe that elements of neo-classical theory can be salvaged within an approach that serves feminist ends (Ferber and Teiman, 1981; Folbre, 1994; Woolley, 1993). The proof of this particular pudding is in the eating, and one waits to see whether such approaches can produce fresh insight (Edwards, 1994; Humphries, 1994).

But in the meantime, neo-classical economics itself has been undergoing changes. Rational economic man has been, if not retired, revamped. Even mainstream economists have come to recognise that information is costly to obtain and process. Sometimes there is little basis for a rational judgement. Habit, tradition and culture provide rules of thumb. There are limits on individuals' abilities to process information. Rationality is, as economists say, bounded. Decision-making may not conform to the theory of rational behaviour. The same sum of money may be regarded differently if it is a potential gain than if it is a potential loss, and if people's passions get involved they may act in ways later judged to be 'irrational' (Frank, 1988).

Markets do not work perfectly. Without perfect knowledge and costless monitoring, delegation raises the central problem of economic incentives (Stiglitz, 1987). Principals find it difficult to monitor agents whom they have employed to act on their behalf, let alone motivate them. Contracts are difficult to enforce in both credit and labour markets (Mayer, 1987; Shapiro and Stiglitz, 1984). Barriers to entry and economies of scale in many industries limit competition and safeguard persistent super-profits. Social and private costs diverge, as do social and private benefits. Such externalities are ubiquitous, yet only private costs and benefits figure in market solutions. Nor can markets co-ordinate the efficient production of goods which are collectively consumed; most economies under-produce such public goods.

Markets and exchange, hitherto the be all and end all of economics, now appear as only one solution to the co-ordination problem. A large number of complex social institutions are also seen to meet the same ends as markets, more efficiently in certain circumstances highlighted in the new neo-classical economics. The family is one such social institution, the firm another. More generally, social norms are now included as social institutions facilitating co-ordination. Through these institutions, interest groups as well as individuals bargain, negotiate and exchange.

The meta-similarity between the old and the new neo-classicism is a belief in efficient outcomes. In the past competition and self-interest were relied upon to weed out inefficient practices. In the new neo-classicism the story is more complex. The new realism suggests a variety of ways in which market economies might malfunction and inefficient outcomes persist over time. But in the end individuals and interest groups will respond if more attractive alternatives are possible, shaping and reshaping institutions along the way (North, 1981).

It would be far-fetched to see the shifts within the discipline as prompted by feminist criticisms, but recognition that rationality and markets are imperfect has implications for the analysis of the family and women in the labour market which feminists cannot ignore. Does the new neo-classical economics provide a better framework for understanding these issues, or is it simply the same old wine in new bottles and just as likely to give feminists a hangover?

This chapter looks at the ways in which old and new neo-classical economists have analysed topics of central importance to feminists: male–female wage differentials, and the related issues of the organisation of the family and explanations of discrimination. Feminist responses to old neo-classical models of male–female wage differentials were important stepping stones in their growing recognition that neo-classical methodology itself was problematic, and this dissatisfaction is traced to the core axioms noted earlier. Has the revamping of neo-classical theory made any differences? Looking at recent analyses which bear the hallmarks of neo-classical institutionalism, although new neo-classical economics may be a step in the right direction as far as feminist analysis is concerned, the changes made are far from sufficient to provide a better and more fruitful discipline.

Economics remains some distance from an understanding of discrimination that satisfies feminist standards and, by the same token, from a definition of equal opportunity which commands widespread support. Most depressing of all, it seems that the new neo-classical economics, like its forebear, can be read as rationalising the *status quo* and contributing to the cultural production of gender.

Male–female wage differentials, household organisation and inequality of opportunity

Differences between men's and women's pay and associated employment segregation have probably attracted more attention from neo-classical economists than any other gender-related issue. Observed differences in pay constitute *prima-facie* evidence of inequality and suggest that the labour market may not be a level playing field. Not surprisingly, this issue has spearheaded the whole discussion of equal opportunities. The documentation of wage inequality is not at issue; the problems concern the analysis of its causes, and specifically whether these causes can be interpreted as 'discrimination'.

Economists define as discrimination only those unequal outcomes which are not justified by market processes nor explained by different tastes manifested in different choices. Only in this case do gendered differences in economic outcomes signal inefficiency, and only then would economists consider recommending policies to promote greater equity. But even in this case economists have to be sure that the benefits of reducing inequity outweigh the costs if the policies are to be justified.

Thus most neo-classical economists do not ascribe all of women's lower earnings to injustice; a significant part of the pay gap is justified within the market mechanism. For example, one important approach within neo-classical economics, the human capital school, views women's relatively low pay primarily as the outcome of women's free choice: specifically, their decision to make smaller investments in productivity-enhancing human capital. Earnings commanded in the labour market depend on an individual's productivity, which in turn relates both to his/her innate abilities and to acquired characteristics like education and training, summarised as human capital (Becker, 1964).

A large number of empirical studies of male–female earnings differentials appeared in the 1960s and early 1970s. True to the human capital tradition, they used measurable differences between female and male workers to explain women's lower earnings. Various studies showed that some, much, or virtually all of the differentials observed were caused by factors other than discrimination. (Important studies include Sanborn, 1964; Fuchs, 1971; Polachek, 1973; Malkiel and Malkiel, 1973; Oaxaca 1973; for a review see Ferber and Lowry, 1976.) Although the applied work is by and large beyond the scope of this review, developments in empirical methods and broad conclusions drawn from the studies have interacted with theory to guide the conceptualisation and understanding of inequality of opportunity.

There is now a standard procedure for decomposing an overall average male–female wage gap into:

- a component which is attributable to differences in the endowments of human capital;
- a residual which is identified with discrimination (see Gunderson, 1989).

Summaries of empirical evidence are found in a number of reviews (Lloyd and Neimi, 1979; Treiman and Hartmann, 1981; Madden, 1985; Willborn, 1986; Cain, 1986; Blau and Ferber, 1987; Gunderson, 1985; Agarwal, 1981). A number of important generalisations emerge, several of which have policy implications. First, the greater the number of variables used to control for productivity-related factors (that is, the broader the concept of human capital), the smaller the productivity-adjusted wage gap relative to the observed gap. Thus the process of adding variables tends to reduce 'unexplained variance' and rationalise more of any unequal outcome. But second, even when they use extensive lists of control variables, most studies do find some 'unexplained' residual that is conventionally attributed to discrimination (Gunderson, 1989).

Ferber and Lowry's (1976) essay, written in response to the early literature but continuing to be relevant, provides a good example of feminist reactions to work on gender within this neo-classical framework. They perceive the latter as constraining the range and method of research so as to rationalise the inequality observed and deflect attention from the charge of discrimination. They doubt that 'productivity' differences between male and female workers explain as much of the earnings gap as alleged, and point out that these differences, particularly the educational and occupational patterns of the female workforce, are themselves likely to be the product of discrimination. Consequently, the explanations of earnings differentials involve circular reasoning. What the neo-classical economist sees as free choice, a feminist standpoint theorist understands as the cumulative moulding of behavioural response produced by a history of difference and discrimination.

But what has caused most furore is the way in which human capital theory in particular, and neo-classical economics in general, implicates the division of labour in the family in the determination of women's relatively low pay. Rationally, how much an individual invests in him/herself depends on the costs and benefits. Benefits accrue in the future in the form of enhanced wages. The pay-off is clearly sensitive to lifetime labour force participation: those who work long hours and anticipate many years in the workforce have the highest expected returns. Women then rationally invest less than men in human capital because they spend proportionately less time in the labour force, interrupting paid work to bear and raise children (Mincer and Polachek, 1974). Moreover, while women are out of the labour force they are unable to engage in on-the-job training, fail to accumulate work experience and their human capital depreciates, contributing to an earnings gap should they re-enter.

Much rides on the source of women's interrupted market activity. If it results from so-called free choice, then it is argued that there is no case for policy intervention; if it is the product of market discrimination or social norms constructed to benefit dominant males, it is discriminatory, *a priori* inefficient, and an appropriate target for equal opportunities policy. Economists subscribe to the former view. Their very description of non-participation as 'specialisation' implies rational calculation. By implication, policies which attempt to shift the domestic division of labour would interfere with optimisation by husbands and wives based on their specific preferences and be distortionary.

Early studies simply took the household division of labour as given, reflecting the preferences of men and women. Women choose to be primarily housewives and only secondarily workers, and invest accordingly. If the trained eye of the economist can 'penetrate facades of pompous pretence, cunning deceit and impassioned demagoguery to discern the rational pursuit of self-interest in martyr, merchant and murderer' (Winter, 1987: 616), however unprepossessing her circumstances, the housewife offers small challenge.

But feminists were dissatisfied and sought a deeper understanding of the household division of labour (Ferber and Lowry, 1976). As an explanation, 'tastes' was inadequate. Feminists were drawn to ask where such tastes originated and how they were reproduced. In seeing the formation of tastes as part of the economic project, they joined forces with other critics of neo-classical economics to question the core assumption of stable preferences. But in the New Household Economics, neo-classical economists themselves offered an alternative. The division of labour in the household was to be explained, not taken as given.

The first problem was to explain the existence of marriage as an institution. Why don't men and women buy the services obtained from wives and husbands on specialised spot markets? Economists' interest in this question marks a major step in the new neo-classicism, and their answers have developed alongside the new approaches. People marry because by so doing they increase their welfare. The gain from marriage compared with remaining single is positively related to the incomes of the two individuals, the difference in their wage rates, and the level of non-market productivity-enhancing variables such as beauty. The more complementary are the inputs of husband and wife, the greater the gains from marriage. Complementarity is acute in the case of children; so the gains from marriage are positively related to the importance of children.

Divorce can be handled symmetrically. Marriage-specific capital which increases productivity within the household, but is worthless if the particular marriage dissolves, stabilises marriage and reduces the risk of investment in further marriage-specific capital (Becker *et al.*, 1977; Becker, 1981). Children are the archetypical marriage-specific investment, though Becker *et al.* (1977) also regard working in the home as in this category.

What of the division of labour in these economically-constituted families? Marriage, according to one of the most widely-quoted phrases in economics, is conceptualised as 'a two-person firm with either member being the "entrepreneur" who "hires" the other' (Becker, 1974). Specialisation in market or household activities is an efficient outcome of the allocation of time by family members, and the associated increased output is one of the most important gains from marriage. But why is it that women specialise in domestic labour and men in paid work?

Specialisation is explained by comparative advantage. But the gendered outcomes require gendered comparative advantage. Either the argument is circular – women hire men as breadwinners because they earn more, while women earn less because they opt out of market work to rear children – or it relies on women's comparative advantage in child-rearing following from their biological (absolute) advantage in childbearing. If childbearing and child-rearing are even weakly complementary, it is efficient for the family to have women specialise in both non-market tasks, in which case sex-typed socialisation prepares individuals for anticipated roles rather than being constitutive of unequal opportunities.

Feminists can still challenge the assumption of complementarity in childbearing and rearing. Becker's own argument involves biological determinism disguised as economic analysis: pregnancy is a prior investment which gives women a greater stake in their children and encourages further investment (Becker, 1981; for objections see Humphries, 1982). But it is difficult to argue that there are no complementaries in childbearing and rearing. The family and its division of labour may be an efficient solution to the co-ordination problem, dictated largely by the biological differences between men and women.

The gains from specialisation in the household presumably compensate women for their reduced capacity to earn in the market, otherwise they would not participate in arrangements which were disadvantageous. It is significant that this seminal contribution of the new neo-classicism rationalised the *status quo* at a new level of sophistication.

More recently, Becker has turned to other factors to ensure the consistency of his model with the gendered division of labour characteristic of the real world. Again the starting point is 'intrinsically identical household members' (Becker, 1985: 35). But once the traditional division of labour is adopted, and Becker is deliberately vague about why this occurs (perhaps because of high fertility, perhaps even because of discrimination against women which reduces their relative market earnings), increasing returns to specialised human capital become a powerful force maintaining and exaggerating the division of labour. Moreover, since housework is more labour-intensive than leisure, given again an initial division of labour and a fixed amount of total effort available, married women spend less energy on each hour of market work than married men working the same number of hours. As a result they have lower hourly earnings, and will not only work less than they would have done otherwise but will reduce their investment in market capital even when they work the same number of hours as married men.

Whatever motivates the family division of labour, the distribution of the efficiently-produced household product remains crucial in the description of the arrangements as socially efficient. Feminists were not so sure that women were compensated for the baggage that handicapped them in the market (Ferber and Birnbaum, 1977; Blau and Ferber, 1986), and suspicious of assumptions that women's powers to exit inhibited exploitation in the family. The debate moved inexorably to discussion of household decision-making. Here the New Household Economics was weak.

The difficulty involved in aggregating individual preferences into a collective preference ordering has been widely discussed in economic theory (Arrow, 1951). The aggregation of family members' preferences into a household ordering poses the same problem on a smaller scale, and bedevils all analyses which posit a household decision-maker. Early work cut through this problem by simply postulating a family social welfare function (Samuelson, 1956). But Becker (1981), explicitly concerned with allocation and distribution within the family, developed an alternative 'altruist model'.

A household is understood to contain one 'altruistic' member whose preferences reflect concern with the welfare of the others. This person (the household head) is wealthy enough to control the intra-family distribution of income. Purely selfish but rational family members will then behave altruistically too, as they have an incentive to consider the welfare of the family as a whole, (the 'rotten kid theorem'), and the intra-family allocation will be the one which reflects the altruist's utility function subject to the family's resource constraints. Becker (1981) concludes that individual differences can be ignored and the family treated as a single harmonious unit with consistent preferences – those of the altruist. But this result is deduced not asserted, as in the older approach (see Pollak, 1985; for doubts see Manser and Brown, 1980).

Although simple, this solution fails to live up to the accepted norms of scientific inquiry, which would require discussion of the criteria most appropriate for aggregating preferences: the feminist-empiricist point again. The dichotomous assumptions of perfect selfishness in the marketplace and perfect altruism in the home go back, of course, to Adam Smith (1776) and are only formally elaborated in Becker (1981). But feminist unease with the economists' model of human agency is surely exacerbated by this bifurcation of behavioural norms: all altruism in the family; all selfishness in the marketplace (Strassman, 1993). Not surprisingly, feminists have suspected masculine self-interest as underlying the traditional acceptance of this model (Folbre and Hartmann, 1988). What is most objectionable is the way in which the model debars from the discussion issues of power and control. Significantly, Becker (1981) never considers a family with two household heads, for which the rotten kid theorem would fail in general, with each head providing too little support to offset selfish behaviour (Hammond, 1987).

New institutionalist economics

However, more recent work in the tradition of neo-classical institutionalism highlights the importance, obfuscated in the New Household Economics, of studying the internal organisation of families as a governance structure for economic activities. Initially developed to understand the emergence of hierarchy in the firm, transaction-costs models are readily adapted to explain the existence and stability of marriage. Complex, continuing relationships are difficult to govern via contracts, hence agents resort to a more complete form of integration. Marriage is just such an institution:

> flexible enough to allow adaptive, sequential decision-making in the face of unfolding events and rigid enough to safeguard each spouse against opportunistic exploitation by the other. (Pollak, 1985: 595.)

But does marriage offer the same level of protection to each spouse? The transaction-costs framework allows the feminist point that specialisation may not benefit women equivalently to men to be pressed home. Specialised investments in marital human capital must be made in advance of multi-period intra-household production and trading. The nature of the investment may well depend on the transaction price in terms of the rate of exchange between the wife's specialised contributions and other output, which may in turn depend on information revealed after the investment is made. A limited agreement on investment and trading may be optimal, leaving transaction price to future negotiation. Husbands and wives may not specify precisely the terms on which earnings, domestic labour and childcare are to be shared throughout the marriage, but agree in general terms that they will specialise and then exchange.

This, however, may lead to a moral hazard problem within marriage, as in the case of other forms of incomplete contracts. Restricted or incomplete contracts prevent the assignment of full damages (benefits) and allow individuals to maximise their own utility to the detriment of others. Opportunistic behaviour by the spouse who has not specialised in marriage-specific capital may lead to termination of trading or unfavourable contract terms for the spouse who has invested in specialised capital. Women who are trapped in marriages by their lack of general capital are exploited. But it is not simply that marriage is stabilised at women's expense, but that women, knowing this may occur, have less incentive to invest. A sub-optimal level of investment in marriage-specific capital, essentially in children, results.

If the internalisation of externalities implicit in marriage does not prevent such opportunistic behaviour, other conventional solutions involve third-party policing of the implicit contract. Divorce courts insure women against the bad outcomes implicit in heavy and asymmetric investment in marriage-specific capital. But, as theory predicts, third-party investigation and policing do not provide complete protection. The evidence is overwhelming that women and children suffer economically from divorce much more than men.

Investment in market capital might strengthen women's position within marriage by ensuring that they retain options outside marriage. But any incentive which this greater security provides to invest in marriage-specific capital runs into the constraints of women's available time. A more innovative approach which might produce a better level of investment in marriage-specific capital, albeit at the expense of the gains from specialisation, involves persuading husbands to become less specialised alongside wives. Simply making such options as paternity leave available is consistent with allowing individual couples to optimise, perhaps trading off the efficiency of specialisation for a different distribution of work, household production and leisure, and a better level of investment in family capital. Whether or not families avail themselves of the opportunities to decrease men's specialisation depends on the value of the forgone benefits of specialisation, the power of cultural constraints, and the weighting of spouses' preferences in the process of family decision-making.

Bargaining models have also been used within the new neo-classical economics to investigate intra-household decision-making. They too abandon the concept of a joint-preference ordering and model household decisions as a result of intra-family bargaining (Manser and Brown, 1980; McElroy and Horney, 1981; Pollak, 1985, Lundberg and Pollak, 1992). Formal game-theoretic models and non-formalised bargaining frameworks have been applied to a range of household issues, including topics such as domestic violence, fertility decisions, divorce, divorce settlements, dowries and excess female mortality, but the most common is allocation and distribution within the family.

In the altruist model allocations within households are determined by total income, not the contributions of individuals; in bargaining models and the transaction-cost approach, the allocation depends systematically on the wealth, income and earning power of individual family members as well as on their sum. Partial specialisation in household production makes wives more dependent on their husbands; the earnings which they can command in the market are reduced and the capital built up in marriage is specific and not readily transferable. Women's bargaining power relative to that of their husbands is likely to be reduced. To be credible, their threat points have to conform with the negative economic consequences which such specialised women face on divorce. Again, this suggests that the gains from marriage will be captured disproportionately by husbands.

Empirical evidence that marriage is an increasingly unstable institution has been interpreted in terms of these models. Early contributions chose to steer clear of issues connected with distribution within the family, and explain increased rates of divorce in terms of technical changes which reduced the overall returns from marriage (Becker *et al.*, 1977). But increased instability has been associated with the rise in female activity rates in recent years. Increased participation means improved options for women outside marriage, so they opt out. Tentative evidence of distributional change within marriage also hints at institutional revision in the face of improved opportunities for women. Just as the conventional neo-classical perspective interprets the *status quo* as optimal, so the new institutionalism cannot but help seeing institutional change in Panglossian terms: as an efficient institutional response to individuals' and interest groups' pursuit of their self-interest in changed economic circumstances.

In the meantime, before the best of all possible worlds is reached (perhaps as a result of institutional transition), there seems to be a gap between women's expectations and reality. The drops in income which women and children suffer as a result of divorce are so large that it seems unlikely they could be offset by psychic gains from changed marital status. If there are any offsets to these losses, it is more likely that women's and children's measured share of family income overestimates their actual share and paints too rosy a picture of their economic situation within marriage.

Feminists have deduced an inequality between men and women in their ability to 'bargain' using different reasoning. England has set out a feminist critique of rational choice theory (England, 1993), beginning with four assumptions common to neo-classical theory: selfishness; the impossibility of interpersonal comparisons of utility; the exogeneity and stability of tastes; and rationality. These assumptions, she argues, flow from a separative model of human nature; a model which has been a focus of feminist criticism in other disciplines. A separative self contrasts with a self that is emotionally connected to others. Emotional connections and the skill and work involved in maintaining them are seen as feminine. Rational economic man is not merely generically masculine but displays a masculinised selfhood. Thus both the assumptions and the separative selfhood with which they harmonise are not gender neutral.

The separation/connection dualism is not only gendered but hierarchical. The elevation of separation and therefore masculinity and the deprecation of connection and therefore femininity (and the distorted view of women and their experience this produces) are seen in political theory, developmental psychology, science and the philosophy of science. The feminist critique is of both the claim that all selves are unconnected and the endorsement of the separative self as more valued. So although the asymmetry in men being separative and women emphasising connection contributes to women's subordination, this cannot be corrected by elevating the separative self for both men and women. Instead, connection must be valued for both. Note again that, as in the identification of welfare-improving changes in the division of labour between male and female partners in the transaction-costs model of the family discussed earlier, gains in welfare require men's behaviour to become more like women's rather than women's behaviour to become more like men's.

To the extent that a 'separative self' model more accurately describes men than women, neo-classical assumptions are masculinised and not universally applicable. To challenge the assumption of rationality, England (1993) extends the critique of separativeness from separation between individuals to polar separations between human qualities, and so reaches the feminist post-modern opposition to misleading dualisms like reason versus emotion and its offshoot within neo-classical economics – rationality versus tastes. The problem is that, although breaking down this false dichotomy might well promote a more realistic co-mingling of cognition and emotion, it changes the meaning of rationality and introduces a new level of indeterminacy into conventional economic analysis.

The problems which remain are not just the formidable ones involved in rendering the alternative models amenable to empirical testing. Static models, in which negotiation about possible co-operation occurs just once, after which the players disperse never to interact again, are clearly inappropriate for analysing the ongoing interaction and decision-making families undertake. But both the multi-period bargaining models and the more general transaction-cost approach seem to require a sacrifice in determinacy:

> one in effect abandons the sharp testable implications of... [the conventional model]... without necessarily putting alternative clear-cut predictions in their place. (Killingsworth and Heckman, 1986: 133.)

Moreover, the technical characteristics of game theory and the constraints they impose may well limit the insights about gender relations inside and outside the family produced by this approach (Seiz, 1991). The looser framework imposed by the transaction-costs approach may be preferred by feminists anxious, for example, to integrate institutional and cultural variables into their analyses (see Woolley, 1993). A bigger question for feminists is whether the way forward is to pursue analysis of power relations within the household using models of this kind, or to use structural models in which men as a socio-economic group oppress women. An example is patriarchy theory, which combines men's oppression of women with an historically-specific form of economic organisation to explain gender divisions.

Although its influence on mainstream economics has been only marginal, patriarchy theory has had a major impact in related disciplines such as sociology and history (recent surveys include Walby, 1986; Fine, 1992; Charles, 1993). Much debate has concerned the precise nature of the structural relationship between patriarchal social relations and the economy (Humphries and Rubery, 1984). Hartmann (1979) provides an influential account suggesting that patriarchy exists in articulation with capitalism, and that men have organised things to ensure that they maintain patriarchal power within the workforce and the home. Hartmann and others have linked this interpretation to an older feminist theme: that women's responsibility for unpaid domestic labour is the key to their oppression (for a recent summary of the 'domestic labour debate' see Fine, 1992).

The gendered division of labour in the household is not the rational and neutral outcome of an ahistorical comparative advantage, but a manifestation of male power in a form functional for the reproduction of the capitalist system. Unpaid domestic workers provide crucial services less expensively than could the state or private enterprise. But the status and nature of this work both denigrate the women who undertake it and handicap them in their pursuit of paid employment. Housework is a source of conflict between men and women, and its potential for generating discord has increased historically as women's entry into paid work has not been accompanied by a parallel reallocation of work in the home.

Hartmann's 1979 paper represents an attempt in the feminist standpoint tradition to unravel the complex relationships between capital and labour and between men and women, beginning from housework, that onerous but 'marginal' activity of 'marginal lives'. In so doing it inverts social scientists' emphasis on the home as the domain of altruism by underlining its potential as the site for exploitation and conflict. The relative openness of structural analysis may prove attractive to feminists disillusioned with the restrictions of neo-classical economics. But the same openness has also proved frustrating to authors unable to establish a hierarchy of determinations in the articulation of patriarchy and capitalism (Humphries and Rubery, 1984).

Discrimination, occupational segregation and inequality of opportunity

Discrimination, as defined in neo-classical economics, relates only to that portion of the observed wage gap which cannot be attributed to differences in the endowment of wage-generating characteristics (Becker, 1968). One interpretation of the residual is that it represents differences in the returns that males and females get for the same human capital (Gunderson, 1989). Once attention is focused on explanations of these residuals, the structural incompatibility between neo-classical economics and discrimination becomes apparent. Discriminatory outcomes are not easily deduced from the standard axioms and usual behavioural assumptions (Becker, 1968).

The tension between the existence of discrimination and the neo-classical view of the world explains economists' predilection to question empirical evidence suggesting that discrimination is a widespread and serious problem. Within the human capital model it is possible to argue that even different rewards for the same measured characteristics do not necessarily signal discrimination. They could also be explained by bad measurement and/or unobserved characteristics. Problems with measurement and unobserved characteristics do haunt attempts to estimate female wage offers.

Take non-participation and its counterpart, work experience, which play significant roles in the human capital explanation of women's relatively low pay. Few datasets provide information on an individual's actual amount and timing of non-participation. Experience is usually estimated from current age minus age at leaving full-time education. But although potential experience is a reasonable proxy for men's actual experience, given their continuity of participation in paid work, it is a poor proxy for the actual experience of married women and fails to capture sample variation. Its use will clearly overestimate married women's experience, and therefore underestimate the rewards for experience and imply discrimination where perhaps none exists. Studies using cross-sectional data which included measures of actual work experience (Malkiel and Malkiel, 1973) or longitudinal data (Mincer and Polachek, 1974) suggested that the estimated reward for work experience was seriously biased downwards when incorrect measures were used and discrimination overestimated. Similarly, studies which estimate actual work experience from backwards projection of participation also produce lower estimates of discrimination (Zabalza and Tzannatos, 1985).

The most recent innovation along these lines concerns the incorporation of corrections for sample selection bias into estimates of discrimination. The sample of women for whom wages are observed is not a random sample of all women, but is self-selected on the basis of criteria – participation – which also depend on wages. The bias created by the selection process has been studied by Heckman (1979) in the context of female labour supply, and a correction procedure proposed.

Discrimination studies now commonly include such a correction (Bloom and Killingsworth, 1982).

The Heckman (1979) correction involves including an additional regressor related to the probability of participation in the wage equation to pick up differences in unobserved characteristics revealed through differences in participation behaviour. If women non-participants come disproportionately from the lower tail of the potential earnings distribution, the observed female–male earnings difference understates the difference in wage offers. However, correcting for selection bias changes the parameters of the wage equation and usually means that more of the actual male–female wage differential is accounted for by other independent variables. Male–female earnings ratios which do not control for selection bias are overstated, because of differences in the effects of unobservables which influence wages (Berger and Glenn, 1986). For example, Zabalza and Tzannatos's influential (1985) study correcting for sample selection bias suggested that 70 per cent of the wage gap was explained by periods of non-participation and only 19 per cent left as a residual; whereas without correction 50 per cent was due to non-participation and 39 per cent left as a residual (but see Wright and Ermisch, 1991). But Zabalza and Tzannatos's conclusion that the extent of discrimination is less than suggested by conventional approaches depends on the interpretation of this decomposition.

How do we know that the regressors in such an exercise represent free choice by women and/or optimisation by families, and not discrimination? If measured correctly, women do have less work experience than men and this appears to be significantly correlated with relative pay. Yet this does not demonstrate that work experience accumulates human capital and increases productivity. Lack of work experience could simply be an excuse used by employers to underpay women. The same argument applies *a fortiori* to non-participation, as Zabalza and Tzannatos grudgingly admit (1985). There is no way of knowing whether non-participation really reduces relevant skills. Given that many women work in caring occupations, it seems implausible that the skills acquired and maintained in raising children and managing a home have no carry-over into paid work.

Certainly the opposite does not appear to be the case; witness recent findings that women non-participants, contrary to expectations, appear to have unmeasured attributes which enhance their earnings (Dolton and Makepeace, 1987; Wright and Ermisch, 1991). This suggests a high positive correlation between a woman's reservation wage and her wage offer, which is likely if women who are more productive in jobs are also more productive at home (Wright and Ermisch, 1991). Moreover, even if non-participation does prevent the acquisition of work experience and causes previously-acquired skills to decay, it remains a moot point whether this is discriminatory and inefficient or simply the product of family optimisation, as discussed earlier.

In the end, economists' interpretation of the decomposition of the wage differential hinges on the strength of their belief in the efficiency of markets and their inability to tolerate discrimination. Thus Zabalza and Tzannatos (1985) find support for their (low) estimate of discrimination against married women in its comparability with measured discrimination against single women. In their view it would be strange (that is, inefficient) for markets to treat the two differently.

Statistical analyses are helpful in identifying the components of male–female wage differentials. Different proximate causes imply different types of policy interventions; but they do not answer the difficult question about where discrimination starts and legitimate market response to free choice ends. Economists and feminists draw this line in different places. But whether a narrow or a broad definition of discrimination is read into the evidence, most studies suggest some part of the wage differential falls into this category. There is a need for theories of discrimination.

Taste-based models of discrimination begin with the assumption that the utility of some or all the relevant agents is affected by association with members of other identifiable groups (Becker, 1957, 1968; Arrow, 1971). This is a rather different kind of taste from that usually taken as given by economists, and its interjection as axiomatic devalues the analysis. One is back to the discerning eye of the economist detecting self-interest even in the most peculiar kinds of behaviour!

Economic analysts have generally concluded that customer discrimination plays a minor part in the differences observed in earnings. If customers prefer to avoid contact with a certain group, workers in that group will specialise in the production of goods which have no customer contact to avoid being paid a lower wage, which would be the outcome if they competed with non-group workers in an occupation with customer contact. So long as the number of workers in the group discriminated against is small relative to the jobs that do not have customer contact, the result is some degree of job segregation but no group earnings differences.

Employer discrimination is taken more seriously. The traditional deduction of labour demand in the context of one group of employers having an aversion to (say) female labour implies that discriminating employers will employ higher ratios of men to women than non-discriminating employers, and will employ only men if men and women are perfect substitutes. The final equilibrium depends on the product market structure. Average production costs are greater the greater the employer's discrimination coefficient. With free entry in the product market, competition among firms will ensure that discriminating employers are eventually driven out of business (Arrow, 1972). An important corollary of the no-discrimination equilibrium is that unless one group of workers has monopoly power in the labour market, workers with the same human capital must earn the same wages. Pay differentials unrelated to human capital are incompatible with robust competition. An important policy implication is that equal pay legislation acts as a brake on the market processes which eliminate discrimination, as described earlier, as discriminators can indulge their tastes without any penalty. Non-discriminators are forced to pay the same wages to their female employees and so lose their competitive advantage.

The situation is different if market structure is imperfectly competitive, since excess profit can buffer employers' discrimination costs. But discriminating firms are still threatened in the long term, since non-discriminators can buy them out and earn even larger profits. There are ways in which discrimination can be reconciled with competition, even in the long run (Cain, 1986). But these usually involve assumptions which are themselves threatening to competition, such as non-constant costs, inelastic supplies of entrepreneurship, and inelastic supplies of non-labour factors of production.

The most important empirical prediction from the analysis is that discrimination will be more prevalent in highly-concentrated industries. Empirical studies have focused on correlating measures of discrimination with measures of concentration, with mixed results. US studies have found a positive relationship between the proportion of blacks in total employment and industrial employment (Comador, 1973; Medoff, 1979–80). But Shepherd and Levin (1973) fail to detect any clear structure/discrimination relationship in their sample of large US firms (see also Oster, 1975). They conclude that 'Except for a few "women's" industries, the management of large corporations is in fact a distinctively white male preserve' (Shepherd and Levin, 1973: 422).

Studies focused on relative wages by race and sex produce mixed results (Haessell and Palmer, 1978; Fuji and Trapani, 1978). For the UK, Chiplin and Sloane (1976) found no relationship between male–female wage differentials and industrial structure, and seemed to find that as far as the proportion of women is concerned this was higher in the more concentrated industries! Industrial structure is important (see Paci *et al.*, this volume, Chapter 4), but its effects are more complicated that simple taste-based theories of discrimination might suggest.

Becker (1957) also considers the case where groups of employees dislike working with each other. If members of the two groups are identical as workers, the employment structure will become segregated, with both types of workers getting the same pay. If there are skill complementarities, employment will be mixed but workers will have to be compensated for this violation of their preferences by higher pay, and so there will be lower levels of employment. Unfortunately this intuitively more realistic hypothesis has attracted less attention, probably because it is not easily subjected to formal quantitative investigation (but see Chiswick, 1973).

If competition in the labour market causes difficulties for neo-classical theories of discrimination, market power makes things easier. The classic case of employers paying a wage less than the worker's productivity occurs under monopsony, where a single buyer of labour faces an upward-sloping supply curve (Robinson, 1934). Where two kinds of labour are involved, the degree of exploitation is greater for the workers whose labour supply is more inelastic. But this classic case seems to have little empirical purchase. Pure monopsony is empirically infrequent and, as far as gender discrimination is concerned, there is a good deal of empirical evidence and theoretical support for the finding that women's labour supply is more elastic than that of men – the opposite of the requisite condition for the relative underpayment of women. But explanations in this category should not be discarded too quickly. It is widely known that women are more constrained than men in choice of employer. They work closer to home and may only be available for less than full-time hours. As a result they may face an effective monopsonist, in contrast to men who can travel further to work and be available more flexibly (see Paci *et al.*, this volume, Chapter 4).

In Becker's model of discrimination (1957), men's prejudice against women workers was not a sufficient condition to sustain a discriminatory wage differential. However, by forming a monopoly in the sale of labour to employers, male workers could enforce their tastes and raise their wage above the competitive level. Overall, however, despite many individual cases of discrimination by unions, research suggests that labour monopoly is not a major source of the observed gender earnings gap (see Cain, 1986, for a survey of important studies; Millward and Woodland, this volume, Chapter 10).

But perhaps a distinction should be made between the role of unions in sustaining existing differentials and their historic role in the gendering of jobs, as suggested in structural models of patriarchal capitalism and in some radical descriptions of segmented labour markets. Elements of employee prejudice, combined with the exercise of market power by male-dominated trade unions, and perhaps with 'within-sex altruism' operating between male employees and employers, provide persuasive analyses of historical developments in labour markets (for a discussion of within-sex altruism see England, 1993; relevant historical analyses include Hartmann, 1979; Cockburn, 1986).

Simple models of the labour market assume that employers are able to observe directly the productivity of job applicants. Greater realism is introduced in models where employers use observed characteristics, such as education, as a screen or signal. If such characteristics include innate attributes, like race or gender, they can ground a theory of discrimination based on imperfect information. Unfortunately, statistical discrimination has been widely misunderstood (see Aigner and Cain, 1977). Statistical discrimination does not involve employers mistakenly believing that the average abilities of men are greater than those of women and so mistakenly overpaying men relative to women, though such 'error discrimination' has been hypothesised in feminist literature. While it is a trivial matter to see how error discrimination explains observed differences in men's and women's pay seemingly unrelated to their human capital, as an explanation of discrimination it sits uncomfortably with neo-classical economics. The problem is again to explain the persistence of such mistaken behaviour in competitive markets. Indeed, as an explanation of discrimination, a theory based on employers' mistakes is even harder for neo-classical economists to accept than an explanation based on employers' 'tastes for discrimination', because the tastes are at least presumed to provide utility to the discriminator.

One factor in the confusion is that the basic model, developed by Phelps (1972), cannot explain discrimination between groups as defined in neo-classical economics. The model assumes that hiring is done on the basis of a test score, which is an unbiased predictor of a worker's true productivity. Thus an employer's hiring decision is based on his/her conditional expectation of a worker's productivity, which is a linear combination of a group component and an individual component (his or her particular test score).

Suppose there are two differentiated groups of worker, men and women. Mean productivity is the same for both groups, but the test score is more reliable for men. A male worker will be paid a higher wage than a woman worker if his score was above average, and vice versa. High-quality women workers will earn lower wages than their male counterparts, but the opposite will be true for low-quality workers. Male workers will be more dispersed around the mean than women workers, simply because more weight will be given to individual performance. Workers will get different pay for the same indicated level of skill, which is discrimination at the individual level as Phelps (1972) and others have argued. But as each worker is paid in accordance with expected productivity based on an unbiased predictor, and the two groups with the same average ability get the same average wages, this situation does not constitute discrimination as usually defined by neo-classical economists (Aigner and Cain, 1977). Nor is it capable of generating the kind of empirical phenomenon described earlier in terms of group differences in earnings unrelated to measured attributes.

Phelps (1972) also considered a model in which average abilities differed between groups. Assume that mean ability of men exceeds that of women. Here the systematic effect of femaleness leads to a lower predicted value of productivity for women than men even if test scores are equal, because the test is by assumption a fallible indicator. Competitive market forces lead employers to pay workers according to their expected productivity, thus male workers will be preferred and get higher wages than female workers with the same test score. But again a proportional relation will exist between the average compensation for the groups and their average ability, and the outcome is not discrimination as usually understood.

Although the Phelps model (1972) does not explain sex discrimination as customarily defined by neo-classical economists, extensions which incorporate risk aversion on the part of employers can be shown to be consistent with empirical patterns in pay (see Aigner and Cain, 1977). In another model the combination of lesser reliability for women on tests with truncation of lower-scoring applicants also produces a kind of discrimination. Neither model appears sufficient as an explanation of observed differences in male–female pay uncorrelated with productivity-enhancing characteristics.

Error discrimination and statistical discrimination have radically different policy implications. If women are disadvantaged because of employers' errors, policies such as affirmative action or pay equity simply correct employers' errors, force employers to learn, and benefit women at no cost to efficiency. If there is neo-classical statistical discrimination, obliging employers to change their behaviour will be costly. Employers are already doing the best they can with limited information and on average their mistakes cancel out, even though their actions result in inequitable outcomes for individuals.

The new institutionalism, with its emphasis on costs of adjustment and bounded rationality, provides a framework which is more sympathetic to the persistence of mistaken behaviour. Feminist analyses develop these ideas, arguing that 'error discrimination' can become embedded in institutional structures (for example, protective labour legislation), and that if the mistaken beliefs are widespread and supported by wider cultural presuppositions, violators of the norms may be rare, contradictory evidence seldom available and so corrective feedback mechanisms muted. Market signals get muffled in the fog of gender stereotypes (Woolley, 1993). Within a dynamic context gender discrimination creates self-fulfilling prophecies. Women are hired for low-grade jobs because they are perceived to be less skilled. Once employed in these positions, they do not learn skills because they are in jobs with no possibility of advancement (Grimshaw and Rubery, this volume, Chapter 5).

Although these developments of 'error discrimination' are promising, as an explanation of discrimination they are not universally accepted by feminist economists, as Woolley emphasises (1993). Behaviour which produces systematic mistakes (that is, outcomes which are wrong on average), or fails to make the best choice given current information and the cost of making decisions, is irrational and may not be attractive to feminist economists. Moreover, error discrimination suggests that intervening in markets can improve both equity and efficiency, which might seem an unduly rosy view. Finally, it might seem naive to believe that supporters of discriminatory institutions are honestly mistaken and have no vested interests in the *status quo*. Work on the circumstances under which individuals make systematic mistakes may well be an important item in the feminist research agenda (Woolley, 1993).

An outcome in which segregation reduces market discrimination occurs in several versions of Becker's (1957) model of discrimination. Competition enables segregation to accommodate demand-side prejudice costlessly. But again, this seems inconsistent with the empirical evidence. Differences in the occupational distribution of males and females account for a substantial portion of the earnings gap. A divide exists in the literature as to whether differences in occupational distributions are the outcome of the (free) choices of men and women, and so legitimately viewed as exogenous determinants of earnings differentials, or whether they are manifestations of discrimination. Job choice, as well as productivity-related characteristics acquired by workers, may reflect discrimination in the labour market or in society more generally, or may occur as a rational response to wage discrimination and occupational segregation. Again, investigation of gendered outcomes necessitates opening up the Pandora's box of preferences left closed by neo-classical economics. Instead, neo-classical economics offers a more comfortable explanation for occupational choice.

Human capital theory is used not only to explain differences in human capital formation and so in earnings, but is extended to explain the concentration of women and men in different occupations and industries (Polachek, 1976; Polachek, 1979). Different occupations convey different opportunities for on-the-job acquisition of human capital. But training involves current costs (earnings forgone, disutility, time) and only pays off in the future. Again, it may not be worthwhile if the individual anticipates a relatively short working career. So women choose jobs which combine current returns and capital formation in an optimal way given their anticipated shorter lifetime work experience, and which impose lower penalties for depreciation given their greater employment intermittency (again see Becker, 1985, for a development of this model).

One logical problem with Polachek's extension of the human capital model to explain the occupational segregation of women workers concerns the assumption that women will choose occupations with low rewards for experience. Even if only intermittent experience is planned, greater lifetime earnings accrue in a job which rewards what little experience has been accumulated (England, 1982). For women to avoid jobs with high rates of appreciation, these jobs must exhibit unattractively low starting salaries, an inverse correlation commonly assumed in the human capital literature but not made explicit in Polachek's analysis.

On a deeper level the human capital model of either earnings differences or employment segregation shares the circularity of the New Household Economics' explanations of gender divisions: women invest less in human capital or choose a less demanding job because they anticipate spending more time than their spouses out of the labour force; but they spend more time out of the labour force because their potential earnings are lower. Predictions from the human capital model about the pattern of concentration of women workers have not proved robust (for example, see Zellner, 1975; England, 1982; Beller, 1982; Polachek, 1985: England, 1985).

Human capital theory does not provide the only explanation of the commonly-observed increase of earnings with experience or earnings penalties for intermittent participation. Institutionalist analyses see some of the relationship between employment continuity and earnings as the result of legal, contractual and traditional agreements in the workplace which have little to do with productivity (England, 1982). These analyses can be readily extended to explain employment segregation by sex not only in terms of the incentive structures confronting women in their job choice, but also in terms of institutional barriers to women's entry into certain occupations. These explanations of employment segregation shift attention from the supply side (women's choices) back to demand (employment discrimination), and accommodate those feedback mechanisms from demand to supply which feature importantly in feminist scenarios.

In general, institutional theories of discrimination make more room for historical contexts, pre-labour market discrimination, group bargaining and monopoly elements. Neo-classical economists often view them with a combination of impatience and condescension: arguing first that they implicitly misrepresent neo-classical models which, for example, are not synonymous with perfect competition; and second that they are complements rather than substitutes for neo-classical analysis, contextualising and shading rather than usurping the latter (see Cain, 1986). But such insouciance is unjustified. Neo-classical economists have found it difficult to explain the persistence of discrimination and occupational segregation, and alternatives deserve to be taken seriously.

Bergmann's classic (1974) article represents a hybrid model: neo-classical in the sense that workers receive their marginal products, but institutional in the sense that certain workers are restricted in terms of their employment opportunities and 'crowded' into jobs where their presence is acceptable. Like the human capital model, the crowding hypothesis is an attempt to explain both women's lower earnings and their employment segregation within the same framework. Unlike other demand-side models of discrimination, discriminators here do not automatically make lower profits. When they discriminate against one group of workers, they raise the wages of other groups but lower the wages of the group discriminated against. The paper constitutes a seminal contribution to a tradition which links the unequal treatment of workers to non-competing segments within the labour market.

Piore's (1975) model conceptualises the labour market as containing a primary and a secondary sector. The primary sector offers jobs with relatively high wages, good working conditions, opportunities to advance and employment security. Jobs in the secondary sector pay low wages, have poor working conditions, offer few opportunities for advancement and afford little security. The challenge is to explain how such segmentation withstands the self-interested mobility and hiring of agents in the market, and persists in the face of competitive pressures. Proponents of segmented labour markets argue that, in the context of changing industrial structure and technology, their development benefited both (some) workers and (some) employers, who together had the power to structure employment in their interests.

Segmented labour market theories seek to explain the divisions among groups of jobs. But they do not explain how it is that different kinds of workers occupy different segments of the labour market. Women fit the description of secondary workers: they receive lower pay and are concentrated in less-skilled, dead-end and insecure jobs (Barron and Norris, 1976). Why is this? For some authors women's occupancy of the secondary segment comes out of the historical moment in which they were incorporated into the workforce; others see patriarchy as structuring the supply side of the labour market; yet others see patriarchy as structuring demand in terms of employers and unionised male workers in alliance controlling access to primary jobs.

Early work in this tradition involved grand theoretical overviews with rather unspecific independent variables, such as capitalism, patriarchy and industrialisation. Recent work has involved detailed case studies. The aim is to use such micro-analysis to demonstrate how earnings differentials come into being and are maintained in firms or industries. Studies of women's pay and employment in the UK (Craig *et al.*, 1985) suggest that pay inequalities are rooted in the system of industrial organisation and the system of social reproduction of the labour force. Labour supply conditions interact with product market and technical conditions (Grimshaw and Rubery, this volume, Chapter 5), and with the structure and functioning of the welfare state, to mould the segmented employment structure (McLaughlin, this volume, Chapter 13).

Quantitative analyses suggest that factors exogenous to the labour market itself, such as differences in household responsibilities, are an important source of earnings differences between men and women (Gunderson, 1989). Feminist critics have long been irritated by neo-classical economists' depiction of these factors as reflecting preferences perhaps moulded by pre-market discrimination, and demand that they be studied as important contributors to economic discrimination. For example, Corcoran and Courant (1987) have shown the importance of pre-market discrimination and sex-role socialisation. It is necessary to discover more about the interaction between what goes on in the labour market and what happens before employment, because an adequate policy response to inequalities in pay and occupational segregation must reach into these areas.

Similarly, feminists have long demanded that closer attention be paid to the nature of variables commonly viewed as unproblematic indicators of productivity. Research has suggested that the conceptualisation and measurement of these characteristics may not be gender neutral. In particular, the meaning of 'skill' has been shown to be socially constructed within a gendered culture. Activities and processes performed by women tend to be defined as 'unskilled' simply because they are performed by women (see Craig *et al.*, 1982; Phillips and Taylor, 1980; Game and Pringle, 1983; Coyle, 1982). Male-dominated trade unions have played a part in the establishment and maintenance of skill divisions on gendered lines. Studies have also shown that mapping from job content to perceived skill depends not just on gender but also whether the job is full- or part-time (Horrell *et al.*, 1990).

Focusing on preferences as the Trojan horse introducing gender bias into otherwise objective economic analysis makes it easy for economists to side-step the issue: they work with given tastes, and it is for other social scientists to understand the formation of preferences. But this kind of work forces recognition that even standard economic variables in both conceptualisation and measurement have already been contaminated by being socially constructed.

Economics and equal opportunities

Feminists and economists are often said to disagree about the causes of inequality, thus blocking an agreed policy response (see Woolley, 1993). But this is not strictly accurate. Economists would probably agree among themselves and even with feminists about the proximate causes of gender differences in economic outcomes. What they would disagree about is which of these proximate causes represent discrimination and which simply reflect joint optimisation by husbands and wives, and/or differences in men's and women's preferences.

As this chapter has shown, economists read economic inequality between men and women firstly as an opaque manifestation of efficient co-ordination, and only secondly as an indication of discrimination and injustice. This is not because economists are male chauvinists. Discrimination entails inefficiency, and inefficiency as a permanent and serious feature of an economy suggests that there are problems with economists' ways of modelling the world. Circular reasoning strikes again. Discrimination equals inefficiency, inefficiency will be eliminated by individuals rationally pursuing their self-interest in markets and other social institutions, so discrimination must be a minor and temporary problem.

The new neo-classical economics, because it offers insight into why economies may seriously malfunction for long periods of time, provides more scope for the analysis of inequality and injustice. To the extent that Panglossian aspects of the new neo-classicism appear to be in retreat (North, 1990), there is hope that future developments within this approach may be even more useful. But to the extent that they are retained the new neo-classicism fails feminists for the same reasons as the old. By interpreting the *status quo* as efficient in the case of conventional neo-classicism, or on its way to becoming efficient, or as nearly efficient as possible in the case of the new neo-classicism, and by suggesting that men and women have different preferences, both approaches have obfuscated inequality and dressed it up as difference. In the process they have shored up conventional gender standards and helped to create the phenomena they study.

References

Agarwal, N. (1981). 'Pay discrimination: evidence, policies and issues' in Jain, H. and Sloane, P. (eds.) *Equal Employment Issues: Race and Sex Discrimination in the United States, Canada and Britain*. New York: Praeger.

Aigner, D. J., and Cain, G. C. (1977). 'Statistical theories of discrimination in labor markets' in *Industrial and Labor Relations Review*, 30 (2).

Amsden, A. H. (ed.) (1980). *The Economics of Women and Work*. Harmondsworth: Penguin.

Arrow, K. J. (1951). *Social Choice and Individual Values*. New York: Cowles Foundation, John Wiley and Sons.

Arrow, K. J. (1971). *Some Models of Racial Discrimination in the Labor Market*. RAND document RM-6253-RC, Santa Monica, California.

Arrow, K. J. (1972). 'Models of job discrimination' in Pascal, A. H. (ed.) *Racial Discrimination in Economic Life*. Lexington, Mass: D. C. Heath and Co.

Barron, R. D. and Norris, G. M. (1976). 'Sexual divisions and the dual labour market' in Barker, D. L. and Allen, S. (eds.) *Dependence and Exploitation in Work and Marriage*. London: Longman.

Becker, G. S. (1957). *The Economics of Discrimination*. Chicago: University of Chicago Press.

Becker, G. S. (1964). *Human Capital*. New York: Columbia University Press.

Becker, G. S. (1965). 'A theory of the allocation of time' in *Economic Journal*, 75 (200).

Becker, G. S. (1968). 'Discrimination, economic' in *International Encyclopedia of the Social Sciences*, 4. London: Macmillan.

Becker, G. S. (1973). 'A theory of marriage: part I' in *Journal of Political Economy*, 81 (4).

Becker, G. S. (1974). 'A theory of marriage: part II' in *Journal of Political Economy*, 82 (2).

Becker, G. S. (1976). *The Economic Approach to Human Behavior*. Chicago: University of Chicago Press.

Becker, G. S. (1981). *A Treatise on the Family*. Cambridge, Mass: Harvard University Press.

Becker, G. S. (1985). 'Human capital, effort, and the sexual division of labor' in *Journal of Labor Economics*, 3 (1).

Becker, G. S., Landes, E. M. and Michael, R. T. (1977). 'An economic analysis of marital instability' in *Journal of Political Economy*, 85 (6).

Beller, A. (1982). 'Occupational segregation by sex: determinants and changes' in *Journal of Human Resources*, 17 (3).

Berger, M. C. and Glenn, D. E. (1986). 'Selectivity bias and earnings differences by gender and race' in *Economic Letters*, 21 (3).

Bergmann, B. R. (1974). 'Occupational segregation, wages and profits when employers discriminate by race and sex' in *Eastern Economic Journal*, 1 (1–2).

Bergmann, B. R. (1987). 'The task of a feminist economics: a more equitable future' in Farnham, C. (ed.) *The Impact of Feminist Research in the Academy*. Bloomington: Indiana University Press.

Blau, F. and Ferber, M. A. (1986). *The Economics of Women, Men and Work*. Englewood Cliffs: Prentice Hall.

Blau, F. and Ferber, M. A. (1987). 'Discrimination: empirical evidence from the United States' in *American Economic Review*, 77 (2).

Bloom, D. E. and Killingsworth, M. R. (1982). 'Pay discrimination research and litigation: the use of regression' in *Industrial Relations*, 21.

Boserup, E. (1987). 'Inequality between the sexes' in Eatwell, J., Milgate, M. and Newman, P. (eds.) *The New Palgrave: A Dictionary of Economics*. London: Macmillan.

Cain, G. C. (1986). 'Labor market discrimination', in Ashenfelter, O. and Layard, R. (eds.) *Handbook of Labor Economics*. Amsterdam: North Holland.

Charles, N. (1993). *Gender Divisions and Social Change*. Hemel Hempstead: Harvester Wheatsheaf.

Chiplin, B. and Sloane, P. (1976). *Sex Discrimination in the Labour Market*. London: Macmillan.

Chiswick, B. R. (1973). 'Racial discrimination and the labor market: a test of alternative hypotheses' in *Journal of Political Economy*, 81.

Cockburn, C. (1986). 'The relations of technology: what implications for theories of sex and class' in Crompton, R. and Mann, M. (eds.) *Gender and Stratification*. Cambridge: Polity.

Comador, W. S. (1973). 'Racial discrimination in American industry' in *Economica*, 40.

Corcoran, M. E. and Courant, P. N. (1987). 'Sex-role socialisation and occupational segregation: an exploratory investigation' in *Journal of Post Keynesian Economics*, 9, (3).

Coyle, A. (1982). 'Sex and skill in the organisation of the clothing industry' in West, J. (ed.) *Work, Women and the Labour Market*. London: Routledge and Kegan Paul.

Craig, C., Rubery, J., Tarling, R. and Wilkinson, F. (1982). *Labour Market Structure, Industrial Organisation and Low Pay*. Cambridge: Cambridge University Press.

Craig, C., Garnsey, E. and Rubery, J. (1985). 'Labour market segmentation and women's employment: a case study from the United Kingdom' in *International Labor Review*, 124 (3).

Dex, S. (1985). *The Sexual Division of Labour*. Brighton: Wheatsheaf.

Dex, S. (1988). 'Gender and the labour market' in Gallie, D. (ed.) *Employment in Britain*. Oxford: Blackwells.

Dolton, P. J. and Makepeace, G. H. (1986). 'Sample selection and male–female earnings differentials in the graduate labour market' in *Oxford Economic Papers*, 38 (2).

Dolton, P. J. and Makepeace, G. H. (1987). 'Interpreting sample selection effects' in *Economic Letters*, 24 (4).

Edwards, P. (1994). 'Review article: economic theory, the labour market and inequality' in *Work, Employment and Society*, 8 (2).

England, P. (1982). 'The failure of human capital theory to explain occupational sex segregation' in *Journal of Human Resources*, 17 (3).

England, P. (1985). 'Occupational segregation: rejoinder to Polachek' in *Journal of Human Resources*, 20 (3).

England, P. (1989). 'A feminist critique of rational choice theories: implications for sociology' in *The American Sociologist*, 20 (1).

England, P. (1993). 'The separative self: andocentric bias in neo-classical assumptions' in Ferber, M. A. and Nelson, J. A. (eds.) *Beyond Economic Man: Feminist Theory and Economics*. Chicago: University of Chicago Press.

Feiner, S. F. and Roberts, B. B. (1990). 'Hidden by the invisible hand: neo-classical economic theory and the textbook treatment of race and gender' in *Gender and Society*, 4 (2).

Ferber, M. A. and Lowry, H. M. (1976). 'The sex differential in earnings: a reappraisal' in *Industrial and Labor Relations Review*, 29.

Ferber, M. A., and Birnbaum, B. G. (1977). 'The "New Home Economics": retrospects and prospects' in *Journal of Consumer Research*, 4.

Ferber, M. A. and Birnbaum, B. G. (1980). 'Housework: priceless or valueless?' in *Review of Income and Wealth*, 26 (4).

Ferber, M. A. and Teiman, M. L. (1981). 'The oldest, the most established, the most quantitative of the social sciences – and the most dominated by men: the impact of feminism on economics' in Spender, D. (ed.) *Men's Studies Modified: The Impact of Feminism on the Academic Disciplines*. New York: Pergamon.

Ferber, M. A. and Nelson, J. A. (eds.) (1993). *Beyond Economic Man: Feminist Theory and Economics*. (*Op. cit.*)

Fine, B. (1992). *Women's Employment and the Capitalist Family*. London: Routledge.

Folbre, N., and Hartmann, H. (1988). 'The rhetoric of self-interest: ideology and gender in Economic Theory' in Klamer, A., McCloskey, D. N. and Solow, R. M. (eds.) *The Consequences of Economic Rhetoric*. Cambridge: Cambridge University Press.

Folbre, N. (1994). *Who Pays for the Kids: Gender and the Structures of Constraint*. London and New York: Routledge.

Frank, R (1988). *Passions Within Reason. The Strategic Role of the Emotions*. New York: Norton.

Fuchs, V. R. (1971). 'Differences in hourly earnings between men and women' in *Monthly Labor Review*, 94 (5).

Fuji, E. T. and Trapani, J. M. (1978). 'On estimating the relationship between discrimination and market structure' in *Southern Economic Journal*, 45.

Game, R. and Pringle, A. (1983). *Gender at Work*. London: Allen and Unwin.

Granovetter, M. (1985). 'Economic action, social structure and embeddedness' in *American Journal of Sociology*, 93 (3).

Gunderson, M. (1985). 'Discrimination, equal pay, and equal opportunities in the labour market' in Riddell, C. (ed.) *Work and Pay: The Canadian Labour Market*. Toronto: University of Toronto Press.

Gunderson, M. (1989). 'Male–female wage differentials and policy responses' in *Journal of Economic Literature*, 27 (1).

Haessell, W. and Palmer, J. (1978). 'Market power and employment discrimination' in *Journal of Human Resources*, 13.

Hammond, P. (1987). 'Altruism' in Eatwell, J., Milgate, M. and Newman, P. (eds.) *The New Palgrave: A Dictionary of Economics*. (*Op. cit.*)

Harding, S. (1986). *The Science Question in Feminism*. Ithaca: Cornell University Press.

Harding, S. (1992a). 'After the neutrality ideal: science, politics, and "strong objectivity"' in *Social Research*, 59 (3).

Harding, S. (1992b). 'Rethinking standpoint epistemology: what is "strong objectivity"' in Alcoff, L. and Potter, E. (eds.) *Feminist Epistemologies*. New York: Routledge.

Hartmann, H. (1979). 'The unhappy marriage of Marxism and feminism: towards a more progressive union' in *Capital and Class*, 8.

Heckman, J. J. (1974). 'Shadow prices, market wages and labor supply' in *Econometrica*, 42 (4).

Heckman, J. J. (1976). 'The common structure of statistical models of truncation, sample selection and limited dependent variables and a simple estimator for such models' in *Annals of Economic and Social Measurement*, 5.

Heckman, J. J. (1979). 'Sample selection bias as a specification error' in *Econometrica*, 47 (1).

Heckman, J. J., Killingsworth, M. R. and MaCurdy, T. E. M. (1981). 'Empirical evidence on static labour supply models: a survey of recent developments', in Hornstein, Z., Grice, J. and Webb, A. (eds.) *The Economics of the Labour Market*. London: HMSO.

Hirshleifer, J. (1985). 'The expanding domain of economics' in *American Economic Review*, 75 (6).

Horrell, S., Rubery, J. and Burchell, B. (1990). 'Gender and skills' in *Work, Employment and Society*, 4 (2).

Humphries, J. (1982). 'Review of *A Treatise on the Family* by G. S. Becker' in *Economic Journal*, 92 (367).

Humphries, J. (1994). 'Review of *Beyond Economic Man: Feminist Theory and Economics*, Ferber, M. A. and Nelson, J. A. (eds.)' in *Journal of Economic History*, 54 (2).

Humphries, J. and Rubery, J. (1984). 'The reconstitution of the supply side of the labour market: the relative autonomy of social reproduction' in *Cambridge Journal of Economics*, 8 (4).

Killingsworth, M. R. and Heckman, J. J. (1986). 'Female labor supply' in Ashenfelter, O. and Layard, R. (eds.) *Handbook of Labor Economics*. (*Op. cit.*)

Lloyd, C. and Neimi, B. (1979). *The Economics of Sex Differentials*. New York: Columbia University Press.

Lundberg, S. and Pollak, R. A. (1992). *Separate Spheres, Bargaining and the Marriage Market*. Mimeo, Department of Economics, University of Washington.

Madden, J. (1985). 'The persistence of pay differentials: the economics of sex discrimination' in Larwood, L., Stromberg, A. and Gutek, B. (eds.) *Women and Work: An Annual Review*. Beverly Hills: Sage.

Malkiel, B. and Malkiel, J. (1973). 'Male–female pay differentials in professional employment' in *American Economic Review*, 63 (4).

Manser, M. and Brown, M. (1980). 'Marriage and household decision-making: a bargaining analysis' in *International Economic Review*, 21 (1).

Mayer, C. (1987). 'The assessment: financial systems and corporate investment' in *Oxford Review of Economic Policy*, 3 (4).

McElroy, M. B. and Horney, M. J. 1981. 'Nash-bargained household decisions: towards a generalisation of the theory of demand' in *International Economic Review*, 22 (2).

Medoff, M. H. (1979–80). 'On the relationship between discrimination and market structure: a comment' in *Southern Economic Journal*, 46.

Mincer, J. and Polachek, S. (1974). 'Family investments in human capital: earnings of women' in *Journal of Political Economy*, 82 (2).

Nelson, J. A. (1992). 'Gender, metaphor, and the definition of economics' in *Economics and Philosophy*, 8 (1).

North, D. (1981). *Structural Change in Economic History*. New York: Norton.

North, D. (1990). *Institutions, Institutional Change and Economic Performance*. Cambridge: Cambridge University Press.

Oaxaca, R. (1973). 'Male–female wage differentials in urban labor markets' in *International Economic Review*, 14 (3).

Oster, S. M. (1975). 'Industry differences in the level of discrimination against women' in *Quarterly Journal of Economics*, 89 (2).

Phelps, E. S. (1972). 'The statistical theory of racism and sexism' in *American Economic Review*, 62 (4).

Phillips, A. and Taylor, B. (1980). 'Sex and skill: notes towards a feminist economics' in *Feminist Review*, 6.

Piore, M. J. (1975). 'Notes for a theory of labor market stratification' in Edwards, R., Reich, M. and Gordon, D. (eds.) *Labor Market Segmentation*. Lexington. Mass: D. C. Heath and Co.

Polachek, S. (1973). *Work Experience and the Difference Between Male and Female Wages*. Unpublished PhD dissertation, Department of Economics, Columbia University.

Polachek, S. (1976). 'Occupational segregation: an alternative hypothesis' in *Journal of Contemporary Business*, 5.

Polachek, S. (1979). 'Occupational segregation among women: theory, evidence, and a prognosis' in Lloyd, C., Andrews, E. and Gilroy, C. (eds.) *Women in the Labour Market*. New York: Columbia University Press.

Polachek, S. (1985). 'Occupational segregation: a defence of human capital predictions' in *Journal of Human Resources*, 20 (3).

Pollak, R. A. (1985). 'A transactions cost approach to families and households' in *Journal of Economic Literature*, XXIII (2).

Poovey, M. (1988). 'Feminism and deconstruction' in *Feminist Studies*, 14 (1).

Robinson, J. (1933). *The Economics of Imperfect Competition*. London: Macmillan.

Samuelson, P. A. (1956). 'Social indifference curves' in *Quarterly Journal of Economics*, 70 (1).

Sanborn, H. (1964). 'Pay differences between men and women' in *Industrial and Labor Relations Review*, 17 (4).

Sap, J., Cuelenaere, B. and Schreurs, P. (1993). 'Economic theory: assumptions, contents and concepts' in *Out of the Margin: Book of Abstracts*. Amsterdam: International Scientific Conference.

Sawhill, I. V. (1977). 'Economic perspectives on the family' in *Daedalus, Journal of the American Academy of Arts and Sciences*, 106 (2).

Seiz, J. A. (1991). 'The bargaining approach and feminist methodology' in *Review of Radical Political Economy*, 23.

Shapiro, C. and Stiglitz, J. E. (1984). 'Equilibrium unemployment as a worker discipline device' in *American Economic Review*, 75.

Shepherd, W. G. and Levin, S. G. (1973). 'Managerial discrimination in large firms' in *Review of Economics and Statistics*, 60 (4).

Smith, A. (1776). *An Enquiry into the Wealth of Nations*. London: W. Strahan and T. Cadell.

Stiglitz, J. E. (1987). 'Principal and agent' in Eatwell, J., Milgate, M. and Newman, P. (eds.) *The New Palgrave: A Dictionary of Economics*. (*Op. cit.*)

Strassmann, D. (1993). 'Not a free market: the rhetoric of disciplinary authority in economics' in Ferber, M. A. and Nelson, J. A. (eds.) *Beyond Economic Man: Feminist Theory and Economics*. (*Op. cit.*)

Treiman, D. and Hartmann, H. (eds.) (1981). *Women, Work, and Wages: Equal Pay for Jobs of Equal Value*. Washington: National Academy Press.

Walby, S. (1986). *Patriarchy at Work*. Oxford: Polity.

Willborn, S. A. (1986). *A Comparable Worth Primer*. Lexington, Mass: D. C. Heath and Co.

Winter, S. G. (1987). 'Natural selection and evolution' in Eatwell, J., Milgate, M. and Newman, P. (eds.) *The New Palgrave: A Dictionary of Economics*. (*Op. cit.*)

Woolley, F. R. (1993). 'The feminist challenge to neo-classsical economics' in *Cambridge Journal of Economics*, 17 (1).

Wright, R. E. and Ermisch, J. F. (1991). 'Gender discrimination in the British labour market: a reassessment' in *Economic Journal*, 101 (406).

Zabalza, A. and Arrufat, J. L. (1985). 'The extent of sex discrimination in Great Britain' in Zabalza, A. and Tzannatos, Z. (eds.) *Women and Equal Pay: The Effects of Legislation on Female Employment and Wages in Britain*. Cambridge: Cambridge University Press.

Zabalza, A. and Tzannatos, Z. (1985). *Women and Equal Pay: The Effects of Legislation on Female Employment and Wages in Britain*. (*Op. cit.*)

Zellner, H. (1975). 'The determinants of occupational segregation' in Lloyd, C. (ed.) *Sex, Discrimination, and the Division of Labor*. New York: Columbia University Press.

CHAPTER 4

Pay Gaps Facing Men and Women Born in 1958: Differences Within the Labour Market

Pierella Paci, Heather Joshi and Gerry Makepeace

This chapter explores the role of conditions in the labour market in setting differential rates of pay for men and women as observed in survey data. The study allows for pay differentials attributable to productivity-related personal characteristics, or 'human capital'. Pay differences not accounted for by such human capital characteristics would reflect unequal treatment if no other relevant factors remained unobserved. Although differential accumulation of these personal assets may also be the result of unequal treatment ('pre-entry discrimination'), it is unequal remuneration of these attributes in the labour market which is conventionally defined as discrimination by economists ('post-entry discrimination').

The introduction of labour market conditions into the explanation of wage differentials is primarily intended to identify channels through which unequal treatment occurs, but it can also indicate the existence of some otherwise unobserved non-discriminatory factors. Although this approach can account for pay differences arising from the sorting of male and female workers into different types of job, it would still leave any unequal treatment within jobs unexplained.

The notion of discrimination in law is not defined in exactly the same way as in economic analysis. The Equal Pay Act, 1970, made it illegal to offer different wages for the same work on the grounds of sex. This resulted in the disappearance of different nationally-negotiated rates for men and women, but pay gaps remained – particularly between jobs done mainly by women and less segregated types of employment. These gaps were addressed in many countries by laws enjoining equal pay for work of comparable worth: in the UK the legislation was the Equal Pay for Equal Value amendment to the Equal Pay Act, 1983. Under the amended law, a woman can claim that her low pay is discriminatory by producing a male comparator doing comparable work for greater pay. An employment tribunal accepts as evidence of discrimination case-by-case detail on what work is actually performed and, since the Equal Value amendment, assesses whether the skills are comparable.

The economist, by contrast, does secondary analysis of less detailed material for a large number of cases. Unequal treatment is deemed to occur if, allowing for observed attributes that are expected to lead to equivalent productivity, workers are not in fact equally rewarded. These attributes are not specific to particular jobs, but are more general determinants of earning power, education and experience which ought to bring an equivalent return in a competitive labour market. Wage differentials adjusted for such characteristics are often used to measure discrimination. However, wage differences between equally productive workers may arise from a large array of labour market conditions, and these are often neglected.

This chapter addresses the topical question of how far the gender pay gap experienced by young adults in Britain is a result of:

- different observable personal characteristics of male and female workers;
- differences in the employers they work for, the jobs they do, and the labour markets in which they operate;
- unexplained differences, possibly unequal treatment, within each sector of the labour market.

The study brings an important new source of evidence to bear on this issue: the fifth sweep of the National Child Development Study (NCDS5), which reports gross pay at the age of 33 and gives an unusually wide array of information on jobs and personal characteristics. Although the cohort only provides evidence on people who were 33 in 1991, they are not unrepresentative of the labour force as a whole in terms of gaps between the wages of men and women (see Paci *et al.*, 1994).

Evidence on the type of firm, the characteristics of the particular contract, proxies for the degree of monopoly power, and the occupation of 33-year-old workers is used to investigate the theoretical background. One job characteristic pervading the analysis is whether a woman's job is part-time. This factor is a major correlate of low pay, and also affects the relationship of women's pay to other variables. This analysis therefore allows for interactions between personal and job characteristics and part-time employment. Do job characteristics help explain the gap between part-time and full-time rates for women as well as the gap between full-time women and full-time men, and thereby the gap between full-time men and part-time women? Too few men were employed part-time (around one per cent) to be included in the analysis.

The combined effect of systematic gender differences in all these variables was found to account for a 17 per cent lead of men's wages over women's, leaving 19 per cent of women's pay unaccounted for. The product of these two differences is the observed gap of 39 per cent. The 19 per cent is an upper measure of unequal treatment within jobs, expressed as a percentage of women's pay (averaged over full-time and part-time jobs). Pay differentials between jobs are more apparent for part-time workers.

Theoretical background

What leads to unequal wages between men and women? In a competitive labour market with perfect information and identical working conditions, wages could be expected to differ only between workers with different productivity-related endowments. If the available jobs differ in their degree of desirability, differences in wages are required to compensate workers in the less desirable jobs (Rosen, 1986). When the assumption of perfect information is removed, wage differentials between similar workers may arise from the presence of internal labour markets (Siebert and Addison, 1991). Finally, in non-competitive labour markets wage differences may be the outcome of the differential degrees of monopoly power in different sub-markets.

The effect of trade unions on the relative wages of otherwise similar workers is well known in the literature on wage differentials (see Lewis, 1986, for a survey). The theory of discriminatory monopsony (monopoly of demand) is also important in this context. According to this theory, if both men and women operate in a monopsonistic labour market, the gender wage gap would reflect the different elasticity of supply for labour attributed to the two groups by empirical studies. Furthermore, if (due to different family commitments and attachment to the labour force) the monopsonistic conditions apply only (or predominantly) to women, gender pay differentials reflect 'exploitation' by the monopsonist employer. Women may be paid less than their marginal value product, compared to the competitive treatment of men (see Reagan, 1978, for some empirical evidence in this area).

Even in the absence of any of these mechanisms, wage differentials may arise out of various forms of discrimination. Becker's well-known 'taste-based' theory (Becker, 1957) proposes three types of discrimination:

- employer discrimination – employers have a preference for male workers rather than female workers;
- employee discrimination – male workers 'dislike' being in a hierarchically-inferior position to women;
- consumer discrimination – consumers prefer to deal with men rather than women.

Employer discrimination implies that the employer is maximising some more general form of utility than just profits: the objective of the employer lies in increasing profits and decreasing the proportion of women employed. Women are then employed only if the employer can compensate the disadvantage derived from doing so by increasing profits. This is only possible if a wage differential exists between equally productive workers of the two groups. Depending on the prevailing labour market conditions, this wage differential may arise from women being paid their marginal value product and men receiving higher pay, or women being 'exploited'. The latter option is only available to the monopsonistic employer facing an upward-sloping supply curve for women. If the supply curve for both groups is perfectly elastic (if the labour market is competitive) the employer's taste for discrimination results in men being paid more than the competitive wage.

Two main conclusions follow from this: employer discrimination is inefficient, since it results in a misallocation of resources; and it can only survive in the long run if either the employer enjoys some degree of monopoly power in the output market, or all producers in that market have an identical taste for discrimination. If this is not the case, less discriminatory employers would force the others out by employing a higher percentage of women and therefore reducing labour costs.

Employee and consumer discrimination provide different explanations of gender wage differentials. In the former, employment of women would cause the marginal value product of other employees to decline. In the latter, the marginal value product of women is reduced by the consumer's preference for men. In both cases the result is employment discrimination, with women being segregated away from discriminatory male employees and into occupations where consumers are more willing to accept them (such as sales and caring work).

If women are segregated into a relatively small number of occupations and/or employers, the abundant supply of labour in these sectors would push wages down and the employer would acquire some degree of monopsony power, reinforcing the possibility of discriminatory wage policy. This is the 'crowding' hypothesis, put forward by Edgeworth in 1922 and later developed by Zellner (1972), Bergmann (1971) and others, from which the hypotheses of labour market segmentation and dual labour markets are derived (Chiswick, 1973; Stiglitz, 1973).

Finally, statistical discrimination may occur in markets where information on an individual worker's productivity is imperfect (Phelps, 1972). The employer pays higher wages or has a preference for hiring men because the expected productivity of individual male workers is higher. The difference in the expected productivity of men and women can be due to the employer knowing the average productivity of women to be lower than that of men, and/or individual variations around the mean to be larger; or the employer using weaker signals to predict individual productivity for women. The extent of statistical discrimination thus depends on how far men and women differ in terms of their productivity and their ability to provide signals of comparable strength.

Figure 4.1 summarises the potential sources of wage differentials. The lightly-shaded area indicates that part of the differential which is explained by differences in personal characteristics between the two groups. In the initial human capital model this amounts to 31 per cent of the total differential between men and women (0.108 out of a total log-wage differential of 0.354). Such differentials are not normally thought of as discriminatory, except to the extent that they reflect pre-entry discrimination (the magnitude of which cannot be measured). The darker shade represents the unexplained component of the gender wage gap which, conventionally, would pick up discriminatory practices.

But the unexplained component may not all result from discrimination: it may reflect differences in the degree of desirability of the jobs done by the

Figure 4.1 Potential components of the pay gap

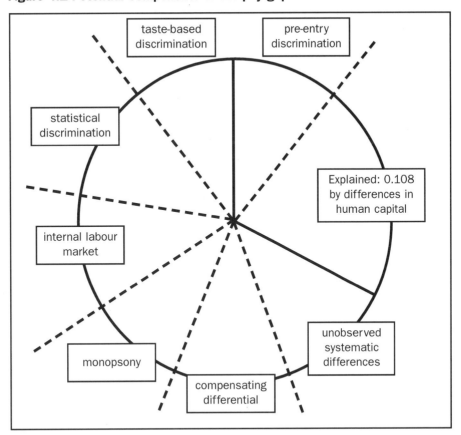

two groups (compensating wage differentials); differences in their elasticity of supply (monopsonistic price discrimination); differential access to internal labour markets; or a wider variation in the productivity of the members of the two groups or a difference in their mean productivity (statistical discrimination). Even after all these factors are taken into account, differences in wages may result from systematic differences in the productive characteristics of the two groups of workers, which the data available fails to capture. However, the possibility of unequal treatment resulting from a pure 'taste for discrimination' cannot be excluded.

The different sources of unequal treatment are not easily quantified, and any one element could be positive or negative. On a narrow definition of discrimination one might be concerned only with the 'taste-based' segment of Figure 4.1; on a broader definition the concern may be with the segment on either side, including pre-entry discrimination. What Figure 4.1 does not illustrate is the distinction between unequal treatment occurring within jobs, and in the process of sorting between jobs. This implies a different set of categories in the shaded areas which the regressions presented here do not attempt to chart.

The conceptualisation and modelling of pay differentials

How can the various determinants of unequal pay be decomposed?

The standard method of accounting for the gender wage gap involves estimating separate earnings equations for male and female employees. This permits the decomposition of the aggregate pay differential into explained (endowment) and unexplained (residual) components – the measure of discrimination and other market imperfections reviewed earlier. The implicit assumption is that wage gaps arising from differences in endowment are a separate problem from those arising from differential remuneration of that endowment.

This view is supported by efficiency as well as equity considerations. Horizontal equity within the labour market would require workers with equal endowments to receive equal pay, independent of personal characteristics such as gender, age or race. For the labour market to operate efficiently, equally productive workers should receive equal pay. Failure to do so will, amongst other things, reinforce if not influence gender differences in allocating time between paid and unpaid work, acquisition of skills and accumulation of human capital. Low returns on the latter for women may inhibit the development of their full potential to contribute to the economy.

What should be allowed to vary in the assessment of equal pay?

It is not conventional to include controls in the earnings equation for employer and job characteristics in general, nor for occupational differences in particular. Human capital theorists argue against the inclusion of such controls, on the grounds that the explanatory variables should solely reflect supply-side differences. While it is possible that different occupational distributions arise from individual choice, many see the fact that women tend to concentrate in a relatively limited number of poorly-paid activities as a demand-side phenomenon, caused by employers' tendency to 'segregate' women by denying them access to the more desirable jobs (employment discrimination).

The decision whether or not to include occupational and other variables in the earnings analysis depends on subjective views of what constitutes discrimination. Bloom and Killingsworth (1982) divide overall workplace discrimination into within-group discrimination, defined in terms of 'unequal pay for equal work'; and unequal access, defined in terms of 'unequal work for the same qualifications'. If the concern is simply with the former, one would control for occupation and job characteristics. When the focus shifts to the broader workplace-wide view of discrimination, however, the rationale for inclusion of job-related variables lies in the extent to which supply determines gender differences in these variables. The outcome of individual choice should be allowed for, but employment discrimination on the demand side should not. In a context of no differential access, discrimination would only occur within groups. The opposite view is taken in the most strict human capital specification: by not controlling for any occupational and job-related differences, this implicitly treats them all as vehicles through which discrimination occurs.

In reality any gender differences in occupational distribution and other job characteristics are likely to reflect both employment discrimination and different preferences between the two groups. The initial human capital specification, by treating all job-related differences as discriminatory, may thus overestimate the extent of discrimination. On the other hand, the more extensive model with job-related controls may underestimate the full magnitude of gender discrimination, to the extent that there are discriminatory processes in the gendering of occupational and job-related outcomes (Blau and Ferber, 1987).

This study adopts an agnostic position as to whether job characteristics are the outcome of constrained opportunities or individual choices. The point of departure is an analysis in terms of personal characteristics only; followed by exploration of other potential determinants of the gender wage gap. The unexplained component of the differential was expected to decline as more extensive specifications were used. Contrary to the standard approach to gender discrimination, the study distinguishes between women employed part-time and full-time, and computes three decompositions to reflect differential treatment between full-time women and men; full-time women and part-time women; and full-time men and part-time women. Tests enquire whether each group is systematically differently remunerated, then separate equations are run where the statistical test indicates this is appropriate.[1]

Definition of data and variables

The NCDS data used in the study comes from the most recent survey of a cohort born in 1958, when they were aged 33 in 1991. For further study details, see Ferri (1993). Over 18,000 people have at some stage taken part in the NCDS, though only 11,407 people participated in the 1991 interview (NCDS5), and not all gave complete information. The estimates used here are based primarily on data derived from the main cohort questionnaire. The work experience and job tenure variables, however, derive from retrospective employment history information given at age 33 in a separate self-completed form. Altogether, usable data on the wages of employees was collected for 6,800 cases.

The estimates of the male–to–female pay ratio among full-timers which emerge (1.203 in the regression sample, 1.223 when all NCDS5 respondents with good wage data are considered) are close to the all-age

---

[1] The hypothesis of selectivity bias amongst women is tested using a Heckman procedure, extended to allow for an Ordered Probit selection into full- and part-time employment. The consistently insignificant coefficient of the lamba term in the earnings equation of both part-time and full-time women has led to the rejection of the possibility of selection bias into both part-time and full-time employment. The estimation results for the selection-adjusted models are therefore not reported.

median of 1.266 as reported from the New Earnings Survey. This suggests that analysis of the cohort probably does have some applicability to a wider age group, and is unlikely to overstate the wage gap phenomenon.

The availability of detailed information on human capital variables, such as the extent and type of general training undertaken by individual workers and their actual job experience and tenure, is a major advantage of using NCDS for analysing gender wage differentials. These represent crucial explanatory variables in any form of human capital earnings function, but unfortunately are very rarely available. Most previous studies have been forced either to ignore them (as for the training and tenure variables), or use proxies (with potential experience often used in place of actual experience). Neither of these solutions is satisfactory, given the wide gender differences in the proportion of those with training (54 per cent of men and 47 per cent of women full-timers, but only 23 per cent of women part-timers), length of service (7.7, 7.0 and 3.4 years respectively), and career interruptions (female full-timers and part-timers have only 8.9 and 5.6 years of average experience after the age of 23 respectively, compared to 10.0 years for men).

The earnings function was estimated for cohort members currently employed as employees with valid information on wages (gross pay per hour). The simplest human capital earnings function specifies hourly pay to depend upon the worker's ability, educational achievements (and any vocational training undertaken), record of attachment to the labour force, and seniority with the current employer. Years of employment experience are counted only from age 23, as the earlier years were less completely covered in the retrospective histories collected in 1991. For such cases as could be included, employment experience before age 23 was not a significant term in wage equations.

Separate earnings functions are estimated for full-time men, and women working full-time and part-time, since the two sectors have been shown to remunerate women's human capital unequally (Ermisch and Wright, 1992). The relevant sample sizes are 2,946, 1,441 and 983, after excluding 1,375 cases with missing data on at least one regressor and discarding the 35 men employed part-time. The dependent variable in the earnings equation is the log of the gross hourly wage earned in a typical week by the cohort member. This is derived by dividing the wage per period reported by the number of hours worked in that period (including overtime). Additional details on the explanatory variables are given in Table 4.2.

The second specification estimated includes variables reflecting the characteristics of the employer (see Table 4.2). These are designed to reflect the extent of monopoly power both in output and in the labour market, and any additional institutional factor which may operate on the demand side. Thus the employer's size may also be taken as a proxy for the extent to which the employer operates some form of internal market, as this is more common in larger firms where full information on individual productivity is more difficult to achieve. The inclusion of a

Table 4.2 Variable definition and rationale for inclusion

Variable	Definition	Designed to capture
Dependent variable		
Log hourly wage	Gross wage per hour of workers (including overtime)	
Explanatory variables		
Personal		
Ability at 11	General ability as measured at age 11	Innate ability
O levels	Dummy = 1 if highest educational qualification O level	Education
A levels	Dummy = 1 if highest educational qualification A level	Education
Diploma	Dummy = 1 if highest educational qualification FE diploma	Education
Degree	Dummy = 1 if highest educational qualification degree	Education
Training	Dummy = 1 if any training longer than three days undertaken at any time	General and specific training
Years employed since age 23	Recent work experience (in years)	On-the-job training + experience
Years in this job	Length of service with current employer (in years)	Internal labour market (ILM) + seniority
Employer		
South East	Dummy = 1 if living in London or South East	Degree of monopoly in labour market Compensation for high living costs
Small firm	Dummy = 1 if working in small business (<25 employees)	Monopsony power (MP) + ILM
Large firm	Dummy = 1 if working in large estab. (>100 employees)	MP + ILM
Private sector	Dummy = 1 if working in the private sector	Degree of monopoly power in output market + flexibility
Training paid by firm	Dummy = 1 if employer paid for any training undertaken	ILM
Job		
Fringe benefits	Dummy = 1 if fringe benefits available	Compensating differential (CD)
Hours flexible	Dummy = 1 if contract allows for flexible working hours	CD
Supervision	Dummy = 1 if job involves supervising other workers	CD
Travel to work	Time spend travelling to work each day (in minutes)	CD + MP
Union member	Dummy = 1 if member of union	Degree of monopoly in labour market
Occupational hierarchy		
Professionals inc. teachers	Dummy = 1 if in professional occupation or teacher	CD + MP + output market conditions
Other intermediate	Dummy = 1 if in other intermediate occupations	CD + MP + output market conditions
Clerical-related	Dummy = 1 if clerical or related	CD + MP + output market conditions
Service and shop	Dummy = 1 if in retail or other services not above	CD + MP + output market conditions
Skilled occupations	Dummy = 1 if in other skilled occupations	CD + MP + output market conditions
Occupational segregation		
Feminised	Dummy = 1 if women represent over 50 per cent of the labour force	Extent of segregation as discriminatory device

variable for the South East reflects some form of compensating differential for working in an expensive area, of which the London weighting allowance is a clear example. Controlling for private ownership of the firm allows for the higher degrees of flexibility in the pay structure of this sector, and for the fact that the output market in which private firms operate tends to be more competitive than that faced by public organisations.

Differences in job characteristics are allowed for by controlling for the availability of fringe benefits and other job 'amenities' (including the provision of employer-financed training), time spent travelling to work each day, and unionisation. The inclusion of these variables is intended to reflect differences in the degree of desirability of the job, and account further for any differential degree of monopoly power on either side of the labour market. The time spent travelling to work is presumed to reflect the area over which the employee could search for other jobs, and thus indicates those who may be exposed to local monopsony power because they are unwilling or unable to travel. It could also reflect a compensating differential for travel costs. Fringe benefits include the chance to buy company shares; the availability of a company vehicle for private use and any other travel benefits; provision of subsidised meals, private medical insurance or an employer pension scheme; offers of help with childcare; and discounts on goods and services. Pension cover is among those mentioned most frequently. Union membership is expected to increase the worker's degree of bargaining power; and the provision of training is seen as a proxy for the presence of some form of internal market.

Finally, occupation is introduced into the earnings equation. Occupations, defined in terms of the three-digit standard occupational classification (SOC), were grouped into seven roughly hierarchical bands, with semi-skilled and unskilled jobs as the reference category (unskilled jobs on their own being too small in number to treat separately). Likewise, 'top' professional jobs were a small category banded with teachers, most of whom are graduates in this generation. Nurses, despite including some equivalently qualified to teachers, were classed with other intermediate non-manual occupations, some of whom may also be highly qualified. Shop workers are grouped with less-skilled service workers rather than clerical workers (as in the Registrar General's social class scheme), to reflect their relative labour market status (Joshi and Newell, 1987).

A further dimension of occupational information is added by characterising the occupation in terms of whether it is likely to be done mainly by women or not. The idea is to see whether occupational segregation is the mechanism making equal pay legislation less than perfectly effective. Even with the Equal Value ('comparable worth') amendment to the Equal Pay Act, it is more difficult to claim equal pay when male comparators are hard to find.

The likely segregation of the NCDS cohort's occupations has been imputed by reference to the British all-age sex ratio of employees in each of the 350

OPCS 1980 occupational groups, taken from the 1981 Census (at the time of the study, the 1991 Tables on Economic Activity had not yet been published). Occupations which had more than 50 per cent female incumbents in the national data were classified as 'feminised'. It is worth noting that this definition of occupational segregation does not identify workplace segregation.

Results

Starting with the analysis of wage differentials in terms of personal characteristics only, Table 4.3 gives details of 2,946 men employed full-time, 1,441 women employed full-time and 983 employed part-time. Their hourly wages at the geometric mean were £7.17, £5.95 and £3.92 respectively. Male wages were 20 per cent higher than those of full-time women, and 83 per cent ahead of the part-timers.

Table 4.3 Model of wage differentials explained by personal characteristics: men and women employed full-time and women employed part-time, aged 33 in 1991, NCDS

Variable	Coefficient			Means		
	Full-time men	Full-time women	Part-time women	Full-time men	Full-time women	Part-time women
Dependent variable log hourly wage				1.970	1.785	1.367
Constant	1.271	1.096	0.960			
Ability at 11	0.004	0.005	0.002	45.28	48.61	44.16
O levels	0.099	0.030	0.069	0.24	0.32	0.39
A levels	0.153	0.077	0.069#	0.20	0.10	0.05
Diploma	0.275	0.289	0.511	0.16	0.19	0.13
Degree	0.452	0.437	0.640	0.16	0.17	0.06
Training	- 0.015#	0.112	0.103#	0.54	0.47	0.23
If employer paid	0.158	0.066#	0.028#	0.51	0.45	0.19
Years employed since age 23	0.025	0.016	0.019	10.01	8.95	5.64
Years in this job	0.002#	0.011	0.011	7.68	6.97	3.44
Adjusted R^2	0.280	0.377	0.397			
n	2946	1441	983			
F	128.498	97.638	72.737			
Differences between	Men/FT women	FT/PT women	Men/PT women			
Raw differential of which:	0.185	0.418	0.603			
unexplained*	0.168	0.192	0.360			
explained	0.017	0.233	0.250			

Note 1 # denotes not significantly different from zero; *coefficient differences weighted by means of full-time women.

It is more convenient to express these differentials in terms of logs because their components can be added up; when differentials are expressed as percentages, their components must be multiplied together. For example, a total differential of 44 per cent could be the product of explained and unexplained components of 20 per cent each (because 1.2 x 1.2 = 1.44). If expressed in logs, the total gap would be 0.36 and each component 0.18. The analysis is thus conducted in terms of logs, and the log differentials are translated into percentages in the summary Table 4.9.

The raw ratio for men to full-time women was 0.185, full-time women to part-time women 0.418, and men to part-time women 0.603. At the outset, therefore, the gap between full-timers and part-timers is larger than any gender gap amongst full-timers. Full-timers, whether female or male, seem relatively well paid in comparison.

How much of the gender wage gap is explained by personal characteristics?

The personal characteristics allowed for in Table 4.3 explain 28 per cent and 40 per cent of the variance within each sub-sample. The coefficients have the expected signs (at least where significant). The existence of structural differences of parameters across full-time men, full-time women and part-time women was tested using traditional F-tests.[2] These rejected the hypothesis that the coefficients were the same across the sub-samples. A closer look surprisingly reveals some coefficients to be more favourable for part-timers than for full-time women – for example, the minority of cases with higher education. Likewise, the parameters for men are not unambiguously more favourable than for full-time women.

On balance, differences in 'human capital endowment' account for very little of the full-time male–female gap of 0.185 (20.3 per cent). Such factors as a one-year lead in work experience, and a seven per cent lead in the proportion having been trained, raise log-pay by 0.017 (1.7 per cent), leaving 0.168 (18.3 per cent) unexplained. The magnitude of the unexplained component – derived as the weighted sum of the differences between the coefficients for the two groups – provides an estimate of the extent of unequal treatment of men and women in the labour market.[3]

---

[2] The F-test is designed to test the hypothesis H0 that the regression parameters are the same across two (or more) sub-samples, versus the alternative hypothesis H1 that they differ. The test is based on a comparison of the 'sum of squares' for the pooled sample with that resulting from running separate regressions for each of the relevant sub-samples. The test score is compared with the critical values of an F-distribution with the relevant number of degrees of freedom. A test score lower than the critical value implies acceptance of H0, and vice versa. Accepting H0 implies that the sub-samples can jointly be treated as a unique, homogeneous sample, since there are no structural differences in the coefficients of the separate regressions. If H0 is rejected, however, a separate regression for each sub-sample is required. In this analysis the F-values were 9.73, 5.80 and 4.24 for tests of structural difference in the parameters of the earnings equations of the three groups, the full-timers and the part-timers respectively. Since the degrees of freedom were [9,5343], [9,4369] and [9,2406], leading to a critical value of F of 1.88 at five per cent significant level, the hypothesis of the coefficients being the same across all groups was rejected.

[3] Throughout, parameter differences are weighted by the means of the relevant explanatory variable for full-time females. In this case the difference in means is weighted by the men's parameters.

Human capital gaps are much more apparent among part-timers: 3.3 years less employment experience, and a 25 per cent shortfall in training and lower educational attainments, for example, compared to women full-timers. Thus it is not surprising to find that 25.4 per cent of the 51.9 per cent gap is explained by such factors, but this still leaves 21.2 per cent unexplained – more than the unequal treatment found to exist between men and full-time women. Moreover, most of the unexplained component stems from the constant term, an otherwise unexplained 'part-time job effect' operating for all part-time work. Adjusting for personal characteristics reduces the total gap between men's and part-time women's pay from 83 per cent to 43 per cent.

Are these differences explained by the women being in different sorts of firm?

The next step is to include information about the firm, as shown in Table 4.4. While there are very few gender and part-time/full-time differences in the proportion of the sample interviewed in the South East, the mean values of the other additional variables vary considerably across groups. Part-timers are much more likely than full-timers to work in small firms, and less likely to be in the largest. Men are most likely to be in the private sector, and women full-timers are more likely to be in this sector than are part-timers. It is therefore not surprising that the inclusion of firms' characteristics increased the variation explained in each sample noticeably (by one to three percentage points).

As the F-test for structural stability did not allow the rejection of the hypothesis that women in full- and part-time jobs may share common parameters on these firm characteristics,[4] an earnings equation was estimated for the pooled female sample, allowing for differences in the coefficients of some variables by including all significant interactions with the part-time dummy. The proportion of variance explained in the pooled regression was 52 per cent (as approximated by the adjusted R^2). Separate terms were needed only for the intercept and three other variables. Firm variables have thus helped to account for differences in parameters between sub-samples, and to reduce more of the unexplained difference between full- and part-time women's wages. For example, employment in either a small firm or the private sector reduces any woman's wage by about five per cent. That more part-timers are in small firms helps account for their low wages. The unexplained component of the full-time/part-time log-wage gap thus comes down to 18.4 per cent (from 21.2 per cent).

The increase in the explained component of the gender gap amongst full-timers is more modest. Unexplained differences remain at 0.159 (17.2 per cent), compared with 0.168 without firm characteristics. There are interesting gender differences in the coefficient for private sector employment: the term is significantly positive for men, and negative (but significant only for part-timers) for women. One possible explanation lies

---

4 The F-value was 2.31, against a critical value of 2.37 for [4,2354] degrees of freedom.

in the different degree of flexibility of labour contracts in the private and public sectors – more centralised in the latter and less likely to escape the letter of equal pay legislation. Another is that private and public employers have a different 'taste' for discrimination.

Table 4.4 Model of log hourly wages explained by personal and employer characteristics

Variable	Coefficient					Mean of X		
	Men	Split samples		All women		Men	FT women	PT women
		FT women	PT women		if part-time			
Dependent variable log hourly wage						1.971	1.784	1.368
Constant	1.216	1.098	1.028	1.100	- 0.082#			
Personal								
Ability at 11	0.004	0.005	0.002	0.005	- 0.003	45.33	48.64	44.21
O levels	0.097	0.029#	0.061	0.043		0.24	0.32	0.40
A levels	0.142	0.072	0.078#	0.074		0.20	0.09	0.05
Diploma	0.270	0.279	0.458	0.276	0.180	0.16	0 19	0 12
Degree	0.441	0.421	0.614	0.422	0.176	0.16	0.17	0.06
Training	0.114	0.157	0.107	0.140		0.54	0.47	0.22
Years employed since age 23	0.023	0.015	0.019	0.017		10.00	8.95	5.65
Years in this job	0.002#	0.010	0.010	0.010		7.68	6.97	3.42
Employer								
South East	0.182	0.108	0.087	0.102		0.20	0.21	0.18
Small firm	- 0.093	- 0.082	- 0.030#	- 0.057		0.23	0.28	0.52
Large firm	0.077	0.053	0.049#	0.054		0.51	0.47	0.29
Private sector	0.059	- 0.021#	- 0.092	- 0.052		0.68	0.52	0.57
Adjusted R^2	0.335	0.407	0.420	0.520				
n	2919	1429	953	2382				
F	123.55	82.57	58.47	162.48				
Differences between		Men/FT women	FT/PT women	Men/PT women				
Raw differential of which:		0.187	0.416	0.603				
unexplained*		0.159	0.169†	0.328				
explained		0.028	0.247	0.275				

Note 1 # denotes not significantly different from zero; * coefficient differences weighted by means for full-time females; † decomposition of full-time/part-time wage gap used parameters from the more parsimonious model.

Table 4.5 Wage differentials explained in terms of personal, employer and job characteristics

Variable	Coefficient					Mean of X		
	Men	Split samples FT women	PT women	All women	if part-time	Men	FT women	PT women
Dependent variable log hourly wage						1.990	1.804	1.394
Constant	1.133	0.999	0.953	0.986				
Personal								
Ability at 11	0.003	0.005	0.002	0.005	-0.004	45.67	49.11	45.12
O levels	0.076	0.005#	0.062	0.034#		0.23	0.33	0.38
A levels	0.113	0.027#	0.042#	0.038#		0.19	0.09	0.06
Diploma	0.217	0.236	0.444	0.248	- 0.080	0.16	0.19	0 13
Degree	0.377	0.381	0.550	0.385	0.170	0.17	0.17	0.06
Training	- 0.068#	0.120#	0.194	0.150		0.55	0.48	0.23
Years employed since age 23	0.021	0.015	0.015	0.015		10.04	9.06	5.89
Years in this job	0.002#	0.008	0.006#	0.008		7.93	7.17	3.60
Employer								
South East	0.161	0.080	0.119	0.095		0.20	0.20	0.14
Small firm	- 0.097	- 0.065	- 0.019#	- 0.044		0.22	0.26	0.49
Large firm	0.082	0.038#	0.016#	0.033#		0.53	0.48	0.31
Private sector	0.044	- 0.030#	- 0.087	- 0.049		0.67	0.53	0.57
If employer paid for training	0.168	0.012#	- 0.088#	0.025#		0.52	0.46	0.20
The job								
Fringe benefits	0.088#	0.062#	0.038#	0.035#		0.98	0.98	0.92
Hours flexible	0.076	- 0.004#	0.049#	0.011#		0.34	0.33	0.27
Supervision	0.093	0.082	0.012#	0.084	- 0.080	0.63	0.57	0.26
Travel to work (minutes)	0.002	0.004	0.003	0.004		26.11	24.95	15.58
Union member	- 0.041	- 0.026#	0.135	- 0.022#	0.131	0.42	0.36	0.22
Adjusted R^2	0.375	0.447	0.482	0.555				
n	2553	1234	671	1905				
F	86.09	55.85	35.65	104.17				

Differences between	Men/FT women	FT/PT women	Men/PT women
Raw differential of which:	0.185	0.410†	0.595
unexplained*	0.152	0.173	0.325
explained	0.033	0.237	0.270

Note 1 # denotes not significantly different from zero; * coefficient differences weighted by means for full-time females; †
decomposition of full-time/part-time wage gap used parameters from the more parsimonious model.

Could the gender wage gap be explained by differences in the type of job?

Table 4.5 addresses this issue. It shows that fringe benefits of some sort were reported by nearly all full-timers, male or female, and by 92 per cent of part-timers. Some degree of choice over hours was reported by around one-third of all full-timers and 27 per cent of part-timers. Supervision was most common among men (63 per cent) and least among part-timers, though as many as 26 per cent of these women reported supervising others. Travel-to-work time is similar for both sets of full-timers, around 25 minutes at the mean, whereas part-timers average barely more than 15 minutes. Finally, union membership is least common among part-timers.

Contrary to expectations based on the compensating differential hypothesis, 'amenities' such as fringe benefits and flexible working hours were positively remunerated for both men and women. This may indicate the existence of another sort of mechanism, such as a segmented labour market where 'good jobs' compensate well in terms of working conditions as well as pay. Compensation for the degree of responsibility involved in the job, however, works in the hypothesised direction (unless supervising others has positive non-pecuniary attractions): supervisors get paid around nine per cent better in full-time jobs, male or female, though there is no significant effect for part-timers. As expected, time and (presumably) distance travelled are correlated positively with higher pay; indeed the combination of this factor and the shorter travelling time of part-timers could help account for the low pay of the part-timers. Contrary to expectation, only among part-timers is membership of a union positively associated with wages.[5]

The inclusion of this set of job characteristics reduces the number of terms for which part-time and full-time parameters differ. Graduates no longer appear relatively well paid in part-time jobs once these job characteristics come into account. The variance explained is further increased, as are the explained wage gaps. However, it should be noted that in the slightly reduced sample for which these variable are all measured, the raw gaps are also slightly smaller. The unexplained wage gaps are still substantial: 16.4 per cent between male and female full-timers, and 18.9 per cent between full- and part-time women, or 38.4 per cent between full-time men and part-time women.

How far do gender differences in occupational distribution account for wage differentials?

Table 4.6 presents the result of including hierarchical occupational banding in the earnings equation. The three groups are unevenly distributed over these occupational levels. Men tend to be over-represented in intermediate and manual jobs; full-time women are

---

[5] The effect of this term on explaining wage gaps is ambiguous, depending on which coefficient is taken to weight the variable difference (here, part-timers' low unionisation will appear to help account for their low pay).

relatively most common in the intermediate and clerical groups; part-timers are least common in the top group and concentrated in clerical and service jobs.

Inclusion of occupational level in the model again adds to the variance explained, raising the three adjusted R^2s on the unpooled samples to 0.40, 0.46 and 0.55 (men full-time, women full-time and women part-time respectively). Occupational level makes the greatest contribution to explaining differentials between women part-timers. When the samples of women are pooled, occupational premiums remain significantly different in full-time and part-time jobs, but the effects of almost all other variables are found to be similar across full-time and part-time labour markets. The impact of qualifications is partly shifted on to occupation.

Does occupational level account for pay gaps? Comparing Tables 4.5 and 4.6, the answer must be 'not much'. The model in Table 4.5 explained a 3.4 per cent differential for full-timers, and 26.7 per cent among women. Inclusion of occupational level raises these to 3.5 per cent and 36.1 per cent in Table 4.6. These job characteristics are better at accounting for the low pay of female part-timers than the relative disadvantage of female full-timers. The remaining unexplained premiums are 16 per cent for male full-timers over women full-timers, and 10.9 per cent for the latter over part-timers.

Table 4.7 allows for occupational segregation. Not surprisingly, the feminisation of the occupation in general 'discriminated' well between the samples. Thirteen per cent of men, 62 per cent of female full-timers and 90 per cent of part-timers were in jobs mainly done by women: confirmation of the 'female ghetto' constituted by most part-time jobs. The estimates also confirm expectations that employment in a female ghetto is worse paid than other jobs, even for men, by a factor of around five to six per cent. An interesting result is that once job segregation is taken into account, many differences across sub-samples in coefficients disappear.[6] The whole sample is pooled together and two separate sets of interaction terms are included, contrasting women in either full- or part-time jobs with men.

The model accounts for 52 per cent of the variance in log-wages, with unexplained components of 14.7 per cent for full-timers and 11.2 per cent between part-time women and men. The unexplained component of the full-time/part-time differential derives almost exclusively from differences in the intercept. There are only a few effects working through a handful of other variables, which tend to cancel each other out.

Inclusion of this measure of segregation finally makes a noticeable difference to the explained component of the gender wage gap, which was 3.5 per cent in Table 4.6 and becomes 4.6 per cent in Table 4.7. This confirms the crucial role played by segregation in determining wage differentials, as outlined by the 'crowding' theory of discrimination.

---

6 The very low values of the relevant F-test (0.34) do not allow the rejection of the hypothesis of the coefficients being the same for the three groups.

Table 4.6 Full model including occupations in broad groups

Variable	Coefficient					Mean of X		
		Split samples		All women				
	Men	FT women	PT women		if part-time	Men	FT women	PT women
Dependent variable log hourly wage						1.987	1.804	1.393
Constant	1.133	0.936	0.945	0.972				
Personal								
Ability at 11	0.003	0.004	0.002	0.004	- 0.003	45.59	49.14	45.0
O levels	0.076	- 0.009#	0.028	0.010#		0.24	0.33	0.3
A levels	0.113	0.008#	- 0.005	0.010#		0.19	0.09	0.0
Diploma	0.182	0.173	0.368	0.187	0.115	0.16	0.19	0.13
Degree	0.332	0.267	0.348	0.285		0.17	0.17	0.06
Training	- 0.066#	0.103#	0.187	0.140		0.55	0.48	0.23
Years employed since age 23	0.021	0.012	0.012	0.012		10.04	9.07	5.8
Years in this job	0.002#	0.009	0.006	0.009		7.94	7.16	3.62
Employer								
South East	0.155	0.081	0.135	0.099		0.19	0.20	0.14
Small firm	- 0.103	- 0.056	- 0.022	-0.039		0.22	0.25	0.49
Large firm	0.079	0.052	0.016	0.043		0.53	0.48	0.31
Private sector	0.043	- 0.013#	- 0.061	- 0.031		0.67	0 53	0 57
If employer paid for training	0.162	0.022#	- 0.107	- 0.024#		0.52	0.46	0.20
The job								
Fringe benefits	0.085#	0.132#	0.048	0.054#	0.0002#	0.98	0.97	0.91
Hours flexible	0.060	- 0.004#	0.033	0.009#		0.34	0.34	0.27
Supervision	0.055	0.078	0.019	0.061		0.63	0.57	0.26
Travel to work (minutes)	0.002	0.004	0.002	0.004	- 0.003	26.08	24.99	15.51
Union member	- 0.027#	- 0.020#	0.120	- 0.017#	0.119	0.42	0.36	0.22
Occupation								
Professionals, including teachers	0.141	0.245	0.452	0.249	0.231	0.11	0.11	0.05
Other intermediate	0.163	0.094#	0.163	0.117	0.015	0.35	0.39	0.17
Clerical	- 0.009#	0.051#	0.201	0.072#	0.111	0.05	0.29	0.27
Service and shop	0.030#	- 0.097#	- 0.017	-0.076#	0.033	0.03	0.06	0.34
Skilled occupations	0.023#	- 0.033#	- 0.010	0.000#	- 0.053	0.35	0.10	0.07

Variable	Men	Split samples		All women
		FT women	PT women	
Adjusted R^2	0.396	0.462	0.546	0.580
n	2497	1219	664	1883
F	72.14	46.44	35.1	82.37

Difference between	Men/FT women	FT/PT women	Men/PT women
Raw differential of which:	0.183	0.411†	0.594
unexplained*	0.149	0.103	0.252
explained	0.034	0.411	0.342

Note 1 # denotes not significantly different from zero; * coefficient differences weighted by means for full-time females; † decomposition of full-time/part-time wage gap used parameters from the more parsimonious model.

Table 4.7 Full model, including occupation classified into likely segregation of occupation

Variable	Coefficients All persons	Interactions Additional effects for women		Means		
		Full-timers	Part-timers	Men	FT women	PT women
Dependent variable log hourly wage				1.99	1.80	1.39
Constant	1.149	- 0.075#	- 0.235			
Personal						
Ability at 11	0.003			45.59	49.14	45.03
O levels	0.059	- 0.061		0.24	0.33	0.38
A levels	0.094	- 0.078		0.19	0.09	0.06
Diploma	0.184		0.194	0.16	0.19	0.13
Degree	0.316			0.17	0.17	0.06
Training	- 0.066#	0.165	0.273	0.55	0.48	0.23
Years employed since age 23	0.020	- 0.008#	- 0.009	10.04	9.07	5.89
Years in this job	0.003	0.006		7.94	7.16	3.62
Employer						
South East	0.151	- 0.071		0.19	0.20	0.14
Small firm	- 0.086		0.062#	0.22	0.25	0.49
Large firm	0.067		- 0.056#	0.53	0.48	0.31
Private sector	0.037	- 0.064	0.107	0.67	0.53	0.57
If employer paid for training	0.164	- 0.140	- 0.296	0.52	0.46	0.20
The job						
Fringe benefits	0.083			0.98	0.97	0.91
Hours flexible	0.051	- 0.063		0.34	0.34	0.27
Supervision	0.059			0.63	0.57	0.26
Travel to work (minutes)	0.002	0.002		26.08	24.99	15.51
Union member	- 0.021#		0.155	0.42	0.36	0.22
Occupation						
Professionals, including teachers	0.154	0.113#	0.294	0.11	0.11	0.05
Other intermediate	0.167	- 0.050#	- 0.034#	0.35	0.39	0.17
Clerical	0.047#	0.070#	0.143	0.05	0.29	0.27
Service and shop	- 0.003#	- 0.044#	- 0.011#	0.03	0.06	0.34
Skilled occupations	0.025#	- 0.038#	- 0.040#	0.35	0.10	0.07
Occupation						
Feminised	- 0.056	- 0.013#	-0.013#	0.13	0.62	0.90
Adjusted R^2	0.52					
n	4380					
F	124.48					

Differences between	Men/ women	Men/ FT women	Men/ PT women
Raw differential of which:	0.328	0.183	0.594
unexplained*	0.175	0.138	0.244
explained	0.153	0.045	0.350

Note 1 # denotes not significantly different from zero; * coefficient differences weighted by means for full-time women.

Discussion

The overview in Tables 4.8 and 4.9 summarises the steps involved in this study, and expresses wage differentials – explained and unexplained – in terms of percentages of the lower-paid group's average (at the geometric mean, since the mean of the log is the log of the geometric mean). The starting point was an excess of men's pay over women's of around 40 per cent. This is a weighted average of 20 per cent among full-timers and 81 per cent to 83 per cent between men and part-timers (the ratios varying slightly as the sample changes between Tables 4.3 and 4.7).

Differences in endowment alone explain more than half (0.226 out of a total differential in log-wages of 0.418) of the difference between part

Table 4.8 Summary of decompositions in terms of log wages

Explanatory model	FT men/ FT women	FT/PT women	FT men/ PT women	FT men/ All women	FT men FT women PT women
	logarithms	logarithms	logarithms	logarithms	sample numbers
Table 4.3 – Personal characteristics					
Gross differential	0.185	0.418	0.603	0.355	2946
Unexplained by model	0.168	0.192	0.360	0.246	1441
Explained by model	0.017	0.226	0.243	0.108	983
Table 4.4 – Personal and firm characteristics					
Gross differential	0.187	0.416	0.603	0.353	2919
Unexplained by model	0.159	0.169	0.328	0.227	1429
Explained by model	0.028	0.247	0.275	0.127	953
Table 4.5 – Personal, firm and job characteristics					
Gross differential	0.185	0.410	0.595	0.330	2553
Unexplained by model	0.152	0.173	0.325	0.213	1234
Explained by model	0.033	0.237	0.270	0.116	671
Table 4.6 – Personal, firm and job characteristics, and broad occupation					
Gross differential	0.183	0.411	0.594	0.328	2497
Unexplained by model	0.149	0.103	0.252	0.185	1219
Explained by model	0.034	0.308	0.342	0.143	664
Table 4.7 – Personal, firm and job characteristics, and likely segregation of detailed occupation					
Gross differential	0.183	0.411	0.594	0.328	2497
Unexplained by model	0.138	0.106	0.244	0.175	1219
Explained by model	0.045	0.305	0.350	0.153	664

Table 4.9 Summary of decompositions as percentages (of the average of the lower paid group)

Explanatory model	FT men/ FT women	FT/PT women	FT men/ PT women	FT men/ All women
	per cent	per cent	per cent	per cent
Table 4.3 – Personal characteristics				
Gross differential	20.3	51.9	82.8	42.5
Unexplained by model	18.3	21.2	43.3	27.9
Explained by model	1.7	25.4	27.5	11.4
Table 4.4 – Personal and firm characteristics				
Gross differential	20.6	51.6	82.8	42.4
Unexplained by model	17.2	18.4	38.8	25.4
Explained by model	2.8	28.0	31.7	13.5
Table 4.5 – Personal, firm and job characteristics				
Gross differential	20.4	50.7	81.4	39.1
Unexplained by model	16.4	18.9	38.4	23.7
Explained by model	3.4	26.7	31.0	12.4
Table 4.6 – Personal, firm and job characteristics, and broad occupation				
Gross differential	20.1	50.8	81.1	38.8
Unexplained by model	16.0	10.9	28.6	20.3
Explained by model	3.5	36.1	40.8	15.4
Table 4.7 – Personal, firm and job characteristics, and likely segregation of detailed occupation				
Gross differential	20.1	50.8	81.1	38.8
Unexplained by model	14.8	11.2	27.6	19.2
Explained by model	4.6	35.7	41.9	16.5

timers and full-time women, but explain very little of the gap between full-time men and female part-timers (only 0.017 out of 0.185). Personal characteristics account for a 12 per cent lead, mostly over the women working part-time, but leave about 28 per cent unaccounted for. Including information about the firm, the job, bargaining power and the broad level of occupation makes only a modest additional contribution to the explanation of wage differentials, and again mainly in terms of why women's part-time jobs are less well paid than full-time jobs. The introduction of a term inferring occupational segregation made the greatest single contribution to the explanation of the wage gap, and operates on the gap between men and women full-timers. About half the total gap between men and women is explicable once this term is introduced. In Table 4.7 a total raw gender differential of 39 per cent appears to be the product of about 1.17 and 1.19 from explained and unexplained terms respectively.

This exercise has drawn attention to the different rates of pay in full- and part-time employment for women. To understand the impact of gender in the labour market, both these segments must be taken into account. In the 1958 cohort, full-time employees of both sexes had equivalent education and experience. Most of the pay gap between them seems to arise from unequal treatment of equivalent human capital, as far it can be measured.

The pay gap between women employed full- and part-time is larger, but more of it can be explained at almost all stages. In terms of personal attributes that might raise productivity, such as education and experience, part-timers are less well endowed than full-timers. They also tend to be found in labour market situations where their employers may be unable to pay, and they are unable to demand, high wages. They are almost all in low-level, female occupations, where wage discrimination would have its greatest impact. Even after allowing for these factors, 33-year-old part-timers suffered an otherwise unexplained mark-down on their wages of 14 per cent, compounding the unexplained gender mark-down among full-timers.

The remaining unexplained differentials cannot be thought of as estimates of discrimination, because some of the estimated effects working through occupation or firm size may themselves be the mechanism through which discrimination works. The unexplained components of Table 4.3 would be nearer such an estimate, provided one accepts that there are no other omitted determinants of excess male productivity. Perhaps this failure to account for all the gaps is due to inadequate information on labour market segment and undue collapsing of details of occupation.

The contrast between men and women is partially explained by the high level of gender segregation in the labour market: the few men doing 'female' jobs are penalised to the same extent as the majority of women. Thus some unequal treatment is the result not so much of the gender of workers but of gendered jobs. Nevertheless, women full-timers in non-feminised jobs are still, all else being equal, paid 13 per cent less than equivalent men.

By contrast, the low pay in part-time jobs is not well accounted for by gender segregation. Despite the fact that most part-time jobs are of a type normally done by women, even the few in less-segregated occupations tend to be less well paid than full-time jobs for women. Part of the explanation seems to be that part-time jobs are only offered at the bottom of the occupational hierarchy, whether in segregated occupations or not. This is crudely and doubtless imperfectly indicated by the supervision and other terms introduced in Table 4.6. In addition there still may be a mechanism, analogous to the unequal treatment of the sexes, whereby the wages of part-timers are marked down. Whether this is part and parcel of the treatment of women, or whether it would apply to male part-timers as well, cannot be disentangled with the evidence here.

Conclusions

What has this evidence from the 1958 cohort explained about why men's and women's wages still differ?

Combined with evidence on the personal circumstances of the 1958 cohort members, the different composition of their employment accounts for about half the wage gap. It adds surprisingly little once the individual's experience and qualifications are controlled for. No explanation has been found for why the average 33-year-old women would have been paid 19 per cent better if she had the same attributes in the same job as a man – perhaps due to the failure of this analysis to take all relevant factors into account. It could also been seen as evidence of some form of differential treatment of women and men in the labour market.

However, a comparison of these findings with those from the previous National Cohort Study is comforting. The 'full model' of Joshi and Newell (1989) revealed a male–to–female lead among 33-year-olds in 1978 of 58 per cent, of which 24 per cent was explained by personal and job characteristics, and 28 per cent remained unexplained. If the unexplained portion (19 per cent in this study) includes any unequal treatment, things would seem to have improved over time, though there may still be a way to go.

What evidence is there for the various hypotheses advanced to explain male–female gaps?

The availability of fringe benefits seems to magnify rather than compensate inequalities in pay. This result may appear somewhat surprising, since it contradicts so clearly the predictions of the theory of compensating wage differentials. It is, however, consistent with the hypothesis of fragmentation of the UK labour market into two sub-markets: one offering high pay and good working conditions, and another which offers neither of these 'amenities'. Females, especially part-timers, are on the less desirable playing field. But of course one could argue that the part-time aspect of the job is in itself an 'amenity' which generates a negative compensating wage differential; although this is hard to reconcile with a positive premium on flexibility of hours for men, and the general lack of support for compensating differentials elsewhere in this study.

If one accepts the interpretation of the travel-to-work term as a measure of the degree of monopsony prevailing in the market, the evidence is consistent with the prediction of the discriminatory monopsony model, which suggests wages to be lower for workers with lower elasticity of supply. In this context the particularly small travel radius of part-timers leads inevitably to them being paid less. The significantly positive coefficient of the union term for part-timers reinforces this interpretation. Unions introduce an element of counteracting supply-side monopoly, which in a monopsonistic labour market keeps wages higher than they would otherwise be.

Finally, there was a significant association between occupational segregation and differential returns to other determinants of earnings. Coupled with the concentration of women (especially part-timers) in 'feminised', low-return occupations, this provides clear evidence of a strong correlation between occupational segregation and the low pay of women in general and part-timers in particular.

Part of the remaining unexplained gap may be due to the higher degree of uncertainty associated with the productivity level of women, especially part-timers – 'statistical discrimination'. The wage differential would then derive from employers perceiving the productivity level of women to be lower, or less predictable, than that of men. The fact that employers appear to be relatively less prepared to finance training of women (especially part-timers) supports this view. The possibility cannot be excluded, however, that the unexplained differential is simply due to outright discrimination on behalf of the employer, other employees, or consumers themselves.

Some wage gap remains unexplained before and after allowing for the sorting of individuals into better- and worse-paying parts of the labour market. These findings suggest that there is likely to be some within-firm unequal treatment; unequal pay does not arise wholly from sorting within the labour market.

Acknowledgements

This work is part of a project funded by the Employment Department, whose support is gratefully acknowledged. The views expressed are solely those of the authors and should not be taken to represent those of the Department. A full report of the project is in preparation. The authors are also grateful to Louisa Blackwell for allowing the use of her recoding of occupation according to national sex ratio.

References

Becker, G. (1957). *The Economics of Discrimination*. Chicago: University of Chicago Press.

Bergmann, B. R. (1971). 'Occupational segregation, wages and profits when employers discriminate by race or sex' in *Eastern Economic Journal*, 1.

Blau, F. D. and Ferber, M. (1987). 'Discrimination: empirical evidence from the United States' in *American Economic Review*, Papers and Proceedings, 77 (2).

Bloom, D. E. and Killingsworth, M. R. (1982). 'Pay discrimination research and litigation: the use of regression' in *Industrial Relations*, 21 (3).

Chiswick, B. R. (1973). 'Racial discrimination and the labour market: a test of alternative hypotheses' in *Journal of Political Economy*, 81.

Edgeworth, F. Y. (1922). 'Equal pay to men and women for equal work' in *Economic Journal*, 32.

Ermisch, J. F. and Wright, R. E. (1992). 'Differential returns to human capital in full-time and part-time employment' in Folbre, N., Bergmann, B., Agarwal, B. and Floro, M. (eds.). *Women's Work in the World Economy*. London: Macmillan.

Ferri, E. (ed.) (1993). *Life at 33: The Fifth Follow Up of the National Child Development Study*. London: National Children's Bureau.

Joshi, H. and Newell, M.-L. (1987). 'Job downgrading after childbearing' in Uncles, M. (ed.) *London Papers in Regional Science, 18. Longitudinal Data Analysis: Methods and Applications*. London: Pion.

Joshi, H. and Newell, M.-L. (1989). *Pay Differentials and Parenthood: Analysis of Men and Women Born in 1946*. Institute of Employment Research Report. Coventry: University of Warwick.

Killingsworth, M. R. (1987). 'Heterogeneous preferences, compensating wage differentials and comparable worth' in *Quarterly Journal of Economics*, 102 (4).

Killingsworth, M. R. (1993). 'Analyzing employment discrimination: from the seminar room to the courtroom' in *American Economic Review*, 83 (2).

Lewis, G. H. (1986). 'Union relative wage effect' in Ashenfelter, O. and Layard, P. R. G. (eds.) *Handbook of Labour Economics*, 2. North Holland.

Paci, P., Makepeace, G., Joshi, H. and Dolton, P. (1994). *Is Pay Discrimination Against Women a Thing of the Past? A Tale of Two Cohorts*. Paper presented to the EMRU workshop, July.

Phelps, E. S. (1972). 'The statistical theory of racism and sexism' in *American Economic Review*, 62.

Reagan, R. B. (1978). 'Two supply curves for economists? Implication of mobility and career attachment of women' in *American Economic Review*, 65.

Rosen, S. (1986). 'The theory of equalising differences' in Ashenfelter, O. and Layard, P. R. G. (eds.) *Handbook of Labour Economics*, 1. North Holland.

Siebert, J. T. and Addison, W. S. (1991). 'Internal labour markets: causes and consequences' in *Oxford Review of Economic Policy*, 7 (1).

Stiglitz, J. (1973). 'Approaches to the economics of discrimination' in *American Economic Review*, Papers and Proceedings, 63.

Zellner, H. (1972). 'Discrimination against women: occupational segregation and the relative wage' in *American Economic Review*, 62.

CHAPTER 5 # Gender and Internal Labour Markets

Damian Grimshaw and Jill Rubery

Most economists now recognise the importance of organisational or internal labour markets (ILMs) in the employment system. Such labour markets can be described as those that favour the existing workforce over the external labour force, and/or those providing conditions of employment that are related to internal corporate objectives. These objectives include increasing effort and commitment, and retaining workers with specific skills or knowledge.

Economists have concentrated on modelling ILMs, but discrimination within them has been left for analysis by industrial relations and personnel specialists or sociologists (Cockburn, 1991; Collinson *et al.*, 1990), while economists still concern themselves with more macro labour market data for detecting discriminatory practices. Research increasingly points to the significance of industrial and organisational factors in explaining wage differentials (Millward and Woodland, this volume, Chapter 10), even within individualised earnings data (Paci *et al.*, this volume, Chapter 4), but this has not led to systematic explorations of how and why gender discrimination may be linked to employers' pay determination and employment policies.

ILM systems can be expected to impact upon broader labour market data, casting doubt on approaches which emphasise personal characteristics as the main determination of pay differentials. Even if personal characteristics are still associated with different pay levels, in a labour market characterised by ILMs it is necessary to analyse how these personal characteristics are recognised and rewarded through employer pay policies, as the existence of market wage rates for particular categories of labour no longer provides an adequate explanation. Equally, the identification of systematic disadvantage for women within the broader labour market data (as indicated by the persistence of gender discrimination even after all other explanations have been examined) suggests that organisations, which operate within this discriminatory environment, are likely to be influenced by external labour market (ELM) structures in constructing their own ILMs. Despite the plausibility of a linkage between ELMs and ILMs, the existence of or scope for such links have not been explored either theoretically or empirically.

The case for developing a more integrated approach to the analysis of internal and external labour markets has more general applicability than to the specific case of gender discrimination (Rubery, 1994). However, this chapter focuses primarily on the issue of gender inequality for a number of reasons.

Firstly, gender is one of the more persistent and pervasive bases for differentiation in the labour market, and in some senses men and women constitute archetypical non-competing groups within the labour force. This discrimination also manifests itself in patterns of gender segregation by occupation, establishment or employment contract, which may facilitate the responsiveness of ILMs to ELM conditions. Discrimination by gender is pervasive outside as well as inside the labour market, and gendered social attitudes and values may enter consciously or unconsciously into all employment decisions and practices.

Secondly, ILMs are characterised by requirements for continuity and time commitment to a particular organisation; requirements that it may be argued are specifically designed around a typical male worker and thereby cause particular difficulties for women.

Thirdly, there is a specific and major policy interest in this area, but the theoretical and conceptual tools are underdeveloped for an appropriate analysis of the implications of ILMs for gender equality policy.

Theories of the internal labour market and equal opportunities

New institutional theories of ILMs represent a significant development of the orthodox neo-classical model of the labour market (see Sawyer, this volume, Chapter 2). The neo-classical model assumes a price-taking firm in which the wage paid reflects the reward for the worker's contribution, or marginal productivity of labour. In contrast, recent new institutional theories have made a concerted effort to integrate the institutional construction of the labour market within a neo-classical framework. For example, some ILM models attempt to integrate the impact of custom and fairness on the employment contract. Another theme is that the wage paid is not simply a signal of a worker's productivity; higher wage rates will also induce higher levels of effort. Much attention has also been devoted to assessing the impact of company-specific skills on the employment relation, which introduces a new indeterminacy in the relation between wages and productivity. It would thus appear that the mainstream economics framework has become more conducive to a broader treatment of the relation between different institutional arrangements and labour market inequality.

A review of the literature on ILMs reveals, however, that surprisingly little attention has been paid to the analysis of labour market discrimination at the company level. ILM structures are seen as potentially restrictive to the operation of equal opportunities policies, since they inhibit open competition between employees. Opening up vacancies to external competition is therefore often seen as consistent with good practice for an equal opportunities employer (Straw, 1989). This raises the question of why issues of equity and fairness are absent in economic models of the ILM.

The answer may be found in the underlying assumption in ILM models of a competitive, harmonious ELM as the natural state of play. Under this assumption, the development of ILM structures is explained exclusively by employers' maximisation of efficiency. It follows that once a given ILM arrangement is rationalised as efficiency-maximising, questions of discrimination are either excluded or subsumed within a discourse where equity improvements are a necessary trade-off with efficiency gains. It thus appears that policies aimed at equitable outcomes in the labour market would encounter serious obstacles if the efficiency formulations of ILMs were accepted uncritically.

This chapter challenges the mainstream analysis of ILM structures on two grounds. Firstly, the market for labour existing 'externally' to the ILM is neither perfectly competitive nor harmonious; instead, discrimination is embedded in this ELM. Secondly, it is erroneous to claim that ILM structures arise exclusively from efficiency-maximising concerns of employers. For example, it is implausible to argue that employers, in structuring their ILMs, are uninfluenced by the broader ELM and the relationship of their internal employees to external opportunities. The interdependent relations between the ILM structure and the divisions that exist within the ELM are thus fundamental to a theory of the ILM (Rubery, 1994). It is necessary to analyse how various ELM opportunities affect both the shape of an ILM and the position of a worker within it. From this analysis it is possible to consider how different types of ILM structures act to exacerbate, reinforce or offset inequalities in workers' ELM opportunities.

Skill specificity

The work of Doeringer and Piore (1971), in the tradition of Becker (1967), provides the classic formulation of the way in which ILM structures are established in response to firm-specific skills. In general, skill specificity refers to skills that are learned through an informal process of on-the-job training. The costs of training provide an incentive for employers to promote employment stability, so they can recoup their investment. The labour market is divided between a primary sector where workers acquire firm-specific skills and have access to job ladders and high pay, and a secondary sector where an absence of firm-specific skills is accompanied by low levels of pay and limited opportunities for promotion.

There are two main problems with developing this type of approach, particularly from a perspective that recognises gender inequality. First, the proposition that labour market duality or differentiation reflects the absence or presence of skill specificity ignores empirical studies which argue that idiosyncratic skills are a commonplace feature of many secondary-sector jobs. For example, restaurant work may lack an identifiable ILM structure, yet it does involve idiosyncratic team, process and communicative elements (Jacoby, 1990). Moreover, any empirical or abstract measurement of firm-specific skills will encounter problems similar to those faced in general by economistic accounts of what constitutes skill. Studies of skill differences between men's and women's work reveal that it is necessary to understand the historical associations between 'male work' and skill, as well as the relation between the downgrading of skill content of women's jobs and women's inferior socio-economic status in society (Armstrong, 1982; Phillips and Taylor, 1980).

The second problem concerns the manner in which differences in expected job tenure by group determine differential access to recruitment and promotion. Doeringer and Piore (1971) argue that skill specificity leads to the wage varying in relation to marginal productivity over time, according to

> an equality between the discounted present value of expected cost and productivity streams calculated over the distribution of expected employment tenure for various *groups* within the enterprise. (Doeringer and Piore, 1971: 78, emphasis in original.)

In other words, wage rates vary between workers with similar levels of productivity according to the employer's expectations of tenure by group.

As it is impossible to know the future employment stability of individual employees, employers assess the risk of separation and potential productivity of each job applicant based on their perceptions of the average employment patterns of the particular labour force group to which they are ascribed. ILMs increase these problems, as investment decisions concerning training are in practice taken by employers under conditions of great uncertainty over whether they will achieve a return on their investment. If employers rely upon conventional wisdom associating women with relatively short employment tenure, the implication is that women will either receive lower wage rates (allowing the firm to recoup the costs of providing training over a short period), or be excluded from on-the-job training where the firm is constrained to offer a single wage rate.

Employer decisions that rely upon a standardised perception of women's employment patterns, whether accurate or inaccurate, discriminate against women. Even in the unlikely case that employers' decisions are based on an accurate assessment of women's average job tenure, the assignment of women to low-wage positions with little access to training denies them the opportunity to advance and change their employment status over time, or indeed to change their level of work commitment. Individual employers are not usually in a position to 'sample' accurately the whole population of women; and even if they decide to risk some investment in women's training, these experiments will not necessarily result in a more accurate assessment of the female population. Given limited sample numbers and the employer's prior beliefs, it is probable that only a marked divergence between behaviour and expectation will lead to a change in practice, and any selection of a female recruit who conforms to expectations may lead to a reinforcement of stereotypes and a curtailment of these experiments.

One of the problematic issues is deciding how to evaluate the actual costs and benefits to companies of employing women in ILMs. To argue that it is necessarily costly for employers to train women (because of their loss of investment returns when women quit the labour market) assumes first that women become automatically deskilled upon motherhood and cannot re-enter the job hierarchy except at the very lowest level; and second that employers always wish to avoid a high quit rate. In practice, women may retain acquired skills during their absence from the labour market. Furthermore, a certain level of turnover may benefit the employer, since it reduces the need to provide extended career ladders to all fully-trained workers, who may otherwise experience demotivation.

A common problem for employers, then, is to get the appropriate balance between retaining a sufficient number of trained employees to avoid potential shortages in higher-level jobs, and having excess supplies of trained employees waiting for promotion who may become disillusioned with the slow pace of advancement up the ladder. Although loss of skills and under-utilisation of women's potential within ILM systems may be a problem, employers have the power to change this system by, for example, offering more promotion to women (increasing the 'carrot' to stay) or better career breaks and part-time work opportunities. These strategies may well result in women becoming a second tier within the ILM, not regarded as fully-committed workers, but employers could benefit from reduced pressure to create career ladders while still being able to draw on these women's skills and experience.

Indeed, current arrangements cannot necessarily be assumed to be in any sense 'optimal' for employers, particularly if the potential economic costs involved in moving to 'more efficient' systems contribute to the inertia of any given arrangement. Thus, for example, whether integrating women into job hierarchies after a career break would actually cause loss of motivation among continuous workers, as may be suggested by management, is a matter for conjecture. It is highly unlikely that such experiments have been carried out systematically.

Efficiency wage theories

Efficiency wage theories provide the second illustration of new institutional approaches to the ILM. In general, efficiency wage models distinguish between different sectors of the labour market by positing an institutionally-embedded relation between the wage rate and labour productivity. Labour is recognised as a peculiar commodity, given the high costs involved in specifying an employment contract for pre-determined levels of effort[1] (Akerlof and Yellen, 1986).

The model of Shapiro and Stiglitz (1984) begins with the assumption that workers' economic behaviour is 'opportunistic': a worker will shirk, and not satisfy the required level of effort for a particular job task. Under conditions of full employment the economic cost of dismissal to the shirking worker is nullified by the ability to gain employment at an equivalent rate of pay. By assuming, however, that the wage paid has a positive effect on productivity and that monitoring of effort is costly and imperfect, Shapiro and Stiglitz (1984) argue that it is profit-maximising

---

[1] The problems of extracting labour from labour power have been subject to exploration since Marx's writings, and experienced a resurgence after Braverman's work (1974). However, the efficiency wage method of substituting new premises into the standard neo-classical model and applying the traditional logistical techniques stands in contrast to the inter-disciplinary paradigm of the labour process debates.

for the employer to pay a wage rate greater than the market clearing wage (or opportunity wage). This 'efficiency wage' system provides the worker with an incentive not to shirk, since the wage premium raises the opportunity cost of dismissal. Furthermore, if each firm's strategy is aggregated to the macro level, the payment of wages above the market clearing rate causes a so-called 'optimum' level of unemployment. This acts as an additional disincentive to shirking, and reduces the costs of supervision to the firm.

Efficiency wage models perpetuate the notion that involuntary unemployment is the result of excessively high wages. They also lend substantial support to policy-makers who defend high rates of unemployment on the basis that they are necessary for an economy to secure faster rates of productivity growth. For the purpose of developing an alternative economic rationale of ILM systems, three points of particular criticism reveal the indifference of this approach to the influence of ELM divisions.

Firstly, efficiency wages are determined not only by technical efficiency considerations, but also by the worker's 'reservation wage' – the minimum wage at which an employee would accept employment. The reservation wage is generally regarded as a function of the average duration of unemployment, the level of unemployment benefits and the availability of alternative employment. The lower the reservation wage, the greater the level of effort for a given wage rate. Similarly, the greater the reservation wage, the greater the efficiency wage level received for a given level of effort. Although this point appears potentially interesting, it is blind to certain aspects of a non-homogeneous labour force. For example, one cannot assume that the official unemployment rate captures the potential excess supply of labour for all jobs. The excess supply of labour for female-dominated jobs, for instance, may include not only unemployed women but also large numbers of 'inactive' women (the 'hidden unemployed') who are not registered as part of the labour force, yet may be willing to work given the opportunity.

It is also problematic to assume that the wage rate is responsive to changes in the reservation position in a consistent fashion. For example, alternative job opportunities generally decline with age, suggesting a reduction in the reservation or opportunity wage as a worker grows older. But contrary to the efficiency wage prediction, conventional employment practice grants wage security with seniority in recognition of a broader social consensus that wages should not decline with age. Hence, an explanation of differential wage rates over time or between groups cannot rely solely upon changes in the reservation wage position; it must also investigate the complex interplay between social norms of fairness or inequity and reservation positions.

The second criticism concerns explanations of persistent wage differentials. Efficiency wage theories are best suited to explaining wage differentials that occur as a result of inter-company characteristics.

Attempts to explain wage differentials that exist between groups of workers, like the gender pay gap, run into trouble almost as soon as the standard assumption of worker homogeneity is relaxed.

Shapiro and Stiglitz (1984) argue that efficiency wage differentials exist between industries because the technical conditions which necessitate wage incentives differ in form. In their words:

> Firms which find shirking particularly costly will offer higher wages than other firms do. (Shapiro and Stiglitz, 1984: 434.)

Similarly, Bulow and Summers suggest that the responsibilities of primary-sector jobs make detection of shirking important, whereas 'secondary-sector jobs are menial so that monitoring is costless' (Bulow and Summers, 1986: 382).

It follows that the gender pay gap must be the result of women's concentration in jobs that are easy to monitor or do not involve much responsibility. This logic implies that effort and performance in caring occupations are easier to monitor than in male-dominated production jobs, and do not involve much responsibility. Evidence shows, however, that men are more likely to have access to output-related bonuses (IRS, 1991), which are easier to introduce in occupations where effort levels are easily measured.

Yellen (1984) argues that efficiency wage models can provide two rationales for a theory of persistent wage differentials based on discrimination if the labour force is non-homogeneous. First, the presence of involuntary unemployment enables employers to exercise discriminatory hiring preferences without suffering the costs of hiring inefficient applicants. Second, employers may know that the 'effort–wage relation' differs between groups and will hire the group which provides cheaper 'efficiency units' of labour (Yellen, 1984).

The former rationale is problematic. If discriminatory recruitment confines one group of workers to relatively high levels of unemployment, it will lower their reservation position. As a result, employers can offer a lower efficiency wage to this group for a given level of effort. In the long run, the competitive forces that underpin the efficiency wage approach must also, within this framework, eliminate discrimination (Bulow and Summers, 1986).

Bulow and Summers (1986) develop Yellen's second rationale as a model of the gender pay gap. They argue that employers believe women to be less committed to their jobs than men, given the evidence that women have higher separation rates from the job.[2] The lesser degree of commitment

---

[2] Although Bulow and Summers (1986) support this with statistical data for the US, alternative evidence on separation rates undermines their model. Darity (1991) cites several studies that show women are no more likely than men to quit a job after adjusting for personal and work characteristics, and indeed that white males are more likely to quit than non-white males.

signifies a greater tendency for women to shirk, making them more expensive per 'efficiency unit' of labour. The result is an under-representation of women in the high-paying primary sector (Bulow and Summers, 1986).

This explanation is also inadequate. The relatively high rates of job separation experienced by women are treated as exogenous to the model; yet it is not clear to what extent these high rates are a function of employment conditions in the secondary sector. This illustrates a general weakness with new institutional approaches to ILMs: differences in employment experience and expectations are treated as exogenous, and the interrelations between the cumulative impact of employer strategies and the experience of different labour force groups are not considered (Rubery, 1994).

Finally, the behavioural assumption of opportunism, common to all new institutional analyses of the labour market, can be criticised. Once efficiency wage theorists have assumed that a problem of individual opportunistic behaviour exists, the economic agenda is restricted to identifying the most efficient means of correcting the natural impulse to shirk. In contrast, economic action can be conceptualised as being embedded in the social system and influenced by the established relationship between production and the institutional environment (Bowles, 1985; Granovetter, 1985; Green, 1988; Hodgson, 1988). This alternative notion of human action has been partially incorporated in recent developments to efficiency wage theories which recognise the influence of custom and fairness in the wage-setting process. Nevertheless, this 'fairness approach' fails to endogenise social norms and expectations.

Fairness

This literature introduces a norm of fairness as an additional factor in the worker's utility function: the less workers perceive their wage as unfair, the more effort they will exert voluntarily. For a non-homogeneous workforce, this approach suggests the employer's wage-setting decision could be affected if different standards of fair pay are held for men and women. Equally, it may be that the employer and/or male employees rely upon customary notions of women's work in the design and perpetuation of discriminatory ILMs.

Akerlof (1982) argues that, for a homogeneous workforce, inter-industry wage differentials are determined by the various notions of fairness underpinning each 'gift exchange' of extra effort for extra pay between the employer and a group of workers. This thesis is derived from a sociological study of young women working in an electricity company, but Akerlof still fails to identify gendered norms of fairness as an important factor. Indeed, he treats the observation that promotion was not a relevant consideration for most women in the company as an exogenous factor, and does not comment on the fact that where promotion did occur there was no change in the wage rate paid (Akerlof, 1982). Although one can extrapolate the logic of this model of wage-bargaining to assert that different 'rent-sharing' agreements are exacted for non-competing groups of workers according to a gendered norm of fairness, an alternative approach is still needed to understand the full role played by fairness in relation to ILMs.

A more recent model (Fehr and Kirchsteiger, 1994) shows how norms of fairness impinge upon the wage negotiations of workers with a strong ILM position ('insiders') and those who are newly recruited ('entrants'). Insiders compare their wage rates with the firm's tradeable income, and possess the power to extract a wage above their reservation position; whereas entrants consider a similarly-skilled insider to be their 'natural reference agent'. Given these conditions, if a two-tier wage system exists entrants will perceive their wage as unfair and will shirk. The employer responds by paying an efficiency wage premium, and the result is a smaller wage differential and the possibility of a non-clearing labour market.

Fehr and Kirchsteiger (1994) are aware that their model would require considerable modification to be applied to a non-homogeneous labour force. Consider a male-dominated firm where new entrants are predominantly women. The natural reference agent for the female entrants is unclear. On the one hand, these women may believe that the firm's ILM structure offers shelter from their external disadvantaged position, and thus refer to similarly-skilled male insiders as a fair standard of comparison. On the other hand, their expectations may be deeply influenced by notions of women's inferior socio-economic status, so their fair reference point would be rooted in their unequal labour market position.

Attempts to extend both approaches to encompass a labour market characterised by inequality and division reveal the need to elaborate the interrelations between norms and various levels of institutional arrangements. Norms of fairness are not necessarily mainly or solely related to notions of 'a fair rate for the job'; they also apply to notions of needs (Kessler-Harris, 1990). Divisions of the labour force by gender may facilitate the payment of different wages to workers employed on different jobs requiring the same levels of skill, not only because of a lack of identification between the two groups, but also as a result of strong normative views that male workers have higher needs and thus deserve more income.[3] Such notions can also underpin differentiated career opportunities within ILMs. Higher-tier workers who fear that the lower tier may be used in the long term to undermine their insider position may be reassured if the lower tier is not given access to the full range of training and career opportunities.

---

[3] Although the empirical validity of the male breadwinner has weakened, particularly for low-income families, it is still powerful as an ideological tool. This was illustrated in 1993 when the UK government argued that the abolition of Wages Councils would not cause hardship within households, as the majority of employees affected were married women with part-time jobs.

The degree to which a society is characterised by a patriarchal norm of fairness is also contingent upon the particular collective bargaining or pay determination system in place. In general, the system of ILM organisation will affect the boundaries across which workers identify collectively when pressing for better conditions. Pay bargaining structures which separate men's and women's jobs are likely to reinforce patriarchal norms of higher pay levels for men.[4] Solidaristic pay bargaining may act against sex inequality in the broader social system, and provide women with an escape from their unfavourable ELM position. These influences are yet more evident in the case of race, where the historical experience of integrating different racial groups into the labour market results in differences in the intensity of racism as well as in the ranking of racial groups within societies (Castles and Kosack, 1973).

This discussion of the endogeneity of preferences is important, as it may be that norms of fairness change over time between the sexes or between labour force groups within the sexes. Firms are now less able to pay women lower rates than men for explicitly the same work than before the equal pay legislation of the 1970s, but they can still maintain lower wage structures for women through job segregation. Perhaps, in the future, employers may be obliged to provide more career ladders for women with higher qualifications, as a continuous employment career becomes accepted as a new norm.

Integrating the ELM into ILM models

Table 5.1 provides a very general guide to the differences between the approach used here and that which characterises new institutional theories of the ILM (the ILM approach). The ILM approach generates a stylised dichotomy of the labour market driven by employer practice to improve efficiency within a perfectly competitive, homogeneous labour market. The ILM typically has two characteristics. First, it provides a form of shelter to internal employees, protecting them from ELM conditions. Secondly, it satisfies the firm's aims to achieve strong worker attachment, boosted by strong incentives such as high pay and access to job ladders and training opportunities. Where ILM structures are absent, the secondary labour market operates much as the traditional neo-classical model, where low pay is directly equated with a low acquisition of human capital.

In contrast, this chapter argues that ILM structures may be found across the full spectrum of occupational differences, industrial structures and organisations. Two characteristic and polar forms of ILM structure – one strong and one weak – may exist within the same company, or serve to distinguish different firms' employment organisation.

A strong ILM system appears much like the stylised ILM structure: again, shelter is provided to the employee through beneficial incentives,

---

[4] The division of the pay-bargaining system into areas covering mainly male and areas covering mainly female jobs is itself likely to be a reflection of patriarchal values and gender inequalities. Where more integrated bargaining exists, however, these structures may have been established for reasons other than attempts to break down patriarchal norms. For example, integrated pay for clerical and manual workers may stem from a period when clerical workers were male.

Table 5.1 The ILM approach taking into account employee internal and external bargaining power

Stylised ILM approach	
ILM	*Secondary labour market*
• Strong incentives (high pay, job ladders)	• Low pay, low skills
• High employment stability	• Weak attachment

ILMs taking into account employees' internal and external bargaining power	
Strong ILM	*Weak ILM*
• Same as stylised ILM	• Weak incentives (low pay, and so on)
• Also responsive to workers' strong ELM and ILM position	• Strong worker attachment

contributing to high employment stability. These conditions of employment, however, are created and reinforced by the workers' strong ELM position, whether by the power of collective trade union organisation, membership of a professional body, or the influence of widely-held social norms of fair employment practice.

In a weak ILM system, low pay and few training opportunities prevail. However, in contrast to the traditional model of the secondary labour market, the employer is able to exploit the vulnerable position of the workforce to achieve strong attachment to the firm. This may characterise a captive labour force of married women seeking short working hours due to domestic responsibilities, or workers living in a residential area with limited transport facilities. In these circumstances it is unnecessary for the employer to pay a premium to retain skilled workers, and the lack of formal qualifications restricts the opportunities for workers to use their acquired skills to transfer to better jobs in the ELM.

Forms of ILMs and equal opportunities

Recognition of the interactions between the ELM and the ILM considerably increases the complexity of studying the institutional form of the ILM, and of determining its effects in perpetuating or offsetting gender inequalities in the wider labour market and society. These problems can be illustrated by considering three different dimensions to the shape and form of an ILM: the pay and job grading structure; the promotion system; and the payment system.

Pay and job grading structure

Figure 5.2 shows the different forms an ILM can take, depending upon the source of labour recruitment and the ILM's sensitivity to outside or ELM

Figure 5.2 Impact of external opportunities on the form of the internal labour market

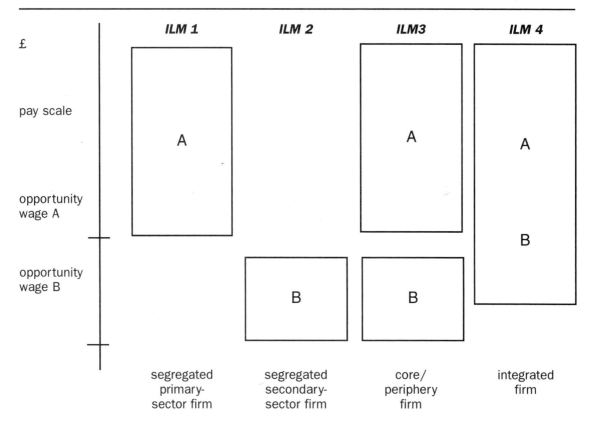

Group A – high opportunity wage; strong expectations of advancement in ELM
Group B – low opportunity wage; low expectations of advancement in ELM

influences. For simplicity it is first assumed that the ELM consists of two non-competing groups: group A has generally good labour market opportunities and its members have expectations of lifetime advancement in the employment system; while group B workers have limited opportunities or indeed expectations for advancement. Employers can minimise the cost of securing a stable labour force if they can establish separate ILM structures for these two groups, as in both cases the employer must provide a premium over and above the pay the group members could expect to receive in the ELM. For group B workers this premium is potentially very small, while group A workers require a much larger immediate premium and greater pay promotion opportunities over time. The separation of the groups into different ILM structures can be achieved through the establishment of segregated organisations (similar to ILM1 and ILM2 in Figure 5.2), or through multiple ILMs within an organisation similar to a core/periphery model (ILM3).

Under both separation systems employers can gain advantages from the fragmented pay structures. Primary-type firms specialising in operations where group A workers are normally recruited can still gain the advantages of utilising group B workers at lower wage rates by sub-contracting out activities to secondary-type firms whose ILMs are geared to the group B labour market. Organisations using a core/periphery model can gain these advantages even for internalised activities.

If, however, employers for various reasons provide an integrated ILM they have to decide how to link the two labour markets to give an entry rate which is sufficiently high to attract group A workers, but which does not 'unnecessarily' raise the costs of hiring group B workers. One possibility is to establish the entry rate somewhere in between the 'going rate' for both groups, and attract group A workers with the offer of accelerated promotion. This suggests that even when integrated ILMs are established, the ELM position of the two groups of workers may still influence the rate of promotion up the integrated hierarchy. Nevertheless, it can be seen from Figure 5.2 that the establishment of an integrated ILM (ILM4) is potentially considerably more beneficial to group B workers than the establishment of separate ILMs either within an organisation or through decentralisation of production and subcontracting. Only in the last example of an ILM, where groups A and B have the same entry rate of pay, does the establishment of an ILM significantly offset the disadvantages faced by group B workers in the ELM.

Figure 5.2 describes forms of ILMs that can evolve in an abstract or ideal world with two non-competing groups in the labour market. These possibilities must be tied into actual ILM systems, and the extent to which men and women can be expected to form respectively A and B groups in the labour market must be established. As argued earlier, gender is a particularly important division in the labour market. Not only is there evidence that women command a different rate of pay, even after 'adjusting' for differences in skill levels, but they also tend to undertake different jobs from men. One of the main ways in which employers can take advantage of different labour force groups' employment opportunities is if these groups are recruited into clearly different types of jobs within the ILM, or if different types of employers draw upon one or other group. Thus segregation by occupation or establishment is an important criteria for establishing ILMs that differentiate by ELM position.

Some labour force groups with low ELM opportunities are still paid within an ILM according to the value of the job they are doing, and not the value of their labour outside the firm. An example is older workers who, although skilled and undertaking valuable work for the firm, would command a very low wage if made redundant. However, except where workers are recruited at old age into specific jobs designed for older workers such as pensioners, this ELM division does not correspond to either occupational or establishment-level segregation. Thus taking advantage of the declining opportunities with old age would require the introduction of variable wages within the same ILM structure as younger workers employed in the same job area. Such an adjustment, although possible by making rates decline with age after a certain point on a grading scale, would make the fact that the organisation was taking advantage of the individual's ELM opportunities more explicit; for example, paying an older but more-skilled worker less than a younger but less-skilled worker in the same job.

Empirical evidence does provide support for the notion that firms will try to establish different ILM structures to take advantage of the different labour market positions of men and women. Research for the EOC reveals that firms in the UK use more than one payment structure, and that the most important factor in determining how jobs are clustered into different payment structures is whether they are male- or female-dominated (IRS, 1991, 1992a). The 1990 Workplace Industrial Relations Survey revealed that gender segregation at establishment and occupational levels is strongly associated with different levels of pay (see Millward and Woodland, this volume, Chapter 10). One of the few systematic studies of an ILM for gender effects in the USA found that women were concentrated in different pay and job hierarchies, and that women's hierarchies tend to have fewer rungs in the ladder (Hartmann, 1987). Indirect evidence is found in the system of job classification that women's jobs are compressed into a narrow range of grades offering few opportunities for advancement.

It has become almost a truism of occupational classification research to observe that women's occupations are less differentiated by skill levels and experience than are men's (Foxon, 1989; Rubery and Fagan, 1993; Plantenga *et al.*, 1992). These classification systems tend to follow the practice within organisations of grouping women's job areas together in much broader clusters, and women's training and skills are more generic and less specific. These differences may reflect women's lower bargaining power, and thus more limited scope to differentiate their position from other workers, both currently and historically.

Much of the trend towards sub-contracting in private and public sectors can be seen as a means of giving organisations the opportunity to benefit from the lower costs associated with firms specialised in female-dominated areas of work (such as cleaning or catering) which fix their pay levels at the 'market rate' for this labour force group (Hunter *et al.*, 1993). Even in the late 1970s sub-contracting catering firms were explicit that the main advantage they offered employers was the opportunity to pay a lower minimum wage rate to these workers than to their shop-floor staff (Craig *et al.*, 1982). Catering firms often adopted practices such as having different anniversary dates of pay rises to prevent any real comparison between directly-employed workers and those employed by the sub-contractor but working on the same site. Subsequent abolition of the fair wages clause has legitimised such policies in the public as well as the private sector.

While the existence and likelihood of ILMs that reproduce and reinforce women's ELM position can be shown to have empirical relevance in the UK and elsewhere, these effects are not automatic or predetermined but depend upon specific institutional arrangements and the actions of agents at both the organisational and the broader sectoral or country levels. For example, where grading systems established at a sectoral level restrict the opportunity for firms to operate different pay and grading structures for male- and female-dominated grades, the potential effect of different external opportunity wages for men and women will be limited. Italy and France have well-established grading structures covering both manual and non-manual employees, and by tradition non-manuals are graded higher than manuals. This contrasts with the UK, where the tradition of separate pay structures allows clerical workers often to be paid less than manual workers (Rubery and Fagan, 1994).

Differences in these grading systems may also affect the broader ELM, such that gender differences in external opportunity wages may be narrower as ILM systems structure the ELM as well as vice versa. Legal or collectively-negotiated minimum wages may restrict the advantages to be gained from sub-contracting services to specialist firms, as the minimum wage rate may reduce the gap between men and women's entry wage rates (Rubery and Fagan, 1994). Thus firms which adopt the more integrated grading structures associated with the fourth example in Figure 5.2 may do so either because of institutional constraints which restrict options to fragment the job structure, or because changing patterns of ELM opportunities and occupational segregation act independently of institutional constraints to reduce the opportunities for establishing segmented structures.

Labour-market-based institutions may in some cases limit managerial discretion to set up fragmented structures, but in other contexts such institutions may reinforce discrimination. This conflict can currently be seen in the health service in Britain. There is considerable evidence, and indeed current litigation, suggesting that pay structures in the health sector do not follow the principle of equal pay for work of equal value. This arises at least in part from the practice of separate pay-bargaining structures, and thus separate ILMs, for different skill groups. There are thus potential gains for women from moving towards individual hospital-based internal grading and pay structures (towards ILMs and away from occupational labour markets), particularly if these offered 'gender-sensitive' job evaluation and the creation of a single pay spine (IRS, 1992b). However, these potential gains must be set against the potential for greater discretion for management in setting pay implied by the break-up of the national system.

The promotion system

Another ILM dimension is the promotion system. The ideal model of an ILM suggests that all workers with firm-specific skill have good chances of promotion. However, empirical research reveals relatively few organisations where all workers recruited at the bottom of a job ladder are likely to move significantly up the system (Rubery, 1994). Providing promotion opportunities for all is very expensive, and many firms restrict the number of workers expecting promotion by creating rules or other criteria which differentiate the 'stayers' from those with 'career potential', or by establishing different entry routes into the ILM structure.

The development of rules or criteria for promotion, such as geographical mobility, have the effect of restricting upward mobility for household second-income earners. This means that promotion to the next rung on the ladder is not linked to performance in the current job, or even to potential performance in the next grade, but to potential suitability for further promotion. These criteria could be argued to conflict with the notion of equal opportunities, as individuals are not being treated on their current merits or allocated according to current efficiency.

Crompton and Sanderson (1990) have argued that the establishment of a separate managerial recruitment and training system may in fact benefit many women clerical workers, by freeing higher-level clerical jobs previously reserved for clerical workers selected for mobility into higher management. This change in practice allows jobs to be allocated to those most likely to carry out senior clerical jobs effectively, often not those who are 'destined' for management, which provides the basis for the 'consolidation of the clerical career' (Crompton and Sanderson, 1990). The cost to women of the creation of more intermediate promotion opportunities may be the separation of clerical and managerial ILMs, thereby limiting in principle the level to which clerical workers can be promoted. This highlights the problems of assessing the equal opportunities implications of different forms of ILMs, as the consolidation of clerical careers may benefit more women, but perhaps at the expense of the exclusion of a small minority from the opportunity for much greater occupational mobility.

Payment systems

ILM systems provide employers with discretion in the determination of pay and job grading. They are no longer assumed to be price-takers in respect of wage setting. Much literature on ILMs has stressed how this discretion needs to be constrained, through its codification into rules and procedures based closely on custom and practice, if employees within the ILM are to trust the firm not to exploit its potential bargaining position and to provide a reasonable reward for firm-specific skills in return for stability and commitment. Moreover, Williamson (1975) suggested that employers have an interest in creating bureaucratic systems to avoid the transaction costs of employees engaging in opportunistic bargaining.

It could be argued that one of the important advantages of ILMs for women is the existence of rules and procedures, in contrast to the alternative model of casualised labour markets. For example, within ILMs there is most scope for introducing job evaluation systems, which arguably provide women with some protection against being paid wages which reflect their position as disadvantaged workers in the ELM and not the value of the job they perform for the company. However, research on the application of the principle of equal pay for work of equal value has revealed that codification is not in itself sufficient to provide protection against discrimination. Job evaluation schemes are probably the most highly-codified systems of job grading, but research shows the importance of the actual scheme adopted and the method of implementation; within any schemes there is scope for discretion in its application as well as in its design (Acker, 1989; Blum, 1991).

Recent institutional developments have on balance pointed away from the codified and job-related hierarchies predicted by both Doeringer and Piore (1971) and the transaction-costs models of Williamson (1975). Instead, systems are becoming more individualised, which according to the Williamson model increases the risk to employers of more opportunistic bargaining. However, the merits of the collective model have usually been discussed within an assumption of socially homogeneous labour in the workplace. The assumption that it is better for employers to establish a common pay structure for all to pre-empt opportunistic bargaining may be open to question if more individualised pay systems allow firms to discriminate negatively as well as positively in pay determination. The costs to employers of meeting demands from a few key workers to pay ever-higher wages may be offset by the opportunity to take advantage of the low bargaining power of those without good ELM opportunities.

Discretionary systems not codified by rules do potentially increase discrimination by gender, if only because they reduce the possibility of monitoring systems for discrimination and establishing notions of fair pay and equal pay for work of equal value. ILM systems almost axiomatically add to the opaqueness of labour markets, as pay depends upon the organisation and not on occupation, and thereby increase the difficulty of obtaining information at a labour market level. Discretionary payment systems further reduce the amount of relevant information. Moreover, research conducted for the EOC revealed the potential for both conscious and unconscious discrimination in the design and application of performance-related payment systems (Bevan and Thompson, 1992). Not only are women and men differentially assessed, but also different criteria appear to be applied for good performance, even within similar jobs. Such assessments are often so subjective that even an employer who in principle wishes not to discriminate may not know to what extent his or her judgment is based on prejudice and assumptions.

Conclusions

Introducing a gender perspective into ILM analysis reveals the diversity of forms that ILMs can take, and suggests the implications of such labour market forms for gender equality are essentially a contingent issue. ILMs may shelter women from the ELM, in which sex-stereotyping and historical patterns of discrimination consign them to low-wage jobs. Alternatively, ILMs may codify and reinforce discrimination in the broader labour market. Gender inequality may acquire internal organisational legitimacy through the assignment of women's jobs to low points on a grading structure, and organisations may use gender divisions as a means of wage discrimination to reduce the high labour cost implications of the ILM and efficiency-wage models. The costs and benefits of ILM systems thus need to be investigated empirically, but within a methodology which recognises the historically contingent nature of organisational structures. Empirical enquiries must be wary of the spurious scientific assumption, found in most efficiency wage and ILM models, that if labour markets are efficient then any institutional structure must be explicable according to efficiency or technical criteria.

This alternative picture of a labour market characterised by a diversity of ILM systems is generated by the interplay between internal and external factors: the workers' bargaining position; the strength of expectations of pay and career opportunities; and the impact of discriminatory managerial practices. In contrast to new institutional approaches, these factors interact according to a labour force differentiated by gender, race and skill.

Moreover, it follows from this approach that there is the potential for ILM structures to persist in a state of inefficiency. Attempts to improve conditions of wage equity may demand substantial 'transaction costs' of institutional change. The costs of ceasing discriminatory practices may in the long term be outweighed by unseen efficiency gains accruing from more optimal labour allocation, but the uncertainty attached to such gains may deter employers from incurring the transaction costs of moving from a tried and tested system to a new system. Recruitment screening devices which reduce the costs of acquiring information about all individual applicants may be retained, even in the face of evidence that they under-represent the skill potential of female applicants and thus lead to less than optimal resource utilisation. The potential costs of developing a more refined screening system may still outweigh the benefits in the short to medium term.

This does not mean that questions of economic costs or efficiency gains should be ignored in the pursuit of greater equity in the labour market. Rather, it draws attention to how costs should be regarded in an economic system. The new institutional literature persistently fails to identify how economic cost decisions take place within a political or historical context. Yet where institutional change generates transaction or transitional costs, the decision whether or not to press ahead with these changes, through for example the provision of public funding, would be determined by the political environment and political objectives. The influence of political ideology may be the major determinant of institutional change:[5] in the positive sense that transitional costs will only be funded if institutional change fits with a more overriding objective; and in the negative sense that, in the absence of wider support for institutional change, agents involved in assessing the costs and benefits will, in the face of uncertainty

---

[5] The continuing privatisation of public services is difficult to defend theoretically on the grounds that it minimises the technical costs of an organisation. Sub-contracting services in local government and the health sector was ostensibly introduced to minimise public expenditure. However, the specification of all conditions of service to be satisfied, such as price, quantity and quality of service, incurs relatively high transaction costs (Pankhurst, 1990).

regarding all future costs and benefits of organisational change, tend to fall back upon the dominant norm of employment practice.

These tendencies have been well recognised over recent years in other aspects of employment policy and practice. The extensive programme of industrial relations legislation and labour market deregulation has been introduced with the precise objective of providing the appropriate wider institutional and political environment to stimulate employers to institute change at company and plant levels. Without such incentives, firms could reasonably be expected to choose the softer option of inertia rather than major organisational change. It can equally be argued that without wider social change and support for equal opportunities programmes, action at the individual firm level may be expected to be limited.

References

Acker, J. (1989). *Doing Comparable Worth: Gender, Class and Pay Equity*. Philadelphia: Temple University Press.

Akerlof, G. (1982). 'Labour contracts as partial gift exchange' in *Quarterly Journal of Economics*, 97.

Akerlof, G. and Yellen, J. L. (1986). *Efficiency Wage Models of the Labour Market*. Cambridge: Cambridge University Press.

Armstrong, P. (1982). 'If it's only women it doesn't matter so much' in West, J. (ed.) *Work, Women and the Labour Market*. London: Routledge and Kegan Paul.

Becker, G. (1967). *Human Capital and the Personal Distribution of Income*. Ann Arbor: University of Michigan Press.

Bevan, S. and Thompson, M. (1992). *Merit Pay, Performance Appraisal and Attitudes to Women's Work*. IMS Report 234. Brighton: Institute of Manpower Studies.

Blum, L. M. (1991). *Between Feminism and Labour: The Significance of the Comparable Worth Movement*. Berkeley: University of California Press.

Bowles, S. (1985). 'The production process in a competitive economy: Walrasian, neo-Hobbesian, and Marxian models' in *American Economic Review*, 75 (1).

Braverman, H. (1974). *Labour and Monopoly Capital*. New York: Monthly Review Press.

Bulow, J. and Summers, L. H. (1986). 'A theory of dual labour markets with application to industrial policy' in *Journal of Labor Economics*, 4 (3), part 1.

Castles, S. and Kosack, G. (1973). *Immigrant Workers and Class Structure in Western Europe*. London: Oxford University Press.

Cockburn, C. (1991). *In the Way of Women: Men's Resistance to Sex Equality in Organisations*. London: Macmillan.

Collinson, D. L., Knights, D. and Collinson, M. (1990). *Managing to Discriminate*. London: Routledge.

Craig, C., Rubery, J., Tarling, R. and Wilkinson, F. (1982). *Labour Market Structure, Industrial Organisation and Low Pay*. Cambridge: Cambridge University Press.

Crompton, R. and Sanderson, K. (1990). *Gendered Jobs and Social Change*. London: Unwin Hyman.

Darity, W. A. Jr. (1991). 'Efficiency wage theory: critical reflections on the neo-Keynesian theory of unemployment and discrimination' in Cornwall, R. R. and Wunnava, P. V. (eds.) *New Approaches to Economic and Social Analyses of Discrimination*. New York: Praeger.

Doeringer, P. B. and Piore, M. J. (1971). *Internal Labour Markets and Manpower Analysis*. Lexington: Heath.

Fehr, E. and Kirchsteiger, G. (1994). 'Insider power, wage discrimination and fairness' in *The Economic Journal*, 104.

Foxon, J. (1989). 'The new standard occupational classification' in *OPCS Survey Methodology Bulletin*, 24.

Granovetter, M. (1985). 'Economic action and social structure: the problem of embeddedness' in *American Journal of Sociology*, 91.

Green, F. (1988). 'Neo-classical and Marxian conceptions of production' in *Cambridge Journal of Economics*, 12 (3).

Hartmann, H. I. (1987). 'Internal labour markets and gender: a case study of promotion' in Brown, C. and Pechman, J. A. (eds.) *Gender in the Workplace*. Washington, DC: The Brookings Institution.

Hodgson, G. M. (1988). *Economics and Institutions: A Manifesto for a Modern Institutional Economics*. Philadelphia: University of Pennsylvania Press.

Hunter, L., MacInnes, J., McGregor, A. and Sproull, A. (1993). 'The "flexible firm": strategy and segmentation' in *British Journal of Industrial Relations*, 31 (3).

IRS (1991). *Pay and Gender in Britain*. London: Industrial Relations Service.

IRS (1992a). *Pay and Gender in Britain: 2*. London: Industrial Relations Service.

IRS (1992b). *Single Table Bargaining and Job Evaluation at Manchester Hospitals Trust*. August, 518.

Jacoby, S. M. (1990). 'The new institutionalism: what can it learn from the old?' in *Industrial Relations*, 29 (2).

Kessler-Harris, A. (1990). *A Woman's Wage: Historical Meaning and Social Consequences*. The University Press of Kentucky.

Millward, N. and Woodland, S. (1995). 'Gender segregation and male/female wage differences' in this volume.

Paci, P., Joshi, H. and Makepeace, G. (1995). 'Pay gaps facing men and women born in 1958: differences within the labour market' in this volume.

Pankhurst, K. (1990). *The Quality of Labour: The Economics of Discretion and of Learning During Work*. PhD dissertation, University of Cambridge.

Phillips, A. and Taylor, B. (1980). 'Sex and skill: notes towards a feminist economics' in *Feminist Review*, 6.

Plantenga, J., van der Burg, B. and van Velzen, S. (1992). *Occupational Segregation in the Netherlands*. Report for the European Commission: Network on the Situation of Women in the Labour Market.

Rubery, J. (1994). 'Internal and external labour markets: towards an integrated framework' in Rubery, J. and Wilkinson, F. (eds.) *Employer Strategy and the Labour Market*. Oxford: Oxford University Press.

Rubery, J. and Fagan, C. (1993). 'Occupational segregation of women and men in the European Community' in *Social Europe*, supplement 3/93.

Rubery, J. and Fagan, C. (1994). *Wage Determination and Sex Segregation in Employment in the European Community*. V/408/94-EN. Brussels: Commission of the European Communities.

Sawyer, M. (1995). 'The operation of labour markets and the economics of equal opportunities' in this volume.

Shapiro, C. and Stiglitz, J. E. (1984). 'Equilibrium unemployment as a worker discipline device' in *American Economic Review*, 74 (2)

Straw, J. (1989). *Equal Opportunities: The Way Ahead*. Exeter: Short Run Press.

Williamson, O. E. (1975). *Markets and Hierarchies: Analysis and Antitrust Implications*. New York: The Free Press.

Williamson, O. E. (1985). *The Economic Institutions of Capitalism*. New York: The Free Press.

Yellen, J. L. (1984). 'Efficiency wage models of unemployment' in *American Economic Review*, Papers and Proceedings, 74 (2).

Part II

Costs and Benefits of Equal Opportunities

CHAPTER 6

The Costs and Benefits to British Employers of Measures to Promote Equality of Opportunity

Sally Holtermann

This chapter summarises the quantitative evidence available on the costs and benefits to British employers of implementing measures to promote equality of opportunity. Other chapters in this volume consider the wider benefits of equal opportunities practices, but the focus here is on the private costs and benefits to employers.

The baseline

In Britain the current situation – usually taken as the point of departure in cost-benefit analysis – results from legal standards universally applicable to all employers. These are embodied in the Sex Discrimination and Equal Pay Acts; and, more pertinently here, in legislation providing employees with rights in the workplace. On top of the statutory minima many employers provide better conditions through contractual arrangements with employees and/or discretionary provision of benefits and services.

Improvements in employment rights and working conditions seem to advance through a cycle whereby some companies, keen to be 'good' employers and establish a competitive lead in attracting scarce workers, provide better conditions than the statutory minimum; other companies move in the same direction to avoid appearing as poor employers and to remain competitive in recruitment; statutory standards are improved (in some cases leap-frogging over good employer practice, but in others following); employers with standards below the new minimum have to improve; the leading employers upgrade their terms to restore their position ahead of the new minimum, and so on.

In this process both employers and government are key players in initiating change, and both need information about the benefits and costs to employers. For employers, this information is a key determinant of action; for government it is necessary for an understanding of the reasons for employer action (or inaction). As the government has wider economic and social objectives than employers, it also needs to have information on the wider costs and benefits – which fall on the employees (and their families), on other employers, and ultimately therefore on the whole economy.

The working conditions and employment rights defining the current situation on equal opportunities in Britain include a wide range of measures.

Maternity provisions

Statutory provisions have been improved in the last year to comply with the EC Pregnant Workers directive. The changes extend the right to 14 weeks' maternity leave to all women who work during pregnancy, increase the proportion of women who will qualify for earnings-related maternity pay, and increase the lower rate of maternity pay (IDS, 1994b).

Contractual terms offered by employers often go beyond the minimum requirements, especially in the public sector and former nationalised industries. The 1988 Maternity Rights Survey (McRae, 1991) found that 14 per cent of women received maternity pay above the statutory level, and some 18 per cent of employers gave the right to reinstatement on more generous terms than the statutory minimum. Incomes Data Services (IDS) has found that there have been continued improvements in contractual terms for maternity leave and pay despite the recession, and report more use of innovations such as bonuses for women returning after maternity leave and flexible working time (IDS, 1992b, 1994b).

Paternity leave

There is no statutory provision for short-term leave for fathers at around the time of the birth. McRae (1991) found that 77 per cent of fathers took time off work around the birth date: 54 per cent took it as part of their holiday (leaving them with less time to spend with their children at other times of the year); 16 per cent had access to paternity or other forms of paid leave (the majority being in non-manual occupations); and 15 per cent took unpaid leave (the majority being in manual occupations). (Some fathers took more than one kind of leave, hence the figures total more than 77 per cent.) IDS (1994b) reports that more employers are granting paid paternity leave and that the number of days is increasing, with three days now most common.

Parental leave

This is leave for either fathers or mothers taken after the end of maternity leave. There is no statutory provision, and the UK is expected to exercise its right to opt out of the EC directive on parental leave when the rest of the EU adopts it. Under the terms of the draft EC directive, all parents in employment – fathers as well as mothers – would have the right to at least three months' leave. The leave can only be taken if the other parent is at work, and need not necessarily be paid. The entitlement is not transferable between parents, can be subject to a service requirement, and must be taken before the child is aged two (five in the case of adoptions and disabled children). Very few employers make provision for parental leave, but many now have schemes for career breaks, the nearest equivalent. These are often aimed at increasing retention of women in categories of skill shortage, and do not always apply to all employees.

Leave for family reasons

Leave for family reasons normally refers to special short-term leave taken for family emergencies, such as looking after a sick child or elderly relative, or while the usual carer is sick, but it could extend (as in Sweden) to attendance at meetings with school teachers or nurseries. The UK has no statutory scheme, and is again expected to opt out of anything adopted by the rest of the EU when it implements the directive on parental leave, which in draft form also included provision for leave for 'pressing family reasons'. Many employers already allow employees time off in exceptional circumstances, but often on a discretionary and unpaid basis.

Assistance with childcare

The many ways in which employers could help their employees with childcare arrangements include provision of a workplace nursery or out-of-school scheme (or places in such facilities), childcare allowances or vouchers, sponsored child-minding schemes, and information and referral services. Publicly-funded provision, apart from state nursery and primary schooling (which on their own offer only limited hours of care), is restricted to day nursery places (plus a few sponsored child-minding places and out-of-school schemes), predominantly for children 'in need' as defined by the Children Act, 1989.

The majority of working parents rely on informal care by family members, while a significant and growing minority use paid child-minders, day nurseries or out-of-school facilities in the private and voluntary sectors (General Household Survey, 1991; Meltzer, 1994). Employer provision is extremely limited: the General Household Survey, 1991, found only one per cent of working parents of under-fives used facilities provided by their employer, and a further one per cent received some other form of financial contribution from their employer.

The full-time working week

More men in Britain work extremely long hours than in any other EU country (Watson, 1992, 1993). Long working hours make it harder for fathers to increase their share of childcare and domestic involvement, and harder for women to enter and make progress in occupations where long working hours are common.

Terms of employment for part-time workers

Nearly half of all women in employment work part-time. Rates of pay for part-time employees are frequently below those for their full-time counterparts, and benefits such as sick pay, holidays, pension entitlement and in-work training are often lower. There was some harmonisation during the 1980s, when employers faced labour shortages (IDS, 1993b), while equalisation of the statutory right to protection from redundancy and unfair dismissal, and possibly pension entitlement, will have to be introduced following recent legal rulings.

Flexible working arrangements

A variety of practices fall under this heading: flexitime, home working, term-time working, short-term contracts, temporary working, contracting-out, self-employment, zero-hours schemes and annual hours schemes. Agreements incorporating flexibility in the number of hours worked, or when and where they are worked, have been increasing in the last few years (Watson, 1994), and this development has gone further in the UK than other EU countries (Grubb and Wells, 1993). Some of these working practices are helpful to parents juggling work and childcare, but others are definitely unhelpful (how can you plan childcare arrangements in a zero-hours scheme?) (Dickens, 1992). Their damaging impact on equality of opportunity needs much more attention.

In-work training

The position of women in education has greatly improved in recent years, and they are now out-performing men in many respects. Women are currently at least as likely as men to be undertaking job-related training (Gibbins, 1994), which is one of the few areas where employers are allowed to exercise positive discrimination to compensate for past inequality in opportunities.

Many of these employment conditions are the subject of proposed or adopted EC directives, and childcare is the subject of the EC Council of Ministers' Recommendation on Childcare (see Holtermann and Clarke, 1992, for a summary of provisions). The directive on pregnant workers has now been adopted, but Britain is expected to opt out of the directives on atypical workers and parental leave. Britain has also secured a ten-year opt-out in the provision for a maximum working week of 48 hours. This chapter reviews the evidence on the costs and benefits to employers of further progress in these areas, but many other employment practices which have an important impact on equal opportunities (part-time working, flexible working arrangements and in-service training) are beyond its scope.

The benefits and costs of promoting equality of opportunity

The main types of benefit and cost that are likely to arise when adopting measures to promote equality of opportunity can be divided into those affecting employers, those affecting employees, and those affecting other employers and the wider economy.

Employers

Corporate image is an important consideration. Some companies gain praise and esteem by being able to show that they are good equal opportunities employers. However, benefits of this kind may be virtually impossible to quantify. How does an organisation measure and value the gain from having this kind of corporate image? Does a good record on equal opportunities improve profit by generating customer or supplier loyalty? Does it increase the value of shares through greater demand from ethical investment trusts that use equal opportunities policy as one of their criteria? Is it a matter of the personal satisfaction and self-image of the employers?

Employee productivity is another benefit which can be hard to measure. Employees work with greater commitment and goodwill for organisations that they respect and trust to treat them supportively. The day-to-day work atmosphere and labour relations generally may be improved when employees feel valued. Changes in working practices may be rendered more acceptable. But it is difficult to quantify exactly what part of productivity or industrial peace can be attributed to equal opportunities policies.

Cost savings are a major factor. Some benefits to employers may accrue in the form of reduced costs of employing labour, and this has gained most attention in discussions of the benefits to employers of family-friendly employment practices. Labour turnover may be lower because of higher retention of women employees, thus reducing annual expenditure on recruitment, induction and training of new personnel. There may also be lower rates of unofficial absence from work, thereby reducing the costs associated with absence – disruption of work programmes, lost output, the extra cost of temporary workers and their relatively low productivity, and so on.

The final aspect is employment costs. Equal opportunities measures may have direct costs. Workplace nurseries, for instance, require substantial capital and running costs; the wages and salaries of parents on paid leave must be met and other workers paid to do their work; bringing the pay rates and employment conditions of part-time workers to parity with full-timers will increase the wages bill. There are also indirect costs: when parents take leave, for example, employers must carry a vacancy or employ a temporary worker, who will need induction and training and may be in the job for too short a time to reach full productive potential. If working hours are reduced there will be a need to reorganise working arrangements, and costs associated with taking on extra employees to cover the full working week of plant and equipment. The alleged high cost to employers is the main reason the UK government gives for doing so little to improve the statutory base. But are the costs really as high as is claimed?

Employees

Employees gain the benefits of increased equality of opportunity for men and women in the workplace (and at home). All family members gain from an easing of the strain of juggling work and caring responsibilities, and some children will gain the social and development benefits of quality childcare facilities.

Other employers and the wider economy

Other employers capture some of the benefits of equal opportunities measures taken by any one employer, just as they do with investment in training, through the enlargement of the pool of skilled and experienced workers. Ultimately there are widespread economic benefits: national productivity would be increased; the skill shortages that afflict the British economy every time it expands would be eased; and the inflationary pressures that build up all too soon would be postponed. But there can also be adverse effects on output and employment if business costs are raised.

Action to promote equality of opportunity has 'externalities' going beyond the interests of the employer; as with all externalities, the failure of the free market to take account of social costs and benefits requires the government to take a role in ensuring a better allocation of resources. A full social cost-benefit analysis would consider not just the impact on employers, but also the benefits and costs to employees, their families, other employers and the whole economy. The objectives of this chapter are more modest, concentrating on the private benefits and costs to employers taking action.

Existing quantitative evidence on the benefits and costs to employers

Parental leave

The EC draft directive on parental leave makes payment while on leave discretionary for each member state, and requires any payments to be met from public funds. However, even with public funding the payments must ultimately be covered by some form of additional taxation, and part of this may fall on employers through instruments such as a higher rate of National Insurance contributions. The magnitude of aggregate leave payments is thus still relevant in an account of employer costs and benefits.

Holtermann and Clarke (1992) estimated the cost of paying allowances at various rates to workers with an entitlement to parental leave of three months. For each rate of earnings replacement while on leave, a low and a high take-up assumption were taken as alternatives; take-up, especially among fathers, can be expected to be below any of these alternatives if the leave is unpaid. The overall costs were built up from the number of births in 1991, the proportion of women working during pregnancy, the proportions of men and women likely to be eligible for parental leave on the basis of length of service (if that is made a requirement), and the probability that at the relevant time the other parent will be in employment.

With payment at the rate of statutory sick pay in 1992, it was estimated that the cost would be around £136 million (low take-up) or around £176 million (high take-up). With payment at 80 per cent of average earnings in 1992, the cost of low take-up would be around £507 million and with the high take-up rate it would be around £655 million. (Note that these and other cost estimates from Holtermann and Clarke, 1992, were intended to show the Exchequer costs of publicly-funded schemes; to show the cost to employers they should have employers' National Insurance contributions added and payments to the self-employed deducted.)

There is scope for some savings to the Exchequer from the second-round effects of parental leave. Tax and National Insurance would be received from parents on paid leave as well as from any temporary replacements for them. The employment of temporary replacements can lead, directly or indirectly, to some reduction in the numbers of people receiving unemployment-related social security benefits (though this is unlikely to be on a one-for-one basis). Holtermann and Clarke (1992) estimated that the flowback to the Exchequer from income tax, National Insurance and social security benefits, assuming that half the additional spells of leave would lead to someone coming off unemployment-related benefits, would reduce the Exchequer cost of publicly-funded parental leave by about a fifth when earnings replacement is at 80 or 100 per cent.

Holtermann (1986) also considered the cost of parental leave to employers, on top of any payments to parents on leave. This quantified the items arising from a new spell of absence: the personnel costs of recruiting a replacement; any additional costs of a temporary worker; supervisor time spent on induction of a new worker; and loss of output from replacements being less effective than permanent staff (or, if the worker is not replaced, the loss in value-added from reduced activity).

A small-scale telephone survey of employers was carried out to discover the extent to which employees, especially men, would be replaced if they took three months' leave, and how effective temporary workers would be. The answers indicated that about two-thirds would be replaced, and that the time taken for temporary workers to become fully effective would depend greatly on the occupation, with unskilled operatives possibly fully effective within days, and skilled and professional workers perhaps taking months. The average for all types of employees was about six weeks.

A review of the literature on the costs of temporary workers indicated that, when full allowance was made for on-costs associated with permanent employees, the cost of temporary workers would be little different from that of permanent staff. The limited literature of the time was used to gain some idea of the costs of recruiting personnel and other expenses, and the overall result indicated that, on the assumptions made about take-up of parental leave and on the basis of average earnings, the costs to employers would be small, amounting to no more than 0.01 per cent of the payroll. The rise in temporary working and contracting out since then means that employers are nowadays probably better able to find and integrate replacements for employees taking leave.

These estimates were very approximate, as there were many uncertainties in their components. Work done since then on turnover costs (Sheffield Hallam University, 1989; Buchan and Seccombe, 1991) suggests that they underestimate employers' costs: recent work generally arrives at higher costs for the lower effectiveness of temporary workers, especially non-manual employees. But no source covers the full range of occupations of men and women likely to be eligible for parental leave and interested in taking it up.

To offset part of the costs, employers might gain some benefit from a scheme for parental leave through its effect on reducing turnover costs or absence (not covered in 1986). Parental leave could result in a higher rate of women returning after childbirth (for them parental leave is a form of extended maternity leave), and a lower rate of absence among women who do return. Even if turnover and absence were well costed, it would be hazardous to guess how much the rates would be reduced by parental leave.

A novel feature of parental leave is that men will have the right to take fairly lengthy spells of leave. The Maternity Rights Surveys show that only a small and apparently declining minority of employers have problems with maternity rights. In 1988, nine per cent of private sector employers reported problems compared with 18 per cent in 1979 (McRae, 1991). It seems that employers have got used to women taking breaks; with parental leave fathers would take breaks, and in time employers may find it no more difficult to accommodate than women taking maternity leave.

Maternity provisions

In the consultation period before the recent changes in legislation, the Employment Department (1992) issued estimates of the cost to employers of options for improvements in maternity leave, the main change being the extension of the right to maternity leave to a larger group of women by relaxing the qualifying conditions. Its estimates were derived by taking the 1986 estimates of the employer costs of parental leave (Holtermann, 1986) outlined in the preceding section, and applying them to the additional number of women who would qualify for maternity leave under the new legislation. The conclusion was that the costs to employers would be between £100 and £250 million, with a central estimate of £175 million.

However, the 1986 parental leave estimates were designed to cover the costs to employers of additional spells of leave, such as fathers taking parental leave, or a woman taking a spell of parental leave after having returned to work at the end of maternity leave. Most costs arising from a spell of absence are incurred in the first few weeks after the employee's departure. When a woman takes parental leave as a continuation of maternity leave – predictably the majority of cases – the costs are triggered when she stops work for childbirth, and are attributable to stopping work for maternity rather than parental leave. The costs would not vary with whether the employee has the right to return or not. It is therefore inappropriate to apply these costings to a situation where there would be no new spells of absence, only a higher proportion with the right to return.

The EOC has argued that maternity leave of 18 weeks for all employees should have been introduced instead of 14 weeks, which it considers undesirably short for the health of mother and baby (some of these weeks will be taken before the birth) and likely to prevent some women from returning to work (EOC *Annual Report*, 1993). The Employment Department has also inappropriately used the 1986 costings of parental leave to estimate the cost to employers of an extension of maternity leave from 14 to 18 weeks, and its figure of £50 million is unrealistically high.

The Department of Social Security has estimated that recent improvements in maternity pay will cost £55 million. This will be funded by employers through a reduction in the refund they receive for payments made on behalf of the DSS for statutory maternity pay. A possible consequence of this method of funding the additional maternity pay provisions, as pointed out by the EOC, is that employers may become more reluctant to employ women of childbearing age (EOC *Annual Report*, 1993).

Paternity leave

Holtermann and Clarke (1992) looked at the cost of introducing a statutory right to fully-paid paternity leave for all employees. The estimates covered the cost to the Exchequer of a state-funded scheme, but these costs would be borne by employers if a statutory requirement for paid leave were introduced with no public funding. If 90 per cent of employed fathers took paternity leave, and if these fathers earned average male earnings in 1992 (a reasonable assumption in view of the lack of a strong overall social class pattern found by the 1988 Maternity Rights Survey (McRae, 1991) in the proportion of fathers taking time off work at around the birth date), the wage cost would be about £213 million if the entitlement was five days on full pay, and £425 million if the entitlement was ten days (in addition to the figure of around £60 million a year already spent on providing employees with paid paternity leave).

This would not be the whole cost to employers, who will also have to deal with disruption caused by additional absence, during which they must either take on a temporary worker (only an extra cost if the temporary worker is paid more or works less effectively), or lose the value of any output on the days not worked. To put these disruptions into context, it should be noted that over three-quarters of fathers already take time off work around the birth. What is more, if paternity leave is unpaid, employers will still have to meet these costs.

Paternity leave would be beneficial not only for equality of opportunity. By establishing fathers' early involvement with children it can bring lasting benefits for families, and is an important part of any programme to improve family support. The main benefits would be enjoyed by the minority of fathers who at present cannot take leave but would like to, and those who would like to take longer leave.

Leave for family reasons

The draft EC directive on parental leave includes a recommendation that employees should have the right to take leave for pressing family reasons, with the minimum number of days to be at the discretion of member states. Various surveys indicate that the ability to take time off work to deal with family emergencies – a sick child or elderly relative, or the illness of a child's usual carer – is much appreciated by employees combining paid work with family responsibilities. The OPCS survey of day-care services for children (Meltzer, 1994) found that a third of arrangements for pre-school children looked after on domestic premises (by a family member, friend, or child-minder, for example) had broken down in the previous month, and in half these cases the mother looked after the child.

In their survey of women in professional and managerial occupations returning to work after a break for childcare, Hirsh *et al.* (1992) found that 75 per cent of respondents said that emergency time off for domestic reasons was very helpful; 26 per cent said it was already available to them to a considerable extent, 58 per cent that it was available to some extent, and 16 per cent not at all. In a survey of 500 organisations, Berry-Lound (1992) found that 55 per cent of respondents in the private sector and 70 per cent in the public sector offered employees special leave in crisis situations. As with paternity leave, many employers expect parents to take time out of their holiday entitlement (IDS, 1992c).

Holtermann and Clarke (1992) made estimates of the wage cost of giving parents the right to paid leave for family reasons. There is so little information on the terms of arrangements currently offered by employers, and the extent to which a formal scheme would lead to extra days of absence, that any cost estimates must be treated as illustrative rather than predictive. On the assumption that 40 per cent of employed mothers have an average of five extra days absence a year and 20 per cent of fathers have four days extra each, the wage cost at average earnings is estimated at £335 million. (The figures for the number of additional days of absence can be viewed in the context of the 1992 estimated average per employee of eight days unauthorised absence through sickness and so on, and 27 days authorised absence on holidays, maternity leave, study leave and so on (CBI, 1993).) With payment at the statutory sick pay rate, take-up would be lower, and Holtermann and Clarke (1992) suggest that if 30 per cent of mothers take four days and 15 per cent of fathers take two days additional leave, the wage cost would be about £35 million.

Other costs to employers, similar to those caused by paternity leave, would arise from disruption at work when absences – most of which will be at short notice – are taken under provision for family leave. Some absences could be in place of sickness and unauthorised leave, and the cost will be reduced to that extent. More than a third of respondents in a 1993 CBI survey expressed the view that family responsibilities were a moderate or high cause of unauthorised non-sickness absence. But the literature on absence from work normally mentions family responsibilities (if at all) as just one of many causes of absenteeism, while poor motivation, stress and lack of absence-control policies are prominent (IDS, 1992b; Alfred Marks, 1992; Arthur Andersen, 1991; CBI, 1993; Audit Commission, 1993), so the scope for reducing absenteeism through family leave and other family-friendly policies is likely to be limited.

Benefits to employers could arise from a contribution to improved productivity made by lower stress among the workforce, and possibly a reduction in turnover among staff who cannot cope with both work and family commitments, but there is virtually no empirical evidence one way or another on this point.

Assistance with childcare

The difficulty of finding quality childcare at an affordable price is frequently given as the main reason for women with children taking extended breaks from employment and then returning to what is often only part-time work – a pattern that results not only in the loss to the women themselves of a considerable part of the lifetime earnings they could expect without children, but the loss to employers of the skills, training and experience invested in those women (Joshi and Davies, 1993).

Employers have become aware of the potential for making savings in turnover costs if, through family-friendly working practices and the provision of help with childcare, a higher proportion of their skilled and experienced employees return to work after a break for child-rearing.

Concern about the impact on women's employment of caring for elderly relatives is also coming to more prominence with the ageing of the population and the increase in women's labour force participation. There is growing awareness of the costs that employers can bear by failure to support employees caring for elderly relatives (for example, Berry-Lound, 1994).

Some studies have shown that the savings in turnover costs can outweigh the costs of the measures adopted to help parents with childcare. Work by Sheffield Hallam University (1989) for Bradford City Council estimated replacement costs for a variety of occupations among the Council's female employees. This study covered recruitment, induction and training, the limited effectiveness of new recruits, and any extra costs arising from vacancy cover (though not from situations where work was postponed or not done at all). It was found that costs were highly variable, depending primarily on the occupational category, but also on the extent to which training had to be undertaken and the time taken for the new recruit to reach full effectiveness. The estimated costs ranged from £1,326 for a clerk/typist and £3,815 for a cook through to £16,010 for an assistant solicitor and £18,859 for a deputy headteacher. These figures were then used to calculate the cost to the Council of replacing those employees using the nursery who said that they would leave if it were to close. This was found to be higher than the annual subsidy the Council paid towards the running cost of the nursery.

The Institute of Manpower Studies has also carried out work on the measurement of turnover costs (mostly in the context of NHS nurses), and can provide a useful checklist – similar to the Sheffield study but more detailed – for employers who wish to measure these costs (Buchan and Seccombe, 1991). In applying this checklist to the costs of turnover among clinical nurses, the IMS also found considerable variation within the same occupation, with a range from £1,251 to £4,962 in five case studies. The Institute has developed a further checklist for use in calculating the cost of absence (Seccombe and Buchan, 1993). Bruegel and Perrons (this volume, Chapter 7) cite other estimates of turnover costs.

Business in the Community (1993) used the same approach to illustrate the business case for family-friendly employment practices. They show the annual expenditure on personnel recruitment and training (on the basis of the Sheffield work) and, with some indication of the reduction in the number of employees who leave each year because of difficulties with childcare, compare the savings from this source with the annual cost of measures to help parents with childcare. They give an example of a company employing 2,000 staff, 60 per cent of them women, 50 of whom are estimated to leave the company each year because of difficulties with childcare. With an average staff replacement cost of £10,000 the savings could amount to £500,000 a year, which would be higher if allowance were also made for a reduction in sick leave and absenteeism. This is much greater than the estimated cost of £216,000 for a package of measures to help families with childcare: a 40-place nursery with parental fees covering about two-thirds of the costs, subsidies for child-minding for 80 children, childcare vouchers of £30 a week for 40 children, subsidised places in after-school care for 32 children, a holiday playscheme for 50 children, and subscribing to a local childcare information service.

The work on turnover suggests that costs will be greater for professional/managerial personnel (who also tend to be in shorter supply and relatively well paid) than for junior non-manual and manual workers (not usually so scarce or well paid). Employers have an incentive to concentrate support on those categories of employee for whom turnover costs are highest, and people in low-paid occupations risk missing out. This does happen in practice – some employers, for instance, allocate nursery places on a points system that gives weight to particular skills categories – but on equity grounds there is an argument for giving all types of employee equal access to any facilities.

A critical element in the use of turnover and absence costs to assess the employer benefits of childcare, or other forms of family-friendly policies, is an estimate of the extent to which these policies actually alter turnover and absence. There is very little firm evidence on this, and inference from trends is difficult. For instance, the proportion of women returning after childbirth has gone up in many organisations (IDS reported an average of around 70 per cent in 1994 compared with around 50 per cent two years earlier – IDS 1994b), but is this to do with recession or family-friendly practices? As with absence, family responsibility is only one among many influences on turnover; many other aspects of pay and conditions are important, and the scope for limiting unwanted turnover through family-friendly policies has its bounds.

There can be some benefit to the Exchequer from helping parents with childcare. To the extent that the economy can adapt to an increase in the supply of experienced employees without displacing other employees – which should not be too difficult, as these are the personnel most likely to be in short supply – there will be a flowback to the Exchequer from extra tax and National Insurance contributions and savings in unemployment-related social security benefits (Holtermann and Clarke, 1992).

Working time

A 48-hour maximum working week would benefit families by making it easier for fathers to spend time with their children. The Employment Department (1991) has estimated the cost to employers of full implementation of the EC directive on working time at £5 billion, and this figure has been much quoted in the debate about the directive. The four elements of the directive were costed at £3.5 billion for the maximum 48-hour week, £0.4 billion for the minimum daily and weekly rest periods, £1.5 billion for minimum paid annual holiday of 20 days, and up to £0.05 billion for the provisions on night work.

It can be expected that the provisions of the directive will raise business costs. Since employers currently pay for overtime, even at premium rates, rather than hire extra workers on standard hours or make more use of shift working, it must presumably be cheaper. The quality of the work is assured; there is flexibility to raise and lower hours according to demand; and there may be less to pay in National Insurance contributions and redundancy payments. With the introduction of a 48-hour maximum working week and the required rest periods, employers will consider how to adapt and assess whether the additional cost of doing the work within the new constraints is worthwhile. Some work will continue but at higher cost, some will be given up, and the overall cost will come from a combination of the higher cost of continued work and lost profit or value-added on work forgone.

The Employment Department's estimates of the costs to employers of the maximum 48-hour week and the rest periods are based on two unwarranted assumptions, which mean the estimates could be seriously wrong. The estimates of the other items are sound.

The first assumption is that half of what it calls the 'full cost' of the 48-hour maximum is borne by employers and half by employees. This assumption is described as 'reasonable', but this particular fraction is not supported by any reasoning or evidence, and is essentially arbitrary.

The fraction is in any case irrelevant because the 'full cost' referred to (the value, at average wages, of the total paid hours worked per week in excess of 48) is not a valid measure of the cost of introducing a maximum of 48 hours. A valid measure of the cost to employers could be derived by working out, first, the additional cost to employers (not the gross cost as in the Employment Department paper) of covering the hours at present worked in excess of 48 by hiring additional workers in standard hours, part-time top-up, or shift working and so on; and second, modifying this by some allowance for the extent to which employers would react to the new regulations by maintaining output, and how far they would forgo the work. There would be some pressure on employers to raise wage rates for basic hours. Exempt categories would be allowed. None of these considerations appear in the Employment Department paper.

The second unrealistic assumption is that hours in excess of 48 per week are paid at the level of average wages. This is unnecessarily simple. Evidence from the Labour Force Survey on patterns of overtime working by sex and occupation, and from the New Earnings Survey, could have been used to give a better estimate.

The maximum 48-hour week would have wider ramifications not addressed by the Employment Department. Some employees (and therefore their families) would lose income from the reduction in hours (it is unlikely that hourly rates would rise enough to compensate fully). The measure could make some contribution to reducing unemployment (though see Gregg, 1994, for scepticism on this point), with consequent savings for the Exchequer in unemployment-related social security benefits.

The trade-off between equality and efficiency

When considering initiatives that could be made to promote equality of opportunity, whether by employers or through government policies, the potential cost incurred by employers certainly has to be addressed. Even when the state covers the cost of allowances paid to parents on leave, there may still be costs to employers that are not covered by benefits. It is important not to give exaggerated estimates of the employer costs, and there is concern about some of the Employment Department costings, as indicated earlier. It is also important to count the economic benefits to employers, which have not been included in government cost assessments even though they are claimed by independent researchers to be substantial, as described earlier. Government assessments also ignore the potential for wider economic benefits, such as the gain to the national economy from utilising more fully the skills and experience of women with children, and the contribution that a reduction in working hours could make to reducing unemployment.

It is in the interest of employers to subject any kind of organisational initiative aimed at promoting equality of opportunity to cost-benefit or cost-effectiveness analysis, to assess both the expected contribution to improving equal opportunities and all the other benefits and costs to employers (the 'efficiency costs and benefits'). Such analysis will reveal that in some cases there will be a net cost in efficiency terms from improving equality of opportunity, while in others there will be a net benefit.

It is natural that employers will be more favourably inclined towards those measures that have the fortunate outcome of improving their business position. The conclusion reached in the IMS case study examination of 'family-friendly working' (Hillage and Simkin, 1992) is that most practices under this heading which have become widespread – flexitime, job-sharing, part-time working – provide benefits to employers that outweigh the costs (a view supported by IDS studies of these subjects (1993b; 1994a)), and that the label is a new disguise for employers acting in their own self-interest. Other types of family-friendly arrangements –

leave entitlements, childcare assistance – are much less common, and pressure for them is meeting resistance from employers and government alike. This is perhaps simply an indication that the balance of benefits and costs for employers is less favourable. However, it could be that only informal assessments have been made, which understate the benefits employers could gain from taking these further practical steps. Hillage and Simkin (1992), for instance, found that few employers had conducted a full audit of the advantages and disadvantages of policy changes.

Is it acceptable from the point of view of equal opportunities policy for measures that have a favourable cost-benefit ratio for employers to be given priority? The risk is that while the more expensive types of measure may stay on an organisation's agenda for social responsibility, they will be repeatedly pushed to the bottom of the list because there is insufficient financial reward to the employer. There is a danger of a shift in attitude towards a position where equality of opportunity is no longer seen primarily as a matter of social justice, desirable in its own right, but merely as something that can be pursued if, and only if, it coincides with the employing organisation's own self-interest.

It does, however, have to be accepted that there are situations where a gain in equality of opportunity can only be made by individual employers incurring some net cost, and there is a trade-off between competing objectives: improvement in one objective (equality of opportunity) can only be gained by some reduction in another (cost-efficiency). Subject to complying with legislative constraints, employers will have to decide what balance to choose according to their own priorities.

It is precisely where this efficiency/equity trade-off is to be found that there is greatest need for the government, which has a wider set of objectives than individual employers, to introduce (and enforce) national minimum standards. However, even within this wider framework there may be equal opportunities policies where the social and economic benefits (aside from equality) do not outweigh the social and economic costs. The government will then have to take explicit responsibility for choosing a balance, reflecting what it judges to be the preferences of the population, between competing objectives.

Accuracy in measuring costs and benefits, and the most comprehensive coverage feasible, should be the aims. Any tendency to overstate the costs of equal opportunities policies, or to understate their contribution to national economic performance, will bias the estimate of the trade-off between equality of opportunity and economic efficiency against equal opportunities, even if a fair interpretation of the balance of public preferences is made.

There is also a need for advocates of further measures for promoting equal opportunities to assess the relative contribution various measures can make to meeting the objective of equality of opportunity. There is a tendency for measures to be listed as if they were all of equal value, but that is unlikely to be the case. Of the various policies discussed in this chapter, which have the most potential to increase equality of opportunity? They appear to vary in their efficiency costs – but how do their equality benefits vary? If a limited sum of money (in the form of net costs to the Exchequer and employers) were available for enhancing equality of opportunity, how would it best be spent?

Finally, a note of caution. There is a risk that increasing equality of opportunity in the workplace through some of the measures discussed here could serve to make other forms of inequality in our society worse. Elsewhere in this volume, Gregg and Wadsworth (Chapter 15) describe the increased polarisation of households in Britain into 'work-rich' and 'work-poor'. Adding to employment benefits for those in work will increase the distance between these two types of household. Even among employed people there is a risk that well-off households could gain more than the low paid if, following their own interest, employers select experienced workers in categories of skill shortage for favourable treatment. This provides another argument for the government to use statutory instruments, or publicly-funded forms of assistance, to ensure fair access to employment benefits across the earnings spectrum.

Conclusions

Three main points emerge from this study. Firstly, many of the existing cost-benefit accounts of equal opportunities are incomplete in their coverage, and some are inaccurate in their accounting. More good-quality, comprehensive empirical work is needed. Secondly, some costs are high – it is easy to get figures in the billions. While there can be offsetting benefits from reduced turnover and absence, there is considerable uncertainty about the extent to which turnover and absence can really be reduced by family-friendly policies beyond those, such as flexitime and part-time working, that are already common. Thirdly, as full evaluation may show that there are net efficiency costs from some equal opportunities policies, there is a need to consider carefully the relative contribution each can make in achieving the objective of equality of opportunity.

References

Alfred Marks (1992). *Absence from Work: A Survey of Office Staff Absenteeism*. London: Alfred Marks.

Arthur Andersen (1991). *Absenteeism Research Survey*. London: Arthur Andersen.

Audit Commission (1993). *Get Well Soon: A Reappraisal of Sickness Absence in London*. London: HMSO.

Berry-Lound, D. (1992). *Work and the Family: Carer Friendly Employer Practices*. London: Institute of Personnel Management.

Berry-Lound, D. (1994). *An Employer's Guide to Eldercare*. Horsham: Host Consultancy.

Bruegel, I. and Perrons, D. (1995). 'Where do the costs of unequal treatment for women fall? An analysis of the incidence of the costs of unequal pay and sex discrimination in the UK' in this volume.

Buchan, J. and Seccombe, I. (1991). *Nurse Turnover Costs: A Review for the Royal College of Nursing*. IMS Report 212. Brighton: Institute of Manpower Studies.

Business in the Community/Institute of Personnel Management (1993). *Corporate Culture and Caring: The Business Case for Family Friendly Provision*. London: Business in the Community.

Clarke, K. (1991). *Women and Training: A Review*. Research Discussion Series 1. Manchester: Equal Opportunities Commission.

Confederation of British Industries (1993). *Too Much Time Out?* London: CBI.

Dickens, L. (1992). *Whose Flexibility? Discrimination and Equality Issues in Atypical Work*. London: Institute of Employment Rights.

Employment Department (1991). *Costing of the Directive on Working Time*.

Employment Department (1992). *Compliance Cost Assessment: Directive on the Entitlement to Maternity Leave and Dismissal Protection of Pregnant Workers and Workers who have Recently Given Birth*.

EOC (1993). *Annual Report*. Manchester: Equal Opportunities Commission.

General Household Survey (1991). London: HMSO.

Gibbins, C. (1994). 'Women and training – data from the Labour Force Survey' in *Employment Gazette*, November.

Gregg, P. (1994). 'Share and share alike' in *New Economy*, 1 (1), January.

Gregg, P. and Wadsworth, J. (1995). 'Gender, households and access to employment' in this volume.

Grubb, D. and Wells, W. (1993). 'Employment regulation and patterns of work in EC countries' in OECD *Economic Studies*, 21, Winter.

Hillage, J. and Simkin, C. (1992). *Family-Friendly Working: New Hope or Old Hype?* IMS Report 224. Brighton: Institute of Manpower Studies.

Hirsh, W., Hayday, S., Yeates, J. and Callender, C. (1992). *Beyond the Career Break: A Study of Professional and Managerial Women Returning to Work After Having a Child*. IMS Report 223. Brighton: Institute of Manpower Studies.

Holtermann, S. (1986). *The Costs of Implementing Parental Leave in Great Britain*. Manchester: Equal Opportunities Commission.

Holtermann, S. and Clarke, K. (1992). *Parents, Employment Rights and Childcare*. Research Discussion Series 4. Manchester: Equal Opportunities Commission.

Incomes Data Services (1992a). *Continuing Improvements in Parental Leave Despite Recession*. Report 622, August, 25 (8).

Incomes Data Services (1992b). *Controlling Absence*. Study 498, January.

Incomes Data Services (1992c). *Time-off Arrangements*. Study 506, May.

Incomes Data Services (1993a). *Childcare*. Study 521, January.

Incomes Data Services (1993b). *Part-time Workers*. Study 540, October.

Incomes Data Services (1994a). *Job-sharing*. Study 548, February.

Incomes Data Services (1994b). *Maternity Leave*. Study 550, March.

Joshi, H. and Davies, H. (1993). 'Mother's human capital and childcare in Britain' in *National Institute Economic Review*, November.

McRae, S. (1991). *Maternity Rights in Britain: The Experience of Women and Employers*. London: Policy Studies Institute.

Meltzer, H. (1994). *Day Care Services for Children*. London: HMSO.

Seccombe, I. and Buchan, J. (1993). *Absent Nurses: The Costs and Consequences*. IMS Report 250. Brighton: Institute of Manpower Studies.

Sheffield Hallam University (Survey and Information Analysis Unit) (1989). *Childcare: The Management Issue of the 1990s*. Sheffield.

Watson, G. (1992). 'Hours of work in Great Britain and Europe: evidence from the UK and European Labour Force Surveys' in *Employment Gazette*, November.

Watson, G. (1993). 'Working time and holidays in the EC: how the UK compares' in *Employment Gazette*, September.

Watson, G. (1994). 'The flexible workforce and patterns of working hours in the UK' in *Employment Gazette*, July.

CHAPTER 7

Where Do the Costs of Unequal Treatment for Women Fall? An Analysis of the Incidence of the Costs of Unequal Pay and Sex Discrimination in the UK

Irene Bruegel and Diane Perrons

One of the major rigidities in the British labour market lies in the sex-typing of jobs. The processes shaping such sex-typing have been extensively explored in feminist and equal opportunity literature, but the issue is hardly mentioned in any discussion of the vitality of the British economy in an increasingly competitive world market. This blind spot is understandable: sex-typing of jobs is seen as an enduring aspect of all modern economies. Its causes are taken to be external to the economy: a reflection of preferences, with no meaningful economic cost. In this chapter it will be shown that there are economic as well as individual costs associated with the unequal treatment of women and men, and where these costs lie.

To forestall misinterpretation, sex-typing is not the main problem confronting the British economy, nor should the case for equal treatment of women rest on instrumental arguments. The issue is ultimately an ethical one.

The high costs of unequal treatment fall on individual women, but this chapter is more concerned with exploring the wider social costs and the view that one of the solutions 'to economic problems depends on enhancing women's economic role' (OECD, 1991: 7). The argument is that the British economy is locked into a 'gender order' through interactions between labour market processes, household decisions and state policies. This gender order is not just harmful to women, but is reflected in high levels of male unemployment and the prognosis that the male share of unemployment will continue to rise (Wilson, 1994).

The economy is locked into this gendered division of labour because of the benefits offered to men as a whole. The 'insider/outsider' division between men, identified in the analysis of unemployment, is in part a reflection of this wider, gendered division of labour. Gendered division of labour is not immutable, however, but subject to a variety of pressures for change, and throws up in turn a variety of defence mechanisms. Its form and rigidity vary – for example, between economies across Western Europe – and it both reflects and reinforces broader, historically-based institutional structures shaping labour market operations.

The costs of this gendered division of labour impinge at a variety of levels, including that of the firm or enterprise. Equal opportunities can make sound business sense and unequal opportunities have inflicted costs at the level of the enterprise. But the business case for providing equal opportunity measures varies with cyclical economic change and styles of management practice, and is highly dependent on the wider system of economic regulation. In particular, the scope for enlightened business-oriented equal opportunity policies is narrowed by developments in the organisation of production, for example sub-contracting and the decentralisation of decision-making.

Figure 7.1 The costs of unequal opportunities

level of impact	short term	long term
within company	high turnover	under-investment in labour-saving technologies
national economy	skill shortages	under-development of skills
		constraints on growth in domestic capacity and income

In Figure 7.1 the costs to employers and the economy of the current gender order are disaggregated into those private to each firm and those that have a more general incidence.

The gender order of employment

Figure 7.2 sketches out the interactions which reinforce the sexual division of labour within the household and the economy. This picture draws on both human capital theories and the wider literature on the gendering of work to illustrate cumulative causation processes. The gendered character of all labour means that the bald propositions of human capital theory and New Household Economics, with their narrow perception of rational action, are limited. Nevertheless, taking that type of model to its logical conclusion, small initial differences in the relative pay of men and women become exacerbated as households rationally supply more male labour to the market. As the labour market rewards experience, the process is cumulative. That process is characterised by the outer ring of Figure 7.2. Such choices reflect and reinforce the 'structures of constraint' governing socially acceptable choices, set out in the central area of Figure 7.2.

This central core of sex-typing of jobs can be analysed as a specific form of 'market failure' limiting the degree to which individual women are able to take full advantage of the theoretically equal access to jobs provided by sex discrimination legislation. Women's pay is higher where they work in

Figure 7.2 The 'gender order' of employment

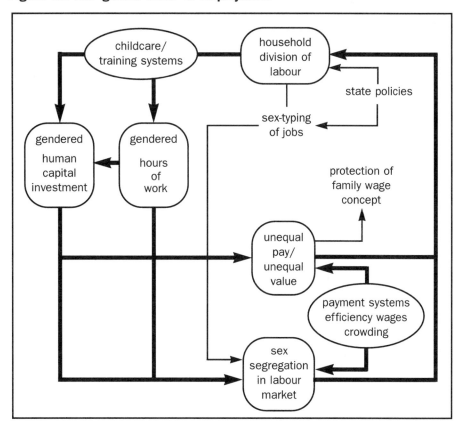

jobs that are predominantly male (Sloane, 1994). In monetary terms, individual women have much to gain from attempting to cross gendered work boundaries. However, in practice the gendered construction of jobs and labour puts a high psychological cost on such entry, especially where a challenge is being made to long-standing discrimination.

Women who work in 'male jobs' continue to face a range of barriers, including sexual harassment (Cockburn, 1992). Once sufficient women are employed in a particular type of work, the rate of entry may accelerate. There is an asymmetry between the costs and benefits to individual women who work in 'male' areas. Their actions in pursuing cases of sex discrimination are likely to be of more benefit to other women, and indeed the wider economy, than to the individuals themselves. The costs of unequal treatment, though recognised by many women, are thereby sustained in practice.

A degree of private housework and childcare is of course necessary (see Figure 7.2). However, the level and distribution of housework and childcare between men and women is determined both by economic factors and cultural norms. One cost of the current division of household labour, raised by feminists (Coote *et al.*, 1990) but ignored by most economic analysts, is the absence of men from involvement in day-to-day childcare.

Human capital theorists tend to separate the analysis of the labour supply from households and its influence on sex differentiation in jobs and pay (the left-hand side of Figure 7.2), from the 'new household economics' of the right-hand side; namely, the way differential pay itself influences the household division of labour. Even without the social, political and cultural structures that reinforce such patterns, narrow economic logic produces a cumulative cycle of gender role differentiation.

It is possible to argue, on the basis of human capital theory, that the under-utilisation of women's potential and actual skills can be mitigated, even within this culture, by the way childcare provision and training systems affect gender differentiation in skill levels and hours of work. This need not be a one-off effect, but can bring in train a cumulative set of changes in the locked-in gender differentiation system.

Economists from different traditions have identified mechanisms which allow sex segregation and unequal pay to become self-reinforcing, including segmented labour markets, crowding, and efficiency wage models. But sex segregation does not necessarily imply unequal pay. Feminist analysis shows how different types of payment system foster different degrees of linkage (Blau, 1993; Rubery, 1992a). It is worth analysing the institutional processes which reinforce the link between unequal pay, the household division of labour and sex-typing of jobs.

In the face of a gender-differentiated labour market, firms would clearly benefit from employing women rather than men. Such a market makes women's labour cheaper per unit of output. Where the work does not require (or no longer requires) skills and attributes normally associated with masculinity, and where it can be organised on a part-time basis, unit labour costs can be lower precisely because women are 'crowded' into relatively few occupations. What is more, equal opportunity policies can bring benefits to employers, even if unequal wage rates in the same job are not admissible. Short-term returns may be low, because women would be paid the old male rate, but in the longer term wage pressures are likely to diminish as the job becomes feminised. This is evident when the relative pay rates of feminised occupations are compared to others (Routh, 1980). Such arguments, which stem from a neo-classical account of the labour market, imply that unequal value will be evened out through the operation of the market. Some people believe that it has been, virtually by definition.

It is more interesting to consider why only a minority of firms use equal opportunity policies to realise the potential benefits of lower wage pressures; why unequal value (unequal pay for work of equal value) and unequal returns (inequality in pay in relation to potential) persist. Historically it is possible to point to the institutionalisation of the male-breadwinner and family-wage concepts as the legitimisation of male trade unionists' endeavours to restrict competitive entry by women to high-wage and well-organised areas of employment. Though little resistance of this kind remains, its historic influence on what counts as a suitable job for a man or woman is still very evident (Lovering, 1994).

Moreover, the social security system, while no longer discriminating formally, continues to uphold the male breadwinner norm by insisting on household income aggregation. As is now well established (Gregg and Wadsworth, this volume, Chapter 15; Morris, 1990; McLaughlin, 1994), partners of unemployed people are severely discouraged by unemployment benefit rules from seeking employment. Thus male unemployment not only results in wasted male skills, but contributes to under-utilisation of women's skills and high levels of family poverty.

There are, however, a number of reasons why firms in a modern economy may not seek to undercut an existing workforce or recruit equally able but cheaper women to traditionally male jobs. Neo-classical explanations rest on the incompleteness of labour contracts, the costs of high dismissal and high turnover regimes, and the problems of linking individual pay to individual effort. This implicit recognition that labour is not just another factor of production, and that the 'human relations' of work are significant, opens up the possibility of analysing the gendering of work and workers more critically.

While not necessarily endorsing efficiency wage theory, it can be argued that the forces which differentiate 'insiders and outsiders' in the labour market are linked to the household division of labour. The means of generating a loyal and stable labour force are gendered, so market forces, far from equalising returns to male and female human capital, tend to stabilise and reinforce differences. The processes which generate efficiency wages are those which allow for systematic divergence between the wages paid and the human capital stock of the workers.

Most discussion of efficiency wages is conducted in abstract genderless terms, but it is possible to suggest that women may be constituted as loyal, conscientious and stable workers in ways which do not raise their pay above the 'spot market' level. Akerlof's (1982) early contribution to the theory of wages and effort describes a group of women who work harder than required, without extra pay, as part of a gift exchange and sense of a 'fair wage'. Women are more directly paced. Women manual workers in manufacturing are much more likely to be on piece-rates and closely supervised, while in service industries women are directly paced by client requirements or care needs (Horrell and Rubery, 1991). Hence there may be less need to raise the cost of dismissal for poor work or use efficiency wages to extract high performance.

Efficiency wages are paid to raise the opportunity cost of job loss. Insofar as women are segregated into jobs where lengthy tenure is not valued, they will have less access to them. But where stability is desired, the premium will depend on the income workers can expect if they lose their jobs. This depends on benefit entitlements, the size of the potential job search area and the wages obtainable within it. Gender role assumptions make the social and personal cost of unemployment especially high for many men. Yet women's lower geographical mobility and lesser entitlement to benefits are likely to result in a lower efficiency wage premium at any given wage level.

While the argument is not all one way, the link between size of unit, pay and gender suggests that an efficiency wage/gender filtering effect may be operating in the UK. Thomson and Sanjines (1990) found that pay was lower for smaller establishments within given industries, and that women were three times more likely to be working in small establishments than in large. Part-time work is found disproportionately in smaller private sector establishments (Blanchflower and Corry, 1986–7). This, plus the lower training levels amongst smaller firms (Storey, 1994; Dougherty, 1994), even after allowing for industry differences, suggests a process that reinforces the segregation of women into lower-skill and lower-value areas of the economy.

Costs and benefits to the individual firm

The arguments for greater equal opportunities lie within the more progressive human resource management literature in Britain (Cooper and Lewis, 1993; Handy, 1994), and have found some resonance amongst larger firms with a national or international reputation to protect. Such arguments generally reflect the issues raised by efficiency wage theorists, though equal opportunity policies have also proved to be good business in other ways. The clearest example is Hersch's (1991) finding that the share value of US companies indicted under equal opportunities legislation declined relative to others. Whether this was because a poor record on equal opportunities was taken as a signal of poor management in general, or whether it was the result of the growth of 'ethical' investment, it shows that reputation matters.

In the short term, the major costs to UK firms of this gender order lie in replacing skilled and trained women who have children. This chapter designates these as costs, while Holtermann (this volume, Chapter 6) considers a reduction in staff turnover as one of the benefits individual firms could derive from equal opportunity measures. Her concern is largely with deriving realistic estimates for the direct cost to firms of implementing a variety of 'family-friendly' provisions, while this chapter concentrates, in effect, on the costs of not doing so.

Estimates of the turnover costs associated with women leaving to have children vary with the type of business and level of the staff concerned. Some companies experience turnover levels of around 2.5 per cent a year as a result of women leaving for this reason (Business in the Community, 1993). Barclays Bank estimates replacement costs for the senior clerical grade or above as £17,000 (Opportunity 2000, 1993a). More generally, the cost of replacing a junior manager is £6,600, allowing for recruitment costs, training, and the initial limited functioning of the new employee (Business in the Community, 1993). For less-skilled positions, such as sales assistants, Boots estimated the cost to be £3,000 per lost employee; a one per cent annual turnover of staff costs them £1 million on this basis.

A number of such progressive firms have found that the savings arising from higher retention rates more than offset the costs of providing appropriate services (Business in the Community, 1993). Nursery provision has been shown to reduce absenteeism (SIAU, 1989; Business in the Community, 1993). Enhanced maternity leave raised the proportion of maternity returnees in Barclays Bank from 33 per cent to 66 per cent and in Boots from seven per cent to 50 per cent between 1989 and 1993 (Opportunity 2000, 1993b).

One reason for high returns found in family-friendly retention policies is that the forms of assistance requested are quite modest; for example, leave when existing childcare arrangements break down (Hirsh *et al.*, 1992). Given the low level of provision generally made by firms, those which provide minimal help and display family-friendly attitudes may prove more attractive as employers, particularly in a tight labour market. 'Work–family programmes' have also been found to have a positive spillover effect, since all employees with or without childcare or similar commitments are more content, less stressed and more satisfied with their jobs (Harker, forthcoming).

Given the effects of childcare breaks on the lifetime earnings of women and the full utilisation of their qualifications, experience and potential (Joshi and Davies, 1993), the wider social benefits of family-friendly policies extend over a long period. These may outweigh the private benefits to the firm, and private provision will remain below the socially desirable level, partly because of the uncertain effects of individual enterprise initiatives on future labour supply. Even in tight labour markets there is an element of 'prisoners' dilemma' unless virtually all firms competing for good-quality labour provide career breaks and/or childcare. The supply of skills will be increased overall and normal turnover will not threaten longer-term returns from such investment. If only a small minority of firms provide these benefits, they may get shorter-term benefits from retention and be subject to poaching by labour market competitors. As with training, the belief that this may happen can reduce the incentive for family-friendly policies, especially in small companies.

Where these policies are part of a general ethos of good employment practices which foster loyalty, high motivation and goodwill, such fears are less well grounded. Collective approaches by employers within individual labour markets can mitigate some of these effects; for example, with nationally-negotiated parental leave schemes in the public sector and the small but growing number of combined workplace nursery schemes. For the most part, however, the time period over which firms might expect to recoup financial returns of such human resource investment will be shorter than the timespan of benefits to the economy as a whole (Joshi and Davies, 1993; Holtermann and Clarke, 1992), which reach into retirement years.

While the aggregate benefits to the economy as a whole from family-friendly policies may be affected by recession, the scale of the effect will be limited because they also imply higher household consumption levels and tax payments (Holtermann and Clarke, 1992). In contrast, financial returns for individual firms from efforts to improve recruitment and retention are closely related to the tightness of labour market conditions for specific groups of workers or periods of skill shortage (Clement, 1992). Thus a number of schemes set in train at the height of the fears of the 'demographic time bomb' did not survive the recession of 1990–3.

In its second annual report, Opportunity 2000 pointed out that progress had been hindered because at least one third of its members had experienced redundancies, financial constraints and limited promotion opportunities. In particular, Midland Bank halted its programme for 200 creches 'halfway'; National Westminster Bank cut staff in its equal opportunities unit and abandoned plans for crêches; and Sainsbury's put trials of term-time working 'on ice'. Birmingham City Council explicitly reduced the priority given to childcare when its specific retention and recruitment problems were over.

The recession also brought a greater concern to retain staff with company-financed training. As a result, United Biscuits increased maternity pay for those in senior management. Rather than a wholesale abandonment of 'women-friendly' policies, the emphasis has shifted to lower-cost schemes such as after-school clubs, and especially to flexible working arrangements. These bring companies more visible short-term benefits.

In many ways family-friendly policies can be seen as specifically gendered forms of efficiency wages, albeit partially in the form of payment-in-kind. They are tied very closely to the development of internal wage structures and targeted on a very specific set of employees. The initiative for such schemes usually comes from management, and organisations can be reluctant to publicise them, preferring to be able to make individual arrangements with valued employees when the need arises (Simkin and Hillage, 1992). The shopworkers' union USDAW states that the scheme developed by Boots is not aimed at 'ordinary shopworkers' (Labour Research, 1993). Even in the public sector, where an equal opportunities ideology is often thought to be inclusive, differential access to family-friendly policies is common (Local Government Management Board, 1993). The 1988 Maternity Rights Survey found that career break schemes were rarely available to all employees (Holtermann and Clarke, 1992), and the minority of Opportunity 2000 members who provided help with family care tended to restrict it to certain grades (Opportunity 2000, 1993a).

Such targeting, however understandable, will barely help to loosen the gender order. Only women already working in positions which might justify such individual support will benefit; it will have little effect on expectations or women's willingness to invest in their own education and training outside traditional fields. Individual performance-related family-friendly policies also carry with them all the problems associated with individual appraisal schemes for women. While the formalisation of appraisal systems can sometimes bring stereotyped assumptions about women into question and improve their promotion chances, as has apparently occured at Boots (Opportunity 2000, 1993b), all appraisal schemes contain a subjective element (Bevan and Thompson, 1992), so the introduction of more discretion into previously formal pay structures could have precisely the opposite effect (Rubery, 1992a).

If family-friendly policies are seen by middle managers as a special privilege, women with children could well have more difficulty justifying their worth. The pressures on all managers to work long hours and the increasing intensity of work, plus decentralisation to cost and profit centres, may render family-friendly policies empty gestures which individuals become wary about taking up. These pressures help to explain the recent decline in the proportion of managers who are women (Institute of Management, 1994).

Many leading firms recognise that they can benefit financially from policies which help women combine a career with motherhood. Such recognition can help raise wider awareness of the complex links between equality and efficiency. But, apart from organisations with a very specific interest in equal opportunities (for example, Childcare Vouchers and Jennifer Griffiths Recruitment), all the private sector organisations subscribing to the goals of Opportunity 2000 (Opportunity 2000, 1993a) are large firms, and most are household names. Insofar as small firms, rightly or wrongly, see themselves as particularly burdened by statutory maternity leave, it is reasonable to infer that they would not identify the benefits of family-friendly policies as readily as larger firms. The evidence on other fringe benefits (Storey, 1994) suggests that few will offer positive family-friendly policies. The long time-scale for the full fruition of the benefits of such policies means that small firms will not necessarily benefit individually in line with the costs they incur. And yet collectively it is small firms in particular which stand to benefit from a larger supply of skilled labour.

For the bulk of the female workforce, family-friendly policies consist of jobs on a part-time basis and some provision of unpaid leave during school holidays. These policies, often described as flexible working, imply a form of feminisation that operates largely within the cycle of gender differentiation outlined in Figure 7.2. In practice, part-time work may yield a more stable workforce than one made up of younger people, but part-timers are still viewed as a flexible workforce with no interest in career development. This form of family-friendly policy contributes to the overall problem of skill development in the British economy and, while valuable to firms in the short term, is not collectively in their long-term interests. This contrasts with policies which help to untangle the vicious circle and contribute to the longer-term perspective of raising overall skill levels and utilising women's potential.

The costs to the economy as a whole

Since sex segregation is common to all advanced industrial societies, it is not surprising that it never figures as an aspect of the competitive performance of the British economy, but there are three reasons why it should. Firstly, differences between European countries in their utilisation of women's potential are not static. Secondly, though the expansion of part-time work is common across all economies, the way it is structured in Britain adds to the problems of continuous upskilling. The third reason for analysing sex segregation as a potential macro-economic problem for Britain relates to the system of wage setting and the inflationary pressures associated with lower levels of unemployment. Debates about the degree to which high levels of unemployment reflect mismatches within the labour market and limited mobility between areas (Jackman, 1990) and occupations have a neglected gender dimension.

Table 7.3 Women's pay as a proportion of male pay, 1991

	Selected manufacturing industries manual* (ratio 1991 as percentage ratio 1980)			Selected service industries non-manual†		
	Electrical engineering	Food, drink and tobacco	Clothing	Credit institutions	Insurance	Retail distribution
Belgium	86 (104)	85 (104)	82 (108)	77	77	73
Denmark	85 (96)	87 (102)	94 (97)	na	na	na
France	85 (102)	82 (104)	83 (101)	73	68	68
Germany	78 (100)	72 (102)	81 (104)	79	78	70
Netherlands	84 (102)	75 (99)	na	68	61	66
UK	70 (91)	74 (96)	79 (101)	53	57	64

Source: Eurostat 1992

Notes 1 Some countries include part-timers in their earnings data; others, including the UK, exclude part-timers.

2 * indicates gross hourly earnings; † indicates gross monthly earnings.

3 The Netherlands uses data from 1990.

High levels of gender segregation appear to characterise all Western European economies (Rubery and Fagan, 1993; Hakim, 1992). What is apparent, however, is that higher levels of occupational gender segregation are associated with lower differences in male and female full-time workers' pay rates, both across the economy (Blau, 1993; Meulders *et al.*, 1993) and within given industries (Table 7.3); and that the relative pay and conditions of part-time women workers are generally better outside the UK (Gregory and Sandoval, 1994; Schoer, 1987; Thurman and Trah, 1990). These lower gender wage differentials, when set against the generally higher rate of female unemployment relative to men in other parts of Europe (Eurostat, 1993), suggest a different gender order. Certainly the impact of unemployed husbands on married women's labour force participation is much lower in other EC countries (Commission of the EC, 1991). Women's work may be more accessible to men, partly because it is not so badly paid but also because female contributions to household income, where both partners work, may be more equal.

Speculatively there is a hint that the gender order is more open to change elsewhere in Europe.

Though information on skill formation rates in different European countries is scant, there is some evidence (Maier, this volume, Chapter 9) that male/female differentials in training and further education tend to be greater in Britain, at least for younger people (Eurostat, 1993). This suggests that the tightness of linkages in the gender differentiation cycle may vary with wider institutional structures. While women are disproportionately employed in low-paid jobs across the EC (Gregory and Sandoval, 1994), the process of feminisation in Britain, with its emphasis on the expansion of low-level part-time employment, appears to be closely related to the development of a low-pay economy.

Only in the Netherlands is there a higher proportion of women in the part-time labour force (22 per cent to 20 per cent: Eurostat, 1993), but the concentration of poor hourly earnings on part-time workers is distinctly lower. In Britain in 1991, 60 per cent of part-time workers earned less than two-thirds of the median hourly earnings of the average worker, three-and-a-half times the proportion of full-time workers; while only 23 per cent of Dutch part-timers were employed at an equivalent rate (Gregory and Sandoval, 1994). This particular British reliance on low-paid part-time women's work, with especially meagre training opportunities (Booth, 1991), has yet to be recognised as part of the ingrained low-investment, low-productivity cycle. At a societal level it is an important cost of the established gender order.

Gender and the low-skills equilibrium

There are two distinct approaches to the idea that the British economy is locked into an unsustainable low-cost, low-value-added competitive strategy. One the one side – the left-hand side of Figure 7.4 – is the notion of a low-skills equilibrium (Finegold and Soskice, 1988); on the other an argument, developed by Wilkinson, Rubery and others in Cambridge, that low wage levels help sustain low investment and a degree of industrial sclerosis. While the Cambridge work is grounded in studies of low-wage, female-dominated industries (Craig *et al.*, 1982) and in the recognition that low pay is gender-related, discussion at the level of the economy as a whole continues to abstract from gender.

The notion of a low-skills equilibrium links skill levels to choices of technology, and choices of technology back to the scale of skill development. It is not just that skill shortages reduce productivity by using backward technologies and work methods in the short term (Haskel and Martin, 1993). The types of technology adopted also mitigate against the development of skills and the appreciation of the benefits of continuous skill upgrading. The argument is based partly on work done at the NIESR (Shipman, 1991) which showed that the lower productivity obtained in British enterprises, compared with matched European ones, could be traced back to the limited ability of UK firms to apply state-of-the-art technology, demonstrating a lack of skill among managers and workforces.

Figure 7.4 The low-skills, low-pay, low-productivity cycle

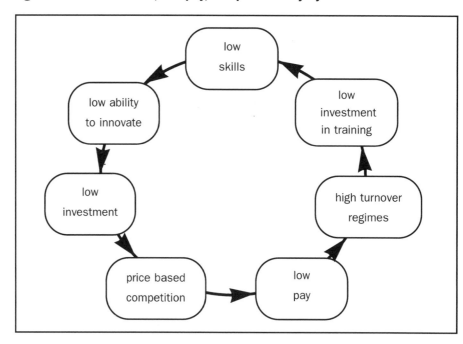

Such constraints limit the ability of UK firms to adopt a quality-based, high-value-added competitive strategy. The Cambridge argument (on the right-hand side of Figure 7.4, flowing upwards) is broadly that low wages reduce the incentive to invest and hence short-term gains in unit costs are quickly dissipated. Low wages encourage high turnover, which reduces the incentive for firms to provide training, fuelling the low-skill, low-innovation cycle.

Figure 7.4 is a characterisation of the British economy as a whole contrasted with other economies. Both arguments would recognise that there are companies which operate on a different trajectory, but neither argument locates the problem within a specific set of secondary industries, and both implicitly recognise that it applies to men as well as women.

Even so, it is possible to see how the overall picture may relate to the way feminisation has developed in Britain. The issue is not only the equal opportunities case – that the pattern of skill formation and relative valuation of different skills fuel differences in pay and in prospects – but that, to a degree, they help to sustain the low-wage, low-value-added competitive strategy.

At the level of the whole economy, the issue relates to the structural shift away from high-value-added manufacturing sectors, a shift stemming from failures to invest and innovate rather than from low wages within those sectors. That structural shift, while explicable at a number of levels, can be connected with the form in which women's labour came to be utilised specifically as low-wage, part-time labour. But the shift in demand for this type of labour, away from male skilled and semi-skilled manufacturing, has not been reflected in any fall in the gender wage gap over the last 15 years; even though shifts in the composition of demand for skilled and qualified labour have made contributions to rising income differentials within men's and women's work (Moll, 1992).

The explanation for this (and some of the limited impact of unemployment on 'insider' wages) may lie in the continuing split in wage expectations at the household level. But for the gendered nature of the two different types of labour, one might expect that pay relativities would even out over a period. But while women's pay remains low, men's wages will continue to be set, as far as possible, at a level which covers the major living costs of households. Thus the imbalance in exits from unemployment will persist (Gregg and Wadsworth, this volume, Chapter 15). Continued gender differentials may contribute to low competiveness in the economy. In the 'male' area of engineering, increases in productivity resulting from large-scale job losses have not led to concomitant reductions in unit costs (Deakin *et al.*, 1992). At the same time, low pay elsewhere in the economy continues to reduce incentives to innovate.

Secondly, the arguments for the links between low wages and low investment, and between low skills and low innovation, operate within 'female' areas of work. The NIESR studies of workforces in retailing, clothing, food processing and hotels show that productivity differentials attributable to skill levels operate in traditional female areas. These studies make almost no reference at all to the gender composition of the workforces in the different companies, and it is unlikely that the differences in productivity can be traced to any differences in gender composition as such. But differences in the skill levels of the workforces could well stem from the greater tendency to use low-paid part-time staff in Britain than elsewhere.

Booth (1991), using the British Social Attitudes Survey of 1987, found that part-time women workers received between one and two days' formal job-related training per year, compared with 22 days for full-time male workers and 21 days for full-time women workers. This huge difference is not explained by a higher turnover rate amongst part-time workers, nor is it a result of their age, educational level, or the type of industry they work in. It reflects the segregation of part-time women workers into 'dead-end jobs' within specific industries.

The link between problems of sex-typing and problems of skill development goes further. Underlying many of the issues raised by the NIESR studies are the advantages to be gained by functional flexibility which transcends traditional sex-segregated jobs. Some of this will be across traditional demarcations, such as those between fitters and operators which have always contributed to stoppages in manufacturing. Despite the development of user-friendly Xerox machines and word-processors, many of the same problems occur within offices and may indeed be amplified by increasingly sophisticated technology. Certainly, the costs of down-time arising from the split in knowledge between those who use machines and those who build, maintain and repair them increase with the sophistication of the machinery.

This problem applies as readily to men as women. Indeed, the need to anticipate, evaluate and communicate potential problems applies to an increasing range of jobs beyond those traditionally classed as skilled, and is also an important factor in quality assurance for products and services (Soskice, 1993). Increased use of 'monitoring' and 'social skills' (Gallie and White, 1994) arises from the decentralisation of responsibility associated with restructuring in the private and public sectors (Soskice, 1993).

The period 1986–92 saw a change in people's perceptions of their work roles and associated responsibilities (Gallie and White, 1994). Nearly 40 per cent of those questioned said they had to exercise some responsibility for others. A large number (66 per cent of men and 60 per cent of women) said they had experienced an increase in the skill requirements of their jobs, much of it associated with social skills. The issue is not so much one of traditional leadership, or direct supervision, since this is becoming less important. Instead it is a need for the traditional 'female' skills of listening, support and understanding. The gender typing of these skills gives women an edge in the graduate labour market in the USA (Soskice, 1993). The problem is not that men cannot acquire these skills, rather that the traditionally low valuation placed on women's skills may lead to their continued underestimation.

Current trends and possibilities

Processes of change are complex and contradictory. The new recognition that 'female' qualities can provide a competitive edge in the market is set in a context of increasing competition, insecurity and stress, particularly in areas of traditionally progressive and stable employment for women. In the public arena, the problem of under-utilised or poorly-utilised labour in Britain is associated with the bleak prospects faced by large numbers of men, rather than the unequal opportunities offered to women. This perception arises partly from the way men and women have been constituted subjectively, and the very different aspirations and expectations they bring to the labour market. The downplaying of inequality between men and women may also be linked to greater differentiation between women in a world of increasing differentials (Humphries and Rubery, 1992). However, the distinct problems of under-utilised potential for men and women are two sides of the same gender order within the labour market, an order which continues to feed into the problems of the economy.

There is a disjuncture between what is rational for some individual enterprises within the pre-existing gender order, and what would collectively benefit employers in their need for a highly-productive workforce. Indeed, it seems that flexibility strategies as well as discrimination fall into such a disjuncture. The disjuncture arises both from the long-term nature of the benefits of equal opportunities and from the uncertainties of many individual employers about the likely distribution of benefits. In some ways it is a textbook case of market failure, as is implicitly recognised in the collective provision of maternity benefits, education and training, whether directly by government or through associations of employers negotiating collectively on nationally-agreed conditions of service.

There is not the space here to discuss how the varied processes of externalisation impact on the division of the benefits of family-friendly policies between those internal to each employer and those which benefit the entire business community. A growing body of literature points to the specific impact of compulsory competitive tendering within local government and the health service on the conditions of service and fringe benefits available to female manual workers (Pulkingham, 1992; Milne and McGee, 1992; Walsh and Davis, 1993; Escott and Whitfield, 1995). But it is also possible to see these effects (within the public sector as well as among contractors) as examples of the way reductions in the size of accounting units may counteract both the growing recognition of the value of equal opportunity and family-friendly policies and the applicability of the equal value provisions of the Equal Pay Act (McCormick, 1990; Rubery, 1992b).

The general process of fragmentation and localisation of accounting units will tend to increase the disjuncture between private and social gains from such policies. Its impact is likely to be more visible within the public sector because of a longer (but distinctly patchy) tradition of 'good employer' policies, but the issue relates also to the growing weight of the small-business sector within the economy.

Differences in the provision of positive equal opportunity strategies between large and small firms, discussed earlier, are likely to affect the overall outcome of current fragmentation and localisation. Decentralised accounting frameworks within large companies may inhibit women's progress along organisational or company-based career paths, since the long-term benefits are likely to accrue to the company rather than the local unit. Localised budget-holding within the public sector is likely to lead to a preference for women unlikely to incur the additional costs associated with maternity and childcare (Audit Commission, 1994).

There are a number of ways to mitigate such effects by defraying the costs through the organisation or company, but in general a tension remains. While some individual employers are adopting family-friendly policies, at least for a select group of employees, processes of externalisation are limiting the internal benefits of such policies for firms. There is a rich tradition of firms adopting a wider view of their social role and a long-term perspective regarding the benefits of public-spirited action. The development of a locally-based business community with a developed infrastructure could as easily encompass family-friendly policies, such as extended maternity leave and childcare, as they now encompass shared catering, sports facilities and specialised services. Indeed, the expansion of employer-based childcare facilities in recent years has almost exclusively taken the form of shared financing of schemes which individual firms buy into as and when they require (Harker, forthcoming).

However, despite some exceptions, the record of TECs in providing training for women (Felstead, this volume, Chapter 8) and especially in providing women-only training facilities in non-traditional skills (Lewis, 1992), suggests that few local business communities recognise how equal opportunity family-friendly provision can be in their long-term shared interests. To a large extent they continue to view such provision as 'social', and better financed and organised by the public sector. By implication, a concerted effort is required to infuse gender-related equal opportunities and 'family-friendliness' into business and community partnerships. But private provision of family-friendly employment, individual or collective, must be underpinned by public policies. In Denmark, where when 'governments do more to help parents combine their work and family lives then employers are encouraged to do more', a more family-friendly environment or set of expectations is established (Harker, forthcoming).

The process of unlocking the gender order to tap into beneficial cumulative effects for the economy as a whole must also recognise the increasing income differentiation between women as well as between men. A range of measures could decouple the link between gender and interruptions in working life and reduce the degree of horizontal and vertical sex segregation. The need to shift the economy out of a low-skills equilibrium through increases in the level and quality of training is widely acknowledged, though the detrimental effects of low pay on the long-term competitiveness of the economy is much more hotly contested.

Given the historical entrenchment of gender differentiation, single policies will have limited effects. Any attempt to foster labour-saving technological investment by providing a strong floor for wage levels has to be linked to a programme of upskilling that will enable those displaced in the short term to take advantage of the consequential expansion in the economy. But the benefits of such increases in productivity should not be exclusively fed into market consumption. In part they need to be translated into shorter working hours and parental leave for men (Hewitt, 1993). Failing such measures, the current differentiation between households in which men are employed for long hours and those in which men are unemployed will persist, and as a result many possibilities of reversing the vicious circle of the gender order and making the most of women's potential contribution to economic well-being will perish.

References

Akerlof, G. (1982). 'Labor contracts as partial gift exchange' in *Quarterly Journal of Economics*, xcvii (4).

Audit Commission (1994). *Adding Up the Sums*. London: Audit Commission.

Bevan, S. and Thompson, M. (1992). *Merit Pay, Performance Appraisal and Attitudes to Women Workers*. IMS Report 234. Brighton: Institute of Manpower Studies.

Blanchflower, D. and Corry, B. (1986–7). *Part-time Employment in Great Britain: An Analysis Using Establishment Data*. Department of Employment Research Paper 57.

Blau, F. (1993). 'Gender and economic outcomes: the role of wage structure' in *Labour*, 7(1).

Booth, A. (1991). 'Job-related formal training: what is it worth?' in *Bulletin of the Oxford Institute of Economics and Statistics*, 53 (3).

Business in the Community (1993). *Corporate Culture and Caring: The Business Case for Family-friendly Provision*. London: Business in the Community and Institute of Personnel Management.

Clement, B. (1992). 'How to make opportunity knock' in *The Independent*, 29 April.

Cockburn, C. (1992). *In the Way of Women – Men's Resistance to Sex Equality in Organisations*. London: Macmillan.

Commission of the European Community (1991). *Employment in Europe*. Luxembourg: Commission of the European Communities.

Cooper, C. and Lewis, S. (1993). *The Working Revolution*. London: Kogan Page.

Coote, A., Harman, H. and Hewitt, P. (1990). *The Family Way*. London: IPPR.

Craig, C., Rubery, J., Tarling, R. and Wilkinson, F. (1982). *Labour Market Structure, Industrial Organisation and Low Pay*. Cambridge: Cambridge University Press.

Deakin, S., Michie, J. and Wilkinson, F. (1992). *Inflation, Employment, Wage Bargaining and the Law*. London: Institute for Employment Rights.

Dougherty, C (1994) 'The Economic Value of Education and Training' in Layard, R., Mayhew, K. and Owen, G. (eds.) *Britain's Training Deficit*. Aldershot: Avebury.

Escott, K. and Whitfield, D. (1995). *The Gender Impact of CCT in Local Government*. EOC Research Discussion Series 12. Manchester: Equal Opportunities Commission.

Eurostat (1992). *Earnings: Industry and Services*. Luxembourg: Eurostat.

Eurostat (1993). *Women in the European Community*. Luxembourg: Eurostat.

Felstead, A. (1995). 'The gender implications of creating a training market: alleviating or reinforcing inequality of access' in this volume.

Finegold, D. and Soskice, D. (1988). 'Education, Training and Economic Performance' in *Oxford Review of Economic Policy*, 4 (3).

Gallie, D. and White, M. (1994). *Employment in Britain*. London: Policy Studies Institute.

Gregg, P. and Wadsworth, J. (1995) 'Women, households and access to employment' in this volume.

Gregory, M. and Sandoval, V. (1994). 'Low pay and minimum wage protection in Britain and the EC' in Barrell, R. (ed.) *The UK Labour Market*. Cambridge: Cambridge University Press.

Hakim, C. (1992). 'Explaining trends in occupational segregation: the measurement, causes, and consequences of the sexual division of labour' in *European Sociological Review*, 8 (2).

Handy, C. (1994). *The Empty Raincoat*. London: Hutchison.

Harker, C. (forthcoming). 'Towards the family-friendly employer' in Shaw, J. and Perrons, D. (eds.) *Making Gender Work*. London: Open University Press.

Haskel, J. and Martin, C. (1993). 'Do skill shortages reduce productivity? Theory and evidence for the UK' in *Economic Journal*, 103.

Hersch, J. (1991). 'Equal employment opportunity law and firm profitability' in *Journal of Human Resources*, 26.

Hewitt, P. (1993). 'Flexible working: asset or cost?' in *Policy Studies*, 14 (3).

Hirsh, W., Hayday, S., Yeates, J. and Callender, C. (1992). *Beyond the Career Break*. IMS Report 223. Brighton: Institute of Manpower Studies.

Holtermann, S. (1995). 'The costs and benefits to British employers of measures to promote equality of opportunity' in this volume.

Holtermann, S. and Clarke, K. (1992). *Parents Employment Rights and Childcare*. EOC Research Discussion Series 4. Manchester: Equal Opportunities Commission.

Horrell, S. and Rubery, J. (1991). *Employers' Working-time Policies and Women's Employment*. EOC Research Series. London: HMSO.

Humphries, J. and Rubery, J. (1992). 'The legacy for women's employment' in Michie, J. (ed.) *The Economic Legacy*. Academic Press.

Institute of Management (1994). *National Management Salary Survey*. London: Institute of Management.

Jackman, R. (1990). *Labour Market Mismatch: A Framework for Thought*. London: Centre for Economic Performance, London School of Economics and Political Science.

Joshi, H. and Davies, H. (1993). 'Mothers' human capital and childcare in Britain' in *National Institute Economic Review*, November.

Labour Research (1993). *Whose Equal Opportunity 2000?* May.

Lewis, J. (1992). 'TECs and the provision of training for women' in *Local Government Policy Making*, 19 (1).

Local Government Management Board/SOCPO (1993). *Equal Opportunities in Local Government*. London: Local Government Management Board.

Lovering, J. (1994). 'Employers, the sex-typing of jobs and economic restructuring' in Scott, A. McEwan (ed.) *Gender Segregation and Social Change*. Oxford: Oxford University Press.

Maier, F. (1995). 'Skill formation and equality of opportunity: a comparative perspective' in this volume.

McCormick, B. (1990). 'Comparable worth, deregulation and demography' in *International Journal of Human Resource Management*, 1 (3).

McLaughlin, E. (1994). 'Employment, unemployment and social security' in Glyn, A. and Miliband, D. (eds.) *Paying for Inequality: The Economic and Social Cost of Social Injustice*. London: IPPR/Rivers Oram.

Meulders, D., Plasman, R. and Vander Strict, V. (1993). *Position of Women on the Labour Market in the European Community*. Aldershot: Dartmouth.

Milne, R. and McGee, M. (1992). 'CCT in the NHS: a new look at some old estimates' in *Fiscal Studies*, 13 (3).

Moll, T. (1992). 'Rising earnings inequalities and returns to skills in the UK' in *Labour*, 6 (3).

Morris, L. (1990). *The Workings of the Household*. Cambridge: Polity.

OECD (1991). *Shaping Structural Change: the Role of Women*. Paris: Organisation for Economic Co-operation and Development.

Opportunity 2000 (1993a). *Second Year Report*. London: Business in the Community.

Opportunity 2000 (1993b). *Supplementary Reports on Boots the Chemists and Barclays Bank*. London: Business in the Community.

Pulkingham, J. (1992). 'Employment restructuring in the health service' in *Work, Employment and Society*, 6 (3).

Routh, G. (1980). *Occupation and Pay in Great Britain 1906–79*. London: Macmillan.

Rubery, J. (1992a). 'Pay and gender, the social dimension in Europe' in *British Journal of Industrial Relations*, 30 (4).

Rubery, J. (1992b). *The Economics of Equal Value*. EOC Research Discussion Series 3. Manchester: Equal Opportunities Commission.

Rubery, J. and Fagan, C. (1993). 'Occupational segregation of women and men in the European Community' in *Social Europe*, supplement 3/93.

Schoer, K. (1987). 'Part-time employment in Britain and West Germany' in *Cambridge Journal of Economics*, 11 (1).

Shipman, A. (1991). *Skill Shortages in Britain and West Germany: The Lessons of the Case Studies*. National Institute for Economic and Social Research, DP 192.

SIAU (1989). *Childcare: The Management Issue of the 1990s*. Survey and Information Analysis Unit, Sheffield Hallam University.

Simkin, C. and Hillage, J. (1992). *Family-friendly Working: New Hope or Old Hype?* IMS Report 224. Brighton: Institute of Manpower Studies.

Sloane, P. (1994). 'Gender wage differential in SCELI' in Scott, A. McEwan (ed.) *Gender Segregation and Social Change*. (*Op. cit.*)

Soskice, D. (1993). 'Social skills from higher education' in *Oxford Review of Economic Policy*, 9 (3).

Storey, D. (1994). *Understanding the Small Business Sector*. London: Routledge.

Thomson, A. and Sanjines, C. (1990). 'Earnings by size of company and establishment' in Gregory, M. and Thomson, A. (eds.) *A Portrait of Pay 1970–82*. Oxford: Clarendon.

Thurman, J. E. and Trah, G. (1990). 'Part-time work in an international perspective' in *International Labour Review*, 129.

Walsh, K. and Davis, H. (1993). *Competition and Service*. HMSO.

Wilson, R. (1994). 'Sectoral and occupational change: prospects for women's employment' in Lindley, R. (ed.) *Labour Market Structures and Prospects for Women*. IER/Equal Opportunities Commission.

Part III

Gendered Skill Formation and Access to Employment: The Influence of the Institutions of Training and Education

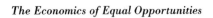

CHAPTER 8

The Gender Implications of Creating a Training Market: Alleviating or Reinforcing Inequality of Access?

Alan Felstead

It is now widely known that girls generally do better than boys at GCSEs, young women are more likely to participate in education at the ages of 16 and 17 than young men and more likely to sit and pass A levels, and women comprise almost half of all undergraduates. Nevertheless, female undergraduates are more likely to study arts and humanities and less likely to study sciences than their male counterparts (Department for Education, 1993: 1; Employment Department, 1994e: 35–43).

However, on entering the workforce the relative equality achieved by women in the education system is not maintained. According to one estimate, young women are between a third and three-fifths less likely to receive job-related training than men with similar attributes (Green, 1991: 300; Green, 1993). Women are also far less likely to get vocational qualifications. Moreover, when both academic and vocational qualifications are taken into account women do rather poorly compared to men. For example, eight percentage points separate the percentage of young males and young females who get at least two A levels (or their equivalent) and there are 13 points difference when all age groups are considered (see Table 8.1). This has been noted as a cause for concern by the government's qualification watch-dog and an area where 'early action to address this imbalance' needs to be taken (NACETT, 1994a: 17).

The aim of this chapter is not to review and synthesise the literature on women, training and skills, which would simply serve to update or extend existing work (such as Wickham, 1986; Clarke, 1991; McGivney, 1994; Istance and Rees, 1994). Instead, it explores the gender implications of exposing government-funded training delivery and take-up to market forces, focusing particularly on women's overall participation rate in government-funded training, the pattern of this participation and, as far as possible, qualification outcomes. It thus draws attention to the human capital aspect of skill formation, and the government's direct role in this process.

During the 1990s the government has consciously sought to create a training market. This began with the formation of the Training and Enterprise Councils (TECs) and has since been extended to the introduction of particular training programmes such as Youth Credits (YCs). The first phase involved setting up legally-independent businesses – TECs – to which public funds are allocated for the delivery of government training programmes. The second phase saw the introduction of particular training programmes which TECs deliver, and which are

Table 8.1 Progress towards the National Training and Education Targets (NTETs) by gender

Targets		Percentage	
	All	Male	Female
Foundation target one			
By 1997, 80 per cent of young people to reach NVQ II or equivalent	64	64	64
Foundation target three			
By 2000, 50 per cent of young people to reach NVQ III or equivalent	39	43	35
Lifetime target three			
By 2000, 50 per cent of the workforce qualified to at least NVQ III or equivalent	39	45	32

Source: Labour Force Survey, Winter 1993/1994 as reported in *Labour Market Quarterly Report* (August 1994: 11)

Note

1 The academic equivalent for NVQ II is five GCSEs at grades A to C, while for NVQ III it is two A levels or three Scottish Highers. Traditional vocational qualifications – BTEC Higher Nationals, RSA Higher Diplomas, City and Guilds craft certificates, and so on – are also translated into NVQ levels for monitoring purposes.

intended to empower individuals to demand training of their choice. These two aspects of the government's programme will form the subject of this chapter. In particular, the chapter will set out the main implications each aspect is having for women's access to training and the institutional determinants which lie behind.

Creating a training market: enter the TECs

Exposing the delivery of government-funded training programmes to market forces is a logical step for a government committed to the supremacy of the market mechanism. However, this process pre-dates the formation of TECs.

Institutionalising patterns of inequality before the TECs

Well before the introduction of TECs, women's participation in government-funded training programmes was lower than men's and concentrated in a narrower range of occupational areas. Furthermore, the opportunities for women to enrol on government-funded training schemes in non-traditional areas were shrinking. Eligibility rules were changed and more of the women-friendly training programmes had their funding cut. For example, the Youth Training Scheme (YTS) – which offered a year's training to all 16-year-old school-leavers who failed to find either a job or a place in further education – was divided into two types or modes of provision, each with a different record on, and scope for the promotion of, equal opportunities.

Mode A initially accounted for around two-thirds of YTS places (Wickham, 1986: 62). It was provided by employers or groups of employers, who acted as managing agents for the scheme and gave trainees work experience and 13 weeks' off-the-job training. The latter was normally purchased from local colleges of further education. But it was recognised that not enough employer-based places could be provided, so Mode B YTS provision was initiated. These schemes were not based around an employer or group of employers but around a community project, training workshop, information technology centre or college of further education. Trainees operated in a simulated working environment and were periodically sent out for work experience on employers' premises. Training providers offering Mode B YTS were paid more than those offering Mode A. Out of these payments providers had to pay the trainee allowance (at that time £27.50 a week).

Since Mode B schemes were workshop-based rather than employer-based, they were less dependent on the sex-stereotyped wishes of employers. Although less popular than Mode A schemes – they were seen as a further step removed from a 'proper job' – evidence suggests that they were able to exploit their relative autonomy by offering women more training opportunities in occupations dominated by men. For example, Mode B schemes took many more steps to encourage young women to participate in non-traditional areas, and had a keener awareness of equal opportunities issues than Mode A schemes (Labour Movement National Inquiry into Youth Unemployment and Training, 1986: section IV).

However, in 1986 the YTS was revised and expanded to a two-year scheme open to both 16- and 17-year-olds. All trainees were required to work towards a recognised vocational qualification, or part of one, and the trainee allowance was raised to £29.50 for 16-year-olds and £35.00 for 17-year-olds. More importantly, the funding system was also revised, with a single uniform payment replacing the original two-tier system. Managing agents were paid a basic grant for each trainee, topped up where an individual trainee was deemed to be disadvantaged in some way and therefore defined as having special training needs (STNs). Moreover, the funding was not intended to cover the entire costs of providing YTS; indeed, it was expected that managing agents would have to obtain a contribution from employers.

This meant that many Mode B schemes with the best records in terms of giving women access to training in occupational areas normally dominated by men were faced with a choice of either closing down or seeking to place their trainees with employers. Managing agents were no longer financially independent of employers, so confronting an employer's sexual prejudice could prove costly. This funding regime had the effect of forcing managing agents to pander to the wishes of employers: 'if an employer says he wants a girl, boy, black or white, send him what he orders' (Cockburn, 1987: 67). The launch of the two-year YTS programme marked the end of the Mode B concept with its potential for opening up many more occupational areas to women. Instead, market forces served to reinforce rather than alleviate the gendering of YTS places, with higher than average proportions of women found in occupations involving people and paper, and lower than average proportions in occupations involving machines (Cockburn, 1987: 8–11).

A slightly different story surrounds government-funded adult training programmes, but with a very similar outcome. Originally the Training Opportunities Programme (TOPS), launched in 1972, was open to all men and women aged 19 or over. Eligibility was cast widely, including all those who had been out of full-time education for at least three years, and were not in work or were willing to give up their job to enrol on a TOPS course. Courses catered for two groups: people who wanted to refresh or update existing skills after an absence from the labour market; and those already in employment who either wished to change careers or develop their existing career prospects. All involved intensive training in classrooms or workshops, and unlike other government-funded schemes (such as YTS, Employment Training and Training for Work) there were no employer placements and the role of employers was minimal. By all accounts the TOPS programme was popular; by the end of the 1970s around 90,000 adults were completing TOPS courses every year, 43 per cent of whom were women (Payne, 1991b: 13–14).

Nevertheless, an evaluation of the TOPS programme concluded that the courses

> were highly segregated by sex. Nine out of ten trainees on clerical and secretarial courses were women; nine out of ten on technological and manual courses were men. Men training on clerical and secretarial courses and women training on technological courses were clustered in particular occupations: for example, most women on manual courses were doing catering or sewing machining. (Payne, 1991a: 10.)

The relative absence of employer involvement thus had little effect on which training courses women and men 'chose'. Even so, when TOPS was eventually swallowed up by Employment Training (ET) in 1988 women's options were severely curtailed. The eligibility criteria for ET focused on the long-term unemployed. Fewer unemployed women than unemployed men register as unemployed, as they are less likely to be eligible for unemployment benefit: career interruptions make women less likely to have clocked up sufficient National Insurance contributions, on which eligibility for benefit is based, and many women have earnings which fall below the National Insurance threshold. As a result numerous women fell outside the definition of registered unemployed on which entry to ET was based. Whereas women made up around 45 per cent of TOPS trainees in the mid-1980s, by 1993 they accounted for only 33 per cent of those on ET. Access to government-funded adult training for women had therefore become more restricted.

Institutionalising patterns of inequality after the TECs

The formation of a network of TECs in England and Wales, and the creation of Local Enterprise Companies (LECs) in Scotland,[1] served to underline further the government's commitment to shifting the responsibility for training delivery on to the shoulders of employers.[2] By the end of 1991, the complete network of 82 TECs and 22 LECs was in place. Yet greater employer representation on TEC boards of directors does not mean autonomy to decide the nature of the programmes delivered. Despite governmental rhetoric that 'planning and management of enterprise and training need to shift from the public to the private sector' (Training Agency, 1989: 4), it was never likely that significant amounts of public money would be handed over with no strings attached.

In 1992–3 TEC budgets varied between £3.7 million and £48.6 million, with £27 million on average (Bennett, 1994: 42). In 1993–4 the national training budget was £2.4 billion, of which £1.8 billion was paid to TECs for the delivery of government training schemes for young and adult workers (Employment Department, 1993c: 66). The activities of TECs are regulated by the TEC Operating Agreement (TOA), which sets the parameters for the programmes TECs deliver and the grounds on which they are allocated funds. Around 80 per cent of TEC budgets are paid for the delivery of training programmes, with the remainder allocated to support for educational initiatives, business and enterprise support, funding for local initiatives and a management budget.

The two main training programmes are Youth Training (YT, soon to be replaced by Youth Credits) and Training for Work (TfW). The former is the modern version of YTS, geared to provide young people with vocational qualifications at or above National Vocational Qualification (NVQ) level II, while the latter is today's equivalent of ET, designed to help the unemployed back into jobs and/or improve their work skills. In both cases the eligibility criteria are set out by the government in the TOA.

In the main, the TOA restricts entry to YT to 16- and 17-year-olds who have left school and registered their wish for a place with the Careers Service. These eligibility criteria, as such, do not disadvantage women's access. However, since more young women stay on longer at school it is not surprising that they are outnumbered on YT by young men – young women accounted for only 41 per cent of YT starts in 1992–3 (unpublished Employment Department figures).

---

[1] LECs have a much wider remit than TECs (extending to environmental and economic regeneration) and deal with intermediary bodies rather than directly with government, thereby allowing them to exercise more autonomy, and have built up stronger partnerships with other local agents such as local authorities. Given these differences this chapter will focus attention on the workings of the TECs (for more on LECs see Bennett *et al.*, 1994: 113–16, 300–3; Danson *et al.*, 1989, 1992).

[2] The average TEC board of 15 directors has ten or 11 private sector representatives compared to five on the institution it replaced – the Area Manpower Boards (AMBs). However, women's representation has not improved. Only five out of 55 AMB chairs and ten per cent of AMB members were women in the mid-1980s (Cockburn, 1987: 86). The situation is remarkably similar today: women account for 12 per cent of TEC board directors, while only two of the board chairs and 12 (15 per cent) chief executives are women (Employment Department, 1994e: 44; Bennett *et al.*, 1994: 56).

Figure 8.2 YT starters by the Employment Department's standard occupational classification (SOC) groups and by sex, April 1992–March 1993

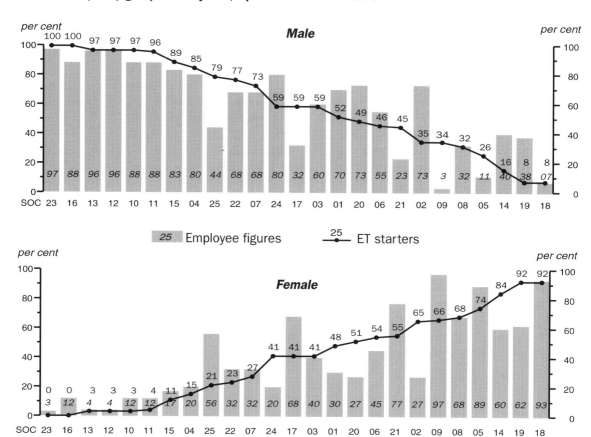

Source: Calculated from data supplied by the Employment Department (SSDE5); figures for employees calculated from the Quarterly Labour Force Survey, Spring 1992

Note 1 The absolute figures on which these percentages have been calculated were rounded to the nearest 100, hence the apparent absence of women from SOC 16 and SOC 23.

It is a different story for TfW. To enter the TfW programme, individuals must be aged 18 to 63 (18 to 59 in 1993–4) and have been unemployed for a continuous period of 26 weeks or more. As noted earlier, this is more of a hurdle for women than for men, as women are less likely to have made sufficient NI contributions to entitle them to register as unemployed. But TfW does offer eligibility on other grounds, such as lone parenthood and returners to the labour market. On the whole, these are more likely to favour women. Even so, lone parenthood alone is not sufficient, as an individual also needs to be in receipt of Income Support and/or 'deemed available for work' for 26 weeks or more. Despite these concessions TECs are still required to give the long-term registered unemployed top priority. Women's participation on government-funded adult training programmes is therefore limited – in 1992–3 only 33 per cent of adult trainees were women (unpublished Employment Department figures).

Key to Figure 8.2

For reporting purposes the ED collects information on YT starters by grouping SOCs into 25 SOC groups (Employment Department, 1994: Annex J).

SOC 01	Corporate managers and administrators
SOC 02	Managers/proprietors in agriculture and services
SOC 03	Professional occupations
SOC 04	Science and engineering associate professionals
SOC 05	Health associate professionals
SOC 06	Legal, business, social welfare and other associate professionals
SOC 07	Literacy, artistic and sports professionals
SOC 08	Clerical occupations
SOC 09	Secretarial occupations
SOC 10	Skilled construction
SOC 11	Skilled engineering, metal machining and instrument-making, electrical and electronic trades
SOC 12	Metal-forming, welding and related trades
SOC 13	Vehicle trades
SOC 14	Textiles, garments and related trades
SOC 15	Printing, woodworking, food preparation, horticultural and other craft and related occupations
SOC 16	Protective service occupations
SOC 17	Catering, waiting staff and travel attendants
SOC 18	Health, childcare and related occupations
SOC 19	Hairdressers, beauticians, domestic staff (excluding cleaners) and other personal service occupations
SOC 20	Buyers and sales representatives
SOC 21	Sales assistants, checkout operators, market traders, door-to-door salespersons and other sales occupations
SOC 22	Industrial plant and machine operators and assemblers
SOC 23	Transport operatives and drivers
SOC 24	Agriculture, forestry and fishing occupations
SOC 25	Other elementary occupations

Once on government-funded schemes the types of occupation for which men and women are trained differ significantly. Women are trained for certain occupations, men for others. According to figures supplied by the Employment Department, two-thirds or more of YT trainees in health (SOC 05), clerical (SOC 08), secretarial (SOC 09), textiles (SOC 14), health care (SOC 18) and hairdressing (SOC 19) are women. Other occupations are almost exclusively the preserve of men, such as skilled construction (SOC 10), skilled engineering (SOC 11), metal-working (SOC 12), vehicle trades (SOC 13), protective services (SOC 16) and transport occupations (SOC 23) (see Figure 8.2). Another way of putting it is that 77

Figure 8.3 ET starters by the Employment Department's standard occupational classification (SOC) groups and by sex, April 1992–March 1993

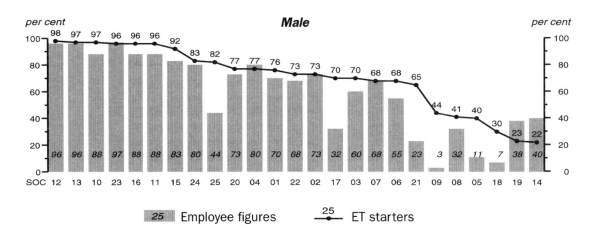

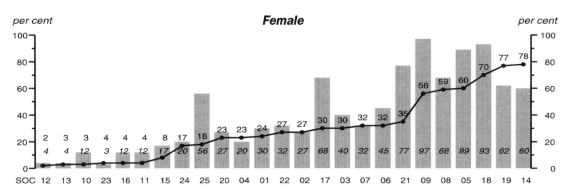

Source: Calculated from data supplied by the Employment Department (SSDE5); figures for employees calculated from the Quarterly Labour Force Survey, Spring 1992

per cent of female YT trainees are in 'office' and 'sales' occupations (SOCs 08, 09, 18, 19 and 21), which account for 44 per cent of all YT places. But women are poorly represented among 'male' occupations: only five per cent of all women YT trainees can be found in these areas (SOCs 04, 10, 11, 12, 13 and 15), yet they make up 36 per cent of all YT places. More worryingly, women YT trainees are under-represented in each of these occupations compared to their representation in the employed workforce.

In other words, YT may in fact be contributing to rather than alleviating existing patterns of occupational and employee segregation (shown as columns in Figure 8.2).[3] This suggestion has been corroborated by a recent survey of over 2,500 school pupils eligible to leave school during the spring or summer of 1993. It found that gender stereotyping was 'more extreme amongst those on YT than those in employment' (Shaw, 1994: 22).

---

[3] To examine this proposition in detail would require the construction of an index of segregation for YT starters and the workforce, and a statistical test between the two to be carried out (the same applies to ET and TfW).

Key to Figure 8.3

For reporting purposes the ED collects information on ET/TfW starters by grouping SOCs into 25 SOC groups (Employment Department, 1994: Annex J).

SOC 01   Corporate managers and administrators

SOC 02   Managers/proprietors in agriculture and services

SOC 03   Professional occupations

SOC 04   Science and engineering associate professionals

SOC 05   Health associate professionals

SOC 06   Legal, business, social welfare and other associate professionals

SOC 07   Literacy, artistic and sports professionals

SOC 08   Clerical occupations

SOC 09   Secretarial occupations

SOC 10   Skilled construction

SOC 11   Skilled engineering, metal machining and instrument-making, electrical and electronic trades

SOC 12   Metal-forming, welding and related trades

SOC 13   Vehicle trades

SOC 14   Textiles, garments and related trades

SOC 15   Printing, woodworking, food preparation, horticultural and other craft and related occupations

SOC 16   Protective service occupations

SOC 17   Catering, waiting staff and travel attendants

SOC 18   Health, childcare and related occupations

SOC 19   Hairdressers, beauticians, domestic staff (excluding cleaners) and other personal service occupations

SOC 20   Buyers and sales representatives

SOC 21   Sales assistants, checkout operators, market traders, door-to-door salespersons and other sales occupations

SOC 22   Industrial plant and machine operators and assemblers

SOC 23   Transport operatives and drivers

SOC 24   Agriculture, forestry and fishing occupations

SOC 25   Other elementary occupations

Moreover, sexual inequality is reflected in what trainees actually achieve. While young women on YT are more likely to gain a full NVQ than men (34 per cent compared to 30 per cent), closer analysis reveals a different picture. Women's qualifications are more likely to be at the lower end of the spectrum (NVQ levels I and II) than are men's (83 per cent for women compared to 69 per cent for men) (Murray, 1994: 8). This no doubt reflects the occupational segregation of YT places by gender, with young women in occupations with little tradition of training and young men in occupations with a historical commitment to skills training.

The pattern of participation in adult training schemes is also highly segregated by sex. Women account for a large proportion of adult training places in the 'paper' and 'people' occupations, while men are concentrated in occupations related to 'machines' (see Figure 8.3). Women in clerical, secretarial and caring occupations (SOCs 08, 09 and 18) represent about two-thirds of the total number of female adult trainees, yet these occupations make up around one-third of all available places. Women have also made few inroads into 'male' occupations (SOCs 04, 10, 11, 12, 13 and 15): they account for five per cent of these training places, but 30 per cent of all adult training placements are in these occupations. Once again, women employees record a proportionately greater presence in all but one of these 'male' occupations, thereby suggesting that the government's adult training programme may be adding to rather than countering existing patterns of occupational segregation.[4]

The question then arises as to why this is so, especially when TECs (and training providers) have an equal opportunities commitment written into their contracts. The TEC commitment reads:

> The TEC shall... agree, and ensure that its Providers agree, to promote equality of opportunity between individuals in access to, treatment on and outcome from the training and enterprise programmes covered by this Agreement. (Employment Department, 1994c: 6.)

The short answer is that TECs and their training providers operate in a funding environment, with programmes which impose severe constraints on their ability to deliver equal opportunities in practice. The eligibility criteria have already been discussed, but the funding mechanisms are an explanatory factor which need to be considered in some detail.

TECs are paid by government for the delivery of training programmes in two ways: for a specified number of training weeks delivered, and for a specified number of outputs achieved. Payments for training weeks are simple enough – TECs supply attendance cards for whole or part weeks (30 hours being deemed a full week for payment purposes), and are paid the agreed rate for each completed week. However, while there is no differentiation between training weeks, paying for outputs is quite different – the higher the qualifications, the larger the payment (see Felstead, 1994: Tables 1 and 2). For example, a YT trainee achieving an NVQ level III carries double the payment of an NVQ level II (four as opposed to two output points). Similarly, for TfW trainees the achievement of a 'positive outcome' – that is being in 'employment or self-employment of 15 hours per week or more ... or full-time education ... or full-time training' (Employment Department, 1994c: 103) 13 weeks after finishing their course, prematurely or otherwise – carries double the payment of a trainee who achieves NVQ level I (four as opposed to two output points).

---

4 A similar point has been made with regard to the European Union's training programmes (Rees, 1995).

The multiplier (the number of points per output) used to determine actual payments is also used by the Employment Department (ED) to set TECs' targets and measure their relative performance. Every year TECs agree with the ED a rate for the number of completed training weeks and the rates to be paid for the achievement of each output point delivered. Negotiations take place for YT and TfW. Volumes – the number of output points to be delivered from the number of training weeks – and prices for each unit delivered are then set for the year. The ED appears more concerned with these figures than it is with how these targets are achieved. In the words of a recent evaluation of TEC planning procedures:

> there are two different negotiation processes which go on in the planning round. One is centred around numbers – prices and volumes – and the other is centred around words – the content of TEC plans. Regional offices [of the ED] tend to pay more attention to numbers than they do to words. (Pearson, 1994: 7.)

The planning profile of TEC training delivery therefore appears to do little to influence financial negotiations. Training, qualifications and jobs (volumes) have the same value in the government's eyes whatever the occupation and whoever the trainee (apart from some categories of STN trainees). The emphasis is on ensuring that these volumes are delivered for the lowest possible price. The publication of TEC performance tables makes this clear (Employment Department, 1993a, 1994c).

The government's 'accent on performance' principle (Training Agency, 1989: 4) is based on measuring TEC performance according to seven separate criteria, six of which relate to YT and TfW. These include indicators such as the cost per output point, the number of NVQs per 100 leavers, and the number of positive outcomes per 100 leavers. Every TEC is given a 'score' on each of these indicators, from which seven separate league tables are then drawn up. The tables have two roles.

Firstly, by highlighting the relatively 'efficient' TECs they help the ED reward the best performers (Bennett *et al.*, 1994: 118). Those with the best performance are likely to be allocated a larger share of the budget and more outputs for the next financial year. This acts to encourage 'lower performers to achieve the standards of the best' (Employment Department, 1994b: 2). Secondly, the tables are used to determine whether or not a TEC will be issued with a three-year licence to operate, supported by annual service agreements for government-funded training and enterprise programmes. The first of these licences began in April 1995, replacing the annual planning round in which TEC corporate and business plans are produced and annual service agreements negotiated. The granting of a licence is dependent on a TEC meeting certain performance criteria. Examining the criteria in detail reveals that only those TECs with above-average performance will qualify (Employment Department, 1994d: 26–34). From 1997 the government intends to contract only with those TECs which have met the criteria for a licence.

The emphasis on rewarding the most 'efficient' TECs and penalising the least 'efficient' helps to explain the gendered pattern of participation identified earlier. Under the Sex Discrimination Act (SDA), 1975, it is lawful to provide women-only training for occupations in which women are significantly under-represented (sections 47 and 48 of the SDA). However, the present means of measuring TEC performance makes the launch of such programmes financially unattractive to TECs. By their very nature non-traditional training courses are likely to yield fewer positive outcomes per 100 leavers than sex-stereotyped courses, since sexual stereotyping continues to influence the recruitment process (Curran, 1988; Collinson *et al.*, 1990). Similarly, the cost of single-sex training courses leading to employment in non-traditional occupations is likely to be high, as they are more likely to be classroom- rather than workplace-based.

Given these factors, it is not surprising that in 1992 only a few TECs (17 per cent) had set up courses for women in non-traditional areas (EOC, 1993: 31). With performance indicators now assuming even greater importance it is unlikely that the situation has improved since then. After all, positive action programmes carry the risk of putting downward pressure on a TEC's performance rating, which may ultimately threaten its very survival.

In addition, on both YT and TfW training programmes TECs are contractually required to pay for trainees' travelling expenses, accommodation, tools, clothing and safety equipment and childcare costs (Employment Department, 1994c: 34, 46). These payments can be made directly by the TEC or indirectly through training providers. Some TECs include a notional amount to cover childcare costs in their payments to providers. Potentially this will induce training providers to discriminate against lone parents, since they are more costly to maintain than 'mainstream' trainees (EOC, 1993: 50). This discrimination is likely to affect women most.

As already noted, payments are made to TECs on the basis of the numbers of training weeks completed and output points achieved. The balance between the two has been shifting ever since the TECs were first established, gradually giving more emphasis to output-related funding (ORF). In 1993–4 ORF accounted for between 25 and 40 per cent of TEC budgets. This serves to underline further the importance of producing outputs (jobs and/or qualifications). In some TEC areas ORF now accounts for 75 per cent or more of TfW and/or YT budgets. Moreover, some TECs are piloting funding arrangements for TfW which make it financially attractive for TECs to recruit the longer-term unemployed rather than simply making them a top priority (Employment Department, 1993b). Once again, this will be to the disadvantage of women, since they are less likely to be able to register as unemployed for the reasons outlined earlier.

In addition to the general funding arrangements for YT and TfW, TECs which meet targets in relation to certain categories of trainee are entitled to a bonus payment under the title of performance-related funding (PRF). The designated categories include trainees from inner cities or special areas, trainees with disabilities, and ethnic minority trainees. Given that PRF is designed to offer some safeguards to special needs groups and the disadvantaged, it is surprising that the TECs' performance in relation to equality of opportunity does not warrant a target worthy of attracting some PRF. Indeed, its absence prompted the EOC to recommend that:

> the proportions overall of men and women in training and enterprise programmes, and the proportions of men and women in non-traditional occupations, be added to the designated categories for performance-related funding. (EOC, 1993: 62.)

So far this section has focused almost exclusively on the contractual relationship between the government (the ED) and TECs for the delivery of government-funded training programmes in a well-defined geographical area.[5] However, it is not the TECs which carry out the training, but a network of training providers with which TECs contract. For YT the TECs contract with managing agents, for TfW they contract with training managers. These can be employers, groups of employers banding together to form local training groups (usually based around a single industry), local authority employers, colleges of further education, voluntary organisations catering for those with special needs, or private sector training organisations whose goal is to make a profit from training delivery.

Providers seek to secure placements for trainees and give them a training programme which can be conducted either on placement, in colleges of further education, or at the provider's premises. For this service, providers typically aim to charge employers £35.00 per week per trainee, or failing that whatever they can get (Felstead *et al.*, 1994b). On the YT programme providers are required to pay trainees a weekly allowance of £29.50 for 16-year-olds and £35.00 for 17-year-olds (the same as in 1986). What they are able to get from employers and what they get from the TEC goes to pay for the allowance, and the training and administration costs they incur. The same goes for the TfW programme, with one important difference: the training allowance (unemployment benefit plus an extra £10 per week bonus) is paid by the Employment Service rather than the training provider. In other words, on the TfW programme training providers do not have to worry about covering the cost of the training allowance, whereas YT providers do.

As soon as a managing agent takes on a young person on the YT scheme, they take on an immediate cost – the trainee allowance. Balanced against this, most TECs pay training providers for each training week delivered and each output achieved (but TEC-provider contracts vary, see Felstead, 1994). The balance of these payments is shifting from training weeks to outputs in line with the government's shift towards ORF for TECs. In

---

[5] The parallels with franchising are striking (see Felstead, 1993b). This has led some writers to suggest that setting up the TECs is part of a wider movement of 'state franchising' (see Vickerstaff and Ainley, 1994, for a review).

other words, in the absence of a paying placement many managing agents may find themselves taking on a YT trainee at a loss, with most of the payment triggered by outputs achieved at the end of the programme. A paying placement will therefore help to make a managing agent's participation in YT economically viable.

Managing agents thus have no financial incentive to challenge existing sexual prejudices with regard to 'women's' and 'men's' work. Those who do so will pick up fewer paying placements and, unless they can draw on financial resources from elsewhere, will eventually go out of business. There is mounting evidence that managing agents who cater for trainees with special needs are suffering a similar fate (*Financial Times*, 4 July 1994, 22 July 1994; *Independent on Sunday*, 3 July 1994). Furthermore, the new Modern Apprenticeship – to be launched nationally in September 1995 and designed to offer young people training to NVQ III instead of NVQ II under YT – will rely heavily on employer funding. It is estimated that it could cost employers 'up to 60 per cent of the cost of training in addition to paying the wages of the apprentices' (*Employee Development Bulletin*, August 1994: 10). In these circumstances the entry of women into non-traditional occupations will be difficult to achieve.

Similar arguments also apply to TfW, but with two differences. First, the financial pressures on training managers are not as great as those on managing agents, at least initially. Under TfW the Employment Service, not the training provider, pays the trainee allowance, making training managers less reliant on employers than their counterparts delivering YT. Secondly, though, training managers are more reliant on employers triggering their bonus payments by offering trainees jobs, whereas YT bonus payments are paid simply for qualifications achieved. Indeed, existing evidence suggests that TECs give training managers greatest reward for positive outcomes and the government, in turn, does likewise in its contracts with TECs (Felstead, 1994). To challenge employers' sexual stereotypes and prejudices is therefore economically risky in the absence of any financial incentives to do so.

Creating a training market: enter individuals

TECs organise the delivery of the government's training and enterprise programmes, but in recent years the government has chosen to change the nature of some of these programmes in several respects. These changes have been designed to empower individuals to take the lead in their own training and development. Indeed, the aim is explicitly set out as one of the government's priorities for action:

> Individuals must be persuaded that training pays and that they should take more responsibility for their own development. (Employment Department, 1991a: 6.)

Three groups of policy initiatives can be identified centring around this aim: providing consumers with information about training opportunities;

making it easier for individuals to pay for training; and giving consumers both the funds and the advice to get the training of their choice (for more detail see Felstead, 1993a).

Providing consumer information

The first group of initiatives is designed to create a new generation of well-informed training customers. It includes initiatives such as Gateways to Learning and Skill Choice (see Coopers and Lybrand, 1992a, 1992b, 1994b; Employment Department, 1992). In short, these are intended to give adults advice and guidance with regard to their skills potential, thereby prompting individuals to think seriously about taking up training or retraining opportunities.

Making it easier to pay

These policy initiatives are designed to iron out some of the imperfections in the capital market. Unlike other forms of capital, 'human capital' is inseparable from the individual in which it resides. Hence the risks of lending money to individuals to invest in their own skill development are great. Human capital offers the lender no collateral to be seized in the event that the loan remains outstanding – human capital cannot be repossessed and is certainly not at risk if repayments are not kept up. Self-sponsored training events therefore face a large financial barrier – about a quarter of employees cite funding as an obstacle to undertaking training, rising to well over half of the unemployed (Rigg, 1989: 75–6, Table 11.21). Offering Career Development Loans (CDLs) to individuals who want to invest in their own skills and giving tax relief on fees paid by individuals for courses leading to NVQs are intended to make self-sponsorship financially easier (Employment Department, 1994a; Inland Revenue, 1994).

Giving consumers funds and advice

By far the most ambitious attempt to put individuals in charge of their own training and development is the award of Youth Credits (YCs) to all 16- and 17-year-olds by 1995, replacing the existing YT scheme. Under the YC scheme every 16- and 17-year-old leaving full-time education is given a training voucher to cash with any approved training provider (managing agent). Initially, ten TECs and one LEC were chosen to run YCs as three-year pilot schemes from 1 April 1991. Within weeks of this launch the government announced that the scheme would be extended to a further nine TEC/LEC areas from April 1993, and eventually extended to all young people by 1996 (the national scheme was later brought forward to 1995). It is claimed that this will 'give young people the power to choose and "buy" their own career training' (Employment Department, 1991b: 1). Alongside the introduction of YCs has been increased emphasis on careers guidance in schools as the best means of informing young people of their consumer rights and opportunities.

The scheme is intended to place consumer sovereignty at the heart of delivering young people's training in the Britain. One of the main principles of consumer sovereignty is free information, to ensure that consumers are well-informed about the products the market has to offer. The establishment of a training market for the young is no different. Hence enhanced careers guidance has been given a high priority across the pilot schemes and will play a significant role once YCs become nationally available from April 1995. Indeed, the government requires all YC areas to provide all 16- and 17-year-old school-leavers with an in-depth interview with a careers officer.

To meet this requirement most of the pilots have funded the Careers Service to recruit extra staff to provide an enhanced service. Typically this involves helping the young person to review his/her achievements, set personal goals and determine their learning needs. As a result an individual action plan (IAP) is drawn up, with the intention of assisting young people identify progression goals, the choice of training opportunities available, and how YCs can pay for their chosen training route (see Figure 8.4). The CBI is pressing the government to go further by providing a universal entitlement of eight-and-a-half hours contact with a careers officer throughout a young person's schooling (CBI, 1993: 37).

YCs are issued by TECs, usually via the Careers Service, to young people in their area. Some issue them to all 16- and 17-year-olds, some only to those who express their intention of leaving full-time education. The credits themselves differ in appearance – they can take the form of passports with tear-off slips, cheque books, multiple-part vouchers, credit cards, and so on. However, the credit must show its monetary value. This usually means specifying a maximum and minimum value, with the actual amount determined by the occupation for which the training is aimed and the TEC area in which the young person happens to live.

Equipped with greater knowledge of what training opportunities are on offer and where, as well as the power to 'buy' the training of their choice, young people are supposed to negotiate with prospective employers how their plans might fit in with the employer's. Once a match has been found a training plan (TP) is drawn up and sent to the TEC. So long as the training is carried out by an approved provider (a managing agent) the YC can be activated. The monies allocated to it are released on a weekly basis, and also when NVQs are achieved (as in the case of YT). The managing agent receives these payments in return for the training carried out on behalf of the employer.

There are, however, several important differences between the market for training and those for consumer products which make the YC scheme 'a gamble with long odds on the futures of young people and with the skill of the nation' (NATFHE and Youthaid, 1993: v). First, the YC idea was originally suggested at a time when the British economy was booming and the number of young people was shrinking. The theory was that young people would be able to shop around for the employer offering the best package, of which training would be a key element. Those employers who offered little or no training would see their labour supply shrink. Giving

Figure 8.4 The Youth Credit route

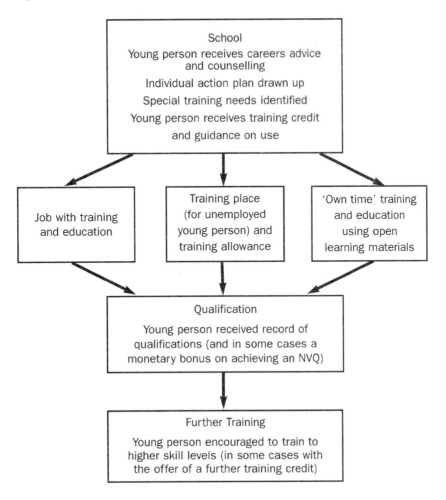

Source: Employment Department, Department for Education and Welsh Office (1991: 36)

young people YCs would therefore 'be a powerful influence on persistent non-training employers. Young people in short supply would simply go to other employers offering training' (CBI, 1989: 24).

However, today's labour market is very different. Young people do not have a range of job vacancies from which to choose, and therefore have little ability to press home their training demands. Many are simply happy to get a job no matter what. To rely on shrinking labour supply to push training on to the business agenda is a precarious strategy, since any success is unlikely to be long-lasting – as the recession of the early 1990s goes to prove (Felstead and Green, 1994).

Secondly, YCs are based on the notion that individuals 'negotiate' with employers about their training, thereby pressuring employers into providing training. However, to demand training individuals need self-confidence and good communication skills to press their case. It is unlikely that the average 16-year-old school-leaver has these abilities. Indeed, the national evaluation of the first-round pilots admitted that:

> young people have been unable to use their TC [YC] as a negotiating tool in discussion with employers. Thus the objective for young people to negotiate their own training or influence the decisions of others in the area does not seem to have happened to any significant extent. (Coopers, Lybrand and Deloitte, 1992, quoted in NATFHE and Youthaid, 1993: 29.)

In any case, there is no requirement on the part of employers to yield to workers' training demands if not compelled to do so (nor to any other of their employment demands for that matter). Instead, YCs provide young people with an unenforceable entitlement, not an enforceable right, to demand the training of their choice. It depends on employers whether young people are given the necessary time off and encouragement to take up their training entitlement. In the absence of either, taking up one's entitlement in one's own time is risky, since most of the rewards for training come from one's existing employer. Vocational training is, by definition, bound up with work. Lack of support at work will weaken the incentive to train in one's own time. Those who get support are likely to be the best qualified, employed in the 'better' jobs where training is taken more seriously and well rewarded. Those disadvantaged in the labour market – groups such as ethnic minorities and women, for example – are likely to be further disadvantaged in their access to vocational education and training. Training will therefore continue to be unevenly spread in spite of the rhetoric that YCs provide '*all* young people with an entitlement and greater control over their own development' (CBI, 1989: 24, their emphasis).

Thirdly, in any other market one person's money is as good as another's. A consumer faces a range of products – in the case of soft drinks, Coca-Cola, Pepsi-Cola, Seven-Up and so on. Provided the customer has the necessary money, a supermarket will gladly sell the consumer the product of their choice. However, in the training market this is not so. Making payments according to achievements discriminates against those most in need (this is at its most extreme in the case of some TECs where YC funds are paid out wholly on the basis of achievement). In such circumstances, training young people with special needs, for example, is a gamble based on whether the trainee will achieve the trigger points necessary to release the funding within the time available. Despite additional funding for young people with special needs, the risk is too great for some training providers (Further Education Unit, 1992).

While YCs encourage the individual to vet the training provider, the funding arrangements prompt the provider to assess the consumer. Will the young person stay the course, will young women leave if they become pregnant and/or get married, and what are their chances of success? These are the types of questions that will be asked. On this basis, those with poor school performance, those with designated special needs and young women will be considered 'bad risks', and hence are least likely to get the training they choose. While there may be plenty of choice in the training market, one person's YC has greater buying power than another's. This is certainly not a feature of conventional consumer product markets.

Similarly, YCs appear to reproduce and reinforce existing patterns of sexual inequality. Young women are still being channelled almost exclusively into those poorly-paid segments of the labour market associated with 'women's work' where there are few training opportunities, while young men are channelled into higher-paid craft occupations where training is given a higher priority (Coopers, Lybrand and Deloitte, 1992: para 35). A subsequent evaluation of YCs found that 'one of the main effects of TCs [YCs] appeared to be reflecting and perhaps reinforcing traditional gender differences' (National Foundation for Educational Research, 1993: 98). Indeed, according to a survey of 122 school pupils in one of the first areas to launch YCs, far fewer girls than boys intended to use their credits to 'buy' training (Sims and Jamison, 1991: 5).

Despite these difficulties, the use of credits as a means of channelling public funds into training seems set to continue:

> Our present training credits [YCs] are focused on *young people who have left full-time education*, and before going further we need to gain more experience in that area. But as we gain more experience it will be important to keep our options open so that we can review the idea of extending credits further. (Michael Forsyth, Employment Minister, July 1992, quoted in Further Education Unit, 1993: 3, emphasis added.)

As a result, development work is currently under way in individual TECs and LECs on extending training credits to adult workers. There is also a suggestion that credits be introduced for all 16- to 19-year-olds' education and training, so all post-16 education and training providers have to compete for young people's custom (CBI, 1993: 29–32). Indeed, there is apparently considerable support for the idea of 'universal credits' among those who run the TECs: 77 per cent are in favour of giving all 16- to 19-year-olds credits to 'buy' full- or part-time education and training of their choice (*FT Survey of Directors of Training and Enterprise Councils 1994*).

The aim of 'putting individuals in charge' of their own training relies on the notion that training markets are like any other and consumers can insist on getting the products of their choice. It assumes that individuals are best placed to pressurise reluctant employers into providing training. Apart from times of labour shortage, it is difficult to envisage circumstances in which individuals alone will have sufficient clout to make this happen. Only those indispensable to the organisation will have the bargaining power to make their training demands stick. Those already facing disadvantages in the labour market will face further disadvantages in their access to career development. Black workers, women, workers with special needs and the low skilled will be poorly placed to negotiate training with their employer – despite appearances to the contrary, their 'buying power' will carry less weight than others.

Conclusion

Rhetorically at least, the government is committed to raising the skills of the British workforce to the levels of our international competitors (see Felstead *et al.*, 1994a). For example, in the recent White Paper *Competitiveness: Helping Business to Win*, the government was critical of past performance in this area:

> For too long the UK's levels of participation and achievement have dragged us down the international education and training league. (President of the Board of Trade *et al.*, 1994: 30.)

The setting of National Targets for Education and Training (NTETs) in 1991 was designed to focus the minds of employers, education and training providers, TECs, government and others on correcting this deficiency. Quite apart from whether the NTETs are set high enough or will be achieved within the given timescales, the disparities between the achievements of men and women are alarming. Just to achieve the existing targets will require

> a significant narrowing of the existing disparity in the attainment of vocational qualifications at level III and above by women in the workforce relative to men. (NACETT, 1994b: 9.)

As far as government-funded training schemes (YT, TfW and YC) are concerned this will be difficult to achieve under existing arrangements, not least because some government training programmes put women at a disadvantage on entry. As already seen, TfW, for example, is directed primarily at the long-term unemployed, so fewer women are eligible for entry. Perhaps more importantly there are no financial incentives for TECs to support programmes which seek to open up training opportunities for women in non-traditional occupations. Indeed, the financial incentives work in the opposite direction – positive outcomes are more likely to be achieved by placing individuals in sex-stereotyped occupations, single-sex courses are more costly, and reliance on employer contributions makes challenging sexual prejudice financially risky. In other words, it makes economic sense for TECs to reinforce rather than alleviate patterns of inequality.

Initiatives to empower individuals are similarly unlikely to break down occupational stereotypes. The fact that a young person carries a Youth Credit does not mean that he or she will get the training they choose. This will depend on the job for which they are recruited by the employer or the occupation which offers the managing agent the best chance of getting a paying placement. Despite the rhetoric, the individual has little power to get the training of their choice.

This chapter has described what, in large part, can be summarised as the 'economics of *inequality*' as far as women's access to and participation in government-funded training is concerned. While the consequences of this inequality have been directly felt by women in terms of relatively poor pay and few promotion prospects for many years, only now have the consequences for Britain's skills base been fully realised. Here the government could take a lead by providing TECs with economic incentives to promote equal opportunities, instead of relying on a vague – albeit contractual – commitment and the weak powers of the individual to press their case.

Acknowledgements

The author would like to thank Irene Bruegel, Francis Green, Chris Rowley, the editors of this book and the participants at the EOC seminar for helpful comments on an earlier version of this chapter. The usual caveat applies. Material from the Quarterly Labour Force Survey, made available through the Office of Population Censuses and Surveys (OPCS) and the ESRC Data Archive, has been used by permission of the Controller of HM Stationery Office.

References

Bennett, R. (1994). 'Training and Enterprise Councils: are they cost-efficient?' in *Policy Studies*, 15 (1).

Bennett, R. J., Wicks, P. and McCoshan, A. (1994). *Local Empowerment and Business Services: Britain's Experiment with Training and Enterprise Councils*. London: UCL Press.

CBI (1989). *Towards a Skills Revolution*. London: Confederation of British Industry.

CBI (1993). *Routes for Success – Careership: A Strategy for All 16–19-Year-Old Learning*. London: Confederation of British Industry.

Clarke, K. (1991). *Women and Training: A Review*. EOC Discussion Series 1. Manchester: Equal Opportunities Commission.

Cockburn, C. (1987). *Two-track Training: Sex Inequalities and the YTS*. Basingstoke: Macmillan Education.

Collinson, D., Knights, D. and Collinson, M. (1990). *Managing to Discriminate*. London: Routledge.

Coopers and Lybrand (1992a). *Gateways to Learning: National Co-ordinator's Report – Evaluating the Impact*. Sheffield: Employment Department.

Coopers and Lybrand (1992b). *Gateways to Learning: National Co-ordinator's Report – The Development Stage: Lessons Emerging*. Sheffield: Employment Department.

Coopers and Lybrand (1994). *Gateways to Learning: National Evaluation: Final Report*. Sheffield: Employment Department.

Coopers, Lybrand and Deloitte (1992). *Training Credits Evaluation: National Co-ordinator's Report of 11 Case Studies, Final Report*. Sheffield: Employment Department.

Curran, M. (1988). 'Gender and recruitment: people and places in the labour market' in *Work, Employment and Society*, 2 (3).

Danson, M. W., Lloyd, M. G. and Newlands, D. (1989). '"Scottish Enterprise": towards a model agency or a flawed initiative?' in *Regional Studies*, 23 (6).

Danson, M. W., Lloyd, M. G. and Newlands, D. (1992). 'Privatism in business development and training: a new approach' in *British Journal of Education and Work*, 5 (3).

Department for Education (1993). 'Statistical bulletin on women in post-compulsory education' in *Statistical Bulletin*, 26/93, December.

Employee Development Bulletin (August 1994). 'Modern Apprenticeships: the new route to a skilled workforce', 56.

Employment Department (1991a). *A Strategy for Skills, Executive Summary: Guidance from the Secretary of State for Employment on Training, Vocational Education and Enterprise*. Sheffield: Employment Department.

Employment Department (1991b). *Training Credits – A Guide*. Sheffield: Employment Department.

Employment Department (1992). *Assessment and Guidance Credits: Prospectus*. Sheffield: Employment Department.

Employment Department (1993a). Press Notice – *TEC Comparison Tables*, 13 September. London: Employment Department.

Employment Department (1993b). *The Training for Work Funding Pilots 1993–4: Paying TECs for Results – 18 Questions and Answers About the TfW Funding Pilots*. Sheffield: Employment Department.

Employment Department (1993c). *Training Statistics 1993*. London: Employment Department.

Employment Department (1994a). *Career Development Loans: Annual Report 1993–4*. Sheffield: Employment Department.

Employment Department (1994b). Press Notice – *TEC Comparison Tables*, 25 August. London: Employment Department.

Employment Department (1994c). *TEC Operating Agreement 1994–5*. Sheffield: Employment Department.

Employment Department (1994d). *TECs: The New Contract Framework – 3-Year Licences*. Sheffield: Employment Department.

Employment Department (1994e). *United Nations Fourth World Conference on Women – Beijing 1995: Report of the United Kingdom of Great Britain and Northern Ireland*. London: Employment Department.

Employment Department, Department for Education and Welsh Office (1991). *Education and Training for the 21st Century, Volume One*. Cm 1536. London: HMSO.

EOC (1993). *Formal Investigation into the Publicly-funded Vocational Training System in England and Wales*. Manchester: Equal Opportunities Commission.

Felstead, A. (1993a). 'Putting individuals in charge, leaving skills behind? UK training policy in the 1990s' in *University of Leicester Discussion Papers in Sociology*, S93/7.

Felstead, A. (1993b). *The Corporate Paradox: Power and Control in the Business Franchise*. London: Routledge.

Felstead, A. (1994). 'Funding government training schemes: mechanisms and consequences' in *British Journal of Education and Work*, 7 (3).

Felstead, A. and Green, F. (1994). 'Training during the recession' in *Work, Employment and Society*, 8 (2).

Felstead, A., Ashton, D., Green, F. and Sung, J. (1994a). *International Study of Vocational Education and Training in Five Countries: the Federal Republic of Germany, France, Japan, Singapore and the United States*. Leicester: Centre for Labour Market Studies, University of Leicester.

Felstead, A., Maguire, S. and Goodwin, J. (1994b). 'Providing training in Leicestershire' in *Leicester Economic Review*, 2 (3).

Financial Times (22 July 1994). 'Training cuts "cause destitution"'. Lisa Wood.

Financial Times (4 July 1994). 'Catholic training body faces closure'. Neil Buckley.

FT Survey of Directors of Training and Enterprise Councils 1994. London: Financial Times.

Further Education Unit (1992). *The Action Planning Process and Training Credits*. London: Further Education Unit.

Further Education Unit (1993). *Training Credits: The Implications for Colleges*. London: Further Education Unit.

Green, F. (1991). 'Sex discrimination in job-related training' in *British Journal of Industrial Relations*, 29 (2).

Green, F. (1993). 'The determinants of training male and female employees in Britain' in *Oxford Bulletin of Economics and Statistics*, 55 (1).

Independent on Sunday (3 July 1994). 'Church closes training body'. Barrie Clement.

Inland Revenue (1994). Number of vocational training relief claims, 1992–3 and 1993–4. Provided to author on request.

Istance, D. and Rees, T. (1994). *Women in Post-Compulsory Education and Training in Wales*. EOC Discussion Series 8. Manchester: Equal Opportunities Commission.

Labour Market Quarterly Report (August 1994). 'The national targets for education and training.'

Labour Movement National Inquiry into Youth Unemployment and Training (1986). *Report of the National Labour Movement Inquiry into Youth Unemployment and Training*. Birmingham: Trade Union Resource Centre.

McGivney, V. (1994). *Wasted Potential: Training and Career Progression for Part-time and Temporary Workers*. Leicester: NIACE.

Murray, I. (1994). 'Training the unemployed? Low-level qualifications and high drop-out' in *Working Brief*, 57.

NACETT (1994a). *National Advisory Council for Education and Training Targets: Report on Progress*. London: National Advisory Council for Education and Training Targets.

NACETT (1994b). *Review of the National Targets for Education and Training: Proposals for Consultation*. London: National Advisory Council for Education and Training Targets.

NATFHE and Youthaid (1993). *Credit Limits: A Critical Assessment of the Training Credits Pilot Scheme*. London: NATFHE and Youthaid.

National Foundation for Educational Research (1993). *Evaluation of the Second Year of Training Credits*. Slough: National Foundation for Educational Research.

Payne, J. (1991a). *Adult Off-the-Job Skills Training: An Evaluation Study*. Sheffield: Training Agency.

Payne, J. (1991b). *Women, Training and the Skills Shortage: The Case for Public Investment*. London: Policy Studies Institute.

Pearson, I. (1994). *The Role of Evaluation in TEC Planning: Final Report*. Employment Department Research Series 26. Sheffield: Employment Department.

President of the Board of Trade, the Chancellor of the Exchequer, the Secretaries of State for Transport, Environment and Employment, the Chancellor of the Duchy of Lancaster, and the Secretaries of State for Scotland, Northern Ireland, Education and Wales (1994). *Competitiveness: Helping Business to Win*. Cm 2563. London: HMSO.

Rees, T. (1995). 'Policy update: women and training policy in the European Union' in *Gender, Work and Organisation*, 2 (1).

Rigg, M. (1989). *Training in Britain: A Study of Funding, Activity and Attitudes – Individuals' Perspectives*. Sheffield: Training Agency.

Shaw, C. (1994). *Changing Lives 2*. London: Policy Studies Institute.

Sims, D. and Jamison, J. (1991). *School Data Report: A Summary of the Main Findings*. London: National Foundation for Educational Research in England and Wales.

Training Agency (1989). *Training and Enterprise Councils: A Prospectus for the 1990s*. Sheffield: Training Agency.

Vickerstaff, S. and Ainley, P. (1994). *The Depoliticisation of Vocational Education and Training (VET) in the Contract State: Will it Work?* Paper presented to the Employment Research Unit 1994 Annual Conference, Cardiff.

Wickham, A. (1986). *Women and Training*. Milton Keynes: Open University Press.

CHAPTER 9

Skill Formation and Equal Opportunity – A Comparative Perspective

Friederike Maier

To examine processes of skill formation and equal opportunities in a comparative way is important, as women's participation in these processes includes a variety of dimensions.

Firstly, all member states of the EU can be assumed to need a highly-skilled and flexible workforce, and demand for unskilled labour in both production-related and service-related industries can be expected to decline. Investment in skills and the maintenance of skills will be even more crucial for the labour market position of women if the demand for unskilled labour decreases, and labour market entry and employment opportunities are structured more than today via skill levels. As long as women have lower skill levels than men, their employment and career opportunities will remain unequal.

Secondly, it is important to recognise that the increase in women's educational levels in the past 20 years has had a positive impact on women's labour force participation: the higher the educational level, the higher the level of work activity and labour force attachment. Comparing different countries, women with higher education are more likely to remain in the labour market, less likely to withdraw in case of childbirth, and less likely to become unemployed than unskilled women.

Thirdly, however, women's higher levels of education and training, and the decreasing gap between the sexes in the quantity of education in most countries, are only one factor influencing women's position in labour markets. Other factors, such as gender-specific patterns of skill formation, different types of education and training for women and men, and gender segregation in labour markets (in part a result of gender-specific training), influence the impact of women's higher levels of training and education on their labour market position.

This last aspect seems to be crucial. It is necessary to understand how training systems in European Union member states influence gender-specific processes of skill formation, how the skill-formation process is interrelated with the employment system, and how processes of segmentation and segregation are linked to different training systems and women's economic position, especially earnings. This chapter analyses the linkages between skill formation and labour market position, and discusses the political implications for equal opportunity policies in this field.

Data problems

The comparative analysis of women's participation in education and training is a difficult task, as data on these subjects is not available on a level comparable to other data. Eurostat's published Labour Force Survey does not include data on educational and training levels for the employed, unemployed, or certain age groups in European Union member states, so the database for comparative research is limited. The study described in this chapter uses various data sources, most of which have some methodological problems due to the fact that member states have very different national systems of education and training. The data quality is best for general education up to the third level (higher education), and not very good for vocational training, especially initial vocational training.

General education and vocational training

Women's participation in general education has been rising in all European Union member states – in many countries the participation and performance of young women now surpasses that of young men. In the last 20 years each new cohort of young women has had a higher proportion in general education, especially in general education above the lower secondary level. In parallel with an overall increase of the number of pupils in secondary education and students in third-level higher education in most European countries, there has been an even faster increase in the number and proportion of women in higher education, so young women's share in all levels of general education (lower secondary, higher secondary and third-level higher education) is today around 50 per cent.[1]

However, the links between general education and the labour market are quite different between countries. Whereas in some countries a high proportion of young people enter the labour market directly after the completion of general education, in others labour market entry is more common after the completion of a vocational training programme, either in a school-based form, a dual system (schools and firms), or an apprenticeship. This difference influences the 'labour market relevance' of general education.

For example, in German-speaking countries labour market entry into a skilled position is based on the completion of vocational or university training – a person who has only completed higher secondary general education (the *Abitur*) with no vocational or professional education is counted (for statistical purposes) as unskilled, and will have difficulties in getting a job as skilled employee. Women's high participation and good performance in general education in these countries has therefore only limited impact on their opportunities in the labour market; but the

---

[1] It is important to note that in higher education (universities and colleges) women's share is highest in Portugal (56 per cent in 1991), France (53 per cent), Denmark (52 per cent) and Spain (51 per cent), and lowest in Germany (43 per cent), the Netherlands (44 per cent) and Ireland (46 per cent). See Eurostat, 1993b.

position may be different in countries where a higher proportion of young people enter the labour market without any initial vocational or university training.[2]

Eurostat (1993a) provides a more differentiated picture on education and training for 14- to 24-year-olds in 1989, as shown in Table 9.1. This age group was chosen because in most European countries the compulsory school age is between 14 and 16 years old. Young people older than the compulsory school age therefore have the choice of continuing their education beyond this age, entering the labour market, or becoming economically inactive. Eurostat data on economic activity and unemployment for this age group shows high activity rates for women in Denmark (67.2 per cent), the UK (62.7 per cent) and Germany (53.9 per cent) in 1989. Young men in this age group are also active (see Eurostat, 1993a). If participating in some form of training – as apprentices, in a dual system, on a part-time basis or on the job – these young people are counted as economically active.

According to the European Labour Force Survey, between 42 per cent (in Portugal) and 73 per cent (the Netherlands) of all young men and between 44 per cent (Portugal) and 67 per cent (Denmark) of all young women are in some form of education and training.[3] In Belgium, Denmark, Spain, and Portugal young women of this age group have a higher proportion in training and education than young men. In Germany, Greece, France, Ireland, Italy, Luxembourg, the Netherlands and the UK, a slightly higher proportion of all young men are in training and education than of young women.

Looking at the distinction between general education and vocational education/training, it is clear that in most countries young women are more likely to participate in general education than young men: only in Germany and Greece does the share of young men in general education exceed that of young women. In Belgium and the UK the proportions are similar for both sexes.

Table 9.1 also shows the overall relevance of general versus vocational training/education in the member states. The share of all 14- to 24-year-olds in general education ranges from 40 per cent in Belgium to only 13 per cent in Italy. Further training (including institutions providing specific subject training, and all university training) is of greater importance in Italy and the Netherlands for both young men and young women. It also involves high proportions of young people in France, Belgium and Spain. Work-related courses, such as those at part-time colleges, are an

---

[2] According to estimates by the European Centre for Vocational Training (CEDEFOP), vocational training at level two (completion of vocational training for a certain occupation, independent of whether it is acquired in a school, college or apprenticeship) or higher is most common for young people in Denmark, Luxembourg and Germany, leaving only ten to 20 per cent of the 16- to 24-year-old age group without any vocational training. These countries are followed by Belgium, France, Ireland and the Netherlands, with around 30 per cent without any vocational training; then Greece, Italy, Portugal, Spain and the UK with around 50 per cent of young people without vocational training at level two or more (Sellin, 1994). Unfortunately separate data is not available for men and women.

[3] The others are either in employment, unemployed or inactive.

Table 9.1 Education and training of 14 - to 24 - year-olds during the four weeks prior to survey

		Type of training (percentage of total age group)							
		General education	Further education	On-job training	Appren- ticeship	Dual system	Other training	Part-time college	Total
Belgium	F	41.9	20.2	–	(0.5)	–	0.6	–	63.5
	M	41.9	18.7	(0.4)	1.1	(0.4)	0.6	–	61.3
Denmark	F	36.3	14.8	1.5	8.5	5.9	–	–	67.3
	M	31.8	12.6	1.4	13.8	4.2	–	–	64.3
Germany	F	27.1	12.8	0.5	13.7	0.3	2.8	–	57.2
	M	28.5	13.4	0.6	15.8	0.5	2.9	–	61.7
Greece	F	38.9	13.9	–	–	–	1.2	–	54.2
	M	42.4	14.4	–	(0.4)	–	0.7	–	.58.0
France	F	29.1	22.1	–	1.8	–	4.6	–	57.6
	M	27.0	23.0	–	4.2	–	4.4	–	58.6
Ireland	F	39.4	13.7	2.7	–	–	–	–	56.6
	M	35.1	16.4	3.5	1.6	–	–	–	57.7
Italy	F	13.7	32.3	0.4	0.2	0.2	2.3	–	49.1
	M	13.3	35.3	0.4	0.3	(0.1)	1.9	–	51.3
Luxembourg	F	39.2	7.4	–	(2.2)	–	–	–	49.8
	M	38.7	9.8	–	(4.5)	–	–	–	55.2
Netherlands	F	24.3	35.4	1.6	0.5	–	3.2	–	65.0
	M	22.7	44.8	1.7	1.1	–	2.8	–	73.1
Portugal	F	36.8	7.3	–	–	–	–	–	44.2
	M	36.2	5.7	–	–	–	–	–	42.1
Spain	F	35.5	20.1	–	–	–	1.0	–	56.6
	M	34.5	19.4	–	–	–	0.5	–	54.4
UK	F	24.8	7.6	2.5	1.3	0.8	3.7	5.5	46.2
	M	24.9	7.0	2.6	5.9	0.8	3.7	5.5	50.4
All	F	27.1	19.0	0.7	3.1	0.4	2.7	1.0	54.0
	M	26.7	19.9	0.8	4.9	0.3	2.4	1.0	56.0

Source: Eurostat, *Unemployed Women in the EC*

Notes 1 General education refers to all persons attending a school which provides general programmes.

2 Further education refers to all persons attending an institution providing training in specific matters not covered by previous classification, and all university students (without complementary training elsewhere).

important source of training in the UK; whereas in Denmark and Germany the apprenticeship system involves higher proportions of young people than the further training system (in Denmark only for young men).

These figures reflect the variety of training systems within the EU. But the question remains of whether the slightly higher proportion of young women in general education (compared to further training and other forms of work-related training, such as on-the-job training and apprenticeships) creates more difficulties in the transition from school to work.

Taking unemployment figures as a first indicator of labour market opportunities, it is obvious that the overall unemployment figures for both young men and young women are lowest in those countries with a higher proportion of young people in work-related training (Denmark, Germany and the UK). Work-related training, whether organised in an apprenticeship system, a dual system or in part-time colleges, integrates young people into the labour market as employees on a substantially lower wage than adult skilled workers or even adult unskilled workers. (In Germany apprentices receive around 42 per cent of the wages of an unskilled person; see Büchtemann *et al.*, 1993). This may create incentives to integrate school-leavers into employment, and simultaneously permits firm- or occupation-specific training targeted to the employer's needs. Although the level of standardisation of apprenticeships and similar training varies between countries, work-related training is more directed towards practical and technical skills in a specific workplace or occupation than school-based further training.

The interrelation between the proportion of young people in general education or further training and youth unemployment is less clear. The Netherlands, with a high proportion of young men and women in further training, had a lower unemployment rate than Italy, where nearly the same proportion are in further training, or Greece, where a higher proportion are in general education.

The relation between youth unemployment and the transition from school or training to work holds true even if one measures youth unemployment as a percentage of total population in the 15- to 24-year-old age group. In Germany, Luxembourg and Belgium less than five per cent of the population of this age were unemployed in 1991, whereas in Ireland, Italy and Spain the relevant figure was higher than ten per cent. A low labour force participation rate among youth does not necessarily imply a low unemployment rate (see OECD, 1993). It seems that in countries with extremely high youth unemployment the transition from school or training to work is influenced by specific labour market structures and institutional arrangements which guarantee high employment stability for people within the employment system combined with high entry barriers for first-job seekers.

To draw a first conclusion, in most EU member states it seems young women are likely to enter the labour market with a level of general education which is as high or even higher than that of young men. Men and women of younger age groups are distributed more similarly across levels of general education in most countries than older age groups. While general education may fall short in providing young people with vocational skills, nevertheless it may instil a range of abilities (such as abstract thinking, problem-solving and interpersonal communication) that have increasing value in the workplace. General education may help to develop these skills, and as more girls acquire these skills the higher proportion of young women in general education may not imply lower labour market opportunities.

However, the relevance of vocational versus general education differs between national labour market systems. If labour markets and their institutional arrangements for job opportunities and earnings are based – as in the German system – predominantly on vocationally-oriented initial training, especially apprenticeships, higher levels of general education will not be sufficient to improve women's employment opportunities.[4]

Segregation in vocational training

EU member states have a broad variety of education and training systems, and thus entry paths into labour markets for young people are quite different. In some countries, like Germany or Denmark, the most common entry path for skilled workers (manual and non-manual) is organised via initial vocational training (in the apprenticeship system or a dual system including firms and schools). In others, such as France, initial vocational training is organised in a school-based system only; while countries such as the Netherlands and Italy have a mixed system of school-based higher secondary vocational training combined with short periods of training in firms. In yet other countries, such as the UK, school-leavers at the lower or higher secondary level do not have initial vocational training but undergo on-the-job training, have part-time jobs which could be combined with part-time colleges, and so on.

Member states vary not only in where vocational training takes place and different forms of vocational training, but also in the degree to which this training is standardised and in how relevant it is for employment opportunities. Two dimensions seem to be crucial for women's employment opportunities: the extent of women's participation in the dominant training system, and the role of training systems in creating or reinforcing the hierarchical and occupational segregation of men and women.

If countries are ranked according to the level of standardisation (the degree of uniformity in the content of vocational training for a particular occupation), Germany and France have the highest standardisation at the

---

[4] Germany is seeing a growing proportion of young women with a completed higher secondary school certificate (*Abitur*) taking up an apprenticeship. In 1989 of all male apprentices 52 per cent had completed the lower secondary school level, 37 per cent the intermediate, and 11 per cent the higher secondary; whereas of all female apprentices 32 per cent had a lower, 48 per cent had an intermediate and 20 per cent a higher secondary school leaving certificate.

national level. In Germany some 330 different occupations, all included in the apprenticeship system, have defined and nationally-agreed contents and curricula[5] which must be followed by both the firm which trains the apprentice and the vocational school which the apprentice attends during apprenticeship. Vocational training outside the apprenticeship system (in Germany only common for nurses, home economics, social and educational occupations, and a few clerical jobs) is regulated and standardised to a similar degree. The same level of uniformity is true in France for vocational training in schools.[6] At the other end of the ranking is totally non-standardised on-the-job training, which is by no means unusual in Ireland and the UK, and which also has some significance for young people leaving school-based vocational training in countries like Italy or France.

Vocational training and labour market structure in Germany

The high degree of standardisation found in Germany (and in other German-speaking countries), and the regulation that completed vocational training leads (via an examination) to the professional status of a skilled employee (either manual or non-manual[7]) in a defined and recognised occupation, have advantages for both employers and employees. Employers know precisely what vocational skills a person with a certified vocational training has, in terms of both quantity and quality. Moreover, beyond information about practical and technical skills, successful completion of an apprenticeship gives a positive signal of the person's ability to work in a 'real' environment, in contrast to purely school-based vocational training.

As the German labour market is firmly anchored in the different constructs of certificated vocational training and broadly-defined occupations, employees with a vocational training certificate have a different status in the labour market to people without vocational training. This can be seen in the regulations relating to unemployment, as labour market agencies may not force the unemployed to take up employment below their certified skills. It is also demonstrated by regulations that only people with recognised vocational training have the right to participate in further training leading to higher certificates like *Meister* or *Techniker*; and finally in the system of wage determination, where the defined wage groups in most collective agreements refer more to skill requirements and completion of vocational training than to job content or tasks.

Inherent in the German vocational training system are strong hierarchical barriers between different levels of skills. It is very difficult for unskilled manual and non-manual workers[8] (people without completed vocational

---

[5] These agreements involve the Federal State, employers' associations and trade unions.

[6] In contrast to this high level of uniformity, workplace-related training after the completion of school-based training is not regulated at all.

[7] The German apprenticeship system is not restricted to crafts-related occupations as in other countries, although it has its roots in the crafts sector. It includes a whole range of clerical, sales and service occupations, and adjusts to changes in occupational structure by developing new curricula or defining new recognised occupations (such as data processing).

[8] It is important to note that having no completed vocational training differs from being employed in an unskilled job (regarded as not requiring any vocational skills). It is very common in Germany for women who have completed vocational training (for example, as hairdressers or salespeople) to be employed as unskilled workers in manufacturing or service sector industries. See Quack *et al.*, 1992.

training either in an apprenticeship or a school, such as nurses and clerical workers[9]) to reach the job status of a skilled person. Even long work experience in a certain occupation seldom substitutes for the lack of a certificate.[10] On the other hand, initial vocational training in the apprenticeship system is the prerequisite for further upward mobility: attending a school of further education like *Technikerschule* or *Ingenieurschule*, or qualifying as a *Meister* (in crafts or manufacturing), is bound to the completion of vocational training in a recognised occupation.

The hierarchical segregation of the German labour market is rather pronounced, with job and career advancement in most cases built upon initial vocational training. The German labour force is divided into three major groups: unskilled, vocationally-trained manual and non-manual workers, and university or higher-level trained professionals. Permeability between these distinct groups (distinct not only in terms of labour market position, but also social status) is very limited, and since the borders between the three skill levels are rather high, upward mobility and employment careers are often limited to a person's initial group categorisation. The German system has adapted to increasing needs for abstract and interpersonal skills by recruiting school-leavers with higher general education into vocational training, and not by opening labour market positions to women (or men) with general education 'only'.

However, the patterns of youth vocational training behaviour are changing slightly, as more (female) school-leavers with a completed higher secondary education (*Abitur*) do not continue with higher education, but enter non-manual apprenticeships first and go on with higher university-based education after completing an apprenticeship. There seems to be a growing overlap between the vocational and university systems for those with a higher secondary education. This pattern is a quite recent development, and points to two problems of the German system: firstly that only those with an *Abitur* have a real choice between different levels of vocational or professional training, and therefore a growing number of young people attend general education; and secondly that the apprenticeship system itself offers only limited career advancement and does not lead to professional positions, for which people have to attend universities and polytechnics.[11]

Since the number of apprenticeships available for school-leavers depends on the development of supply and demand in the market for

---

[9] The alternative to an apprenticeship is to attend a specialised vocational school. This is more common for girls, as these schools offer vocational training in the social and educational occupations, technical/medical assistants, office work, home economics and health care occupations. The completion of a school-based vocational training course counts as recognised vocational skills. One disadvantage of school-based training (and occupations) is the less-developed system of further training leading to career advancement; for other disadvantages see Quack *et al.*, 1992.

[10] The degree of upward flexibility (allowing people without vocational training to participate in further training or employing them in the status of a skilled worker) is clearly connected to the overall development of the labour market and to certain occupations or branches. Once there is a lack of skilled labour, as in the early 1970s, upward mobility is easier than it is today.

[11] Only people with an *Abitur* have the chance to study at universities and polytechnics.

apprenticeship places, empirical studies show that cohorts entering the labour market in years with a general lack of apprenticeship places include a higher proportion of unskilled than cohorts entering the market in years with a sufficient number of places (see Blossfeld, 1989). The impact of this cohort-specific situation at the point of entry to the labour market has been found to be fairly stable, or persistent, over the cohort's employment cycle for both men and women (see Blossfeld, 1992). Additionally, since the proportion of women in the apprenticeship system has risen only very slowly, reaching its peak in recent years with 43 per cent, it comes as no surprise that women are more likely than men to have no vocational training and be unskilled (around 29 per cent of all women and 18 per cent of all men in employment did not have a completed vocational education in 1990).

For the German case it can thus be concluded that one main issue for the promotion of equal opportunities is to increase women's share in the dominant system of vocational training. The lower proportion of women in vocational training will limit women's employment opportunities as long as vocational training is the main entry path into skilled employment and structures the labour market and social status in such a far-reaching way.

However, as can be seen in a series of empirical research studies, the particular occupation in which an apprentice is trained also has an impact on employment opportunities. Equalising formal qualification levels is not sufficient to solve the problem of women's lower employment prospects in terms of access to skilled and well-paid positions. Male and female apprentices in Germany are trained in different occupations, and apprentices registered the highest value on the dissimilarity index of all labour force groups in Germany (see Quack *et al.*, 1992, and the references given in that paper). Analysis of segregation trends within employment shows that the concentration of women in few, often strongly feminised, occupations is particularly evident during initial vocational training. In general, men are more likely to be trained in manufacturing and technical occupations, women in service-related and clerical occupations. Firms' recruitment for apprenticeships is highly gender specific, and only a few clerical and administrative occupations (such as bank clerks) are mixed.

Despite continuous structural change in the German labour market, involving a reduction in manufacturing and an increase in service-related industries, young men with vocational training in manufacturing and technical occupations have better employment prospects (measured by risk of unemployment after completion of vocational training, the rate of unemployment of skilled workers in the occupation, the propensity to stay in the trained occupation, and the proportion of skilled workers with an employment status corresponding to their training compared to average rates) than young women trained in special service jobs like hairdresser, pharmacist's helper or housekeeper (see Quack *et al.*, 1992).

Young women who have completed vocational training are more often employed on jobs classified as unskilled than young men, either because they find employment in a different field (such as medical assistants employed in the chemical industry on assembly lines), or find employment in the same field but at a level below that of their qualifications (such as trained butchers employed as unskilled salespeople, trained cooks as waitresses, administrative clerks as typists, and so on). Only in technical occupations with highly-specialised skills, such as laboratory assistants, and in clerical occupations with specialised skills, such as banking, insurance and foreign trade clerks,[12] is the transition from training to employment less risky for both men and women. Here young women take up employment in positions corresponding to their qualifications as frequently as men. In 1989, 35 per cent of all women who had completed vocational training had been employed as unskilled and semi-skilled workers, compared to 24 per cent of all men with the same qualification level (see Tessaring, 1993).

The continuous structural change towards service-related occupations with specialised qualified fields, and decreasing demand for unskilled manual and non-manual labour in both manufacturing and services, make it even more important to ensure that women get access to administrative, clerical and technical apprenticeships. Their increased level of general education certificates may help in situations when employers recruit apprentices according to their formal educational level; but although this is still sometimes the case, certain firms and sectors in fact exercise 'informal quotas' in favour of men to ensure continued male dominance in the occupation (the banking sector is one example).

Vocational training and labour market structure in other European countries

Only the German-speaking countries, and to a lesser extent Denmark, have the dominant model of apprenticeship as an entry path to the labour market. In France most vocational training takes place in schools, with work-related training acquired on the job. French school-based vocational training has a high degree of standardisation, and school certificates allow a hierarchical structure of job entry qualifications. A similar system (school-based vocational training) is found in the Netherlands, Belgium, Italy and Spain.[13] The UK neither offers a uniform work-related apprenticeship system nor a highly-standardised school-based system as a dominant entry path. It seems that the UK has the highest proportion of school-leavers without any certificated vocational training, and most vocational skills are acquired in on-the-job training or in part-time jobs combined with part-time college work. The Youth Training Scheme is one form of work-related vocational training, but compared to Germany it is not highly standardised in terms of training requirements.

Standardised and certificated systems of school-based training for levels two, three or four of the European classification of vocational training

---

[12] All these occupations are mixed occupations, with at least 40 to 60 per cent women.

[13] In France and the Netherlands, governments have increased training opportunities in the apprenticeship system during recent years.

(skilled manual and non-manual non-academic professions) are developing in all countries, mostly under the quantitative and qualitative control of Ministries for Education (for details see Gordon, 1993). Schools train for a broad range of occupations, classified as clerical/administrative, technical/manual, services (trade/hotel/catering), social/educational and health care. Most schools have highly gender-specific divisions, with young women concentrated in social/educational and service-related training and young men in technical/manual groups. Clerical/administrative training is either male dominated or a mixed subject. The segregation of young people in female- or male-dominated occupations seems to be similar in the different training systems concerned, although there can be variations in the proportion of women in certain occupations (see Rubery and Fagan, 1993).

The gender-specific horizontal segregation of the labour market is also reflected in training systems: the difference is that in work-related training young people gain early experience of employers' recruitment policies, whereas in school-based training this experience comes later; but nevertheless women's distribution by subject is just as much a reflection of employment prospects as it is for men.

As school-based training does not teach practical, workplace-specific or firm-specific skills, young people enter the labour market with a broad occupational skill but without practical experience, which has to be acquired on the job. In contrast to Germany, where every employer expects a person who has completed vocational training to behave and work like a skilled worker (to have not only theoretical knowledge but also practical experience), in countries like France, the Netherlands, Belgium, Italy, Spain and the UK job experience is gained only after initial vocational training via work experience in 'real' jobs.

As the differences between unskilled and skilled workers are not so clearly tied to a vocational certificate, the formal barriers between these workers may be less pronounced in these countries than in Germany, with its rather well-defined skill levels. Comparative studies show that in countries like the UK and France manual and non-manual workers do gain access to skilled jobs via job experience and seniority rules (see Blossfeld, 1992, and the references given there). Labour market entry for first-job seekers seems to be accompanied by higher risks of unemployment, entering part-time employment, and lower employment stability. Italy and Spain have the highest proportion of unemployed school-leavers, as institutional rules guarantee employment stability for those in work but a low rate of new entrants to employment.

Whether school-based training followed by on-the-job training is more favourable for women than the apprenticeship system is difficult to decide. In the latter system the barriers between the hierarchical segments of the labour market are high, so it may be more difficult for women to get access to skilled employment if they are excluded from vocational training when young. The more informal process of on-the-job training, combined with career advancement via job experience, might be more in favour of women if they have the opportunity to participate in these forms of training and accumulate equal job experience. On the other hand, a highly-standardised and recognised skill-based labour market structure has advantages for workers, so women who do have access to vocational training may suffer less downward mobility than in systems in which vocational experience is less defined and advancement is tied more to employment and social status (for example, collective bargaining groups) than individual qualifications.

A recent study by the OECD (1994) links education and training with the structure of labour markets, and concludes:

> in countries where skilled workers are recruited from the external labour market and skills are obtained largely through individual human capital investment, women's increased level of qualification has improved their access to jobs. However, there is some evidence ... that as women have become more qualified the returns to human capital investment beyond initial job access are deteriorating. That is, higher educational attainment does not translate into income improvements at the same rate as 20 years ago...[14] In broad contrast to this external labour-market-oriented system are those where skills are defined by and obtained within the firm. These exclusionary internal labour market systems are most prominent in Japan and Germany, but can be observed in specific industries everywhere. In this type of situation, the relationship between initial qualification, employment access and occupational mobility is quite different. German firms require a general qualification but also a technical qualification which is obtained through an apprenticeship. For instance, people intending to begin a managerial career in banking are likely to take an apprenticeship with a bank following completion of their *Abitur* and then remain with the bank in a part-time position while they complete a university degree... Following this extended educational preparation, during which the job 'candidate' is already tied to the firm, promotion takes place within the firm. Women are disadvantaged in several ways by this system which requires commitment to a particular career path at a young age, with few opportunities for reconsideration on the one hand, and lengthy preparation and personal investment given expected returns on the other. (OECD, 1994: 122.)

Skills and wages

A study by the EU expert network on women's employment on wage determination and sex segregation (Rubery and Fagan, 1994) found that member states use different systems of job classification and grading. In

---

[14] Rubery and Fagan found similar results for some EU member states, especially in professional and public sector jobs: 'New contours of gender segregation are appearing within the professional labour market and, relatively to men, women tend to be better qualified for the jobs they hold. This "overqualification" does not only apply at entry level but over the life cycle as women are less likely to be promoted even within the "feminised" professions.' (Rubery and Fagan, 1993: 120.)

countries such as France and Belgium, educational qualifications are central to all grading structures; in Germany vocational qualifications are central to the division between unskilled, skilled and professional jobs (most jobs are graded according to the vocational level the job-holder needs); whereas in Britain, Ireland and the Netherlands grading is more by job content, and division by qualifications has not been the main source of job and pay hierarchies. These differences reflect different attitudes towards the relationship between skills/qualifications and wages/wage structure in these societies. Both France and Germany have a highly-standardised educational/vocational system, in which different levels of qualifications are seen as legitimate indicators of social status and stratification, and this is also apparent in the job grading system. For both countries, economic position is presumably more influenced by the individual's quantity and quality of education and training than in other countries.

Job grading systems are connected to the hierarchy of jobs and wages in an organisation, but are not the only factor influencing remuneration: seniority and age-related payments, piecework and performance-related pay play a crucial role as well. Payment systems reflect a complex interrelationship between job grading, work organisation, and internal employment and career ladders, and thus include more than a one-dimensional relation.

To illustrate the differences, in France, Belgium and Italy initial entry pay is linked to educational qualification, but thereafter seniority increments take on greater importance than is the case in Germany or the UK. In Italy, for example, movements through job grades depend mainly on seniority, while in Germany and the UK only some promotion with experience or seniority is likely. In Germany such promotion is still tied to the worker's vocational qualification level, so within each skill group some promotion is possibly linked to seniority, but the barriers between the main skill groups remain. Germany, in contrast to Italy, has a labour market and wage structure characterised by occupational grades and skills, whereas in the UK payment structures are more likely to be influenced by a mixture of job-based pay, output or merit-related pay and seniority pay.

This is not the place to examine the impact of different payment systems on women's remuneration and economic position in depth (see Rubery and Fagan, 1994), but to draw some conclusions on the role of skill formation and wages. As Germany has the strongest relation between occupational skills and remuneration,[15] it is important for German women to have access to vocational training and qualifications, and to improve women's access to apprenticeship places and opportunities to acquire a certificated vocational training, even for older age groups. There is little evidence that the German system of skill formation will change dramatically in years to come. As long as the German labour

---

[15] However, in most EU states qualification level and job level are more closely linked in the public service than in the private sector; see Gordon, 1993.

market remains characterised by its emphasis on vocational and occupational skills, it seems necessary to improve women's training situation. It is important to open up opportunities for retraining and further training for women with vocational training in typical female occupations, such as hairdressers, which currently do not offer skilled employment opportunities, or nursing, which does not offer the same promotion opportunities as other skilled non-manual jobs. Moreover, it seems crucial to strengthen the notion of job experience as a basis for the upgrading of women's pay, especially among those employed as unskilled and semi-skilled workers in manual and clerical jobs. Thus in Germany women's higher participation in general education will not be sufficient to improve their labour market situation.

The situation may be different in France, Belgium, Italy and Spain, particularly as regards entry into the public sector. As educational levels are important for the entry level and job grade in these countries, women's higher educational levels, combined with the use of external recruitment procedures, have opened new opportunities in skilled clerical, administrative and professional jobs. It is thus important here to secure women's participation in general and higher education. As seniority pay has greater relevance in these countries, women with stable employment patterns are promoted within seniority schemes, and therefore employment stability combined with lowering withdrawal rates for women with children are important issues.

In the UK there seems to be a relatively weak relationship between educational or vocational qualifications and labour market position. Employers apparently have much greater flexibility to determine the relative pay and grade of jobs than in other countries. Formal training and educational requirements are not the dominant legitimating factor in employment and pay differentials. Nevertheless, it would be wrong to draw the conclusion that participation in education and training has less importance for women in the UK than elsewhere. But the indications are that increasing women's participation in training and education is only one factor, and not necessarily sufficiently important to secure equal opportunities.

Some final remarks

The main emphasis of this chapter has been on formal training and education, leaving aside 'other' processes of skill formation such as socialisation in families (of different social status), the development of different societal attitudes concerning women's roles, and skills associated with 'non-market' work such as affection, patience in dealing with people, caring as emotional labour, and so on. It is clear that most of these are important parts of work-related skills, but are undervalued or used without being paid because they do not reflect formal training. These skills are used heavily, especially in service-sector occupations, but do not translate into higher wages unless they are combined with formal credentials. To aid women's position in the labour market, a positive step would be to move towards a more complex notion of skills, including a revaluation of those learned on the job or in formal training as well as those acquired elsewhere.

As regards equal opportunity policy more generally, concentration on vocational training initiatives is a necessary but not sufficient approach. As this comparison shows, skill formation processes and their interrelation to the labour market are quite different across EU member states, and equal opportunities policies must be embedded in the specific national societal and institutional context if they are to be effective. The first step towards developing a new concept of equal opportunities in training and broader skill formation would be to improve the statistical basis. This could help raise awareness of the effect gender is having on the 'allocation of opportunities' (Rees, 1994). The second step is then to examine national education and training systems with respect to the reinforcement of patterns of gender segregation, and to analyse gender-specific outcomes more carefully. 'Failure to address this issue is in effect operating a system of passive discrimination' (Rees, 1994, 8).

References

Blossfeld, H.-P. (1989). *Kohorten differenzierung und Karrier Prozess – Eine Längsschnittstudie über die Veränderung der Bildungs – und Berufschancen im Lebenslauf*. Frankfurt/New York.

Blossfeld, H.-P. (1992). 'Unterschiedliche Systeme der Berufsausbildung und Anpassung an Strukturveränderungen im Internationalen Vergleich' in Sadowski, D. and Timmesfeld, F. (eds.) *Ökonomie und Politik Beruflicher Bildung – Europäische Entwicklungen. Schriften des Vereins für Socialpolitik*. NF 213. Berlin.

Büchtemann, C., Schupp, J. and Soloff, D. (1993). 'Übergänge von der Schule in den Beruf – Deutschland und USA im Vergleich' in *Mitteilungen aus der Arbeitsmarkt und Berufsforschung*, Heft 4.

Eurostat (1993a). *Unemployed Women in the EC*. Statistical Facts, Theme 3 (population and social conditions), Series D (studies and analyses). Luxembourg.

Eurostat (1993b). *Schnellberichte Bevölkerung und Soziale Bedingungen*. 9.

Gordon, J. (1993). *Systeme und Verfahren der Zertifizierung von Qualifikationen in der Europäischen Gemeinschaft*. Berlin: CEDEFOP.

OECD (1993). *Education at a Glance – OECD Indicators*. Paris: Organisation for Economic Co-operation and Development.

OECD (1994). *Women and Structural Change – New Perspectives*. Paris: Organisation for Economic Co-operation and Development.

Quack, S., Maier, F. and Schuldt, C. (1992). *Occupational Segregation in the FRG and the Former GDR 1980–89*. Report for the European Commission, DGV, Equal Opportunities Unit, Berlin. Manchester: UMIST.

Rees, T. (1994). *Equal Opportunities for Women and Men – Equality in Education and Training Policies*. Report to the European Commission's Employment Task Force (DGV), Brussels.

Rubery, J. and Fagan, C. (1993). 'Occupational segregation of women and men in the European Community' in *Social Europe*, supplement 3/93.

Rubery, J. and Fagan, C. (1994). *Wage Determination and Sex Segregation in Employment in the European Community*. V/408/94 – EN, European Commission, DGV (Employment, Industrial Relations and Social Affairs), Equal Opportunities Unit.

Sellin, B. (1994). *Situation und Trends: Angebot und Nachfrage von Fachkräften*. Berlin: CEDEFOP.

Tessaring, M. (1993). 'Das duale System der Berufsausbildung in Deutschland: Attraktivität und Beschäftigungsperspektiven' in *Mitteilungen aus der Arbeitsmarkt und Berufsforschung*, Heft 2.

Part IV

Pay Structures, Regulations and the Consequences of Employment Segregation

CHAPTER 10 # Gender Segregation and Male/Female Wage Differences

Neil Millward and Stephen Woodland

> Gender segregation ... has proved to be one of the most profound
> dimensions of labour market inequality. (Scott, 1994b: 1.)

The gap between men's and women's pay at the aggregate level is well
known and extensively researched. Much of the gap has been attributed to
occupational segregation, the disproportionate representation of women
in 'women's jobs' and of men in 'men's jobs', plus the generally lower pay
of the former. Factors leading to lower pay for 'women's jobs' include the
relative abundance of the attributes and competencies required for those
jobs (supply), and the level of employers' demand for them. But social
forces and institutions modify the interplay of supply and demand in ways
which generally result in men having greater access to better-paid jobs, in
some cases effectively excluding women from them. Overt discrimination
in selection and promotion is only part of this: other, more subtle,
mechanisms are at work.

Segregation at occupational level has been extensively studied through
nationally-representative datasets based upon individual or household
censuses and surveys (Hakim, 1992). What has not been studied with
anywhere near the same degree of interest is gender segregation at the
level of the workplace or employer. The small literature on this is largely
American (Groshen, 1991; Carrington and Troske, 1993). Indeed, the
work reported here and in Millward (1995) is probably the first attempt to
study gender segregation at workplace or employer level through the
medium of a nationally-representative sample survey of appropriate
units.[1]

It is quite possible that segregation between and within workplaces
reinforces, or perhaps even overwhelms, occupational segregation at the
national or industry level. Jobs performed by both men and women at the
aggregate level may be segregated at workplace level, with some
workplaces employing mostly or only women for them, while others use
mainly or only men. The effects of this segregation may be reinforced by
the presence at the same workplace of other jobs which are themselves
highly gender concentrated. For example, semi-skilled assembly workers
may be predominantly male in a workplace with mostly male unskilled and
skilled workers, but in a workplace with mostly women in other
occupations the semi-skilled workers may be all or mostly women. This
might have the effect of depressing women's pay in the female-dominated
workplace and enhancing men's pay in a male-dominated workplace, even
for ostensibly similar job attributes and levels of skill.

---

[1] Segregation within workplaces has, however, been examined using perceptual questions addressed to
individual employees about their place of work (Martin and Roberts, 1984).

It may thus be reasonable to conceive of a penalty attached to the pay of women, with two components: one arising from the fact of being employed in a predominantly female workplace; and one from working in a predominantly female occupational group within their workplace. Conversely a premium could be attached to the pay of men arising from working in predominantly male workplaces and occupational groups. This chapter concerns the size and nature of these various components of the inter-establishment gender wage gap.

Gender concentration, gender segregation and the wages gap

Gender segregation is usually conceptualised in terms of occupations or industries. It is generally measured by comparing the concentrations of men and women in different occupations or industries, and sometimes referred to as the 'sex ratio'. A less familiar form of segregation is at the level of the establishment[2] or place of work, measured by comparing the concentration of, say, females within an establishment across the whole range of establishments.[3] A high level of inter-establishment segregation in populations occurs where many establishments have a high concentration of women and many others have a high concentration of men. Segregation would be low if there are only a few establishments with a high level of male or female concentration.

Segregation can be defined using two or more dimensions: the usual example is that of occupations within industries. The two dimensions used in this chapter are establishments and occupations. Thus the second measure of segregation concerns occupational groups within establishments, and captures differences in gender concentration for the same occupational group across establishments.

Gender wage differences

Rubery's wide-ranging review of the literature on gender wage differences (1992) highlights the degree to which the effects of segregation on the male/female wage gap have been overlooked by economists, who generally prefer to attribute the gap to differences in productivity between the sexes. Productivity differences are rarely measured directly, but are proxied by, for example, differences in human capital (Becker, 1957), job tenure and experience, different work preferences (Polachek, 1981), differences in physical capabilities (Becker, 1985), and women's family role (Fuchs, 1989). These explanations are not uncontested and do not fully account for the male/female wage gap (see Humphries, this volume, Chapter 3).

An alternative explanation is gender segregation: men and women are segregated into different occupations, establishments and industries, with women disproportionately represented in those that are low paying. The

---

[2] An 'establishment' means the operations of a single employer at a single site or address. See Millward, 1993, for further discussion.

[3] An alternative, subjective measure has been used in a number of recent studies based upon surveys of individuals by asking respondents whether they work wholly or mainly with members of the same sex (Martin and Roberts, 1984; Scott, 1994b).

essential feature of segregation is that males and females do not compete in the same labour market; their wages, as a result, are subject to different forces of supply and demand and different institutional forces. On the demand side, the lower wages of females arise from employers, and perhaps society at large, placing a lower value on the services of women than on those of men. On the supply side, historical forces may restrict the number of entry positions into the workforce available to females, thus resulting in overcrowding in 'female' jobs. The institutionalisation of these processes forms a key ingredient of labour market segmentation.

Bergmann (1986, 1989) emphasises the role of discriminatory factors that cause women to have limited employment opportunities, arguing that women have their own 'labour-market turf', which is narrowly defined relative to that available for men. This leads to overcrowding in traditional female occupations, industries and, to an extent, establishments, with the effect of lowering women's productivity and wages in these units.

Fuchs (1989) dismisses the segregation argument on the grounds that competitive forces will ensure that companies minimise costs. If labour productivity is the same between males and females, a company hiring females at a lower wage will make higher profits relative to a company hiring males at a higher wage. Competition will force the company with a high concentration of males out of business. This argument assumes that competitive forces always prevail over social attitudes towards the valuation of women's work, an argument that is ill at ease even with everyday observation.

An elaboration of the gender segregation explanation of women's relatively low pay is contained within labour market segmentation theory (Doeringer and Piore, 1971; Wilkinson, 1981). In its early formulation this posited a dualist labour market divided into a low-paid, low-productivity, low-skilled and largely female sector, and a separate high-paid male sector. Subsequent formulations abandoned crude dualism for a more complex concept of a spectrum of labour market segments. More recently, Horrell *et al.* (1989) have attributed the existence of segmented labour markets to the historical process of labour market discrimination. Tradition determines where females work, and it does not necessarily follow that this will be in low-productivity or low-skill occupations, or in establishments with low profitability. This more recent strand of labour market segmentation theory implies that female concentration within workplaces will depress the pay levels of both women and men.

Data source and previous analyses

To permit a thorough analysis of the extent of different types of gender segregation in employment and their effects upon male/female wage differences, the ideal dataset would contain a wide range of information on the characteristics of individuals, the jobs they perform, and the establishments and organisations in which they work. Most research examining the gender wage gap has used individual-level data, with almost no information on the employing unit, so the extent of inter-establishment segregation cannot be addressed; nor can the effect upon wages of this type of segregation be assessed. By contrast, the data used here is largely concerned with employing units. While lacking the individual-level measures of the ideal dataset, it allows a statistical estimate of the effects of establishment-level gender segregation on the male/female wage gap.

Data source

The 1990 Workplace Industrial Relations Survey (WIRS3) is a nationally-representative sample survey of just over 2,000 establishments in Britain. The dataset covers a broad range of industries, types of employer and establishment sizes. This is a major advantage compared with the limited employer-based datasets used by Groshen (1991) and Carrington and Troske (1993) to examine gender segregation in the USA: the former was restricted to five narrowly-defined industries; the latter covered only a sub-set of small businesses with less than 100 employees. Besides its comprehensive industry coverage, the WIRS dataset has a wealth of information about various workplace characteristics: employment, earnings, unionisation, pay-setting procedures, organisational structure, and so on. The data is of high quality and very representative, as illustrated by the sample response rate of 83 per cent. An overview of the data is given in the survey sourcebook (Millward *et al.*, 1992), which also contains extensive detail of the survey's design and conduct.

Employment data in WIRS is disaggregated into eight broad occupational groups: three manual groups of unskilled, semi-skilled and skilled; and five non-manual groups of clerical, administrative and secretarial (hereafter referred to as 'clerical'), supervisors and foremen, junior technical and professional employees, senior technical and professional employees, and middle and senior management. Clearly these broad groups contain many different occupations across the population of workplaces. However, since many occupations are highly industry-specific, and industry is finely coded in WIRS, the eight categories capture much of the occupational diversity within establishments. To the extent that this is so, the crudeness of the categories is less of a disadvantage than might first appear.

The WIRS pay levels data consists of managers' reports of the gross weekly earnings of the typical (median) employee for five of the eight occupational groups (unskilled, semi-skilled, skilled, clerical and supervisors). Groups with less than five employees were excluded from the question. Because earnings might differ substantially for men and women (owing to different hours worked or other reasons) the question focused on whichever sex was the majority in the group. Thus for each occupational group in a given establishment there is earnings data for either men or women, but not for both.

Earnings data was collected in banded form. Respondents[4] were asked which of a set of ranges of gross earnings displayed on a card applied to the typical (median) employee in the occupational group. The ranges were in increments of £1,000 per year between £5,000 and £10,000 per year gross earnings, and increments of £2,000 per year towards the upper and lower ends of the distribution.

No information was obtained about the characteristics of individual workers, nor are there any summary measures of their characteristics other than gender. For example, there is no data on the average level of education, job experience or age of the workforce. But the premium or penalty associated with working in a male- or female-dominated establishment and in a male- or female-dominated occupation can be estimated within an establishment. Admittedly, there is no data to control for variations across establishments in the age and experience of the workforce – or in other characteristics that might affect the relative productivity of males and females. But this is no more serious a problem than the lack of controls for workplace and employer characteristics in estimating the gender wage gap from individual-level data.

Previous uses of the WIRS wages data

The WIRS wages data has formed a central interest of the surveys since the series began. The initial report on the 1980 survey devoted more than half a chapter to describing cross-tabulations of data on pay levels for the four occupational groups covered, and concluded, *inter alia*, thus:

> The second major source of variation in the pay of manual workers... was the composition of the workforce as reflected in the proportions of manual workers who were women. The higher was the female proportion of the manual workforce the lower was the level of pay for semi-skilled and skilled workers. The trend was marked and consistent. In cases where all manual workers were women, pay levels were only just over half of those in cases where hardly any or no manual workers were women. (Daniel and Millward, 1983: 268.)

Subsequent multi-variate statistical analysis of this data focused on the impact of trade union bargaining upon pay levels: the size of the 'union wage premium' (Blanchflower, 1984). The gender dimension was given little attention; indeed, the measure of female concentration mentioned in the 1983 quotation was included in the regressions only as a proxy for low labour quality:

> Clearly one would expect that a higher quality workforce would result in higher gross weekly pay of the 'typical' employee. WIRS contains a number of variables that can be used as proxies for the quality of the labour force at the workplace... The ratio of female

---

[4] The respondents referred to here, and when survey responses are used throughout this chapter, are the main management respondents in WIRS – generally the senior manager responsible for personnel or employee relations matters at the sampled establishment.

manual workers to all manual workers (FEMANE) is also expected to have a negative coefficient. Female manual workers tend to have relatively low human capital accumulation in anticipation of lower labour force participation; they also tend to be concentrated in smaller, low-paying establishments, which tend to operate in labour-intensive, low-skill industries. Thus, a high proportion of female manual workers may indicate a low quality labour force.

A similar argument can also be applied to the percentage of the labour force of Asian, African, West Indian or similar origin (BLACK) which is included to pick up the effects of discrimination: the higher the proportion of black workers, the lower the (log) wage is expected to be. (Blanchflower, 1984: 319, emphasis added.)

It is difficult to understand why Blanchflower cast female concentration in the role of a proxy measure of low labour quality, rather than 'to pick up the effects of discrimination', as he did with ethnic minority concentration. But the spirit of this approach has been continued by him and others in analysing the WIRS wage levels data in the more recent surveys. These surveys have included additional questions about the pay of the 'typical' worker in an occupational group, notably whether the typical worker was male or female. In their widely-quoted analysis of manual workers' pay in the 1984 WIRS, Blanchflower *et al.* (1990) used this question to include a majority-male dummy variable; they excluded any further measures of gender concentration in the equations they reported. Their only comment on gender was:

The factors listed under 'other variables' are conventional controls and are consistent with established knowledge about cross-section wage equations. Establishments with part-time workers and female workers pay less, for example... (Blanchflower *et al.*, 1990: 152)

Similarly, Blanchflower and Oswald (1990: 359) reported a parallel analysis of white-collar workers' pay and merely referred to their theoretical starting point as assuming that 'wage rates depend upon [workforce] composition effects'.

Other analysts have used additional variables relating to the gender composition of the workforce, but with little discussion of their choice and no rationale for their inclusion other than as a 'control' (Stewart, 1987, 1990, 1991, 1994; Machin *et al.*, 1992; Metcalf and Stewart, 1992).

In one respect those studies form the starting point for this chapter, since they have established or confirmed the importance of a number of workplace characteristics which can be initially adopted as controls in an investigation of the inter-establishment gender wage gap. The type of trade union organisation and collective bargaining structure, workplace size, sector and ownership, external labour market conditions; these and many others have been shown to affect pay levels. But the notion that gender concentration should be left to one side as a mere 'control' is rejected.

Indeed, from an equal opportunities point of view the most striking feature of the WIRS-based studies of pay determination has been their neglect of their own results relating to gender. All of the more recent studies have estimated wage equations jointly for majority-male and majority-female observations, with a dummy variable indicating that the observation was for a majority-male case. The size of the majority-male coefficient has never been commented on. Moreover, in studies where establishment-level female concentration has been included as a 'control variable' its size and significance have never been discussed. In Stewart's most recent analysis (1994) he reports coefficients on the majority-male variable ranging from 0.29 for unskilled workers to 0.13 for semi-skilled workers in non-union establishments. For the establishment-level female concentration control the range is from minus 0.48 for semi-skilled manuals to minus 0.16 for unskilled manuals in the union sector. In all these studies the majority-male coefficient is substantially greater than the premium associated with working in an establishment with recognised trade unions.

If the Stewart (1994) model is re-estimated with the union and non-union establishments pooled, it is possible to compare the size of the coefficients on union recognition and on the occupation group being majority-male to see the relative importance of the two variables in explaining the variation in earnings across establishments. The gender coefficient is in all cases larger than the union coefficient, with the difference ranging from 0.23 for skilled manuals to 0.12 for supervisors. This is *prima-facie* evidence that the role of gender segregation in male/female wage differences is worthy of investigation.

Estimates of gender concentration and segregation using WIRS

Before addressing the question of the gender wage gap it is helpful to study the picture of inter-establishment gender segregation given by WIRS. Figure 10.1 gives the distribution of female concentration across establishments for all employees, showing high levels of gender concentration for both sexes and a high level of segregation between establishments. This is clearly seen by comparing the actual distribution of establishments with the standard normal curve, which represents approximately what would be expected if there were no 'crowding' by gender.

It is also interesting to note that high concentration is much more common for males than for females, despite the two sexes having almost equal shares of employment.[5] Approximately 34 per cent of males work in establishments where they represent at least 75 per cent of the workforce. This contrasts with approximately 23 per cent of females working in establishments where they represent at least 75 per cent of the workforce.[6] The extent to which the actual distribution differs from the 'expected'

---

[5] The overall establishment female proportion is 44 per cent.

[6] In studies using perceptual measures of workplace gender concentration it is also reported that more employees work in male-dominated than in female-dominated workplaces (Scott, 1994a)

Figure 10.1 Distribution of inter-establishment female concentration

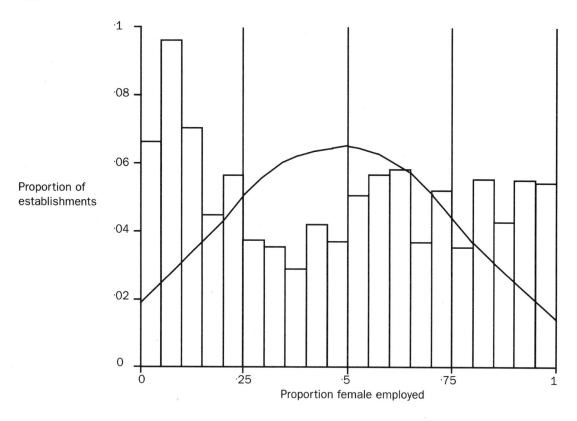

Source: WIRS, 1990

normal distribution is a measure of the degree of gender segregation across establishments. The difference in this case is large and highly significant.

Millward (1995) disaggregates the degree of concentration by type of establishment, finding that the establishments most likely to have a high female concentration are:

- small workplaces, especially those with 25–49 employees (those with less than 25 are excluded from the sample);
- trusts and self-proprietorships in the private sector;
- providing local and central government services;
- where labour costs make up over 50 per cent of total costs;
- where the workplace provides a local rather than a regional or national service;
- where managers reported a relatively high labour productivity compared with their competitors;
- where managers reported very good relations with the workforce generally;
- where the local male unemployment rate was high.

Establishments with a high male concentration are characterised as:

- small enterprises (less than 100 employees) in the private sector;
- very large enterprises (100,000 employees or more), notably state-owned;
- workplaces serving monopolistic product markets;
- situated in an area of high unemployment.

The more detailed employment data by occupational group within establishments can be used to give a finer picture of gender segregation across the economy (Millward and Woodland, 1994). For each of the eight occupational groups the distributions are highly skewed, reflecting the tendency for men to work with men and women to work with women within the same broad occupational group. For all occupational groups the two distributions diverge to the extent that it cannot be said employers' hiring practices approximate a random process with respect to gender.

In summary, inter-establishment gender segregation is widespread among British workplaces, in terms of both the workforce as a whole and specific occupational groups. Segmentation theory implies that this segregation would play an important part in explaining the differences between male and female earnings.

Estimates of male/female wage differences across establishments

In estimating the wage penalty associated with working in establishments and occupational groups with high female concentration, a number of decisions concerning the treatment of the dependent variable and the method of estimation must be made.

Modelling men's and women's pay jointly or separately

All previous known analyses of the WIRS pay data have modelled the pay of men and women jointly, with a dummy variable identifying the majority-male cases when these were recorded. One possible approach to studying the gender pay gap would be to concentrate on the coefficient of this dummy variable and see how it varied among differently-specified wage equations. Alternatively, men's and women's pay could be modelled separately. This second approach has been adopted, as it has the great advantage of avoiding the implicit assumption that the determinants of pay are the same for both sexes. Just as Stewart and others have modelled pay separately in union and non-union establishments, so pay in male-dominated and female-dominated occupational groups within establishments can be modelled.

Defining the dependent variable

Ideally, any estimates of gender differences in pay should focus on pay rates rather than earnings, primarily because of differences in the hours worked by men and women. The WIRS pay data refers to weekly earnings, and there is insufficient information to convert these into an hourly rate of pay. Moreover, the data is banded, which introduces a number of further considerations. Mid-points could be assigned to the bands of weekly pay (as many earlier analysts have done) and divided by hours worked to proxy an hourly earnings rate. An adjustment could also be made for overtime hours at premium rates by assuming a constant overtime premium. Both these manipulations involve making assumptions and some information is lost.

It is preferable to use Stewart's maximum likelihood method for grouped dependent variables on the log of banded weekly earnings data (Stewart 1983), and then add controls for hours of work. Differences in the incidence of overtime hours (and hence overtime pay) are controlled for by including a dummy variable for paid overtime hours. It is very important to include this control when calculating the difference between male and female pay, because women rarely work paid overtime whereas men often do so. As an example, in 49 per cent of establishments where the majority of unskilled workers were male, the typical male worker received overtime pay; the comparable proportion where the majority were female was 12 per cent.

Similarly, differences in standard (non-paid-overtime) hours are controlled for, so the greater incidence of part-time and shorter hours worked by women does not confound comparisons. This has not been the usual practice: most previous analysts have proxied the effect of shorter hours by using the proportion of the establishment's workforce working part-time.[7] For the 1980 WIRS this was justifiable, since no data on hours worked was collected. But in more recent surveys, where total hours and paid overtime hours were recorded, there seems no strong argument for ignoring the data and using the part-time proportion as a crude proxy.

Adding controls to account for additional elements of pay besides the hourly rate

Two further controls attempt to allow for the possibility that differences in earnings (as measured) are not equal to differences in wage rates, which are the objectives of these estimates. The first captures the existence of payment by results, either on an individual or group basis. It is measured separately for each occupational group and entered as a dummy variable. The second recognises the possibility that earnings may include a premium for working shifts. The survey did not record this separately for each occupational group, but simply contains an establishment-level variable denoting that there was some shift working. The expectation is that both the payment-by-results and the shift-working dummy variables will have small positive coefficients.

A further possibility considered was the inclusion of dummy variables indicating the presence of profit-related pay or establishment-wide bonuses. It was judged unlikely, however, that such payments would have been included in reported earnings figures, since they tend to be infrequent.

---

[7] 'The percentage of the workforce at the establishment that work part-time (PARTE) is a factor that is likely to affect the gross pay of a typical employee. As there is no information on the number of hours worked at the plant, this variable is likely to proxy lower average hours per employee and is thus expected to have a negative coefficient.' (Blanchflower, 1984: 319.)

Improving the controls for the role of unions and employers in bargaining

A general, and largely unacknowledged, difficulty in analysing the WIRS pay data is that the dependent variable refers to an occupational group, whereas many of the explanatory variables refer to the establishment as a whole or to a larger sub-unit than the occupational group. This is the case with union recognition. The survey records whether there are recognised trade unions covering manual or non-manual workers, or both; but does not record specifically whether, for example, unskilled manual workers or supervisors have their pay determined by collective bargaining. The conventional solution has been to assume implicitly that the recognition of manual unions at the establishment implies all three groups of manual workers (unskilled, semi-skilled and skilled) are covered by collective bargaining.

Since the survey also contains information on the proportion of manual/non-manual workers covered by collective bargaining, experiments could be conducted with appropriate explanatory variables. These appeared to perform no better than the conventional manual (or non-manual) recognition dummy variable (Millward and Woodland, 1994). The equations reported here revert to this specification, plus the additional dummy variable for the presence of a closed shop or strong management recommendation to employees to join a union, as used by Stewart (1994).

A second modification concerns the structure of bargaining. Where pay is bargained with trade unions, negotiations may be on either a single or a multi-employer basis. A traditional rationale for multi-employer bargaining is that it 'takes wages out of competition' by introducing some degree of uniformity within an industry, either nationally or regionally. The effect of multi-employer bargaining might be to raise or lower wages from what individual employers would otherwise negotiate. However, since multi-employer bargaining has suffered a widespread collapse in Britain in recent decades, largely because some large or dominant firms have left the joint arrangements in order to pay higher wages, the remaining multi-employer arrangements can be expected to result in lower pay *ceteris paribus*. Appropriate control variables were thus included to indicate whether multi-employer bargaining was the most important level of negotiations affecting the most recent settlement for the relevant group of workers.[8] This is regarded as a more appropriate and precise indicator of bargaining structure than affiliation to an employers' association, used by some previous analysts.

Results on gender concentration

The empirical results on the effects of female concentration on earnings are summarised in Tables 10.2 and 10.3, while the full equations appear in Tables 10.4 and 10.5.[9]

---

[8] In fact, the question used relates to the largest manual or non-manual negotiating unit, if there was more than one. The most common arrangement was a single unit.

[9] Usual practice was followed by estimating unweighted equations and including variables that control for disproportionate sampling.

Table 10.2 Earnings premiums by establishment female concentration

	Occupational group			
	Unskilled	Semi-skilled	Clerical	Supervisors
Cases where majority of occupational group is female				
Establishment female proportion				
Base category: 0–19 per cent female concentration in establishment				
20–29 per cent	0.072	–	- 0.034	–
30–39 per cent	0.058	- 0.037	0.016	- 0.417*
40–59 per cent	0.044	- 0.286†	- 0.016	- 0.413*
60–100 per cent	0.007	- 0.305‡	- 0.063†	- 0.493†
Number of establishments	*413*	*163*	*1026*	*203*
Cases where majority of occupational group is male				
Establishment female proportion				
Base category: 0–19 per cent female concentration in establishment				
20–29 per cent	- 0.060†	- 0.070‡	0.043	- 0.089‡
30–39 per cent	- 0.104‡	- 0.106‡	- 0.035	- 0.060*
40–59 per cent	- 0.171†	- 0.154‡	- 0.186†	- 0.103‡
60–100 per cent	- 0.241‡	- 0.181‡*	- 0.167	- 0.189‡
Number of establishments	*517*	*598*	*127*	*580*

Source: 1990 WIRS

Notes

1 For full equation see Tables 10.4 and 10.5.

2 ‡ significant at one per cent, † significant at five per cent and * significant at ten per cent

Table 10.2 gives the results for concentration at the establishment level.[10] The cells show the proportionate difference in earnings between an establishment having a specified female proportion and an establishment in the base category (one with a female concentration of less than 20 per cent). The coefficients are to be compared to a base value of one, so a coefficient of 0.05 represents a five per cent premium; a coefficient of minus 0.05 represents a penalty of five per cent compared to the base category. In the top panel of Table 10.2, for example, unskilled female employees in an establishment with an overall female concentration between 20 and 29 per cent have earnings that are approximately 7.2 per cent more than female unskilled employees in an establishment in the base category (less than 20 per cent female). This result is not statistically significant.

---

[10] In Tables 10.2 and 10.3 there is no report on an equation for skilled manuals because there were too few establishments where the majority of skilled manuals were female.

Turning generally to the cases where the majority of the occupational group was female (top panel of Table 10.2), the results for semi-skilled manuals and supervisors are most in line with expectations. If the effect of female concentration is as predicted by segregation theory, the size of the coefficient was expected to become progressively more negative as the female proportion in the establishment increases. The results are mixed. For both unskilled manuals and clericals there is no significant variation across the categories, and the signs are not always as predicted. Both semi-skilled manuals and supervisors, however, do show the predicted pattern. As the female proportion in the establishment increases, the earnings of these two groups decrease relative to the base category. Where the establishment's workforce is 60 per cent or more female, semi-skilled workers' pay is approximately 31 per cent lower than in an establishment with at least 80 per cent males.

The majority-male equations (lower panel of Table 10.2) are more consistently in line with segregation theory. As establishment-level female concentration increases, male earnings fall progressively. The pattern is clear for all occupational groups. For example, the results for unskilled manuals show that as the establishment's female proportion rises through the bands indicated, the 'establishment female wage penalty' moves from six to ten to 17 and finally 24 per cent. The results for semi-skilled manuals are similarly patterned. Those for clericals and supervisors are less clearly progressive with increasing female concentration, but the general trend is as expected: higher levels of female concentration are associated with lower wages. Interestingly, and in contrast to results reported by Sorensen (1986), there was no tendency for the gender concentration effect to diminish or disappear near the upper quartile of female concentration.

Turning to the depressing effect on earnings of female concentration within occupational groups, the separate majority-male and majority-female equations have different base categories and only half the full range of female concentration is covered in each set of equations. In the top half of Table 10.3, covering majority-male cases, the base category is cases where there are no females in the group, and the bands of female concentration moving down the table represent increasing proportions of females up to 50 per cent. The expectation was that as this proportion increases the (male) wage will fall, as evidenced by increasingly negative coefficients. This expected pattern is apparent in the equation for supervisors, and is approximated in the case of semi-skilled manual workers. For clericals and unskilled there is no clear evidence of a progressive relationship; nevertheless, nearly all the coefficients have the expected sign, and some are significant.

The lower panel of Table 10.3 shows the results for cases where the majority of the group is female. The base category for comparisons here is cases where all employees in the group are female. Cases at the top of the panel are those with the highest proportion of males (between 41 and 50 per cent), which would be expected to have higher wages than the base

Table 10.3 Earnings premiums by occupation female concentration

	Occupational group			
	Unskilled	Semi-skilled	Clerical	Supervisors
Cases where majority of occupational group is male				
Occupation female proportion				
Base category: 0 per cent female in occupation group				
1–9 per cent	- 0.039	- 0.027	0.067	- 0.007
10–19 per cent	- 0.054*	- 0.036	- 0.169*	- 0.017
20–29 per cent	0.020	- 0.038	- 0.111	- 0.056*
30–39 per cent	- 0.003	- 0.145‡	- 0.106	- 0.082†
40–50 per cent	0.016	- 0.087†	- 0.060	- 0.113‡
Number of establishments	*517*	*598*	*127*	*580*
Cases where majority of occupational group is female				
Occupation female proportion				
50–59 per cent	- 0.061	0.153‡	- 0.044*	0.071
60–69 per cent	- 0.013	0.234†	0.023	0.051
70–79 per cent	- 0.067	0.174‡	0.019	0.089
80–89 per cent	- 0.105‡	0.163‡	- 0.007	0.084
90–99 per cent	- 0.045	0.106†	- 0.004	0.032
Base group: 100 per cent female concentration in occupational group				
Number of establishments	*413*	*163*	*1026*	*203*

Source: 1990 WIRS

Notes

1 For full equation see Tables 10.4 and 10.5.

2 ‡ significant at one per cent, † significant at five per cent and * significant at ten per cent

category. The predicted pattern is therefore one of positive coefficients at the top of the panel, decreasing progressively as the base group of 100 per cent females is approached.

The semi-skilled manual results come very close to exhibiting this expected pattern, and all the positive coefficients are statistically significant. For the other three groups there is no evidence of a gender concentration effect at the level of the occupational group. Very few of the coefficients are significant, and these do not have the predicted sign.

Overall the results in Table 10.3, comparing the same occupational group across the sample of establishments, provide quite strong evidence that increasing female concentration lowers the pay of men, but only weak evidence that increasing female concentration lowers the pay of women.

Other findings

Turning now from the effects of female concentration to other factors affecting earnings levels, a number of results are worthy of comment. Firstly, the estimation of separate majority-male and majority-female equations is amply justified. This is most strongly indicated by the different coefficients on the variables capturing the effects of trade union representation and bargaining structure, shown in Tables 10.4 and 10.5. There appear to be important differences in the effects of unions on pay between male- and female-dominated occupational groups.

Indeed, these results point to the conclusion that collective bargaining only has a beneficial effect upon the pay of male-dominated groups of workers. There are no significant positive coefficients on union recognition in the majority-female cases in Table 10.5; on the contrary, some are significant negatives. Only two of the five majority-male equations in Table 10.5 have significant positive coefficients on union recognition. Taken as a whole, the results do not confirm the existence of a generalised 'union wage premium' in Britain in 1990.

On the other hand the results do confirm the continuance of a wage premium in workplaces with strong union organisation, as indicated by a closed shop or strong management encouragement of union membership. But such a premium is confined entirely to male-dominated occupational groups; none of the majority-female equations had significant coefficients on this variable.

The third facet of collective bargaining structure included in these equations, the level of bargaining, also showed important differences between male- and female-dominated groups. For majority-male cases four out of five equations showed significant negative coefficients on the dummy variable, indicating multi-employer bargaining. None of the majority-female equations had significant coefficients on this variable. Broadly speaking, it appears that bargaining structure impacts on men's pay but not women's.

The control for hours worked – included to simulate the effect of converting the dependent variable, weekly earnings, into hourly earnings – naturally had strongly significant positive coefficients in all equations. Paid overtime had the expected effect in three of the five majority-male equations, but not in any of the majority-female equations. Again, this supports the separate estimation for the two gender groups.

Contrary to expectations, there was no evidence of shift work raising pay levels. Indeed, the majority of coefficients on this variable were negative, although none was significant. Similar results are reported by Sloane (1994). The WIRS variable for shift work refers only to the presence of shift work for any employees and is certainly not targeted at the

Table 10.4 Earnings equations – males by broad occupational group

	Occupational group				
	Unskilled	Semi-skilled	Skilled	Clerical	Supervisors
Manual proportion	- 0.116†	- 0.010*	- 0.112‡	- 0.177*	- 0.171
Skilled proportion	- 0.092	- 0.159‡	- 0.040	- 0.105	0.024
Single site	0.014	0.000	0.026	0.188‡	0.090
Establishment has shift work	- 0.010	0.023	0.013	- 0.002	- 0.010
Payment by results	0.017	- 0.001	- 0.008	0.100‡	0.039*
Foreign-owned	0.053	- 0.002	0.028	0.139‡	0.075‡
Private sector	- 0.016	0.045	0.036	0.058	0.011
Union(s) recognised	0.060†	0.038	- 0.004	0.082*	0.032
Negotiate: multiple employers	- 0.097‡	- 0.079‡	- 0.067‡	0.141‡	- 0.065†
Closed shop or management recommends membership	0.047†	0.020	0.028*	- 0.007	0.045*
Male local unemployment rate	- 0.006*	- 0.005†	- 0.003*	0.003	- 0.002
Paid overtime hours	0.107‡	0.049†	0.073‡	0.032	0.018
Total hours worked	0.013‡	0.014‡	0.012‡	0.011†	0.015‡
Establishment female proportion					
20–29 per cent	- 0.060†	- 0.070‡	- 0.059‡	0.043	- 0.089‡
30–39 per cent	- 0.104‡	- 0.106‡	- 0.062‡	- 0.035	- 0.060*
40–59 per cent	- 0.171†	- 0.154‡	- 0.109‡	- 0.186†	- 0.103‡
60–100 per cent	- 0.241‡	- 0.181‡	- 0.085‡	- 0.167	0.189‡
Occupational female proportion					
1–9 per cent	- 0.039	- 0.027	0.004	0.067	- 0.007
10–19 per cent	- 0.054*	- 0.036	- 0.060*	- 0.169*	- 0.017
20–29 per cent	- 0.019	- 0.038	- 0.056*	- 0.111	- 0.056*
30–39 per cent	- 0.003	- 0.145‡	- 0.058	- 0.106	- 0.082†
40–50 per cent	0.016	- 0.088†	- 0.145‡	- 0.060	- 0.133‡
Industry dummies (6–9)	Yes	Yes	Yes	Yes	Yes
Establishment size dummies (6)	Yes	Yes	Yes	Yes	Yes
Number of establishments	517	598	803	127	580
Mean of dependent variable (£/week)	159.65	181.27	214.65	180.55	242.50

Source: 1990 WIRS

Note

1 ‡ significant at one per cent, † significant at five per cent and * significant at ten per cent

Table 10.5 Earnings equations – females by broad occupational group

	Occupational group			
	Unskilled	Semi-skilled	Clericals	Supervisors
Manual proportion	0.041	0.095	- 0.120‡	- 0.067
Skilled proportion	- 0.154†	- 0.333‡	0.072†	- 0.176*
Single site	- 0.009	0.008	0.041†	0.019
Establishment has shift work	- 0.019	0.034	- 0.013	- 0.004
Payment by results	0.028	0.017	0.037†	- 0.012
Foreign-owned	0.095†	- 0.019	0.088‡	- 0.044
Private sector	- 0.005	- 0.008	0.009	- 0.052
Union(s) recognised	0.009	- 0.080*	- 0.002	- 0.107†
Negotiate: multiple employers	0.031	- 0.026	- 0.029	- 0.027
Closed shop or management recommends recognition	0.022	0.037	0.004	- 0.002
Local female unemployment rate	- 0.022‡	- 0.032‡	- 0.018‡	- 0.024
Paid overtime hours	0.001	- 0.106‡	- 0.024	0.055
Total hours worked	0.033‡	0.031‡	0.024‡	0.028‡
Establishment female proportion				
20–39 per cent	0.072	–	- 0.034	–
40–59 per cent	0.058	- 0.037	0.016	- 0.417*
60–79 per cent	0.044	- 0.286†	0.016	- 0.412*
80–100 per cent	0.007	- 0.305‡	- 0.063†	- 0.493†
Occupational female proportion				
50–59 per cent	- 0.061	0.154‡	0.044	0.071
60–69 per cent	- 0.013	0.234‡	0.023	0.051
70–79 per cent	- 0.067	0.174‡	0.019	0.089
80–89 per cent	- 0.105	0.162‡	- 0.007	0.084
90–99 per cent	- 0.045	0.106†	- 0.004	0.032
Industry dummies (6–9)	Yes	Yes	Yes	Yes
Establishment size dummies (6)	Yes	Yes	Yes	Yes
Number of establishments	413	163	1026	203
Mean of dependent variable (£/week)	97.42	116.40	151.87	184.93

Source: 1990 WIRS

Note

1 ‡ significant at one per cent, † significant at five per cent and * significant at ten per cent

occupational groups for which the pay data was collected, making it difficult to suggest any interpretation of this result.

There is a weak negative association between local labour market conditions and earnings levels, the 'wage curve' extensively documented by Blanchflower and Oswald (1995). In the equations reported here the size of the coefficient on the local unemployment rate is very small for all occupational groups (an average of minus 0.006 for males and ranging from minus 0.015 to minus 0.036 for females), and is significant in only five of the nine earnings equations. This is consistent with the WIRS evidence that only a minority of managers cite local labour market conditions as a factor influencing the size of pay settlements (Millward *et al.*, 1992).

Estimates of the male wage premium

From the earnings equations it is possible to estimate a *ceteris paribus* earnings premium associated with working in an establishment where the majority of the occupational group is male. An analogous method to that employed by Stewart (1994) was used for calculating union wage differentials. The results show premiums among occupational categories to be 29 per cent for unskilled manuals; 22 per cent for semi-skilled manuals; 12 per cent for clericals; and 14 per cent for supervisors.

These results highlight the very large effects associated with males and females being segregated into separate establishments. Alternative estimates of the male/female wage gap using individual data have generally taken no account of job segregation at the workplace. Sloane (1994) is a notable exception. The results here suggest that omitting some measure of female concentration at the workplace leads to a serious understatement of the effects of gender on pay.

Carrington and Troske (1993) report similar results on the effect of establishment-level female concentration on earnings. Their analysis is extended by including an economic performance variable to test for two alternative hypotheses. The first relates to discrimination theories which predict that adding a performance indicator would have no effect on the lower pay of female-dominated establishments. The second concerns human capital theories which posit that once performance differences were controlled for the earnings gap should disappear. Carrington and Troske found evidence for the latter hypothesis. Further experiments were therefore conducted to see whether the introduction of economic performance variables would alter the results (Millward and Woodland, 1994).

Subsequent work tested for a possible relationship between various measures of gender concentration and segregation, and establishment financial performance. This approach is used as a more direct method of testing whether establishments with high female concentration generally have lower human capital, lower productivity and hence lower wages: in other words, whether or not there is a negative correlation between female concentration and human capital. If the relationship is negative it was expected that an inverse relationship between female concentration and measures of establishment performance would be found.

The WIRS dataset has information about economic performance of the establishment which has produced a number of robust findings (Machin and Stewart, 1990). The hypothesis stated earlier was investigated by augmenting the Machin and Stewart model (1995), which tested for the effects of unions on financial performance. The dependent variable is the respondent's assessment of the financial performance of the establishment compared with other establishments in the same industry. Table 10.6 gives the results. Column one shows the basic Machin and Stewart model. Column two indicates that establishment performance is not significantly affected by the level of female concentration, giving no support for the hypothesis that higher female concentration is an indicator of lower human capital. The same table (columns three and four) gives the results of tests for the effects of intra-establishment gender segregation on financial performance. One measure shows some evidence that higher gender segregation within the workplace is associated with lower financial performance relative to comparable establishments.

Further developments of the analysis

While the authors are confident that the work so far has confirmed the existence of a substantial establishment-level male wage premium, there are a number of further lines of enquiry to pursue.

Firstly, there is much to be learned from repeating this analysis on the 1984 WIRS data, to detect any changes in the degree of establishment-level gender segregation between 1984 and 1990, and test whether the male wage premium had increased or decreased. The initial hypothesis would be that the decline in collective bargaining and fragmentation of pay-determination processes occurring during the period would have increased the male wage premium, despite the fact that the overall, raw difference between men's and women's hourly earnings has narrowed. Part of the rationale is that segregation has increased, not least because some employers may have sought to avoid exposure to equal value claims by increasingly segregating their workforces into male-dominated and female-dominated establishments.

Secondly, and from a more policy-oriented perspective, it is worth looking for the existence of managerial practices and procedures that reduce the depressing effect of female concentration on women's wages. The prime candidate here is job evaluation. It has long been recognised that formal job evaluation schemes, particularly analytical schemes, might reduce the extent of gender bias in the setting of pay (Incomes Data Services, 1979), and research has supported this view (Ghobadian and White, 1987). Analytical methods are now the preferred job evaluation method under UK equal pay laws and are recommended by ACAS. But they are not widespread; indeed, a mere five per cent of establishments in the 1990 WIRS had an analytical job evaluation scheme covering both sexes and a

Table 10.6 The effects of female concentration and gender segregation on establishments' financial performance

	1	2	3	4
Manual union(s) recognised	0.039	0.032	0.032	0.040
Closed shop or management recommends	- 0.325‡	- 0.335‡	- 0.318‡	- 0.317‡
Working at full capacity	0.336‡	0.339‡	0.334‡	0.339‡
Sales rising in last 12 months	0.323‡	0.324‡	0.310‡	0.326‡
UK-owned	0.244†	0.253†	0.256†	0.255†
Single independent establishment	- 0.379*	- 0.384*	- 0.392	- 0.390*
Proportion of establishments in one-digitindustry with manual union(s) recognised	- 1.033‡	- 1.076‡	- 1.014‡	- 1.007‡
No manual workers	- 0.001	0.010	- 0.049	- 0.002
Establishment female proportion		- 0.100		
Segregation index 1			0.657*	
Segregation index 2				0.382
Establishment size dummies (6)	Yes	Yes	Yes	Yes
Number of establishments	811	811	811	811

Source: 1990 WIRS

Notes

1 The above are Ordered Probit models where the dependent variable is an ordered variable running from zero (a lot below average financial performance) through to four (a lot above average financial performance).

2 Segregation index 1 is a measure of the degree of gender segregation within establishments. It is the absolute value of the difference between female proportion in occupation 'i' and establishment 'j' and the mean female proportion in occupation 'i' across all establishments. This is then summed (weighted by the share of occupation i's employment in establishment j's total employment) across all eight occupational groups.

3 Segregation index 2 is an alternative measure of the degree of gender segregation within establishments. It is the absolute value of the difference between female proportion in occupation 'i' and establishment 'j' and the establishment female proportion in establishment 'j'. This is then summed (weighted by the share of occupation i's employment in establishment j's total employment) across all eight occupational groups.

4 ‡ significant at one per cent, † significant at five per cent and * significant at ten per cent

clear majority of the workforce.[11] This may mean there are too few such cases to detect any impact on male/female differentials within the workplace; initial attempts have been unsuccessful, but further work in this vein is intended.

Implications for equal pay policy

The main results of these analyses are clear and have important implications. Gender segregation between establishments is very substantial, and has an adverse effect upon the relative pay of women.

---

[11] The precise conditions are described in Millward and Woodland, 1994.

When a large number of factors widely known to affect pay levels are controlled for, there are still large differences in pay between men and women that are accentuated by gender concentration within establishments. Controlling for a wide range of other factors, when unskilled workers in an establishment are mostly men they earn nearly 30 per cent more than they would if they were mostly women. Such a gap can hardly be attributed to greater physical demands of male work. Even for clerical workers, the difference is 12 per cent.

The establishment-level male wage premiums estimated are for 1990, and it is not yet known whether they were even greater in the early 1980s. But the continuance of such large gender differences, some 20 years after the Equal Pay Act and six years after more stringent equal pay legislation, indicates an underlying problem with which managerial good practice and current legislation are ill-equipped to deal. Some existing intra-establishment wage differences do appear to arise from unequal treatment of men and women, and could well be addressed by more rigorous application of the current laws. But the limited range of comparisons provided for in current law will never address that part of the female/male wage gap arising from gender segregation, particularly inter-establishment segregation. The pervasive undervaluation of 'women's work' requires more radical changes in employers' practices and in legal provision and enforcement than the changes made since 1970.

Acknowledgements

The authors would like to thank Paul Edwards, Jill Rubery and participants at the EOC conference which led to this volume, and colleagues at the Centre for Economic Performance and the Policy Studies Institute, for helpful comments on an earlier version of this chapter (Millward and Woodland, 1994). Remaining errors and deficiencies are the responsibility of the authors. The work was carried out as part of the Industrial Relations Programme of the Centre for Economic Performance at the London School of Economics and Political Science. The Centre is financed by the Economic and Social Research Council. The authors acknowledge the Department of Employment, the Economic and Social Research Council, the Policy Studies Institute and the Advisory, Conciliation and Arbitration Service as the originators of the 1990 Workplace Industrial Relations Survey data, and the ESRC Data Archive as the distributor of the data. None of these organisations bears any responsibility for the authors' analysis and interpretations of the data.

References

Becker, G. (1957). *The Economics of Discrimination*. Chicago: Chicago University Press.

Becker, G. (1985). 'Human capital, effort, and the sexual division of labour' in *Journal of Labor Economics*, 3 (1).

Bergmann, B. (1986). *The Economic Emergence of Women*. New York: Basic Books.

Bergmann, B. (1989). 'Does the market for women's labor need fixing?' in *Journal of Economic Perspectives*, 3 (1).

Blanchflower, D. (1984). 'Union relative wage effects: a cross-section analysis using establishment data' in *British Journal of Industrial Relations*, 22 (3).

Blanchflower, D. and Oswald, A. (1990). 'The determination of white collar pay' in *Oxford Economic Papers*, 42 (2).

Blanchflower, D. and Oswald, A. (1995). *The Wage Curve*. Boston: MIT Press.

Blanchflower, D., Oswald, A. and Garrett, M. (1990). 'Insider power in wage determination' in *Economica*, 57 (1).

Carrington, J. and Troske, K. (1993). *Gender Segregation in Small Firms*. Discussion Paper, Centre for Economic Studies, 92–13, May.

Daniel, W. W. and Millward, N. (1983). *Workplace Industrial Relations in Britain: the ED/PSI/ESRC Survey*. London: Heinemann Educational Books.

Doeringer, P. and Piore, M. (1971). *Internal Labour Markets and Manpower Analysis*. Lexington, Mass: D. C. Heath & Co.

Fuchs, V. R. (1989). 'Women's quest for economic equality' in *Journal of Economic Perspectives*, 3 (1).

Ghobadian, A. and White, M. (1987). *Job Evaluation and Equal Pay*. Department of Employment, Research Paper no. 58.

Groshen, E. L. (1991). 'The structure of the female/male wage differential' in *Journal of Human Resources*, 26 (3).

Hakim, C. (1992). 'Explaining trends in occupational segregation: the measurement, causes and consequences of the sexual division of labour' in *European Sociological Review*, 8 (2).

Horrell, S., Rubery, J. and Burchell, B. (1989). 'Unequal jobs or unequal pay?' in *Industrial Relations Journal*, 20 (3).

Humphries, J. (1995). 'Economics, gender and equal opportunities' in this volume.

Incomes Data Services (1979). *Guide to Job Evaluation*. London: Unwin.

Machin, S. and Stewart, M. (1990). 'Unions and the financial performance of British private sector establishments' in *Journal of Applied Econometrics*, 5 (4).

Machin, S. and Stewart, M. (1995). *Trade Unions and Financial Performance*. Mimeo, University College, London, Department of Economics.

Machin, S., Stewart, M. and Van Reenen, J. (1992). *The Economic Effects of Multiple Unionism: Evidence from the 1984 Workplace Industrial Relations Survey*. Discussion Paper 66, Centre for Economic Performance, London School of Economics and Political Science.

Martin J. and Roberts, C. (1984). *Women and Employment: A Lifetime Perspective*. London: HMSO.

Metcalf, D. and Stewart, M. (1992). 'Closed shops and relative pay: institutional arrangements or high density?' in *Oxford Bulletin of Economics and Statistics*, 54 (4).

Millward, N. (1993). *Establishment Surveys in Britain*. Working Paper 413, Centre for Economic Performance, London School of Economics and Political Science.

Millward, N. (1995). *Targeting Potential Discrimination*. EOC Research Discussion Series 11. Manchester: Equal Opportunities Commission.

Millward, N., Stevens, M., Smart, D. and Hawes, W. R. (1992). *Workplace Industrial Relations in Transition*: the ED/ESRC/PSI/ACAS Surveys. Aldershot: Dartmouth Publishing.

Millward, N. and Woodland, S. (1994). *Gender Segregation and Establishment Wage Levels*. Working Paper 639, Centre for Economic Performance, London School of Economics and Political Science.

Polachek, S. W. (1981). 'Occupational self-selection: a human capital approach to sex differences in occupational structures' in *Review of Economics and Statistics*, 63 (1).

Rubery, J. (1992). *The Economics of Equal Value*. EOC Research Discussion Series 3. Manchester: Equal Opportunities Commission.

Scott, A. (ed.) (1994a). *Gender Segregation and Social Change*. Oxford University Press.

Scott, A. (1994b). 'Gender segregation and the SCELI research' in Scott, A. (ed.) *Gender Segregation and Social Change*. (*Op. cit.*)

Sloane, P. J. (1994). 'The gender wage differential and discrimination in the six SCELI local labour markets' in Scott, A. (ed.) *Gender Segregation and Social Change*.. (*Op. cit.*)

Sorenson, E. (1986). 'Implementing comparable worth: a survey of recent job evaluation studies' in *American Economic Review*, 76 (2).

Stewart, M. B. (1983). 'On least squares estimation when the dependent variable is grouped' in *Review of Economic Studies*, 50 (4).

Stewart, M. B. (1987). 'Collective bargaining arrangements, closed shops and relative pay' in *Economic Journal*, 97 (385).

Stewart, M. B. (1990). 'Union wage differentials, product market influences and the division of rents' in *Economic Journal*, 100 (403).

Stewart, M. B. (1991). 'Union wage differentials in the face of changes in the economic and legal environment' in *Economica*, 58 (203).

Stewart, M. B. (1994). *Union Wage Differentials in an Era of Declining Unionisation*. Mimeo, University of Warwick.

Wilkinson, F. (1981). *The Dynamics of Labour Market Segmentation*. London: Academic Press.

Workplace Industrial Relations Survey (1990). Sponsored by the Employment Department, the Economic and Social Research Council, the Policy Studies Institute and the Advisory, Conciliation and Arbitration Service.

\

CHAPTER 11 An Economic Exploration of the UK and Australian Experiences

Laurie Hunter and Sheila Rimmer

This chapter is concerned with the comparative experience of Britain and Australia with regard to equal pay, equal opportunity, and the behaviour of the gender pay differential. The difficulties of tracing the economic effects of legislation or other policy actions are formidable. Policy changes interact with the institutional structure, economic agents may adapt their behaviour, and other environmental factors do not remain constant. For these reasons, debate continues about the comparative impacts of the Equal Pay Act, 1970, and the incomes policies of the 1970s on the UK male/female wage ratio (Sloane and Theodissiou, 1994; Zabalza and Tzannatos, 1985, 1988; Chiplin and Sloane, 1988; Borooah and Lee, 1988; Rubery and Fagan, 1994).

A comparative country analysis may lead to a better understanding of some of the major influences on the gender pay gap, and the economic processes by which present-day outcomes have been generated. The comparative perspective arguably raises new questions about the role of institutional arrangements, and forces one to question why the evolutionary paths following similar legislation on equal pay and opportunities have been different.

Table 11.1 Relative award rates of pay for men and women in Australia, 1947–92

1947	60.9
1969	72.0
1972	77.4
1976	92.4
1980	91.6
1986	92.3
1992*	93.6

Source: Norris, 1993
*Source: *Distribution and Composition of Employee Earnings and Hours*, ABS, 6306.0, May 1992

Australia, like Britain, has witnessed a rapid expansion of female employment, and a significant narrowing of the earnings gap between men and women, following legislative changes in the period 1969–76. Until 1969 the Australian system of wage fixing formally discriminated against women, but in that year the Commonwealth Conciliation and Arbitration Commission granted 'equal pay for equal work' (fully effective from 1972). In 1972 equal pay for work of equal value was introduced (effective in 1975). These changes were associated with a 30 per cent rise in the female/male award wage ratio, following a period of 20 years of little change (see Table 11.1). The female/male average weekly earnings ratio increased by a similar amount, taking average female earnings to 83 per cent of male earnings in 1977. Since then, despite a Sex Discrimination Act (1984) and affirmative action legislation (1986), there seems to have been no further progress (see Table 11.2). Indeed, recent earnings data suggests that the gender pay gap may be widening again.

Table 11.2 Female/male average weekly ordinary-time earnings ratios in Australia, 1981–93

1981	81.4
1982	79.6
1983	79.5
1984	81.3
1985	82.7
1986	81.9
1987	82.7
1988	83.4
1989	82.7
1990	83.0
1991	84.5
1992	83.2
1993	83.9
1994a	80.6 (May 1994 private sector)
1994b	88.5 (May 1994 public sector)

Source: *The Distribution and Composition of Employee Earnings and Hours*, ABS, 6306.0, May 1992 and 1994

Note

1 This data refers to the earnings in August for a standard working week and do not include overtime or commission. The figures are for full-time adult workers, thus many of the usual objections to weekly figures do not apply.

In Britain, the Equal Pay Act, 1970 (fully effective from 1975), was followed by the Sex Discrimination Act, 1975. Women's hourly pay rates relative to men's rose by about 17 per cent, thereafter stabilising at around 74 per cent of the male rate. Legislative amendments in 1984 and 1986 provided respectively for equal pay for work of equal value, and for state subsidies to companies engaging in affirmative action programmes, but there is little evidence of any significant effects from these changes.

Legislative changes connected with equal employment opportunity were the dominant policy measures of the 1980s in Australia. But other Acts brought prominence to the expectation of equity for women workers, including the 1972 Child Care Act (funding) and the 1979 provision for 52 weeks' unpaid maternity leave in all awards. A woman was appointed to the High Court in 1987, women flew in the RAAF, and were station leaders in the Antarctic. The ILO 'Workers with Family Responsibilities Convention' was ratified in 1991; provisions for workers to use their sick leave entitlements for absence due to family responsibilities were enacted in 1994. Such milestones signalled a new phase of women's workplace involvement.

The two countries have experienced similar legislation over a similar time period. The effect on the size of the wage gap appears to have been different, but in both cases the initial change has been followed by a period of apparent stagnation. In both countries there have subsequently been very considerable changes in the economic environment, and in labour market policy and institutions.

Wage structure influences in Britain and Australia

After the Sex Discrimination Act, 1975 (apart from the 1981 and 1986 amendments already mentioned), equal pay and equal opportunity legislation *per se* has been absent from British labour market policy. But the government's involvement in the labour market has been widespread.

In the late 1970s the Labour government sought to maintain its 'social contract' with the labour movement, seeking moderate wage settlements in return for TUC participation in policy formulation. The 'contract' broke down finally in the 1978–9 'winter of discontent', paving the way for the incoming radical Conservative government to tackle the perennial 'stagflation' problem and restore an internationally-competitive edge to British industry. Wage dispersion in the economy, which had narrowed during the 1970s, began to widen again as the government pursued its programmes.

Labour market issues were high on the agenda. In broad terms the government's aims were to remove what it regarded as the shackles of rigidity from the labour market, including the (downward) inflexibility of wage rates, the 'floor' to the wage level provided by industry-wide collective agreements on basic pay and by Wages Councils, the reluctance of many unemployed workers (as the government saw it) to search actively for work and accept low-paid jobs, and the feather-bedded security enjoyed by many public sector employees.

The British government sought greater 'flexibility' in the labour market by removing what it saw as constraints on employers' competitive ability deriving from statutory regulation of employment conditions. The main deregulatory legislation was contained in a series of Employment (or kindred) Acts from 1980 to 1993.[1] Probably the most significant step in the present context was the abolition of the Wages Councils, which set minimum wages for around 2.5 million workers (the majority of them

[1] The Employment Act, 1980 (affecting unfair dismissal and maternity rights in small companies); the Wages Act, 1986 (affecting how wages are paid and rules about deductions from pay, and reducing Wages Council scope); the Employment Act, 1989 (removing many restrictions on the employment of women and young people, and amending certain provisions of the Sex Discrimination Act, 1975); and the Trade Union Reform and Employment Rights Act, 1993 (giving new protections against dismissal, maternity leave provision and enhanced protection against dismissal on maternity-related grounds, and abolishing the remaining Wages Councils). In 1982 the Fair Wages Resolution was axed, freeing contractors to the public sector from the obligation to pay the national going rate for the type of work.

women, many of whom were part-time) in 1990, leaving Britain with no wage-floor protection at all.

Evidence suggests that the effect of a minimum wage is to bunch workers at or around the minimum, and that removing the constraint will give rise to a standard normal distribution, leaving scope for formerly 'protected' workers to be shunted down the distribution. In short, the prediction is that the abolition of Wages Councils will further reduce the pay of lower-paid workers, adversely affect low-paid women and part-timers, and add to the earnings inequalities which have been increasing in the last decade (Dickens *et al.*, 1993).

However, while this is a potential factor for the future, the role of Wages Councils in the evolution of the earnings gap in the 1980s would be limited to the removal of under-21-year-olds from their scope in 1986, more restricted terms of reference for Wages Councils, and a poor record of enforcing wage rates as abolition approached. This weakening of the Wages Councils' machinery may well have had some influence, though it is hard to quantify.

Another principal target for government reform in Britain in the 1980s, parallel to the deregulation and privatisation initiatives, was the reform of trade unions and their role in collective bargaining. Unions were regarded by government as contributing to wage inflation through the use of bargaining power, and preventing the flexible (downward) adjustment of real wages in recession, thereby unnecessarily adding to unemployment. In a series of legislative measures, union power was curbed (by the curtailment and ultimately outlawing of closed shop arrangements, requirements for secret ballots before strike action, controls on picketing, and increased liability of unions and officials for a range of activities which previously carried legal immunity). Collective bargaining rights were withdrawn for teachers and nurses (both with a heavy female representation) and more generally the government sought to move away from reliance on collective bargaining as the main influence on wage determination. Where collective bargaining persisted the government encouraged decentralisation, but its preference was for pay to be a reflection of productivity and individual performance.

One reason why the Australian labour market forms a useful and interesting benchmark for comparative work is its uniqueness in having a comprehensive, compulsory arbitration system. The system has seen phases of dominance and weakness, and recently some have speculated that its continued existence is doubtful. The institution of the Industrial Relations Commission (IRC) mostly functions in a gender-neutral manner, but there have been notable occasions when the IRC has introduced policies intended to benefit women.

It is commonly argued that the centralised wage-fixing system emerged as a response to the 'great strikes' of the 1890s (Deery and Plowman, 1991). Throughout its history the IRC has been attempting to strike a balance between the goals of meeting a 'needs' principle of protection for the weak, and the principle of the economy's 'capacity to pay'. When these principles were incompatible, 'needs' tended to yield to 'capacity'. The first award for women's pay was in 1912, when the relativity was set at 54 per cent of the male rate. During the Second World War that relativity eased, to the extent that by 1950 a relativity apparently produced by market forces was institutionalised in the new female basic wage, set at 75 per cent of the male equivalent. The impact of subsequent equal pay legislation on awards and earnings has already been outlined.

A key feature of the Australian system is that the determinations of the IRC create legally-binding minimum standards. Even by agreement, pay rates lower than an award[2] cannot be made. Coverage rates by award of federal or state arbitral bodies are around 75 per cent for men, and over 80 per cent for women. The policies of the IRC are of considerable significance to women, particularly since IRC awards relate to the conditions of work, not merely pay. (For full-time women the award is 96 per cent of total earnings; for full-time men it is 87 per cent.) In their comparative work, Blau and Kahn (1992) argued that the American decentralised wage determination process was a likely source of the relatively large gender pay gap in the USA (compared with more highly-structured systems, as in Australia, which tend to produce a narrower wage dispersion). If so, the very recent labour market reforms in Australia may well compromise the further extension of pay equity in the 1990s.

Since the mid-1970s there have been several distinct episodes in wage fixing. Between 1975 and 1981 a strictly-enforced indexation system was in place, with awards tied to changes in the retail prices index. Women's relatively high dependence on centralised systems, and the fact that 96 per cent of their earnings derive from awards (compared with 88 per cent for men), mean that a tightly constrained system is likely to favour them, or at least preserve the *status quo*. It is certainly a plausible explanation for the rather stable gender pay relativities of the period.

The indexation system was abandoned by the IRC on the basis of the diminishing commitment to the principles of indexation shown by unions, employers and government. In 1982, when unemployment jumped from around 6.5 per cent to almost ten per cent by December, the economic and social circumstances were ripe for the acceptance of a social contract. An Accord between the main union and employer councils and the government was formalised early in 1983. The Accord was a broadly-based prices and incomes policy with indexation provisions. The notion of the wage was extended to allow consideration of taxation reforms and the spread of occupational superannuation.

---

[2] The award rate of pay is the agreed base rate for ordinary time (unless otherwise specified), and includes allowances and shift loadings but excludes overtime, bonuses, commissions, piece-work pay and other similar payments. The Industrial Relations Commission is the dominant institution, making awards in National Wages Cases which affect the pay rates of all workers covered by awards. Some awards are on an industry basis, others cover occupational groups, and many are the formalisation of collective bargaining outcomes. In addition there are state-level tribunals, which generally follow the IRC awards.

By 1993 coverage of full-time employees with superannuation and other standard benefits was virtually universal and gender neutral. However, in part-time work the coverage was 71 per cent of women and 49 per cent of men. Almost half the casual workforce received these non-wage benefits. It must be added that of those not working full-time, the men are likely to be young, still at school, unmarried and without dependants. The women are more likely to be in permanent part-time work, married and with dependent children. The steady growth in non-wage benefits, particularly for women, means that trends in earnings/award gaps do not tell the whole equity story of the 1980s. Again, women seem to have gained from the highly-structured regulatory pay system.

Equal pay experience: Australia and Britain

Some stylised facts

Following the British Equal Pay Act, 1970, fully implemented by 1975, there was a significant increase in full-time women's hourly earnings expressed as a percentage of the equivalent male earnings. From around 63 per cent in 1970, the ratio rose to about 74 per cent in 1976. Equal pay legislation was to be fully implemented in Australia by 1975, but it related to legal minima rather than to earnings. The female award rate of pay rose from 72 per cent of the male in 1969 to 92.4 per cent by 1976. Between 1975 and 1981 a highly-constrained earnings policy was in place, whereby pay movements were confined to retail price indexed adjustments to award pay. Equal pay was implemented to a far greater extent than in Britain.

From the late 1970s until recently, the British full-time female/male earnings ratio remained stable, slightly below its 1976–7 level. As Table 11.3 shows, there was a slight relapse in the late 1970s, but consistent data since 1983 indicates that from 1987 the relative position of full-time women's earnings has improved, standing at 79 per cent in 1993. The female/male award relativity in Australia remained fairly stable throughout the 1980s. Had Australian employers desired it, they could have clawed back the old pay differential for men through 'over-award' pay. This does not appear to have happened to any great extent, since the narrowing gap in award pay rates seems to have been paralleled in terms of earnings. Female workforce participation has grown steadily against this background of rising relative pay.

The increase in the relative female wage has not led to the net substitution of male for female labour. In fact the reverse appears to have occurred, as measured by changes in participation rates and relative changes in male and female employment. While female participation and employment rates grew steadily in the 1980s, men saw slower employment growth than women and falling participation (see Table 11.4).

These trends need to be qualified by reference to the growing importance of part-time jobs, a high proportion of which are filled by women. Between 1979 and 1993 employment in Britain grew by 2.3 per cent. This

Table 11.3 Female/male hourly earnings ratios by employment status and occupational group in Great Britain, 1985–93

	Full-time manual*	Full-time non-manual*	All* full-timers
1975	68.0	60.7	70.6
1976	71.1	62.6	73.5
1977	71.7	63.0	73.8
1978	72.0	61.2	72.2
1979	70.2	61.0	71.3
1980	70.9	61.1	71.8
1981	69.9	61.8	72.8
1982	68.8	61.0	71.9
1983a	69.6	61.4	72.2
1983b	70.6	63.1	74.0
1984	69.9	62.1	73.4
1985	70.9	62.4	73.9
1986	70.7	62.1	74.1
1987	71.1	61.2	73.4
1988	70.8	62.2	74.9
1989	70.5	63.4	76.4
1990	70.3	65.6	77.0
1991	70.4	66.8	78.3
1992	70.8	67.6	79.3
1993	71.2	67.7	78.9

Source: New Earnings Survey, *Employment Gazette*

*Refers to gross hourly earnings excluding overtime for employees on adult rates not affected by absence; figures prior to 1983 and the first set of 1983 figures relate to men aged 21 and over and females aged 18 and over, thereafter figures relate to men and women on adult rates.

comprised a growth of women's employment (an additional 293,000 full-time workers and 1,250,000 part-time) offset by a decline in men's employment (1,888,000 fewer full-time workers and 616,000 additional part-timers; see Table 11.4). Only about ten per cent of part-time women workers would want full-time work if available, compared with over 50 per cent of male part-timers.

In Australia total employment between 1979 and 1993 grew more than ten times faster than in the UK. Overall, women gained more than a million jobs, of which 55 per cent were part-time. Part-time work accounted for 44 per cent of the additional half a million jobs for men (see Table 11.4).

Table 11.4 Economic activity – people of working age, spring of each year, not seasonally adjusted – in Great Britain and Australia

	1979 '000	1984 '000	1990 '000	1993 '000	percentage change 1979–93
Great Britain					
Women (16–59)					
Economically active	9681	10421	11595	11552	+ 19.3
Economic activity rate	63	66	71	71	+ 12.7
In employment	9030	9202	10835	10672	+ 18.2
In full-time work	5603	5221	6200	5896	+ 5.2
In part-time work	3426	3945	4475	4676	+ 36.5
ILO unemployment rate	n/a	12	7	8	–
Men (16–64)					
Economically active	15188	15280	15650	15236	+ 0.3
Economic activity rate	91	88	88	86	- 5.5
In employment	14438	13463	14576	13344	- 7.6
In full-time work	14321	12987	13701	12433	- 13.2
ILO unemployment rate	n/a	12	7	12	–
Australia					
Women (16–59)					
Economically active	2331.3	2699.5	3513.8	3618.1	+ 55.2
Economic activity rate	43.3	45.1	52.3	51.5	+ 18.9
In employment	2148.0	2461.6	3270.8	3267.9	+ 52.1
In full-time work	1402.3	1561.2	1993.5	1905.5	+ 35.9
In part-time work	745.7	900.4	1291.2	1362.4	+ 82.7
Men (16–64)					
Economically active	4115.6	4422.3	4938.0	5046.4	+ 22.6
Economic activity rate	78.3	76.3	75.5	73.8	- 5.7
In employment	3909.6	4064.5	4648.2	4473.8	+ 14.4
In full-time work	3707.6	3807.7	4279.6	4022.7	+ 8.5
In part-time work	202.0	256.8	368.6	451.1	+ 123.3
Australian unemployment rate	6.0	8.9	6.4	10.6	–

Source: Great Britain – Labour Force Survey, revised from Sly, F. 'Women in the labour market' in *Employment Gazette*, November 1993. 1979 figures differ in some respects from later figures; for full details see Sly (1993). Australia – The Labour Force Survey, Australian Bureau of Statistics

In contrast with the UK, full-time work expanded for both women and men. Australian women were (relatively) less dependent on part-time job growth than their British counterparts.

Both long-term trends or structural factors and cyclical effects are clearly influential in both economies. The 1990–3 recession in Britain witnessed falls in male and female participation and employment, but women's employment held up better than men's, and part-time employment continued to increase during the recession (see Table 11.4). In Australia, economic deterioration in the early 1990s was accompanied by falling activity rates and full-time employment for women and men. Part-time work kept employment fairly stable for women. But whereas in 1979 13 per cent of female and 22 per cent of male part-time workers would have preferred to work more hours, by 1993 the relevant proportions were 25 and 40 per cent. Changes in the structure (and health) of the economy, trading patterns, and extensive labour market reforms underpinned these shifts in the shares of full- and part-time work.

Women are more heavily concentrated in non-manual occupations, which tends to increase their relative earnings as non-manual earnings are higher than manual. But within each of these categories, British women are much more heavily concentrated in the lower-paid occupations (67 per cent in lower-paid non-manual occupations and 72 per cent in lower-paid manual occupations; Sly, 1993). Work is also strikingly segregated in Australia into 'men's' and 'women's' jobs, and there is little evidence that this is changing much. The affirmative action and equal opportunity provisions have had only a marginal impact on the gender bias of work.

In combination with differential pay growth for male and female intensive work, there is substantial scope for the erosion of past pay equity gains for women (Rimmer, 1991). Over the year to May 1993, median earnings for full-time adult workers increased by 5.2 per cent for men and 2.7 per cent for women. The gender pay relativity fell from 85.8 per cent to 84.4 per cent. On balance pay grew faster in male-intensive jobs. Occupational segregation in the part-time workforce is high and has been increasing in the last two decades, underlying the need to pay special attention to the market for part-time labour (Hakim, 1993).

At the end of the 1980s and in the early 1990s Australian government policy emphasised labour market reform as part of the micro-economic reform agenda. Male-intensive work at ports, in power generation and other infrastructure was boosted by these reforms; while women gained jobs through the expansion of service work, some promoted through tourism. Labour market policy has not had gender-neutral outcomes. Part of labour market deregulation was aimed at 'structural efficiency', intended to promote productivity growth in exchange for better-paid, more fulfilling work (Deery and Plowman, 1991). The creation of 'career paths for all' was suggested. In nursing this had the effect of providing significantly greater promotion opportunities for women, in an area where pay was already well above average and the gender pay relativity favoured women.

Assessment of trends in the UK
Given the behaviour of the female/male earnings ratio and the employment and participation measures, it can be inferred that the

growth of demand for female labour relative to its supply outstripped that for male labour; and that demand for part-time employees grew rapidly while that for full-time employees fell (though it should be noted that until the onset of the 1990–3 recession full-time employment showed virtually no change). It is clear that economic forces are working differentially on full-time (or male) and part-time (or mostly female) employment.

In the case of full-timers, after a period of minor fluctuation around 72 to 74 per cent, the hourly earnings ratio for full-time women relative to full-time men began to rise from 1987, reaching 79 per cent in 1992 and 1993, a rise of five percentage points. Further analysis for manual and non-manual workers reveals that while the earnings ratio for manual workers showed little variation from just above 70 per cent, the non-manual ratio rose from 62 to nearly 68 per cent (see Table 11.3).

Table 11.5 Hourly pay of part-time female employees on adult rates* as percentage of the hourly pay of full-time female employees, manual and non-manual, in Great Britain, 1985–93

	Manual	Non-manual	All
1985	0.87	0.81	0.78
1986	0.88	0.79	0.76
1987	0.87	0.79	0.76
1988	0.87	0.77	0.75
1989	0.87	0.78	0.75
1990	0.87	0.78	0.75
1991	0.88	0.77	0.75
1992	0.88	0.77	0.74
1993	0.88	0.76	0.74

Source: New Earnings Survey

*Average hourly earnings for those not affected by absence.

In contrast, the hourly earnings ratio for part-time women relative to full-time women declined by four percentage points over the period 1985–93; again, the manual worker ratio remained constant while the decline occurred in the non-manual sector (see Table 11.5). The hourly earnings ratio between part-time women and full-time men showed little trend change, though manual, non-manual and all-worker ratios reveal some gain from 1988.

Full-time women's earnings thus improved relative to those of full-time men and part-time women, in both instances seemingly due to changes in the non-manual sector of employment. What was working in favour of full-time women employees was not apparently working for part-timers. It seems important to explain what factors might underlie this observation.

Assessment of trends in Australia

The implementation of equal pay and the assorted legislative provisions for equal employment opportunity in Australia were, as in Britain, accompanied by faster employment growth for women than men. Women gained more of both the added full-time (62 per cent) and the added part-time (71 per cent) jobs between 1979 and 1993.

Among full-time adult workers the big shift in relative average earnings occurred between 1972 and 1975, rising from about 70 to 80 per cent. These shifts were not uniform across the occupational (or industrial) structure. Pay relativities for professionals and tradespeople barely changed between 1986 and 1993; but over this same period the female/male ratio of ordinary-time earnings for nurses working full-time rose from 0.959 to 1.032.

On a gender basis part-time pay rates are frequently favourable for women. In 1986 the female/male weekly and hourly pay ratios for part-time workers were 0.99 and 0.93 respectively. By 1993 these ratios had risen to 1.10 and 0.96. Superficially at least, women's relative rewards for part-time work are more equitable than for full-time work. However, this leaves out of account promotion prospects and other non-wage entitlements.

The weekly earnings of part-time women were 45 per cent of women's full-time earnings in 1993. This proportion had been as high as 49 per cent in 1988. Relative to full-time men's weekly earnings, part-time women workers' earnings were around 37 per cent. These pay ratios have not changed much in recent years. It is also evident that pay growth for part-time workers tends to be similar for women and men in most occupations.

Another important area for consideration is casual (temporary) employment. Overall, nearly 20 per cent of employed workers in 1990 were casuals, and for women employees the proportion was 28 per cent. Of these, 85 per cent were part-timers. When this is added to the 'permanent' part-timers, nearly 39 per cent of women were employed part-time. Thus the employment of women in Australia is heavily characterised by both casual conditions and part-time work, and concentrated largely in sales and personal service, labouring and clerical jobs. However, in contrast to Britain, many casual workers in Australia enjoy similar conditions of employment to permanent employees and have a career structure. Many are employed as 'regular casuals', and under the award system casuals' wage rates are loaded to compensate for intermittent work, impermanency and non-entitlement to award benefits such as annual leave and sick leave. This loading varies from ten to 50 per cent of the rate for day workers, but averages around 20 per cent (Romeyn, 1992).

A framework for analysis

Much analysis of the wage gap, and the contribution of direct discrimination to its size, is conducted on a cross-section basis, working from the human capital theory of Becker (1964, 1985) and others (for further discussion see Humphries, this volume, Chapter 3). The conventional approach uses the well-known Oaxaca decomposition method which permits estimation of the extent to which the observed (log) wage gap is explained by human capital factors, particularly education and work experience. The unexplained portion is commonly accepted as a measure of discrimination (D_F), though it has also been described as a measure of ignorance (Mincer, 1985). Over time, refinements in method, especially corrections for sample selectivity bias, and better data have narrowed the estimates of the D_F coefficient. Estimates for different years (though differing in method and data quality) suggest a reduction over time in the D_F coefficient in Britain from 51 per cent in 1972 to 21 per cent in 1980 (see Ermisch and Wright, 1991).

For Australia it appears from a range of recent studies that D_F was around 12 per cent in the 1980s. A cohort of young Australians whose working life began after the key equal opportunity legislation was implemented appeared to benefit from the 'enlightened period' (Korosi *et al.*, 1993a). There was evidence of a widening gender pay gap as the cohort matured. This occurred before family responsibilities were evident, but D_F was estimated for this panel to be around nine per cent. It may be that successive cohorts of women will find more equitable labour market outcomes emerging over the very long term, years after the relevant legislative changes were enacted.

However, since the concern here is comparative analysis over time, it is desirable to move beyond the cross-section approach commonly adopted in human capital analysis of the gender gap in a single country. It may be helpful to adapt a conceptualisation developed by Blau and Kahn (1994). In a study of rising wage inequality and the gender gap in the USA, they separate two distinct types of influence on the gender wage gap:

- gender-specific factors, reflecting measured and unmeasured male/female differences in characteristics and differences in the labour market treatment of equally-qualified men and women (thereby including effects of discrimination);

- the overall wage structure within which the rewards for skill, education, experience and so on are determined, which will reflect pay determination mechanisms and their responsiveness to signals generated by the relative factor demand and supply interaction in the system as a whole.

Of these influences, the first is broadly similar to the human capital approach of cross-section studies: in time series it would pick up changes in the female and male rewards for education levels, skill levels (training) and work experience. Presumably legislative measures or behavioural adaptations (such as a reduction in the acceptability of discrimination) affecting the treatment of equally-qualified men and women would also be included here, as might changes in the relative availability (or need) for paid employment. Changing social patterns have meant that more women than in the past must provide for themselves through paid work.

However, the second set of influences, centred on the way the wage structure rewards different characteristics, is largely excluded from normal cross-section studies.[3] Among the factors that may be influential under the wage structure banner are:

- changes in pay-fixing institutions;
- government policy on pay, for example incomes policy;
- changes in employers' labour utilisation policies (which may reflect competitive conditions or response to government policy);
- changes in the industrial or occupational structure of employment which influence the rewards (including rents) to workers in different kinds of employment;
- changes in trade union coverage and/or bargaining power affecting the union wage mark-up;
- changes in labour market arrangements or institutions which affect the processes of adjustment in the labour market (this might include changes in tax or social security provision, or 'deregulation' measures designed to improve the 'flexibility' of the labour market).

The scope of this framework is wider than can be tackled comprehensively here, so this chapter focuses on areas to which less attention has been paid in the literature but where it is believed that important factors have been at work, and in ways that suggest differences in the working out of broad economic forces in the two countries. Although the human capital model approach to the gender gap is valuable in cross-section and even in cross-section-over-time comparisons for a single country, it does not go very far in comparative analysis, which would need to explain why differences arise in the rewards for different characteristics.

Exploring some of the broader forces underlying the changes in these rewards necessitates concentration on the 'wage structure' influences. (For recent work on a comparative scale, see for example Rubery, 1992; Rubery and Fagan, 1994, and other references cited therein.) Policy influences of two kinds can be seen: those that are gender specific, designed to operate directly on inequality; and those with a more general focus, intended to be gender neutral but nevertheless affecting gender outcomes. For example, changes in tariff protection in some industries will shift the occupational/industrial mix of female employment and pay relativities. These indirect effects of policy are particularly important in this analysis.

Structural and institutional influences in Britain and Australia

From an analytic point of view, evolving and multi-faceted policy-making presents the problem that there are few real 'milestones' (like the Equal Pay Act) which might be expected to generate outcomes showing a clear break with the past. However, there are a few main sets of factors.

---

[3] It should be noted that a number of recent cohort studies permit study of the wage gap across time intervals: Paci *et al.*, 1994; Dolton *et al.*, 1994.

Britain

The disposition of the British labour force was affected in the 1980s by two major policy initiatives. First, large parts of the public sector were privatised, many areas of the civil service were converted into agencies designed to be run on business lines, and other parts of the public sector were required to engage in compulsory competitive tendering (CCT) for a range of services they had previously produced by direct internal labour. Whether privatisation and the associated changes are likely to have affected male/female employment and pay differentially is a question beyond the scope of this chapter, but one consequence may be noted.

As the privatised organisations sought profitability, and as CCT led to the contracting-out to private sector organisations of formerly internalised activities, employment cut-backs were enforced. Many workers were taken out of the scope of single-tier national bargaining (the most common bargaining arrangement in the heavily-unionised public sector) into either non-covered or two-tier bargaining, in which the union mark-up tends to be lower. If more men than women were affected by these changes, privatisation may well have contributed to males getting a reduced benefit from unionisation – which would tend to narrow the gender wage gap (Blanchflower, 1986; Beaumont and Harris, 1990). In fact the evidence does suggest such an effect. Male public sector employment fell from 3.7 million in 1982 to 2.8 million in 1990, while comparable female employment declined only marginally from 3.3 million to 3.2 million (*Social Trends*, 1991).[4]

Secondly, partly as a consequence of high unemployment and partly due to government policy, union density dropped substantially in the 1980s, as did the coverage of collective bargaining. Between 1984 and 1990, union membership density as a whole fell from 58 to 48 per cent (a 13 point drop for manual employees, and an eight per cent drop for non-manuals). Over the same period the proportion of employees covered by collective bargaining fell from 71 to 54 per cent. However, these figures (drawn from the Workplace Industrial Relations Surveys for 1984 and 1990) are overstatements since the surveys excluded small workplaces, which employed a total of 6.6 million people in 1990. Thus by 1990 'collective bargaining affected only a minority of employees in Britain' (Millward *et al.*, 1992: 92). The public sector still retained the highest coverage, manufacturing and private services were substantially lower, and all recorded major falls in coverage.

This pattern is reflected in the most important level of bargaining affecting pay. Between 1980 and 1990, multi-employer bargaining declined for both manual and non-manual workers; single employer multi-plant bargaining increased marginally, and plant-level bargaining declined. Pay increases that were not the result of collective bargaining now dominated, affecting 52 per cent of manual employees and 57 per cent of non-manuals (Millward *et al.*, 1992).

---

[4] However, while more men may have been affected by privatisation, the public sector is very feminised. Low-paid workers in areas like catering, cleaning and ancillary tasks, previously protected by unionisation, may find that contracting-out leaves them in a much worse position.

What, then, are the implications of these changes for the gender wage gap? Unions (and collective bargaining coverage) are generally recognised to generate a wage mark-up over non-union pay levels, varying over time with relative bargaining power, and over labour force groups and labour market sectors. Estimates suggest that the public sector mark-up is significantly higher than in the private sector; and the mark-up for women, lower-skilled and disadvantaged groups tends to be higher than in other sectors, presumably reflecting the effects of collective bargaining in pursuit of common pay rates and conditions for covered workers (Blanchflower, 1986; Beaumont and Harris, 1990). Evidence over time suggests the union mark-up saw a strong rise at the start of the 1970s, then remained fairly stable until 1984 before falling in the later 1980s (Layard *et al.*, 1991; Metcalf, 1994). This would accord with the weakening bargaining power of unions as the 1980s progressed, though real wage growth was maintained – arguably as a result of employers winning concessions over manning and working practices, raising productivity in unionised firms (Metcalf, 1994).

Women are much less likely to be union members than men, and unionisation among part-timers is much lower than for full-time workers. Reductions in union density and membership, collective bargaining coverage and union bargaining power are thus more likely to have a negative effect on male than female earnings. A reduced mark-up would tend to reduce male earnings relative to women's, with the exception that women who are unionised and have benefited from a high mark-up may lose out in parallel with men. Much depends on the scale of the union 'spill-over' effects, and the extent to which non-union sectors of employment fare even worse under high unemployment than sectors where unions are well represented.

However, it is also arguable that as unions weaken, their ability to contain differentials will be lessened and wage dispersion will increase, as will wage inequality. The unions' ability to defend the interests of weaker groups in society is reduced, and women in the lower reaches of the earnings distribution may fare worse. There is now widespread agreement that inequalities have increased throughout the 1980s and 1990s in Britain, and the position of women concentrated in low-paid occupations, or segregated into a part-time marketplace, is likely to have deteriorated. Overall, the outcome of weaker trade unions and reduced coverage may be to narrow the gender gap, but this discussion suggests that other effects may be increased divergence within both male and female components of the labour force.

In the 1980s there was considerable debate about the existence and importance of the 'flexible' firm, portrayed as an employing organisation with a core or stable workforce and a periphery of flexible workers to absorb the main fluctuations in demand (Atkinson, 1985; Atkinson and Meager, 1986; Pollert, 1987; Hunter *et al.*, 1993). While there is no doubt that more extensive use of flexible labour (part-timers, temporary workers and self-employed sub-contractors) did occur in the 1980s, evidence suggests this was due less to employers adopting new flexible practices than to relative expansion of industries and occupations in which flexible working arrangements were normal (McGregor and Sproull, 1991). Data for the 1990–3 recession indicates sharp falls in the use of temporary and self-employed workers, though part-time work was less affected (Robinson, 1994; Hunter, 1994).

The economic conditions of the 1980s in Britain underlined for many employers the need to keep labour costs in check, often as a means of survival, commonly as a contribution to competitiveness. Many employers recognised that peaks of activity (whether cyclical, seasonal, or time of week or day) could be covered by flexible labour, such as workers on short-term finite contracts, agency temps, and part-timers to cover peak days or hours, rather than by paying full-time regular workers, whose time and work were not fully utilised. There are of course costs to the use of flexible labour, as well as advantages:[5] temporary workers and sub-contracted personnel may have less loyalty and commitment to the employer, and little incentive to provide high-quality service. But for many types of easily-learned, low-skill and repetitive work (assembly operation, packing, and so on) flexible labour will serve well enough. Part-timers are often more akin to full-timers in their degree of job knowledge, loyalty and commitment, and may be able to aspire to limited promotion and training. They offer scope for flexibility of hours worked, usually without the need to pay a premium overtime rate.[6]

The use of non-standard contract labour has increased, with employers thinning out full-time, standard contract workers (predominantly male) and covering the gaps with part-time (or other 'flexible' contract) workers, predominantly female. While Robinson (1994) argues that there was no clear break in trend in part-time female employment in the 1980s, there was no indication that women were entering the labour force at an unprecedented rate after 1979. However, this does not rule out the possibility of some substitution of part-time female workers for other workers, since the effect of earlier contributions to the growth of part-time female employment (such as favourable structural changes in industrial and occupational employment) may well have weakened by the 1980s. In other words, a stable or even declining rate of growth of part-time female employment could still be consistent with some employers substituting part-time for full-time workers.

This situation would be assisted by a segmentation of the full-time/part-time female labour markets, which employers could exploit. For example, one 'segment' might contain a readily-replenished flow of women available only for part-time work because of the presence of young children, an absence of childcare facilities at affordable prices for low-income households, and being 'locked in' to household tasks through superior

---

[5] Cost advantages are less to do with reduced hourly rates than with reduced costs of pension contributions, sick pay and annual leave. In Britain, unlike Australia, there is no loading factor for temporary workers in most cases (McGregor and Sproull, 1991).

[6] Overtime premium rates in Britain generally only apply after a 'full-time' threshold of weekly hours has been worked. In Australia penalty rates apply to the period when work is on, say, Sundays, whereas an imputation for overtime is often included in hourly pay for part-timers.

skills in such activity; while another 'segment' might comprise a full-time female labour market in which qualifications, work experience (and continuity) and commitment are required to enable women to compete with their male counterparts.

Table 11.6 Shares of workers in low (L), medium (M) and high (H) wage employment

Australia

		Average per annum			
		1975–9	1980–4	1985–9	1993
Men	L	17.69	19.35	22.83	25.97
	M	74.75	73.18	68.58	63.58
	H	7.56	7.47	8.59	10.45
Women	L	26.17	28.46	32.32	32.89
	M	70.27	66.49	59.94	55.45
	H	3.56	5.05	7.74	11.66

Britain

		1976	1981	1986	1994
Men	L	15.0	19.3	23.5	26.0
	M	75.4	69.7	64.0	58.0
	H	9.6	11.0	12.5	16.0
Women	L	17.4	17.0	20.0	24.0
	M	72.6	72.3	68.0	62.0
	H	10.0	10.7	12.0	14.0

Source: Australia – *The Distribution and Composition of Employee Earnings and Hours*, various issues; Great Britain – New Earnings Survey

Notes

1 Australian figures are based on full-time workers earning less than 75 per cent of the median, 75–175 per cent of the median, and more than 175 per cent of the median.

2 British figures are estimates based on NES tables of gross hourly earnings, excluding overtime, for full-time employees on adult rates whose pay was not affected by absence in the period. Like the Australian figures, the British estimates (by interpolation within earnings bands) are for workers earning less than 75 per cent, 75–175 per cent and more than 175 per cent of the median.

On the evidence of Table 11.6, middle-ranking jobs in the British earnings distribution have been declining in importance, rather more rapidly for men than for women. Both higher-paid and lower-paid jobs[7] have been expanding, but the upper range has expanded faster. Table 11.6 shows a similar pattern in the Australian experience.

Given this, a scenario can be ventured in which the middle range of jobs is shrinking, to be replaced in part by a growing proportion of low-paid,

---

[7] Robinson (1994) comes to an opposite conclusion for low-ranked jobs, using a different approach to the pay distribution.

low-skilled jobs in manufacturing and personal service industries fed by a highly-elastic supply of female labour, predominantly part-time. This contrasts with the non-manual sector, containing faster-growing managerial and professional groups, where the evidence suggests the discrimination coefficient against women tends to be lower (for university graduates see Dolton and Makepeace, 1986; for professional workers, see Chiplin and Sloane, 1976). This scenario is certainly in line with the observed improvement in the measured wage gap for full-time non-manual workers, while the manual worker gender gap remains unchanged and the full-time/part-time ratio for women moved against the part-timers, as described earlier.

Alternatively, this situation could mark a change in the way the wage structure rewards skills (including education, qualifications and work experience). A flexible wage structure would certainly be expected to reflect buoyant demand for better-qualified non-manual workers and declining demand for manual skills, in terms of a widening differential and a wider dispersion (greater inequality) in the earnings distribution. This assuredly fits with the evolution of the earnings structure in Britain in the 1980s and 1990s, probably assisted by the changes in wage-fixing mechanisms and practices discussed earlier. And (younger) female full-time workers in general seem to have been in a good position to take advantage of this shift in demand structure: the evidence is that over the last 15 years there has been a reversal of the former superiority of boys' qualifications on leaving school relative to girls' (*Social Trends*, 1994).

Australia

By the early 1990s it was evident that the economy had slipped far down the OECD rankings in terms of growth in output, employment and productivity (Rimmer, 1994). This was the background to the quest for micro-economic reform, or a drive for enhanced efficiency at industry and enterprise levels. In March 1991 the Prime Minister's Economic Statement foreshadowed a phasing-down of tariffs by the year 2000. The government promised 'transitional assistance' in the form of labour adjustment packages (LAPs) for vulnerable industries such as textiles, clothing and footwear (TCF) and motor vehicles. Workers would be entitled to short-term job training with income support, wage subsidies for up to six months, and relocation assistance.

In TCF it is mainly women who bear the adjustment costs. Some have used LAPs for English language training, some have found new jobs in TCF, some have retired or become unemployed, while many others have become outworkers at pay rates well below the industry award. It is anticipated that the men displaced from the motor industry and associated areas of manufacturing will be more mobile across the workplace, and less likely to be unable to find work than women. Thus a policy with clear-cut implications for a gender bias in outcomes was implemented without recognition of the likely uneven burden of the costs of structural change.

The Prime Minister's advisory council suggested a number of micro-efficiency measures, including policies to reduce turnover and absenteeism, improve industrial relations, enhance levels of skill and job training, and encourage better safety standards and the development of an 'export culture' among workers and their managers. Key elements of the labour market reform involved the arrangement of working time, revised shift-working schedules, the reduction or abolition of penalty rates for unsociable hours, and the absorption of overtime pay into wages. The changes in the conditions and organisation of work have clear implications for women, and it is not apparent that these have been thought through.

On the demand side, employers seem to be seeking considerable flexibility about when work will be undertaken and how it can be fitted to changed trading patterns and conditions. Firms expect cost savings and greater efficiency by extending non-standard working patterns. On the supply side, individuals are likely to choose flexible working patterns to help them meet their home responsibilities, to fit into study or retraining, or simply to accept what work is available. For some workers these are short-term options, but for others they may become longer-term traps. The risk of marginalisation is there for both men and women. It is often argued that concerns for these people are unjustified, since when asked only a minority would prefer longer working hours. Of course, the 'choice' of accepting part-time work and the extent of working hours may be notional. Security and the likelihood of future options, as well as the possibility of exploitation, must also be considered.

Quite a lot is known already about work undertaken in Australia on a part-time or casual basis (Romeyn, 1992). The Australian incidence of these working patterns is high by international standards, with the bulk of the work in sales and personal service occupations, clerical work and labouring. Two-thirds of Australia's casual work is in wholesale and retail trades, community services, and the recreation and personal service industries. Almost four-fifths of permanent part-time work is in community services, selling, and the financial sector. Casual employment is distributed in the female-to-male ratio of 60 to 40.

Traditionally Australian unions have opposed part-time work, seeing it as a threat to full-time jobs. It may be that the increasing casualisation of work is the employers' way round such objections. Casual work is paid by the hour, with loadings of typically around 20 per cent to compensate for the lack of the benefits attached to permanent work, whether full- or part-time. Family considerations dominate the female preference for part-time or casual work, but job availability and study are the reasons given by men for these work patterns.

The flavour of the drive to more flexible working patterns and the practical complexities may be captured in the case of retailing. For part-time adult workers, pay is below average for both women and men. About two-thirds of these workers are women, who earn 96 per cent of male pay.

Retailers claim that the system of awards, structured in times of much lower female workforce participation, has inhibited their flexibility. Sales patterns at that time reflected the fact that most women were able to shop at virtually any time of the week. A recent force for structural change for retailers has been a customer preference to shop late in the week, and later in the day than they did years ago. Stores accordingly need experienced staff to be available at these new core shopping times.

To meet changing shopping patterns without significant additional labour costs, broader definitions of ordinary hours have been made and a complete review of loadings has taken place. Employers proposed significant variations to the standard 38-hour week, providing for work to be compressed into fewer days. They sought a total of 152 hours to be worked in each 28-day period, with a minimum of eight days' leave. This still meant 38-hour weeks, but with the possibility of 12-hour shifts. An alternative was packages of part-time work, such as a 28-hour week worked over two-and-a-half days.

The ILO (1990) sees employer demands for greater flexibility as underpinned by the drive to become more competitive. Union focus is on strategies to defend the interests of workers. The ILO has shown that the demands from these parties are not compatible. There is a strong possibility of a transfer to workers, especially women, of the costs associated with achieving increased efficiency. Extended, very lengthy shifts may be so tiring for some workers that cost-efficiency is not attainable. The Women's Electoral Lobby in Australia is concerned that agreements to compress the working week into days involving 12-hour shifts and early starts will disadvantage workers with children. For women, the issues of flexibility, participation, part-time work and caring responsibilities are inseparable. Policy which does not recognise that must permit, if not promote, inequity.

The need for greater workplace flexibility is emerging in all parts of the economy where the bunching of tasks is possible: tourism and hospitality are obvious areas. But employers still seem to think that part-time work is viewed by the unions as under-employment. Flexibility on hours would be viewed by them as a 'loss of their hard-won gains'.

There are a number of avenues for employers to achieve flexibility despite the award system. In the short term at least, they can hire even more casual staff – in line with the predictions of the 'core/periphery' model. Such workers have hourly contracts, and firms may prefer permanent part-time workers. Part-time pay attracts standard benefits, but there is scope for gain from longer-term attachments between workers and their employers. It may be that retailing (and other flexible-time sectors) become more male-intensive. A 12-hour shift in retailing is normally from 10am to 10pm and, at least in central business districts where the bulk of employment is concentrated, problems of transport and safety are already emerging for women.

The trend in Australia appears to be towards more regulation of non-standard-hours jobs. Casual work is becoming increasingly part of the award structure. Unions are starting to recognise that the tide is turning on permanent part-time work to the disadvantage of many unionists, particularly women. The likely outcome is that flexible working agreements, reached at the workplace and registered formally, will regularise arrangements on non-standard work.

It is quite clear that those with least bargaining strength are best protected in a formal system, so the focus now turns to pay-fixing and institutional changes. Workplace reform must be seen against the background of the quests of employers for savings, and of workers for the means to combine their paid working life with domestic roles. The Australian government is stoutly behind the overhaul of the labour market, even if it is unwilling to recognise the uneven costs this is imposing.

The government has argued in the 1990s that workplace reform at the enterprise level of the micro-economy is a key element of the policy mix to achieve macro-economic goals, and would be achieved through decentralisation of wage fixing. At first the IRC chose not to arbitrate enterprise agreements, but at the October 1991 National Wage Case the principle of enterprise bargaining was established. Only the Australian Federation of Business and Professional Women stated outright opposition to the IRC, fearing that the industrially strong would gain from the new system and that women would be disadvantaged. The Women's Electoral Lobby emphasises the generally weaker bargaining power of women, believing that women's concerns will be ignored, that part-time workers are at a relative disadvantage, and that women are more likely than men to trade working conditions for pay.

Progress in registering enterprise bargains has been slow. By mid-1993, 1,000 agreements ratified by the IRC applied to 11.5 per cent of workers. To mid-1992 the bargains were concentrated in metals and manufacturing, where output and productivity measures are easier to obtain and interpret than in sectors like education, health, welfare and other services. Of critical concern are those who work where productivity is not readily measurable, such as government services and non-profit organisations funded by donations, levies and subsidies. If output cannot be measured, except in terms of the cost of inputs used to produce it, there seems little hope that an operational way will be found to demonstrate productivity gains on which to base wage claims. For many workers, enterprise bargains are an empty option. Women are likely to be over-represented in that group.

There is another reason for concern that women will lose out in the new pay arrangements. Reporting on equity considerations, the Department of Industrial Relations (1993) found that where workplaces have a particularly high percentage of female workers, there is a lower than average probability that a workplace agreement will be in place. An 'access gap' has been identified: compared with 24 per cent of men, only

15 per cent of women working at places with at least 20 workers are covered by a negotiated agreement. Not only are women excluded from agreements, but they also appear to work where there are none.

On an industrial basis, women work mainly in community services, wholesale and retail trades, and finance. Only in community services, where pay growth is below average (but the female/male pay ratio is high), is the coverage of agreements above the economy-wide average. But here 13 per cent of men were covered by agreements, compared to only six per cent of women. The most likely jobs to be excluded from agreements have been clerical, sales and personal service workers. Given the large proportion of Australian women's jobs accounted for by these commonly-excluded occupations, the equity consideration is substantial. The vast majority of women have so far remained directly untouched by enterprise bargaining; but given the access gap, which means that relative pay changes must occur, it cannot be inferred that women are not indirectly affected by the enterprise deals negotiated by men.

Distributional data newly released this year provides some evidence that the shift towards a more decentralised bargaining system is favouring men. In the year to May 1993, the female/male relativity fell from 91.9 per cent to 91.1 per cent. For women, 'over-award' pay fell by over 11 per cent; for men it fell by less than two per cent. The dispersion of weekly earnings grew: people in the lowest decile had earnings growth of 1.5 per cent, compared with 3.7 per cent for the top decile. The jobs in the bottom decile are essentially women's jobs, whereas those at the top include many professions where women are greatly under-represented.

In April 1988 the Australian government amended the Conciliation and Arbitration Act. The new Industrial Relations Bill was meant to streamline procedures, overcome deficiencies, and promote the government's industry and industrial relations goals. The aim was to have far fewer unions, and for these to be industrial rather than craft-based. Union amalgamation is supported by the union movement overall, and over time the number of individual unions fell. Male unionisation had risen in the 1970s, but had fallen by a third by 1993; unionisation of women (down by a quarter over the same period) was about the same in 1993 as it had been 25 years earlier.

About 40 per cent of unionists are women, but a far smaller percentage of union officials are female. The union movement has been active at times in promoting women's concerns over training, childcare, maternity and paternity leave, and in 1994 the case for parental leave. The ACTU has formally attempted to raise female representation in its executive by reserving three designated positions for women. A leading woman unionist suggested that, rather than being dealt with as a matter of fairness, giving attention to 'women's matters' is linked to the survival of unions in the context of the rapid rise in the feminisation of the workforce (Deery and Plowman, 1991).

But another view about the ACTU is that its:

> support for enterprise bargaining, its record on casual employment
> and the gender-biased nature of many of its political and industrial
> agendas indicate despite the public rhetoric, gender issues are still
> of marginal concern. (Bennett, 1994: 197.)

The ACTU leadership has openly stated its support for enterprise
bargaining, which is not surprising given its closeness to the government.
What is surprising is the unwillingness to concede the risks to equity,
which appear obvious to many. It is probable that although the main
union body supports enterprise bargaining, some officials involved in
negotiation are less certain that it is appropriate.

There are few studies on gender and unions in Australia, but research
suggests that a premium for unionists of around ten to 15 per cent is likely.
Christie (1992) found no significant difference in the premium for men
and women. Korosi *et al.* (1993b) found the unionist premium was greater
for young men (eight per cent) than for young women (five per cent). Their
Oaxaca decomposition showed that, for both sexes, about 40 per cent of
the pay differences between unionists and others is due to discrimination
in favour of unionists.

One feature of the award system in Australia which is currently being
overhauled is the multiplicity of awards and their often vast range of pay
classifications. At the end of the 1980s work began on restructuring and
simplifying awards. The ACTU produced a 'blueprint' for restructuring.
Skill-related career paths were formalised in awards, as were training and
the possibility of multi-skilling in job descriptions. Employers would deal
with fewer unions and less complex awards, but whether on balance this
helps or hinders equity, and whether it will influence the union mark-up
on gender, remains to be determined.

Predicting the longer-term impact of the industrial relations changes of
the past five years or so is difficult. It is unclear whether the unions will
be more or less powerful or successful under the new arrangements. Given
the 'official line' of the ACTU on enterprise bargains, it is also unclear
how interested unions will be in recognising the pitfalls of labour market
deregulation for Australian women. It is hard to know whether the
replacement of craft-based unions with industrial unions will promote or
inhibit equity. One would suspect that a union representing clerks might
afford more protection for women, than, say, a mining union negotiating
principally for men at workplaces where clerks are present.

Overall, this evidence suggests a number of propositions. Women have
both gained and lost from policies which were supposed to be gender
neutral. They were best protected in Australia in the highly-regulated
arrangements of the indexation phase, and to some extent under the
Accord. They gained from policies which were directed towards efficiency
gains through the restructuring of awards and work organisation. Jobs

(like nursing) which had never provided career paths opened up more promotion opportunities for women in the 1990s than in the past. Women also gained from the drive for multi-skilling, as the training provisions of awards gave them opportunities to extend their skills. Working in teams and cellular methods of organisation extended the scope of their work skills. Finally, women gained in terms of superannuation coverage from the non-wage benefits under the Accord.

On the minus side, there can be no doubt that the decentralisation of bargaining has already reversed some pay equity gains. Without some more substantial 'safety net' provisions than those currently in place, women at the bottom of the pay structure will fall even further behind. The skewing of the gender attachment to work means that, at least in the foreseeable future, women's labour market position will be compromised rather than promoted by enterprise agreements. Bennett (1994) argues strongly that empirical work on the gender consequences of enterprise bargaining shows the pay gap to be widening already:

> decentralised wage fixation is likely to swamp any compensatory effects associated with the introduction of anti-discrimination provisions. (Bennett, 1994: 206.)

Conclusions

Many of these issues require further examination, but three general lessons emerge.

- The comparative approach serves a useful purpose in broadening the scope of inquiry on equal pay by providing a focus on the interaction of policy, institutions and the economic environment which is not highlighted in the standard human capital model.
- Future change in the gender pay gap may well be more influenced by general economic policies (and agent responses), which have no explicit gender intent but may in practice prove not to be gender neutral. The potential gender implications of general policy should be subject to greater attention than in the past.
- The country-specific structure and behaviour of institutions are important intermediaries in the actual implementation and adaptation of policies by economic agents in the labour market. The differences in the two countries with regard to casual employment and pay provide a striking example.

More substantively, it is clear that the labour markets of the 1990s are very different from those of the 1970s, when equal pay and equal opportunities legislation was introduced. The drive in developed industrial countries for a more competitive stance has led governments to 'deregulate' labour markets, albeit in different ways and degrees, to permit greater responsiveness to competition. This has tended to increase the extent of the 'flexible labour force', although the structure may differ. In Britain the dominant form appears to be part-time employment, whereas in Australia the casual (temporary) workforce is more important. This may be due in part to different union attitudes: British unions are more anxious about temporary employment, but Australian unions have been more hostile towards part-time employment – a difference which is surely attributable to the Australian award system, which provides greater protection and compensation for its casual workers. Thus Australian unions can 'afford' to be less fearful than their British counterparts about the casualisation of the workforce.

Wage-fixing institutions have undergone considerable change in both countries, against a background of trade union rationalisation, reduced membership and a reduction in bargaining power. In Australia, the most important effects stem from the shift towards enterprise bargaining, with a growing risk that the prop to women's relative earnings from a centralised system may be removed, widening the gender wage gap. This will be all the more important if the 'access gap' proves to be substantial. In Britain, the considerable changes to bargaining structures are less clear-cut in their implications for the gender gap, although some deterioration may be predicted at the lower-skilled, part-time end of the market; and the abolition of Wages Councils may add to this in time. In both countries there are risks that weaker, less-advantaged groups of women employees will fall further behind, especially if trends in the occupational structure of employment continue to squeeze out middle- and low-skilled jobs and intensify competition for the remaining jobs at the lower end of the market.

These considerations make it difficult to assess the overall implications of 'flexibility' for women's pay and opportunity. It may well have improved the position and prospects of those women who have been able to take advantage of the breakdown in traditional work structures and patterns. Where women have been able to unload their conventional domestic responsibilities, or find ways of working round them, greater market flexibility may enhance earning power. But for less-advantaged women who have greater difficulty in providing continuous market-time commitment, the effect may well be to lock them into a highly-competitive and low-paid segment of the labour market with poor prospects, which may become increasingly detached from the primary labour market sector. Although the Australian system has hitherto provided better protection for these groups, its future ability to do so is a matter of concern, though not yet (apparently) to the trade union movement.

This comparative approach also draws attention to the fact that the crude gender pay gap tells only part of the story. Following the Australian 1983 Accord, non-wage benefits for part-timers and casual workers improved significantly. The coverage (universal among full-time workers) of superannuation offers far superior retirement outcomes for women than were dreamt of a decade ago. But whether non-wage conditions compensate for wage differences, or exaggerate the differential, is a matter requiring further examination.

Overall, there is some evidence to suggest that the relative position of women has tended to improve in recent years; although at least in Britain this may partly be due to an absolute deterioration in the male labour market. But there may also be some suggestions of a 'twist', with women who have better education and who work in expanding, better-paid occupations improving their positions, while those at the bottom end inhabiting the secondary labour market are clearly at risk of doing less well than before. If this is correct (and it would seem consistent with general observations on the greater social and economic inequality of recent years), it suggests that the secondary sector in which women predominate is the area which needs to be watched most carefully. Centralisation of wage fixing, high employment, strong trade unions and legislation providing social protection tend to prevent the secondary market becoming detached from the primary market. In the absence of these conditions – such as has been experienced in recent years – the risk of radical decoupling is high.

An OECD report characterises

> women as principal economic actors... [Recognising this] challenges the traditional assumption that equity and efficiency are mutually exclusive outcomes that have to be traded off against each other. Women are not a problem for the economy. On the contrary, the solution to economic problems depends on enhancing women's economic role. (OECD, 1991: 7.)

Where the role of women in working life is enhanced, it appears that equity is least compromised. But in modern times it is essential to consider the gender implications of new policies, and also to preserve the 'safety nets' of minimum wage laws which have in the past afforded protection for those most vulnerable to structural change. In both countries it is likely that economic forces are impacting differently on different groups of women. An exploration of this is clearly a direction for further work.

Acknowledgements

The authors are grateful to Phil Beaumont, Colette Fagan, Jill Rubery and Diane Sinclair for helpful comments on earlier drafts. Residual errors of omission or commission are the responsibility of the authors.

References

Atkinson, J. (1985). *Flexibility, Uncertainty and Manpower Management.* IMS Report 89. Brighton: Institute of Manpower Studies.

Atkinson, J. and Meager, N. (1986). 'Is flexibility just a flash in the pan?' in *Personnel Management*, September.

Australian Bureau of Statistics (1992). *The Distribution and Composition of Employee Earnings and Hours.* May.

Australian Bureau of Statistics (1994). *The Distribution and Composition of Employee Earnings and Hours*. May.

Beaumont, P. B. and Harris, R. I. D. (1990). 'Collective bargaining and relative wages' in Gregory, M. B. and Thomson, A. W. J. (eds.) *A Portrait of Pay*, 1970–1982. Oxford: Clarendon Press.

Becker, G. (1964). *Human Capital*. New York: Columbia University Press.

Becker, G. (1985). 'Human capital, effort and the sexual division of labor' in *Journal of Labor Economics*, 3.

Bennett, L. (1994). 'Women and enterprise bargaining: the legal and institutional framework' in *The Journal of Industrial Relations*, 26 (2).

Blanchflower, D. (1986). 'What effect do unions have on relative wages in Britain?' in *British Journal of Industrial Relations*, July.

Blau, F. D. and Kahn, L. M. (1992). *The Gender Earnings Gap: Some International Evidence*. NBER Working Paper 4224. Cambridge, Mass: National Bureau of Economic Research.

Blau, F. D. and Kahn, L. M. (1994). 'Rising wage inequality and the US gender gap' in *American Economic Review*, Papers and Proceedings, 84.

Borooah, V. K. and Lee, K. C. (1988). 'The effect of changes in Britain's industrial structure on female relative pay and employment' in *Economic Journal*, 98.

Chiplin, B. and Sloane, P. J. (1976). 'Personal characteristics and sex differentials in professional employment' in *Economic Journal*, 86.

Chiplin, B. and Sloane, P. J. (1988). 'The effects of Britain's anti-discrimination legislation on relative pay and employment: a comment' in *Economic Journal*, 98.

Christie, V. (1992). 'Union wage effects and the probability of union membership' in *Economic Record*, 68 (200).

Commonwealth of Australia (1988). *Labour Market Reform, The Industrial Relations Agenda, 1988–89*. Budget-related paper 9. Canberra: AGPS.

Deery, S. J. and Plowman, D. H. (1991). *Australian Industrial Relations* (3rd edition). New South Wales: McGraw-Hill.

Department of Employment (1985–93). *New Earnings Survey*. London: HMSO.

Department of Industrial Relations (1993). *Enterprise Bargaining: the First 1,000 Agreements*. Canberra: AGPS.

Dickens, R., Gregg, P., Machin, S., Manning, A. and Wadsworth, J. (1993). 'Wage Councils: was there a case for abolition?' in *British Journal of Industrial Relations*, December.

Dolton, P. and Makepeace, G. (1986). 'Sample selection and male–female earnings differentials in the graduate labour market' in *Oxford Economic Papers*, 38.

Dolton, P., O'Neill, D. and Sweetman, O. (1994). *Gender Differences in the Changing Labour Market: Opportunities of Qualified Manpower in Britain, 1960–87*. Paper presented to the EMRU Workshop, July.

Ermisch, J. and Wright, R. (1991). 'Gender discrimination in the British labour market: a reassessment' in *Economic Journal*, 101.

Hakim, C. (1993). 'Segregated and integrated occupations: a new approach to analysing social change' in *European Sociological Review*, 9, December.

Humphries, J. (1995). 'Economics, gender and equal opportunities' in this volume.

Hunter, L. C. (1994). 'The "flexible" labour force in Scotland?' in *Scottish Economic Bulletin*, 48, Winter 1993–4. HMSO.

Hunter, L. C., McGregor, A., MacInnes, J. and Sproull, A. (1993). 'The flexible firm: strategy and segmentation' in *British Journal of Industrial Relations*, 31, September.

ILO (1990). 'The hours we work: new work schedules in policy and practice' in *Conditions of Work Digest*, 9 (2). Geneva: International Labour Organisation.

Korosi, G., Rimmer, R. and Rimmer, S. (1993a). 'Rising inequality? Shifts in the distributions of earnings and income among young Australians' in *La Trobe University Discussion Paper*, 12/93.

Korosi, G., Rimmer, R. and Rimmer, S. (1993b). 'Contributions from gender and unions to earnings differences among young Australians: the analysis of a panel' in *Proceedings of the Conference on Contemporary Issues in Income Distribution*. Sydney: University of New South Wales.

Layard, R., Nickell, S. and Jackman, R. (1991). *Unemployment, Macro-economic Performance and the Labour Market*. Oxford: Oxford University Press.

McGregor, A. and Sproull, A. (1991). *Employer Labour Use Strategies: Analysis of a National Survey*. Research Paper 83. London: Department of Employment.

Metcalf, D. (1994). 'Transformation of British industrial relations? Institutions, conduct and outcomes, 1980–1990' in Barrell, R. (ed.) *The UK Labour Market*. Cambridge: Cambridge University Press/National Institute of Economic and Social Research.

Millward, N., Stevens, M., Smart, D. and Hawes, W. (1992). *Workplace Industrial Relations in Transition*. Aldershot: ESRC/PSI/ACAS.

Mincer, J. (1985). 'Inter-country comparisons of labour force trends and of related developments: the overview' in *Journal of Labour Economics*, 3.

Norris, K. (1993). *The Economics of Australian Labour Markets*. Melbourne: Longman Cheshire.

OECD (1991). *Shaping Structural Change: the Role of Women*. Paris: Organisation for Economic Co-operation and Development.

Paci, P., Makepeace, G., Joshi, H. and Dolton, P. (1994). *Is Pay Discrimination Against Women a Thing of the Past? A Tale of Two Cohorts*. Paper presented to the EMRU workshop, July.

Pollert, A. (1987). 'The flexible firm: a model in search of reality' in *Warwick Papers in Industrial Relations*, 19, University of Warwick.

Rimmer, S. (1991). 'Occupational segregation, earnings differentials and status among Australian workers' in *Economic Record*, 67 (198).

Rimmer, S. (1994). *Australian Labour Market and Microeconomic Reform*. Bundoora: La Trobe University Press.

Robinson, P. (1994). 'The British labour market in historical perspective: changes in the structure of employment and unemployment' in *CEP Discussion Paper 202*. London: Centre for Economic Performance.

Romeyn, J. (1992). 'Flexible working time: part-time and casual employment' in *Industrial Relations Research Monograph No 1*. Canberra: Department of Industrial Relations.

Rubery, J. (1992). 'Pay, gender and the social dimension to Europe' in *British Journal of Industrial Relations*, 30 (4).

Rubery, J. and Fagan, C. (1994). 'Equal pay policy and wage regulation systems in Europe' in *Industrial Relations Journal*, 25 (4).

Sloane, P. J. and Theodissiou, I. (1994). 'A generalised Lorenz curve approach to explaining the upward movement in women's relative earnings in Britain during the 1970s' in *Scottish Journal of Political Economy*, 41 (4).

Sly, F. (1993). 'Women in the labour market' in *Employment Gazette*, November.

Social Trends (1991). London: HMSO.

Social Trends (1994). London: HMSO.

Zabalza, A. and Tzannatos, Z. (1985). 'The effect of Britain's anti-discriminatory legislation on relative pay and employment' in *Economic Journal*, 95.

Zabalza, A. and Tzannatos, Z. (1988). 'Reply to the comments on the effects of Britain's anti-discrimination legislation' in *Economic Journal*, 98.

Part V

The State, the Family and the Labour Market

CHAPTER 12 # Part-time Work and Equal Opportunities: The Case of The Netherlands

Janneke Plantenga

In June 1993, the Dutch Green Left Party introduced a parliamentary Bill to stimulate part-time work. The proposed new Act would anchor in law the right to part-time employment, in the sense that an employee would be entitled to reduce current contractual working hours by a maximum of 50 per cent. The employer would be obliged to concur. In addition, distinctions between personnel arising from differences in working hours would be outlawed. Equal treatment of full- and part-timers would thus be established in law.

The explanatory statement accompanying the proposed Bill emphasised the importance of part-time work. It is seen as offering a solution to rising unemployment, providing industry with the flexibility it needs, and creating the possibility for individuals to combine paid work with caring tasks, further education or voluntary work. A number of problems are nevertheless recognised. To date, the growth of part-time employment has been concentrated in the service sector, and distributed unequally between men and women. In the view of the Bill's designer, however, these are not reasons to reject the concept of part-time work, and in fact make legislation essential. It would lead to the breakdown of employers' unreasonable resistance to part-time work for men and in areas outside service sectors, and result in a real redistribution of paid and unpaid work (*Bevordering van deeltijdarbeid*, 1992–3).

The Bill's most striking characteristic is its optimism; the emphasis lies on the opportunities offered by part-time work, and the fact that this legislation could (uniquely) serve the interests of all concerned – employees, employers and government. However, this optimism is not shared by everyone. A much more pessimistic view is expressed, for example, in the OECD report *Shaping Structural Change* (1991), which rejects part-time work as a 'peripheral adjustment to the employment contract' which in most cases has done little to modify employment norms or gender roles (*ibid.*, 10). Part-time work is viewed only as an improvement of the quantitative position of women in the labour market, whereas in qualitative terms little has changed. It does not actually affect the prevalent social division of labour; in contrast to their full-time working male partners, part-time working women have little prospect of building a career, and thus continue to combine household and caring tasks with a paid job. As a result, there is no question of a breakdown of traditional role patterns.

This discussion of the pros and cons of part-time work from an equal opportunities point of view is the central theme of this chapter. The analysis focuses on the Netherlands, as part-time work is very widespread in that country. However, the part-time phenomenon is much discussed in all countries of the EU, so the implications of this analysis go beyond the national boundary.

Part-time work: the involvement of men and women

An initial impression of the role played by part-time work in the labour market participation of men and women is given in Table 12.1, which shows data for both the Netherlands and the EU to facilitate comparisons. It should be noted that the distinction between full-time and part-time work is usually made on the basis of a spontaneous answer given by the person interviewed. However, a number of countries have a rather more specific classification which is wholly or partially based on the number of hours worked. Employees in the Netherlands, for example, are considered part-timers if they have less than 31 hours per week specified in their labour contracts, or if they work between 31 and 34 hours a week in a specific sector where these hours would be considered fewer than normal (Eurostat, 1988).

Table 12.1 Labour force participation and part-time work in the Netherlands and the EU, 1991

	Participation rate		Proportion of part-time work in the active population	
	NL	EC	NL	EC
Total	56.9	54.6	32.7	13.8
Men	70.0	67.5	15.7	4.0
Women	44.3	42.6	59.9	28.6
Married women	41.6	45.5	75.6	35.2

Source: Eurostat, Labour Force Survey, 1991

As Table 12.1 shows, part-time work is very widespread in the Netherlands; in 1991, 59.9 per cent of women worked part-time. The figure is even higher (75.6 per cent) when married women are considered. This is considerably higher than the European average: only the UK approaches this percentage. In the UK, 42.7 per cent of the active female population works part-time; and 49.6 per cent of married women. Denmark is in third place, with scores of 37.8 and 41.5 per cent respectively.

Table 12.1 also shows that many men work part-time in the Netherlands: 15.7 per cent, compared with a European average of four per cent. In the professional careers of men and women, however, part-time work plays a rather different role. For men, part-time work tends to remain an incidental and temporary phenomenon, while for women it is rather more structural. This difference is illustrated in Figure 12.2, which breaks down the participation rate for various age groups to distinguish between those working full-time, those working part-time and those unemployed.

Figure 12.2 Participation rate by age and position in labour force, 1991

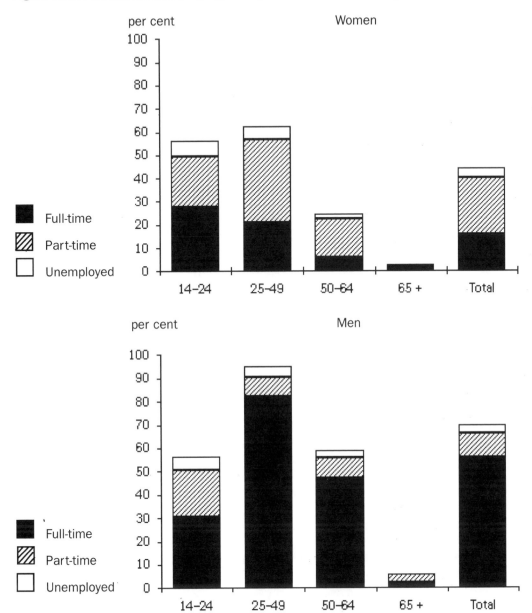

Source: Eurostat, Labour Force Survey, 1991

The graph clearly indicates that part-time work plays an important role for men in the 14 to 24 age group, where more than 30 per cent of the active male population works part-time. This group includes students who are, for example, employed part-time to sort mail for the postal authorities two nights a week or to stack shelves at a supermarket on Saturdays. In older age groups the incidence of part-time work falls to about eight or nine per cent, but rises again (significantly) in the 55-plus group.

For the active female population, however, a rather different picture emerges. The importance of part-time work is relatively limited in the youngest age group, with 38.6 per cent of the active female population aged 14 to 24 working part-time. But this percentage rises to 57.2 for the 25 to 49 age group, indicating that part-time work for women is not a temporary phenomenon restricted to the start or end of a professional career, but rather a very usual method of combining paid and unpaid work.

The demand for part-time work

The spectacular growth of part-time work in the Netherlands during the 1980s must be viewed within the specific economic and political situation of that time. From an economic point of view, the second half of the 1980s in particular was characterised by a significant increase in employment. Simultaneously, however, there was also a fairly significant growth in unemployment figures. For the most part, the increase in employment seems to have benefited new arrivals in the labour market, leaving a substantial number of hard-core long-term unemployed.

Politically, the 1980s can be characterised by an emphasis on the importance of unrestricted functioning of the market. After the 1960s and 1970s, when the government played a prominent part in the economic process, a more limited governmental role was advocated in the 1980s. Flexibility, privatisation and deregulation were the key words. In practice, this particular mix of economic and political circumstances led to a large increase in all manner of flexible labour relations, varying from part-time work to sub-contracting.

Of course, the application of various forms of flexibility may differ by sector. As Table 12.3 shows, the proportion of part-time workers is significantly above average in the service sector, with an especial concentration of part-time work in teaching, health care and other public services. Manufacturing, however, has a relatively low number of part-timers. In this sector, part-time work occurs mostly in the food, drink, tobacco, printing and publishing industries. It remains rare in the heavily-capitalised metal-processing industry, especially amongst personnel working directly in production (COB/SER, 1988).

The question as to what determines the selection of a specific strategy of flexibility is usually answered by reference to the type of work. For example, many services cannot be provided from stock, so in this sector it is important for human resources to be attuned to work demand. If work demand is relatively predictable (for example, in a retail outlet where late shopping and Saturdays could be expected to be busier than Mondays), part-time contracts for those periods are a real solution. In contrast, industry can generally produce from stock, so temporary under-staffing entails lower costs. A sudden rush can be handled potentially by overtime and/or bringing in temporary staff (LTD, 1991a).

Table 12.3 Proportion of people with a part-time job in various sectors, 1991

		Total	Employees
0	Agriculture, hunting, sylviculture and fishing	30.8	29.9
1	Mineral extraction	–	–
2/3	Manufacturing	19.2	18.9
4	Public utilities	–	–
5	Building and civil engineering	12.0	11.3
6	Commerce, catering and hotels, and repairs	37.4	40.0
7	Transport and communications	23.3	23.9
8	Banking, finance and insurance	27.1	24.8
90	Public administration, national defence and mandatory social security	19.7	19.6
91–9	Other services	58.9	58.9
	Total	34.3	33.9

Source: CBS, *Enquête Beroepsbevolking*, 1991

Beyond these objective differences, the selection of flexibility strategies will also be influenced by the gender composition of the labour supply. In more concrete terms, in their choice of strategy companies will take into account the existing personnel composition, so in a 'male job' the strategy will not be part-time work, but more often overtime or (full-time) temporary staff. The opposite obtains in 'female jobs', where overtime would not be the first option; here, bottle-necks are usually solved by part-time working.

Differences in the gender composition of the workforce also explain why there is so little part-time work in industrial sectors and so much in health care. In industrial sectors, the notion of part-time work is often dismissed as an illusion. There is resistance to it, especially when a company operates a shift system, because it would make planning even more complex. Conversely, a part-time nurse in a 'continuous shift' hospital is a fully accepted phenomenon (FNV, 1993b). Thus the selection of a particular strategy (part-time work) is not only based on the nature of the work, but also on the gender composition of the labour supply. As a consequence, flexibility strategies seem to intensify job segregation between the sexes. The lack of part-time work in industrial sectors and in higher, managerial positions makes these 'male' segments hard to reach for the female employee who prefers a part-time job. Instead, she is almost automatically nudged in the direction of the 'female' service sector where part-time work is normal.

The supply of part-time work

The advantages of certain forms of part-time work for government and employers are self-evident. But what causes an individual to work part-time, and to what extent is this a voluntary phenomenon? Table 12.4 shows that almost one quarter of men, 22.2 per cent (79 out of 356) to be precise, work part-time because they cannot find a full-time position; a relatively important proportion of this involuntary part-time work is apparent in the 25 to 44 age group. Over 46 per cent (164 out of 356) say they have taken a part-time position so they can pursue further education. This reason is given mostly by young people: high-school and university students attempting to improve their financial situation by working part-time. Health reasons for working part-time are also put forward, particularly in the older age groups. Finally, housekeeping is mentioned by 3.6 per cent (16 out of 356) of men. For women, however, this is by far the most important reason – close to 50 per cent (589 out of 1,180) of women part-timers mention housekeeping. As one would have expected, this is most common in the 25-plus age group. Involuntary part-time work seems to emerge equally for both men and women: almost 25 per cent (292 out of 1,180) of women said they were unable to find a full-time job.

Table 12.4 Employees (in thousands) by sex, age group and reasons for holding a part-time position, 1991

	15–24 years	25–44 years	45–64 years	Total
Men				
No part-time job	443	1972	803	3218
Part-time job	185	112	59	356
Management of household	–	13	–	16
Health	–	11	24	35
Education	148	15	–	164
Could only find part-time position	28	39	13	79
Other reasons	9	34	19	62
Total	629	2084	861	3574
Women				
No part-time job	362	572	110	1044
Part-time job	230	694	256	1180
Management of household	25	429	135	589
Health	–	10	11	23
Education	130	14	–	145
Could only find part-time position	58	156	78	292
Other reasons	16	84	32	132
Total	592	1266	366	2225

Source: CBS, *Enquête Beroepsbevolking*, 1991

The figures in Table 12.4, however, are more ambiguous than they appear at first sight. For example, giving housekeeping as a reason does not tell us whether part-time work is a voluntary or involuntary phenomenon. In the Netherlands, childcare facilities remain extremely limited. At the end of the 1980s, only about three per cent of the total number of children under four years old were taken care of in institutionalised facilities (European Commission Childcare Network, 1990). Following measures to stimulate childcare provision taken by the Ministry of Welfare, Health and Culture, the number of childcare places has grown rapidly in recent years, but waiting lists remain long. In addition, many day-care facilities are part-time: a child can have a place for three days a week, for example. Given this situation, a part-time position is often the only way to combine paid work with looking after young children.

Another problem arising from Table 12.4 is that the figures lack detail. It is true that a distinction is made according to age, but it would also have been interesting to know how the figures vary according to hours worked. It is possible that involuntary part-time work is more frequent in short hours part-time jobs. After all, a four-hour-a-week position as a French teacher is very different from an 18-hour-a-week job at the same school. Involuntary part-time work is perhaps not related to the phenomenon of part-time work as such, but to a specific variation of it: short hours part-time jobs.

The popularity of long hours part-time jobs is shown by recent research by the FNV (Dutch Federation of Trade Unions), which points out that a full-time working week is ideal for fewer and fewer people. In 1990, the ideal working week was 29 hours (averaged over both sexes); by 1993, the preferred number of working hours had dropped to 24 a week. Among women, the preferred number of working hours dropped from 24 to 19 hours a week, and a majority wanted a job working between 15 and 24 hours a week. Men wished to work on average 33 hours in 1990, and only slightly less then 29 hours in 1993, in which year a majority opted for a job of between 25 and 34 hours a week. Whereas in 1990 about 50 per cent of the men interviewed considered a full-time job as ideal, in 1993 this percentage dropped to little less than one third (FNV, 1993a).

This impression is confirmed by detailed research carried out in 1993 by the NIMMO (Netherlands Institute for Market Research) among 1,879 Dutch people aged 16 and over (Van den Putte and Pelzer, 1993). They were asked about their preferences for length of working hours if all impediments were removed, such as childcare needs, shortage of jobs and the impossibility of working part-time. Table 12.5 gives an initial overview of the findings. A distinction is made between the preferred and actual working hours of men and women and the situation at home.

It appears that women who have a partner and children living at home would like to make considerable changes to their working hours. At present, 63.4 per cent do not have a paid job, while 3.4 per cent work more than 34 hours. There is no enthusiasm for increasing working hours

Table 12.5 Working hours of men and women: ideal and actual

Paid hours per week

	With partner and children at home		With partner, without children at home		Single, no children at home	
	Now	Ideal	Now	Ideal	Now	Ideal
Women						
0 hours	63.4	13.7	47.0	19.4	43.3	7.2
1–14 hours	12.4	18.4	5.3	11.0	3.1	5.2
15–24 hours	14.3	50.3	9.3	38.3	5.2	20.6
25–34 hours	6.5	13.7	12.3	26.9	9.3	47.4
> 34 hours	3.4	3.4	26.0	4.4	39.2	19.6
	100.0	100.0	100.0	100.0	100.0	100.0
Men						
0 hours	9.6	1.3	31.5	9.1	32.3	3.8
1–14 hours	0.6	1.9	0.4	4.7	1.5	6.8
15–24 hours	1.0	21.0	2.2	18.5	3.0	12.0
25–34 hours	3.2	43.3	5.2	40.1	4.5	43.6
> 34 hours	85.7	32.5	60.8	27.6	58.6	33.8
	100.0	100.0	100.0	100.0	100.0	100.0

Source: Van den Putte and Pelzer, 1993

to 34 or more, but below this threshold there is some evidence of 'under-employment'. All but 13.7 per cent of these women would like to work at least some hours, and over 50 per cent regarded a part-time job of 15 to 24 hours as potentially ideal, while only 18 per cent would like to work between one and 14 hours. Men in a similar domestic position also preferred a part-time job but wanted to work longer hours, a result that also emerged from the FNV study. Over 43 per cent of these men chose working 25 to 34 hours a week, while 21 per cent would like to work between 15 and 24 hours.

Of the sub-group of women with a partner but without children at home, 26 per cent worked full-time but only 4.4 per cent considered this ideal. The percentages for men were 60.8 and 27.6 respectively.

Finally, of the single women without children almost 20 per cent preferred a full-time job. Although this percentage is considerably higher than among the other groups of women, the majority still preferred a (long hours) part-time job. Of their male counterparts only 33.8 per cent considered a full-time job as ideal; long part-time jobs were also popular among them.

To summarise, it appears that a part-time job is most popular among all groups, regardless of the presence or absence of partners or children. No more than one-third of any group wanted a full-time job. Half-time jobs (15 to 24 hours per week) were preferred by women with a partner, especially when they had children at home, and short part-time jobs were relatively unpopular with all groups. A longer part-time job (25 to 34 hours) is popular among all groups of men and among single women.

In conclusion, it can be confirmed that part-time work is far from voluntary in all cases. Considering the limited opportunities for childcare in the Netherlands, the percentage of involuntary part-time work shown in Table 12.4 should be considered as a minimum. However, there are indications that involuntary part-time work is most apparent in short hours part-time positions. Longer part-time jobs seem popular, on the other hand, even among those working full-time. A tentative conclusion can therefore be that short hours part-time positions are mainly stimulated by market demand, whilst in the case of longer part-time positions the supply side is most often the catalyst (see WRR, 1990).

Part-time work: some objections

From an equal opportunities point of view, the major advantage of a part-time position is that it allows the combination of paid and unpaid work. Nevertheless, part-time work does have its disadvantages. The legal status of those working part-time, for example, remains worse than that of those working full-time. One could also question the quality of many part-time jobs.

With regard to legal status, it should be noted that the general principle by which part-time and full-time workers must be treated equally is not yet legally established. This leads in practice to a number of different situations. A survey in 1991, for example, concerning the legal status of part-time workers shows that 82 per cent of the investigated companies paid part-time workers on an equal basis with full-time staff (LTD, 1991b). More than 16 per cent, however, paid part-timers proportionally less. Furthermore, 35 per cent of these firms do not pay bonuses to part-timers when they work unusual hours, while this figure was only 22 per cent for full-timers. About one-third of the companies have introduced a minimum-hours threshold for (early) retirement schemes. There are even a few firms where part-timers are obliged to contribute to early retirement schemes but cannot take up these options. Remarkably, 43 per cent of the studied collective agreements include measures supposed to stimulate part-time work, but only five per cent of the firms have in fact taken any concrete steps in this direction.

Besides legal status, the quality of part-time positions is a cause for concern: part-time positions are usually relatively low level. As already noted, part-time work appears to imply a certain continuation of horizontal and vertical job segregation between women and men. In jobs classified as 'typically male', part-time work has had little impact, and in (higher) management positions part-time jobs also remain relatively rare.

According to Table 12.6, 25 per cent of women and eight per cent of men worked part-time in such positions in 1991, against a general average of 61 and 17 per cent respectively working part-time in all jobs.

Table 12.6 People holding director-level and upper-management jobs according to the length of the weekly working schedule, 1991

	Total	Working week less than 35 hours		Share of part-time work in total active population
	absolute (x 1.000)	absolute (x 1.000)	percentage	
Women	69	17	25	61
Men	413	35	8	17

Source: CBS, *Enquête Beroepsbevolking*, 1991

The fact that high-quality part-time positions are relatively rare is also confirmed by a representative survey carried out by LTD in 1988. Of the companies studied, 61 per cent only use part-time labour for low-level positions, 27 per cent have part-time workers at low and middle levels, and eight per cent at low, middle and high levels. Part-time work often remains limited to low-level positions primarily in small companies (LTD, 1988).

The generally poorer legal status and lower level of part-time jobs have, of course, consequences on wages. Research on the effects of career interruptions on wage levels show that an interruption of a few years has considerable consequences. A part-time job does moderate these effects, but in the long term also results in a lower wage level than a full-time position (Groot *et al.*, 1990). The fact that far more women than men work part-time will certainly contribute to the persistent wage gap between men and women.

Part-time work as an emancipation strategy: arguments for and against

The disadvantages of part-time work make the growth of this form of employment in the Netherlands something of a mystery. Who actually wants a job with poor legal status and no career perspectives? In view of these disadvantages, what can explain the fact that 60 per cent of the active Dutch female labour force works part-time, and that enthusiasm for such work is obviously even higher than this?

The peculiar history of women's work in the Netherlands is without doubt an important reason. Up to about 1960, the married woman working outside the home was a rare phenomenon; she was almost always at home. Of course, there have been many changes over the past 30 years, but for many the woman remains first and foremost a spouse, a housewife and a mother. When the question of taking on a professional job is raised, a part-time position is preferred because the identification of a woman with a professional job remains rather diffuse. Women choose a part-time position in order to combine paid work with domestic duties at home, and not in order to lose the spouse-housewife-mother identification. In other words, part-time work allows sexual identity and professional identity to coexist.

The fact that women maintain some distance from 'the professional world' through part-time work also makes them vulnerable. Women working part-time remain *women* first and foremost; in other words, they are people with other commitments, and thus differentiate themselves from their (male) colleagues working full-time. The disadvantages linked to part-time work, such as the more fragile legal status and mediocre wages, can be considered as an exploitation and a confirmation of this difference. The disadvantages can exist because they relate to persons whose identity and livelihood in most cases do not depend (entirely) on their own working activity. From this point of view, part-time work is 'profoundly non-egalitarian' (Jenson, 1988).

Nevertheless, there is another aspect to this problem. The strong social division of labour, where the woman was given the responsibility of the home while the man earned his and her living outside, not only made the identification of the woman with a professional activity difficult, but also gave birth to the implicit concept of the wage-earner with no family or personal obligations. Instead, the point of departure is that a wage-earner has someone else to take care of home and hearth; someone who does this to such an extent that he can function exclusively as a wage-earner. As Holtmaat puts it:

> the wage-earner only functions well in his role of pure wage-earner if he really has no other task on his mind. The wage-earner who can meet expectations 100 per cent is the man who can close the door behind him in the morning and abandon the domestic worries to his spouse, his mother or his sister. When he comes home in the evening, the meal is on the table, the house is clean, the laundry has been put away in the cupboards and the children have been to school, to the doctor and to a swimming lesson. (Holtmaat, 1987: 765.)

As long as such a concept of the wage-earner remains dominant, and domestic obligations are not integrated into the labour system, many women cannot and will not match this model. What is more, according to the figures in Table 12.5 more and more men cannot identify with the role of 'pure wage-earner' either. In such a situation, a part-time position is a rational choice. Moreover, part-time work becomes a first step towards a new employment structure, breaking away from the classical concept of the 'pure' wage-earner and the division between breadwinners and carers.

The fact that part-time work is two-sided makes assessing this phenomenon complicated. On the one hand are the pessimists, like the authors of the 1991 OECD report, who only see more of the same. In their view, part-time contracts are the expressions of frustrating constants in society. Pessimists interpret the figures as reflecting an image of women who, besides their duties as housekeepers, wives and mothers, do not have any choice but to opt for short hours part-time jobs, because on the micro level (in the household) as well as on the macro level (within society) a start has hardly been made on a fundamental re-evaluation of the existing organisation of labour and care. In their view, the part-time employee is a woman whose part-time contract only serves the interests of her employer, because the employer's striving for flexibility seems to mesh perfectly with the unaltered implicit social contract between men and women.

On the other hand, there is the picture painted by the optimists, like the Dutch Green Left. They point to the changes part-time work implies: that for the first time employers are confronted with an employee who also has other responsibilities. In this perspective, part-time work is not so much an exclusive female strategy. The part-time employee is above all a highly-educated professional with a contract of at least three days a week, who is, with her or his partner, trying to create a more evenly-distributed division of work and care. In this scenario the part-time employee gives short shrift to the myths of the 'unemployed carer' and 'carefree employee' by combining work and care in him or herself. The labour structure is thus not so much perpetuated, but rather reformed.

The problem is, as usual, that up to a point both sides are right. Part-time work is usually not more than a consolidation and perpetuation of the marginal position of women. Short hours part-time jobs especially (contracts of less than 15 hours a week) do not guarantee economic independence, and seem to have been introduced merely to serve business interests; they do little more than create a pool of marginal workers. However, it is also true that part-time work can promise a change for the future; this promise may still be hard to underpin statistically, but most people know some supporting personal examples. Starting from the conviction that full-time labour market participation is not the only key to socio-economic equality, part-time work offers both women and men the possibility to escape from the all-or-nothing option in the labour market, and thus shape a life in which work and care take up well-balanced positions relative to one another.

A stimulating backlog ?

The Netherlands is quite an interesting case in terms of female employment. From a European perspective, the Dutch level of female labour force participation was for a long time remarkably low and only comparable with Ireland and the south of Italy. Since the early 1970s, however, a rapid shift is apparent. Influenced by changes in education, numbers of children and relative wages, labour market participation has risen very quickly and the phenomenon of the 'married working woman' has become widely accepted. The special relationship between women and paid work, however, is still expressed in the fact that far more Dutch women work part-time than in any other European country.

The large number of part-timers in the Netherlands has also aroused international attention. In recent months the German media has focused admiringly on the Netherlands' high part-time scores. The direct cause of this interest is primarily the growth of unemployment in Germany, which has forced policy-makers to search for alternative instruments to combat it. In an action plan to generate more growth and employment, part-time work is perceived as one of the most important instruments in reducing unemployment (*Financieel Dagblad*, 1994.) The specific construction of the Dutch labour market, which has often been described as lagging behind others or even as retarded, has suddenly been transformed into an ideal worth striving after!

Against this backdrop, it could be argued that the Netherlands and its deviatory pattern has worked itself, almost by accident, into an interesting situation where current supply-side trends match those found on the demand side of the labour market. The specific history of the nature and extent of female paid work in the Netherlands has resulted in labour market behaviour which meshes perfectly with the demands made on employees in the 1990s. Although it is more than tempting to speculate on this notion, a number of critical observations are relevant. Enthusiasm is, after all, aimed primarily at part-time work as an instrument of flexibility. No one mentions in so many words that it is women especially who work part-time and thus bear the costs of this flexibility. If this flexibility aspect is emphasised too often the pessimists will be proved right, and part-time work will only serve employers' interests.

The agenda for the 1990s has thus been defined. In principle, part-time work has three aims: stimulating employment (in numbers of jobs); stimulating flexibility in companies; and facilitating the combination of paid and unpaid work. Only when potential conflicts between these aims have been reconciled will the optimists be proved right and part-time work become a first step towards the establishment of a different labour structure.

References

Bevordering van deeltijdarbeid (1992–3). Tweede Kamer, 23 216, 1–3.

COB/SER (1988). *Deeltijdwerk in kleinere industriële bedrijven*. The Hague: Commissie Ontwikkeling Bedrijven/Sociaal Economische Raad.

Enquête Beroepsbevolking 1991. Voorburg/Heerlen: Centraal Bureau voor de Statistiek.

European Commission Childcare Network (1990). *Childcare in the European Community 1985–1990, Report Co-ordinated by Peter Moss*. Brussels, Women of Europe supplements, 31.

Eurostat (1988). *Labour Force Survey, Methods and Definitions*. Luxembourg: Office for Official Publications of the European Communities.

Eurostat (1991). *Labour Force Survey 1991*. Luxembourg: Office for Official Publications of the European Communities.

Financieel Dagblad (5 and 7 March 1994). 'Nederland model voor Duitse maatschappijrevolutie'.

FNV (Dutch Federation of Trade Unions) (1993a). *Deeltijd compleet, FNV-beleidsnota deeltijdwerk*. Amsterdam: Stichting FNV-pers.

FNV (Dutch Federation of Trade Unions) (1993b). *Deeltijdwerk vanzelfsprekend ook in ploegendiensten. Roostervoorbeelden*. Amsterdam: Stichting FNV-pers.

Groot, L. F. M., Schippers, J. J. and Siegers, J. J. (1990). 'The effects of unemployment, temporary withdrawals and part-time work on workers wage rates' in *European Sociological Review*, December.

Holtmaat, R. (1987). 'Het individualiseringsbeginsel en verzorgingsbehoeftigheid' in *Sociaal Maandblad Arbeid*, December.

Jenson, J. (1988). 'The limits of 'and the' discourse' in Jenson, J., Hagen, E. and Reddy, C. *Feminisation of the Labour Force: Paradoxes and Promises*. Cambridge: Polity Press.

LTD (1988). *De positie van mannen en vrouwen in het arbeidsproces*. Ministerie van Sociale Zaken en Werkgelegenheid. The Hague: SZW.

LTD (1991a). *De rechtspositie bij deeltijdwerken en de praktijk*. Ministerie van Sociale Zaken en Werkgelegenheid. The Hague: SZW.

LTD (1991b). *Veranderende arbeidstijdpatronen*. Ministerie van Sociale Zaken en Werkgelegenheid. The Hague: Loontechnische Dienst.

OECD (1991). *Shaping Structural Change: The Role of Women*. Expert report to the Secretary-General. Paris: Organisation for Economic Co-operation and Development.

Van den Putte, B. and Pelzer, A. (1993). 'Wensen, motieven en belemmeringen ten aanzien van de arbeidsduur' in *Sociaal Maandblad Arbeid*, July/August.

WRR (1990). *Een werkend perspectief; arbeidsparticipatie in de jaren '90*. Wetenschappelijke Raad voor het Regeringsbeleid. 's-Gravenhage: SDU uitgeverij.

CHAPTER 13   # Gender and Egalitarianism in the British Welfare State

Eithne McLaughlin

Thinking about the welfare state

The 'welfare state' is often described as a set of institutions and provisions which, together with civil and political rights, ensure citizenship: membership of, and participation in, a given society. T. H. Marshall's classic analysis of citizenship (1949), for example, focused on the importance of social, as well as civil and political, rights in securing effective citizenship. Social rights to a minimum income, health care, agreed educational standards, and so on, have the potential to moderate what would otherwise be a very uneven distribution of citizenship caused by differential power in a capitalist market society. In other words, civil and political rights alone in a market economy are not sufficient to ensure citizenship for all. To the extent that social rights are provided by welfare states, welfare states are egalitarian, though not necessarily 'equalising'.

More recent comparative work led by Esping-Andersen (1990) has followed Marshall's early conceptualisations very closely, though with a more developed focus on the twin processes of 'commodification' and 'decommodification'. Commodification may be defined as the lengthy historical process through which people have become equivalent to 'things' (commodities) because one part of them (their labour) is bought and sold in a market (the labour market). People, of course, are not things and the total maintenance costs of people may exceed the particular price paid for units of their labour in the labour market. For example, in the long term people are not in the labour market when they are very young or very old, and their costs at these times have to be met somehow. And at any given time during their working years, the price a person fetches in the labour market may not meet his or her full maintenance costs. While, for example, £17 an hour may more than meet a person's immediate basic maintenance costs, a wage of £2.50 an hour will probably not, especially if that individual is also trying to meet the maintenance costs of children from their labour price. And of course, there are many times during the working years when a person may be unable to sell their labour at all – for example, during times of low labour demand, or because of disability.

Industrialised societies have therefore developed a range of methods by which the costs of maintaining people are spread across the labour market and collective social institutions, such as social security, health care and education systems. These societies also have laws which specify the balance of responsibilities for meeting the full maintenance costs of people between employers, individuals, families and the collectivity represented by the state.

Decommodification, then, is the historical process by which these employment laws, taxation, social security provision, health care provisions and so on moderate the effects of commodification – which, left to its own devices, would not ensure acceptable standards of living for all. From the point of view of individuals, decommodification guarantees certain social rights for all by reducing dependence on, and vulnerability to, capitalist labour markets:

> Decommodification should not be confused with the complete eradication of labour as a commodity; it is not an issue of all or nothing... the concept refers to the degree to which individuals, or families, can uphold a socially acceptable standard of living independently of market participation. (Esping-Andersen, 1990: 37.)

The extent of decommodification achieved in different countries is the result of the interplay of political demands from social groups who would benefit from reduced dependence on the labour market, and the power of those using labour. Some decommodification is likely to be regarded as efficient by the latter, because it spreads people maintenance costs around, even if it were not demanded by other political groups. Welfare states are therefore fundamentally both political and economic settlements.

Such conceptualisations of commodification and decommodification derive from a masculinist tradition of social rights, which fails to recognise the way in which the historical processes of both commodification and decommodification have intertwined with pre-existing gender orders. Pateman (1989), Pascall (1993) and other feminist social policy writers have shown how traditional citizenship analyses have been partial and gender-biased, because discussion of the role of social rights in reducing dependency on the labour market (the relationship between citizenship and social class) has not been matched by discussion or conceptualisation of the role of social rights in reducing dependency on and in the family (the relationship between citizenship and the family). Lewis (1992) and Shaver (1990) among others, for instance, have shown how Esping-Andersen's comparative analyses of welfare regimes have failed to incorporate the way in which welfare regimes have decommodified men and women differently, through the differential development of social rights for husbands and wives, mothers and fathers. In addition, men and women have been incorporated differently into capitalist labour markets: the historical process of commodification itself has also not been gender neutral. Men's incorporation into capitalist labour markets has depended upon them being able to sell their wives' unpaid labour as part of a package underpinning their own availability for paid labour. This assumption of the availability of women's unpaid labour in commodification has been repeated in, rather than challenged by, the development of welfare states' decommodifying provisions.

Lewis (1992) has suggested that an alternative way of analysing modern welfare regimes is to categorise them along a continuum of strong and weak 'male breadwinner' states – that is, in terms of the extent to which welfare provisions either presume or privilege a single earner or a dual-earner couple as the basis of households (especially households with children). Lewis argues that the idea of the male-breadwinner family model has served historically to cut across established typologies of welfare regimes, and further that the model has been modified in different ways and to different ends in particular countries. She describes Britain as a strong male-breadwinner regime because of the high level of part-time employment among women (mothers); a lack of childcare services and maternity rights; and the long-lived inequality between husbands and wives in social security (Lewis, 1992).

The existence in Britain of very different 'rules' around full-time compared with part-time employment will be a central theme in this chapter. It is, however, the case that welfare states do more than regulate mothers' employment; they also regulate the provision of unpaid care for disabled and elderly adults, as well as children (see McLaughlin and Glendinning, 1994), and indeed marriage and sexuality. This latter regulation is visible in welfare states' activities around birth rates, legitimacy and illegitimacy, female 'promiscuity', prostitution, homosexuality, maternal and child health, contraception, abortion and adoption. All these policy areas involve analysis of health care, social care and child protection law,[1] in addition to social security, employment and fiscal policies. To understand the influence of welfare states on the gender order, then, it is necessary to look more broadly at whether, how, and to what extent various social policies alter the terms and conditions of engagement in and with family relationships.

It is beyond the scope of this chapter to deal with all these fields, although in the final section (considering possible strategies for the achievement of an egalitarian welfare state), issues around reproduction, care and family relationships form an implicit backdrop. First, however, it is appropriate, given the orientation of this volume, to concentrate on the more usual topic of relationships between the social security system, employment policy and the labour market.

The origins and nature of the British welfare state

In the hundred years between 1845 and 1945 – the formative period in the establishment of the 'modern' welfare state – the relatively greater political power of working-class men compared to women, the partial overlap of the interests of employers and employees as family men, and the interest of the nation state in women as reproducers and carers, conjoined to make the male breadwinner the key institutional basis of the British welfare state. This was most obvious in relation to employment legislation and the social security system, but it also explains why social rights were not developed in the field of social care.

---

[1] There has been a fascinating upsurge over the last decade in historical analyses of the various ways in which welfare states were formed out of natalist and eugenic policies in the second half of the 19th and first half of the 20th centuries (see, for example, the 1993 volume of national case studies edited by Koven and Michel, and Williams' 1989 British account).

During these formative years, most men could rely on, or expected to rely on, their needs for care labour (whether personal, or for their children or parents) being met through marriage and the services of a wife. Men thus had less interest than women in securing social rights in welfare services (apart from medical care, which depends on specialist knowledge not available to men through marriage). It is still the case that publicly-funded social care services in Britain (and indeed throughout Europe) are not based on individual social rights: access to them remains at the discretion of welfare professionals. Public funding for social care services is also much lower than for social security help, which is based on concepts of individual entitlements. Working-class men in particular had a strong interest in, and influence over, the development of social rights to weaken their dependency on the labour market, which meant employment legislation and cash social security provision, not care services, since these were already available to them through marriage.[2]

The post-war settlement of 1948 did not, of course, produce any kind of 'total' decommodification for working- and middle-class men, but it certainly resulted in greater decommodification for men than women. On the one hand there was no collective development of social care and childcare, which would have given women more choices in the labour market; on the other, the British employment legislation and social security system were modelled around male breadwinners and non-earning wives.

It was assumed that the bulk of employment would be held by working-age men on a '48 hour, 48 week, 48 years' basis, with both workers and employers paying into, and for, the welfare state's collective provisions through National Insurance contributions and income tax: 'A-type' employment in Figure 13.1. Both employment legislation and the social security system enshrined these assumptions; thus employment protection legislation was targeted at those working full-time hours, and part-time workers were to enjoy no, or less, protection. Wage rates were collectively negotiated on the basis of the male family wage (see Land, 1980).

The National Insurance system did not require contributions from women in 'pin-money' jobs – part-time, low-paid and casual work, or 'B-type' employment in Figure 13.1. Thus married women were to be 'covered' by their husbands' National Insurance contributions rather than their own for pensions, and not at all for most other insurance benefits. The coverage achieved by wives in this way was always highly restricted. The assumption that unpaid work was both a woman's main job and that the welfare of the unpaid worker could be satisfactorily secured by transfers of income from husbands to wives was also manifest in other aspects of the social security system. These aspects include:

- the presumption that all women with children are first and foremost full-time mothers meant that working-age mothers claiming social

---

[2] Meanwhile the health care system emerged as a centrally-funded and regulated – in other words, universal – form of provision, unlike social care. But neither was health care like social security, since it was not based on the development of individual rights – rights to specific treatments in specific circumstances. Such an approach would have challenged medical professional discretion and clinical judgment in a politically unacceptable way.

**Figure 13.1 Bearing the maintenance costs of people in the British
post-war welfare state**

1948

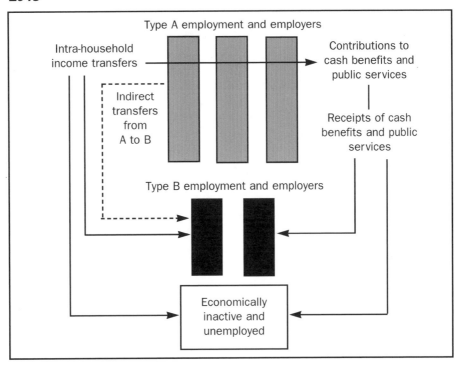

1990s

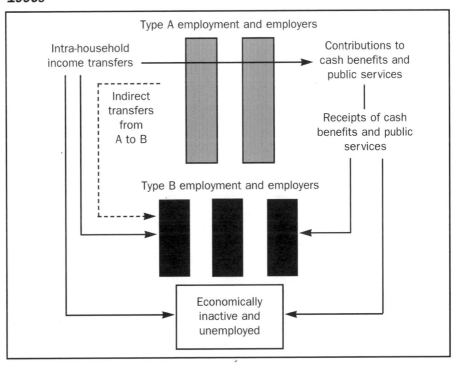

assistance (usually lone mothers) were not, and still are not, required to register for work while they have any children under 16;[3]

- the failure to incorporate periods spent out of the labour market in the performance of 'vital duties' (as Beveridge described them in his 1942 report), such as care of young children or disabled adults, through crediting of full-weight contributions on the individual's behalf, and/or the development of benefits targeted at the risk of labour market interruption and income insecurity caused by the need to provide care;

- the presumption that adult (male) insurance and assistance claimants will have an 'adult dependant' (in other words, a wife), and that any adult woman 'living with' an adult male outside, as well as inside, marriage should receive income from him.[4]

Together, employment legislation and the social security system (the decommodifying package) positioned men and women differently in relation to both the labour market and the family. This was intended to lower women's participation in the labour market, and indeed female employment rates were historically low between the late 1940s and the mid-1960s. However, there was also interplay between the gendered decommodifying package and existing wage and employment differentials between men and women, resulting in a further weakening of women's position in the paid labour market compared with men. Symptoms of this were, for example, women's lower wage rates and the undervaluation of skill in typically female occupations (Phillips and Taylor, 1980; McLaughlin and Ingram, 1991); women's lesser access to occupational welfare provision, such as pensions; and downward occupational mobility for many qualified women as A-type employment continued to be based on a male full-time continuous-employment model.

These weaknesses – the result of the twin processes of gendered commodification and gendered decommodification – are, of course, the problems which the EOC has sought to solve since the mid-1970s. The main tools available to the EOC, however – the Sex Discrimination and Equal Pay Acts – address only a few aspects of this historical legacy.

In fact a major weakness in the post-war settlement (for lower-skilled men as well as for women) has been the existence of relatively 'unregulated' (in other words, highly commodified) forms of employment – B-type employment – in the British system. Here wage rates themselves probably do not cover basic subsistence costs, and certainly not the additional costs of children, and frequently neither the employer nor the employee

---

[3] Britain is not unique in this regard, but many countries do require lone mothers with children of school age to register as available for work. Together with childcare and fiscal policy towards families with children, this contributes to Britain being the only country in the EC where lone mothers have lower employment rates than mothers in two-parent families.

[4] Some of these features of the social security system have been moderated or weakened in recent years – for example, the extension of the invalid care allowance to married women, changes to the definition and implementation of the cohabitation rule, formal changes which have converted the husband-claimant into the '(husband-as-)main claimant'. However, the essence of the system remains; indeed, the new Child Support legislation in 1990, which includes a cash transfer from the absent parent to and for the caring parent as well as transfers to and for their children, represents a new measure based on a notion of mothers-as-dependants-of-fathers.

contribute to collective long-term social provision, such as pensions and health care. From the late 1960s onwards, international economic trends, such as the growth of the service sector, and down-sizing and delayering in the manufacturing and commerce sectors, manifested themselves in Britain through the growth of B-type employment – 'unprotected' casual employment, part-time employment, and employment at wage rates below the basic subsistence cost of the labour supplied.

Changes in the patterns of hours worked between 1979 and 1990, for example, show how employers responded to the 'opportunity' of differential treatment of part-time work in British employment protection legislation. In 1979, 30 per cent of women in part-time manual and 23 per cent in non-manual jobs worked less than 16 hours a week, while in 1990 the figures were 44 per cent and 32 per cent respectively. As regards contributions to the National Insurance system, in the early 1990s an estimated 2.5 million employed women earned less than the lower earnings limit for contributions (Lister, 1992). In European welfare states, such as France and Germany, these same international economic trends have had different outcomes because of higher levels of employment regulation (Balls and Gregg, 1993).

In addition, since 1979 British governments have pursued further deregulatory policies (Deakin and Wilkinson, 1992) which have resulted in even more rapid growth of B-type employment. This has begun to affect not only women but also unqualified manual male workers, whose wage and employment rates have fallen simultaneously (McLaughlin, 1994a). B-type employment now probably accounts for at least 40 per cent of employment and probably a higher proportion of job vacancies (McLaughlin, 1991).

What is more, the reduction in the scope of National Insurance and greater reliance on social assistance (means-tested benefits) have increased the importance of familial position, for unemployed men as well as women. Means-tested benefits are based wholly on couples (Millar, 1989), whereas insurance benefits do not take the earnings of a partner into account. The reduction in the scope of social insurance was part of the strategy of successive British governments to 'deregulate' employment. Eroding the decommodifying function of the social security system for men through contraction of the insurance system, making it more difficult to be eligible for insurance benefits in times of unemployment and incapacity, was seen as part of a package to reduce the ability of male workers to shore up wage levels.

The post-war 'male breadwinner' in the social security and associated system of labour market regulation was the British version of the corporatist or 'social partners' approach in continental Europe. But while the latter was explicit about the relationship between employers, employees and the state, the British system was to embed these relationships less obviously but no less significantly in the social security and employment legislation package. Conservative governments since

1979 have altered both elements of this package, but have done so much more radically in relation to employment legislation than to social security. The result is that new, highly-commodified forms of labour have developed without corresponding new forms of social security to counterbalance them and secure welfare and citizenship for all.

As well as producing low levels of welfare and high levels of insecurity for those engaged in these new forms of labour (mostly women), these contradictory developments are excluding some from these forms of labour, particularly unemployed couples and unskilled women (see Gregg and Wadsworth, this volume, Chapter 15). The unprotected or 'welfare-poor' nature of much non-standard or B-type employment, and general declines in wage rates for unskilled work, have resulted in unskilled and less-educated men and women being squeezed out of the labour market; simultaneously, the proportion of two-earner households is increasing. The result is that the sharing out of people maintenance costs has changed markedly, with more working-age men out of employment, and more B-type and less A-type employment (the lower section of Figure 13.1).

This in turn means fewer incoming contributions to pay for collective welfare provisions, leading to restrictions in the quantity and quality of what can be offered collectively, higher contributions from those (employers and employees) who are paying in, and the extension of the tax base to capture more from those outside A-type employment – for example, through the extension of VAT.

The limits of deregulation

How and why is there a contradiction in the development of highly-deregulated (or commodified) forms of employment and an increased emphasis on forms of social security provision predicated on the male-breadwinner model – a contradiction manifest, it is argued here, in reduced employment rates for lower-skilled men and increased inequalities between women?

Forecasts of future employment growth predict that the largest expansion of job opportunities will be concentrated in managerial, professional and technical areas, but that personal and protective services are expected to grow by 16 per cent by the end of the century (Cm 1810, 1992) and above-average rates of growth are also expected in sales-based occupations. Both these sectors are at the cutting edge of 'flexible' forms of work. They use predominantly highly-commodified labour – the labour is probably paid at a low hourly rate, but even more importantly is probably hired for a relatively low number of hours per week, so that weekly earnings are below those necessary to secure a basic but acceptable standard of living. In addition, the majority of workers in these sectors are unlikely to be offered occupational pension or sickness cover by their employers; many will also be earning less than the threshold of earnings at which National Insurance contributions become payable, and thus cannot acquire rights to statutory social security provision.

What is more, the retail sector has been at the forefront of the development of 'zero hours' contracts of employment, where an employee is not guaranteed any minimum working hours per week or month, but must be available to work whatever hours are offered week to week and even day to day. Such contracts represent the ultimate in labour commodification, because the employer takes no responsibility for the basic maintenance of the employee. In other words, the employer may or may not meet the costs of ensuring that the labour (the employee) is 'reproduced': provided with enough food, heating, adequate shelter, and so on, to enable them to continue to be available for work. By offering zero hours contracts, and hence no specified weekly wage, the employer can off-load the costs of maintaining their workforce on to other sources when he or she chooses, while nevertheless retaining an experienced and adequate pool of labour.

In addition, those working less than eight hours a week are not covered by employment protection legislation, and those working between eight and 16 hours a week until very recently were covered only if they had continuous service of five or more years with one employer. Those on temporary contracts, even if full-time, are of course unlikely to be in occupational pension schemes or to build up sufficient continuous service with a single employer to gain access to statutory provision.

In any case, statutory provision has been eroded. For example, in the field of pensions the failure to link statutory pensions to rises in earnings levels, and changes to SERPS from a value based on the best 20 years of one's earnings to total working life earnings, will both disproportionately affect women (Land, 1989; Groves, 1991). Independent entitlement to pensions (and other forms of long-term welfare provision) are increasingly needed by women because of rising rates of marital breakdown, the fact that widows can now inherit only half instead of all the SERPs component of their husband's pension (Social Security Act, 1986), and because personal pension schemes are not obliged to make any provision for a surviving spouse.

The rise in forms of employment involving little or no occupational welfare (either because the wage involved is very small as a result of low or irregular hours, or the hourly rate itself being low, or because the job carries no entitlements to occupational or statutory benefits, such as retirement or sickness provision, or all of these) poses many serious issues for the future of the welfare state. These issues fall into two categories: on the one hand, long-term welfare matters such as disability and pension provision for future generations; and on the other, more immediate concerns connected with the participation of potentially low-earning women and men in the labour market.

The latter problems are caused by falls in the amount and security of earned income from employment relative to the basic maintenance costs of individuals (especially parents) in the short term, which result in a skewing of labour supply towards these forms of employment from those workers who have other sources of income to rely upon within their households, leading to a polarisation between 'work-rich' and 'work-poor' households (see Gregg and Wadsworth, this volume, Chapter 15). This is a major reason why the distribution of standard and non-standard forms of work between the sexes has altered very little.

The bulk of low-earning, non-standard workers in the UK are women. In the US, this 'junk-job' sector is similarly dominated by women, though it also draws on Hispanic-American men, recent male immigrants and young people of both sexes. The US junk-job sector thus utilises a more heterogeneous mixture of people, though, like the UK sector, it does not generally draw on prime-age, white men (Esping-Andersen, 1990). In the UK, the result is that although the number of full-time male employees has fallen by 20 per cent since 1977, this has not been offset by rising part-time employment and self-employment among men. Various authors (McLaughlin, 1991; Hewitt, 1992; Gregg, 1993) have highlighted the fact that female labour force participation has risen fastest in households with employed male partners; thus the bulk of female part-time work is taken by married or cohabiting women, overwhelmingly with working partners who in turn are disproportionately likely to be of intermediate and high skill and/or educational levels (see Gregg and Wadsworth, this volume, Chapter 15).

The expansion in non-standard labour forms has largely been filled by relatively highly-qualified women rather than by unskilled and less-educated women or men. The much-vaunted sharp rise in female employment has been among graduates. Women of intermediate educational levels increased their employment propensity somewhat, but the unqualified did not – indeed, unqualified women saw a small reduction in their employment propensity (Schmitt and Wadsworth, 1994). Thus the unskilled of both sexes were increasingly excluded from the employment growth which did occur in the 1980s – although the problem was greater for men. This trend towards exclusion occurred despite the fact that much of the employment growth was in unqualified or unskilled occupations, and therefore without rapid and radical changes in social policy this trend is set to continue.

Forms of labour have developed which do not meet even the short-term basic reproductive or maintenance requirements of the workers so employed. Only those with access to other funds – earnings of partners, or parents in the case of young people – can afford to engage in these forms of work. But this is not only a household issue. Employees in B-type employment are relying on subsidies from the wages (and other forms of long-term occupational welfare) of their partners, who are very likely to be in A-type employment. In other words, the wages and other forms of welfare provided by employers in A-type employment are indirectly subsidising the availability, maintenance and use of B-type labour for those employers utilising the latter as their key employment strategy.

This pattern of cross-subsidies between employers is interesting in its own right, but even more interesting is how to interpret it in relation to equal opportunities policies and strategies. Since the B-type labour strategy of some employers in some economic sectors depends upon the existence of A-type employment elsewhere in the labour market, it may be all the harder to attempt to erode differentials in wages and other forms of occupational welfare between those in A-type employment (predominantly though not exclusively men) and those in B-type employment (predominantly women, especially mothers), through equal pay and sex discrimination legislation.

Indeed, the deregulatory policies which have led to the rise in B-type employment have also meant that the wage levels of male full-time workers in some lower-level occupations have fallen.[5] This leaves some men less able to sustain such cross-subsidies and hence constrains their partners' abilities to engage in these forms of work. These trends in wages, and the increase in non-standard forms of employment, have combined with a social security system still predicated on the single-earner family model to produce high proportions of unskilled manual men and women not in employment. This has occurred despite growth in low-wage, low-skill employment, as has the increasing proportion of multiple-earning households in which the female partner is very likely to be over-qualified for the occupation in which she is employed.

Of course, the lower participation and employment rates of unqualified women have many causes, including issues around the lack of public subsidies for childcare provision. What is particularly interesting now, however, is how existing problems for unqualified women are interacting with the reduction in traditional, relatively highly-paid employment in manufacturing for unskilled and semi-skilled men – often their partners. These men and women are caught up in the terminal stages of the demise of the male manual 'family wage'. So long as a less-qualified father manages to hang on to a 'traditional' male job, his partner will be able to engage in non-standard forms of work. Their problems begin when he becomes unemployed, and would have to take a lower-paying job to get work again. At this point the absence of publicly-subsidised childcare (which would allow the woman too to take full-time employment), the low and sometimes uncertain earnings available from non-standard forms of work, and the low level of fiscal support for families with children, combine to make it difficult for these couples to earn enough to meet their 'social reproduction' costs (their basic income maintenance needs; Dawes, 1993).

The government's approach to this problem has been to promote and expand the means-tested in-work benefit system as a supplement to low wages, rather than to address wage rates, conditions of employment, fiscal

---

[5] The extent of differentials in wages between non-manual and educated workers and manual and less-skilled workers, for men as well as women, has risen sharply in the UK in the 1980s. In contrast, continental European countries have sought to prevent this by relatively high minimum wage rates, more restrictive regulations on hiring and firing, more generous unemployment benefits, and replacing private with public sector employment. Thus the OECD's survey of trends in the dispersion of wages (*Employment Outlook*, July 1993) shows the US as having the strongest trend for top wages to rise and bottom wages to fall, with Britain following.

policy and so on. But the in-work benefit strategy encourages, rather than discourages, reliance on a single male wage, which is the cause of the problem in the first place.

The single-earner model of social security provision

The structure of social security provision, both in and out of work, is predicated on a presumption of adult female dependency on male partners (see McLaughlin, 1994b, for a longer discussion). The social security system, and labour market policy more generally, generate a higher level of dependency on male potential earners by allowing for (and, to some extent, creating) dependent adult women. There are many aspects to the creation and maintenance of this dependency (Lister, 1992); this chapter focuses on family credit as a form of financial help designed around one-earner households, and the treatment of female partners as dependants in out-of-work benefits.

Family credit (FC)

The in-work benefits system is based on the idea that it is appropriate for the state to intervene to 'solve' some of the problems caused by low wage levels, but not others. Thus, although Conservative governments have not regarded it as acceptable to intervene in these problems by legislating on wage rates themselves, or through the tax system, they have seen it as acceptable to intervene by subsidising low wages in certain circumstances – where one low earner is supporting other people, either as a sole male breadwinner or as a lone parent. This generates inequities between dual-earning two-parent families and male-breadwinner two-parent families, since it offers help to sole-breadwinner families but none to dual-earner families, and overlaps with issues around maintenance from absent parents.

As Marsh and McKay state (1993), FC is most likely to be claimed by two kinds of family moving through a quite narrow band of time in their life-cycle as they bring up dependent children. It tends to be a benefit useful to lone parents whose children are old enough to look after themselves (for example, after school), and to potentially low-earning couples whose children are not yet that old (pre-school and young primary school children). As such, the benefit is intimately tied up with questions around the provision and financing of childcare.

Marsh and McKay (1993) concluded that for lone parents FC made a significant contribution to labour market participation, but that this contribution tended to occur around the margins of a prior decision to participate – a decision which rested on issues of childcare availability and costs, and hence on the age of children. In effect FC acts as a form of cash childcare allowance for lone mothers (though inadequately so), usually when maintenance from the absent father is not being paid, or not being paid at a high enough level. It is also a form of childcare allowance for couples where FC 'pays' the female partner to stay at home and provide what would otherwise be unpaid childcare, rather than sharing in the more usual pattern of family support (both partners earning, albeit one usually part-time and the other full-time).

In a couple where a single earner (most likely the male) was employed and claiming FC, and the non-employed partner returned to employment, even part-time, entitlement to FC would almost certainly cease at the next six-monthly review of benefit entitlement.[6] Marsh and McKay state that:

> the wives in FC couples have similar problems as have lone parents on income support. True they lose 'only' 70 per cent of family credit (though more if they are on housing benefit and community charge benefit too) for each pound they earn, but they get no £15 a week disregard as do those on income support. The fixed six-month term of FC awards cushions this disincentive a little, but nearly all of the one in six low-income couples getting FC were one-earner families. (Marsh and McKay, 1993: 48.)

At the moment, for two-parent FC couples the options for the woman seem to be to 'get a full-time job and so spring the whole family clear of the FC threshold altogether, or stay at home' (*ibid.*).

Thus FC tends to be received by three groups of people. The first are single-earner couples while their children are pre-school and until the mother makes a successful move towards 'long' part-time or full-time hours of work, which in turn will be when potential childcare costs reduce (when children become older and more self-reliant, or at school for longer hours). At this point the couple move off FC and leave the population of low-income families by becoming a dual-earner couple. The second group are single-earner couples who have either chosen to see their long-term future in terms of a single earner, or have ended up this way by accident because the labour market withdrawal of the mother, facilitated by FC, has lasted too long and she cannot now regain entry to employment. These couples will remain FC recipients for very long periods, and correspondingly remain in the population of low-income families. Thirdly come lone mothers who are not receiving enough maintenance from an absent father to pay for full substitute childcare and/or share the costs of children's subsistence needs.

The general problem with FC, then, is that it has evaded the issue of whether the state should be providing childcare support for families, and whether this should be in cash, services, or both; and relatedly, that for some couples it discourages participation in the dual-earning pattern – the most secure route out of poverty. This discouragement probably occurs in around a third of potentially low-earning unemployed couples with children and up to half of FC-receiving couples (Marsh and McKay, 1993). The most immediate and direct effect of FC is simply to keep low-earning households at low levels of net income. As such, it contributes to rather than lessens the much-reported widening of incomes in Britain in the last

---

6 The provision announced in the 1993 autumn Budget that £40 a week childcare costs (incurred with registered child-minders and nurseries only) may be disregarded from earnings before the calculation of FC (yielding a maximum net £28) could bring some couples with one full-time and one part-time earner into the FC net, or encourage some non-employed partners of FC claimants to take up part-time work. However, the government's own projections do not anticipate a large number of new applicants – a total of 50,000 new claimants are expected, with the majority being lone mothers rather than couples.

decade and the decline in net incomes of people in the bottom decile of the income distribution.

In the long term FC results in:

- perhaps around half of FC couples remaining on FC for very long periods of time;
- such FC couples not joining the majority of families who are two-earner couples (usually one full-time and one part-time);
- the family never entering the moderate, average or higher income strata of working-age households;
- the FC couple, but especially the woman, facing very poor post-retirement income prospects.

Out-of-work benefits

In addition, the discouragement effects of FC interact with other aspects of the social security system which allow for female dependency in 'unemployed couples': the system's assumption that wives are 'legitimate' dependants of husbands, which permits wives who are employed when their husbands become unemployed to leave their own employment without financial penalty and be claimed for by their husbands as adult dependants; and the highly punitive treatment of the part-time earnings of the partners of registered unemployed people (see McLaughlin, 1994b, for more detail).

These presumptions of adult female dependency are of some significance because by permitting, and indeed encouraging, female dependency on men during unemployment, the social security system raises the level of financial dependency on men and hence the level of income they will need to secure from future employment. The majority of unemployed men set the level of the wage they seek by the costs of their household needs, rather than in comparison with out-of-work benefit levels or previously-held wage levels (Dawes, 1993). The lower employment rates of female partners of unemployed men mean that many men must try to find a 'family wage' to cover their female partners' needs as well as those of their children, thus making it unlikely that they can participate in the growing non-standard forms of employment common in the low-skill sectors or move into full-time work in low-skill female-dominated occupations (which pay less than the equivalent male sectors).

The out-of-work benefit system also makes it unlikely that the female partners will participate in these forms of employment. Marsh and McKay (1993) found that 18 per cent of couples knew that earnings of £5 a week each could be disregarded under income support for the first two years of unemployment; another 18 per cent knew that this increased to £15 together after two years; but 38 per cent had no idea whether or what earnings were permitted or disregarded, while 26 per cent guessed incorrect figures for disregarded earnings. Apart from the fact that many unemployed people do not know that they are allowed to earn, or what they are allowed to earn, while in receipt of out-of-work benefits, the levels of earnings permitted are obviously very low.

Such benefit-induced discouragement is not the sole explanation of why so few of the female partners of unemployed men are in employment compared with the partners of employed men (there is also the nature of local labour markets faced by both partners, and partners tending to share characteristics which leave them both disproportionately vulnerable to unemployment; see Gallie *et al.*, 1994). Nevertheless, the assumption of female dependency in social security policy is part of the wider context of sex-segregated labour markets, or gendered commodification, and other social policies (such as low levels of subsidised childcare services) which combine to concentrate paid work in some households.

It is not only the level of permitted earnings in out-of-work benefits which may discourage non-standard forms of work. Dawes (1993), for instance, found that overall a third of people perceived difficulties in the signing-on process as a disincentive to taking a short-term or 'risky' job. Couples with dependants were most likely to think this was a problem. McKay and Marsh (1994) found that parents showed a strong preference towards jobs which offered reliable income, and that reliability or security (which was primarily seen in terms of the job's expected duration) qualified the attraction of wage rates themselves:

> Joining the 'flexible workforce' [temporary and short-term jobs] holds few appeals to people with dependent children... at least for those of them who are main wage earners. (McKay and Marsh, 1994: 19.)

Such 'skewing' of participation caused by the full-time single-earner model of the social security system affects a large number of people. As well as the nearly three million registered unemployed claimants themselves (though not all are parents), Metcalf (1992) estimated that over half a million women living with an unemployed man in receipt of benefits are not included in this claimant count. There are also 1,674,000 claimants of working age on sickness or invalidity benefit and 1,483,000 claimants of working age on income support. In addition 213,000 couples received FC in 1992, among whom as many as half are likely to have been discouraged from working as suggested earlier (see also Metcalf and Leighton, 1989).

Promoting egalitarianism and the development of gender neutrality

It has been argued elsewhere (McLaughlin, 1994a) that the failure of the British welfare state to respond positively to the rise in non-standard forms of work, falling wage rates at the bottom of the labour market, and the continued inadequacies of fiscal policy towards families, will pose major political and social questions in the future. Unless the balance of responsibilities for welfare, or people-maintenance, between employers and the state, and between the state and individuals (especially parents), is rethought, the increasing 'flexibility' of the deregulated UK labour market will result in a polarised and rigid society marked by high levels of exclusion and low mobility as those with the lowest potential earning power discover that their only option (as parents) is to remain on out-of-work benefits.

On the one hand there is a two-tier labour market, with the higher tier of A-type employment paying wage levels which will sustain individuals, both parents and non-parents, in the long and short term; and a lower tier of B-type employment which will not meet the costs of parenting, and in some cases will not even meet the basic costs of individuals, in the long term and often in the short term too. On the other hand, the government is adopting a hands-off policy towards both wage rates and fiscal policy for parents, and relying on an inadequate social security approach which exacerbates the problems instead of solving them. This is creating an ever-wider gap between less-educated and unskilled women and better-educated and skilled women. More and more of the former will be unable to engage in the 'luxury' of non-standard forms of work, while more and more of the latter will be able to do so, even if usually in jobs for which they are over-qualified, and some will even find full-time employment in the higher levels of the labour market.

Yet while their fortunes are in some senses in opposition to each other, the policy changes required to cure both of their ills are the same. Fundamental to the promotion of egalitarianism between women, and between women and men, are the adoption of a minimum wage and the equal treatment of those combining part-time or irregular employment with caring responsibilities in both employment legislation and social security. There are strong arguments in favour of both on efficiency grounds too, not least because they are required to end the skewing of participation caused by the social security system and the long-standing failure of British fiscal policy towards parents. 'Efficiency' in this context refers to both efficiency in the labour market and efficiency more broadly in terms of the requirements of a developed and mature welfare state.

Minimum wage

As well as, or perhaps instead of, the old moral and equalising arguments in favour of a minimum wage, there is now an increasingly compelling argument that such a wage is needed to set a floor expressing the minimum obligations an employer has towards his or her workforce. Changes at the bottom end of the labour market necessitate a definition of what obligations employers have to maintain the labour they draw upon, whether daily or less frequently. If this is not done, as the preceding discussion has shown, some employers will end up paying the costs of such maintenance via their wages to employees who are the partners of underpaid workers; and/or the expense will be met by everyone sharing the costs of social security benefits, such as income support, housing benefit, FC, and other less visible forms of welfare support (see Glyn and Miliband, 1994).

A national minimum hourly wage rate, equally applicable to full-time, part-time and casual employees, at a level which would cover an individual's immediate basic needs when employed for, say, half or more of a week, is a key equal opportunities policy for the future. A minimum wage, in labour market efficiency and egalitarian terms, should not be set so as to include all the costs some individuals have but which others do not. It should thus not follow or repeat the historical legacy of male family wages – as, for instance, any attempt to set a minimum wage by reference to existing male wage rates would do. The level of the minimum wage should assume that where parents are involved, both are employed (though not necessarily both full-time), and that adequate horizontal redistribution between those with and without children has been achieved by the tax and benefits system rather than the wage system.

Social insurance

As important as a minimum wage are changes to the benefit system, changes which should both 'individualise' men and women, and recognise the parental (and other caring) responsibilities of some.[7] This would involve substantial change to the social insurance system, both in contributions and benefits, and movement towards greater insurance coverage rather than the means-tested approach of recent governments. Indeed, it has been suggested elsewhere that the goal should be to restrict the means-tested approach to assistance with housing costs only (McLaughlin, 1994b).

On the contributions side, the lower earnings limit should be dropped and the principle of contributions from all earnings (including those above the upper earnings limit) accepted. Home responsibilities protection, which at present only permits some years to be excluded from the calculations for entitlement to the basic rate state pension, should be transformed into a fully-fledged system of crediting. Credits should be available on both a partial and a full basis for all those engaged in unpaid caring work in the family or wider community, and qualify for all insurance benefits, not only the state pension.

On the payment of benefits side, in the short term the goal should be to make all insurance benefits available on a partial as well as full basis. It is important that this is not done by the use of categories to define full-time and part-time (for example, over 16 hours or over 20 hours a week, or whatever, equals 'full-time') because this creates discontinuities in participation, incentives to some employers to provide jobs at below whatever cut-offs are used, and inegalitarian welfare outcomes for some.

There is not the space here to outline exactly what such a modernised and egalitarian insurance system would look like, but the Commission on Social Justice final report (1994) has gone some way down this road. In the long term, and after the effects of a modernised social insurance system have been assessed, consideration needs to be given to whether a 'carer's benefit' is necessary for those with full-time caring responsibilities (caring responsibilities which preclude even the possibility of part-time employment – for example, those with pre-school children and/or those

---

[7] The benefit system also needs to recognise the extra costs of disability, which impact on some individuals in much the same way as does parenting.

assisting a severely disabled person with extensive care needs; see also Davies and Joshi, this volume, Chapter 14).

Fiscal policy towards parents

Fiscal policy towards parents should address the extra costs of all parents by increasing tax and benefit assistance for parents and the costs associated with pre-school children through public assistance with childcare and nursery education (Hewitt and Leach, 1993). A reasonably substantial increase in child benefit could be achieved by the funnelling of monies released by the ongoing phasing out of the married couples tax allowance (MCTA)(Commission on Social Justice, 1994), monies which at present are not being targeted on parents. However, the extent of redistribution which has occurred in favour of non-parents over the last decade, together with the decline in earnings at the bottom of the labour market, suggest that investment over and above that released by the phasing out of the MCTA is required.

Employment legislation

Employment legislation should treat those working different hours equally because, as with social insurance categories of 'full-time' and 'part-time', anything else creates incentives for some employers to evade basic obligations for the maintenance of their workforce by manipulating work hours. In addition, there is a need for legislation which allows part-time employment to be led by employee demand rather than employers; in other words, reverse the present situation where the bulk of part-time work is available because an employer has decided it should be, rather than because an existing or potential employee has requested work in that form.

The first reason for this is that the main obstacle to the achievement of equal treatment in employment between men and women has been the 'ghettoisation' of mothers into part-time employment, itself only readily available in lower-level occupations (see for example Rubery and Fagan, 1992; Waldfogel, 1993). Existing equal opportunities legislation will not succeed in eliminating the 'family gap' this causes. Legislation needs to be strengthened by measures akin to maternity provision (which has proved successful for those eligible for it; Waldfogel, 1993), to keep mothers 'in the running' for employment advancement. For example, legislation which permitted all employees at any occupational level to request less than full-time hours, only refusable on good grounds by an employer at an industrial tribunal, would make a start in this direction, though it would probably need to be supplemented by a right to lengthier care leave than is embodied in current maternity provision.

The second reason why this form of legislation would have egalitarian outcomes would be its contribution to reducing the present inefficient competition between higher-qualified and less-qualified women for unskilled and intermediate-level jobs. Inevitably, less-qualified women lose out in this competition, jeopardising their whole family income maintenance base, as well as increasing the long-term welfare gap between themselves and other women.

Conclusion

These four strands of reform address the costs of social reproduction for individuals, especially parents, and clarify and change the balance of responsibilities for meeting these costs between individuals, families, employers and government. Throughout, the aim is to 'individualise' people, both in the labour market and within the family. The reforms would change the level of dependency of others on job-seekers and actual or potential low-earning workers, and thus increase flexibility in labour supply and participation by all. In addition, problems of poverty among women would be lessened in the long term through earlier enhancement and protection of their labour supply, whilst still recognising that care is an important and valuable part of people's lives to which they may wish to devote time.

There are, of course, other reforms which are necessary before an egalitarian welfare state could be achieved (the two most critical areas are probably education and training, and social care) but the reforms described in this chapter are essential to the establishment of a new political and economic settlement, and long overdue.

References

Balls, E. and Gregg, P. (1993). *Work and Welfare: Tackling the Jobs Deficit*. Commission on Social Justice, Issues Paper 3. London: IPPR.

Beveridge, Sir W. (1942). *Social Insurance and Allied Services*. Cmd 6404. London: HMSO.

Cm 1810 (1992). *People, Jobs and Opportunities*. London: HMSO.

Commission on Social Justice (1994). *Social Justice: strategies for national renewal*. London: Vintage Press.

Davies, H. and Joshi, H. (1995). 'Social and family security in the redress of unequal opportunities' in this volume.

Dawes, L. (1993). *Long-term Unemployment and Labour Market Flexibility*. Centre for Labour Market Studies, University of Leicester, Leicester.

Deakin, S. and Wilkinson, F. (1992). 'European integration: the implications for UK policies on labour supply and demand' in McLaughlin, E. (ed.) *Understanding Unemployment*. London: Routledge.

Esping-Andersen, G. (1990). *The Three Worlds of Welfare Capitalism*. Cambridge: Polity.

Gallie, D., Marsh, C. and Vogler, C. (1994). *Social Change and the Experience of Unemployment*. Oxford: Oxford University Press.

Glyn, A. and Miliband, D. (eds.) (1994). *Paying for Inequality: The Economic Cost of Social Injustice*. London: Rivers Oram Press.

Gregg, P. (1993). 'Jobs and justice: why job creation alone will not solve unemployment' in Balls, E. and Gregg, P. *Work and Welfare: Tackling the Jobs Deficit*. (*Op. cit.*)

Gregg, P. and Wadsworth, J. (1995). 'Gender, households and access to employment' in this volume.

Groves, D. (1991). 'Women and financial provision for old age' in Maclean, M. and Groves, D. (eds.) *Women's Issues in Social Policy*. London: Routledge.

Hewitt, P. (1993). *About Time*. London: Rivers Oram Press.

Hewitt, P. and Leach, P. (1993). *Social Justice, Children and Families*. Commission on Social Justice, Issues Paper 4. London: IPPR.

Koven, S. and Michel, S. (1993). *Mothers of a New World: Maternalist Politics and the Origins of Welfare States*. London: Routledge.

Land, H. (1980). 'The family wage' in *Feminist Review*, 6.

Land, H. (1989). 'The construction of dependency' in Bulmer, M., Lewis, J. and Piachaud, D. (eds.) *The Goals of Social Policy*. London: Unwin Hyman.

Lewis, J. (1992). 'Gender and the development of welfare regimes' in *Journal of European Social Policy*, 2 (3).

Lister, R. (1992). *Women's Economic Dependency and Social Security*. Manchester: Equal Opportunities Commission.

Marsh, A. and McKay, S. (1993). *Families, Work and Benefits*. London: Policy Studies Institute.

Marshall, T. H. (1949). 'Citizenship and social class', republished in *Sociology at the Crossroads* (1963). London: Heinemann.

McKay, S. and Marsh, A. (1994). *Lone Parents and Work*. London: HMSO.

McLaughlin, E. and Glendinning, C. (1994). 'Paying for care in Europe: is there a feminist approach?' in Hantrais, L. and Mangen, S. (eds.) *Concepts and Contexts in International Comparisons: Family Policy and the Welfare of Women*. Cross-national Research Papers Series 3 (3). Centre for European Studies, University of Loughborough.

McLaughlin, E. and Ingram, K. (1991). *All Stitched Up: Sex Segregation in the Northern Ireland Clothing Industry*. Belfast: Equal Opportunities Commission Northern Ireland.

McLaughlin, E. (1991). 'Work and welfare benefits: social security, employment and unemployment in the 1990s' in *Journal of Social Policy*, 20 (4).

McLaughlin, E. (1994a). 'The demise of the institution of the job' in *The Political Quarterly*, 65 (2).

McLaughlin, E. (1994b). *Flexibility in Work and Benefits*. Commission on Social Justice, Issues Paper 11. London: IPPR.

Metcalf, H. (1992). 'Hidden unemployment' in McLaughlin, E. (ed.) *Understanding Unemployment*. London: Routledge.

Metcalf, H. and Leighton, P. (1989). *The Under-utilisation of Women in the Labour Market*. IMS Report 172. Brighton: Institute of Manpower Studies.

Millar, J. (1989). 'Social security, equality and women in the UK' in *Policy and Politics*, 17 (4).

OECD (1993). *Employment Outlook*. Paris: Organisation for Economic Co-operation and Development.

Pascall, G (1993). 'Citizenship – a feminist analysis' in Drover, G. and Kerans, P. (eds.) *New Approaches to Welfare*. Aldershot: Edward Elgar.

Pateman, C. (1989). *The Disorder of Women*. Cambridge: Polity Press.

Phillips, A. and Taylor, B. (1980). 'Sex and skill' in *Feminist Review*, 6.

Rubery, J. and Fagan, C. (1992). *Occupational Segregation and Part-time Work*. Paper presented to the European Labour Market UK Presidency conference, Glasgow, November.

Schmitt, J. and Wadsworth, J. (1994). 'The rise in economic inactivity' in Glyn, A. and Miliband, D. (eds.) *Paying for Inequality: The Economic Cost of Social Injustice*. (*Op. cit.*)

Shaver, S. (1990). *Gender, Social Policy Regimes and the Welfare State*. Social Policy Research Centre Discussion Paper 26, University of New South Wales, Australia.

Waldfogel, J. (1993). *Women Working for Less: A Longitudinal Analysis of the Family Gap*. Discussion Paper WSP/93, STICERD, London School of Economics and Political Science, London.

Williams, F. (1989). *Social Policy: A Critical Introduction*. Cambridge: Polity.

CHAPTER 14 # Social and Family Security in the Redress of Unequal Opportunities

Hugh Davies and Heather Joshi

Women have three potential sources of income in contemporary Britain: the labour market, the state and the family. This study quantifies the importance of intra-family payments for hypothetical model couples at various stages of the life cycle, and for various different combinations of partners' earning power. The resulting picture of the potential role of the family alongside the state and the labour market will inform policy debate on issues such as derived rights to social security, and provide insight into gender relations (Joshi, 1993; Ward *et al.*, 1993; Arber and Ginn, 1991).

To date there has been little quantification of the family as a source of income (Sorenson, 1993). This chapter provides an illustrative estimate of the cash gains to be made from marriage and the losses to be faced if a marriage fails. If couples pool their incomes and share the proceeds equally, the partner with the lower contribution will be compensated by half the original difference between them. Wives normally receive less from the labour market and state, so they are the beneficiaries of income-pooling, with husbands making payments out of their receipts from the outside world. Husbands' earnings may exceed those of their wives for a number of reasons, including unequal opportunities in the labour market and the prevailing unequal division of domestic responsibilities within marriage. Of particular interest here are the earnings wives forgo, through reduced years and hours of employment and lower rates of pay, to rear children. Unequal treatment because of gender and the financial penalties of motherhood tend to reinforce one another (Joshi, 1991).

The 'earnings opportunity cost of children' has already been explored (Joshi, 1990; Joshi and Davies, 1992a, 1992c, 1993). Allowing for the impact of state transfers, the 'revenue cost of children' can be defined as the difference between the net income of a family without children and that of an identical family with children. The 'expenditure costs of children' signify that adults with dependent children have a lower standard of living than those without children but with the same income. There is a connection between these costs and the recycling of income within the family. The potential importance of income-sharing varies throughout a couple's life cycle and is linked to the process of reproduction.

Within the lifetime of an individual, the lack of earnings after retirement is, to some degree, redressed by transfers from the state and by pensions linked to earnings, which can be seen as a rescheduling of one's own labour market income. When a woman's earning phase is interrupted to rear children, her earnings and earnings-related pensions are reduced. Thus the gaps between spouses are widened while rearing children and in old age. Redistribution between spouses who pool incomes is important at these times. A survivor's (here, always widow's) pension is another, posthumous, form of intra-couple payment.

In describing the flows of purchasing power between spouses as transfers, there is no suggestion that these are mere grants unrequited by an exchange of services. There is no attempt to model household production levels or estimate how much of the income gained in pooling is 'earned' by unpaid work.[1] Nor is there a complete accounting of the (implicit) flows of purchasing power within the family: any such flows between parents and children are ignored, and to emphasise this point the term 'spousal transfer' is used.

Constructing lifetime-income profiles for illustrative couples enables six key questions to be investigated.

- How much of a married woman's lifetime income is derived from her partnership rather than the labour market and the state?
- How does the income forgone by parents, the 'revenue cost of children', compare with the 'expenditure costs' of their consumption?
- Who loses how much when mothers forgo earnings, and how far is their sacrifice shared with the state and their spouses?
- How much of the gap in spouses' incomes is attributable to the revenue costs of children?
- How much of the gap between spouses' incomes arises because of unequal treatment in hourly earnings (gender discrimination), and how much from other sources of disparity?
- Is the gap between spouses' incomes, and hence the scope for intra-family transfer, greater while children are dependent than in old age?

These questions pick up hitherto unworked strands from previous work simulating lifetime incomes and pensions,[2] and blend them with the idea of the within-couple transfer made explicit in an exploration of the conventional assumption that couples always pool their incomes and share consumption (Davies and Joshi, 1994). That work was based upon cross-sectional data on actual couples. The computation of the spousal transfer in this chapter does not imply that equal sharing always takes place, but demonstrates how much the transfer would be if the couple's income were equally shared. By making this explicit, it is implicitly described how the situation would be if there were no sharing. It is of course possible that couples put all their incomes into a common pool, but do not benefit equally from how this income is spent (or saved). The actual ways in which couples pool resources and share consumption may be more subtle than is

---

[1] The authors are grateful to Apps for pointing out this possible misconstruction of terminology. Empirical evidence from the National Child Development Study suggests even higher rates of participation in unpaid domestic tasks by women earning less than their partners than by those who earn about the same as their partners (Joshi *et al.*, 1994).

[2] The method builds on the work of Joshi (1990) and has been applied to pensions and divorce (Joshi and Davies, 1991, 1992b), childcare (Joshi and Davies, 1992c, 1993) and the interaction between pensions and motherhood (Joshi and Davies, 1992c). The model used here is an extended and updated version of that described in detail in Davies and Joshi (1992).

allowed for here, but more elaborate models would produce outcomes between those given by the polar assumptions of equal sharing and no sharing.

Method and assumptions

This study is based on a simulation model. The lifetime earnings of illustrative people are generated from econometric functions. Tax, benefit and pension rules are then applied to simulated gross earnings.

Participation and earnings

Female participation is modelled by a multinomial logit where the outcomes are 'not employed', 'employed part-time' and 'employed full-time'. The key variables are age, marital status, number and age of children, occupational grade and non-labour income. A women is assumed to participate when her probability of doing so is greater than 0.5. Hours simulated for full-time employees are constants depending on occupational grade. For part-timers, hours are estimated by an *ad hoc* method depending on the ratio of the probabilities of full-time and part-time work. Earnings for participants are obtained from separate wage equations for full-time and part-time jobs (Ermisch and Wright, 1991). Earnings depend on work experience, which is generated from the simulated pattern of employment over time. Men are assumed to be employed continuously.

The equation used for male wages is a standard human capital equation from a study of married men and women (Wright and Ermisch, 1991). No allowance is made for any dependence of men's earnings on their marital status, but Wright and Ermisch's equation is modified for younger ages by splicing on extra parameters (Greenhalgh, 1980). Although economic theory suggests that labour market behaviour will depend on the extent of income-sharing in a partnership, neither estimates nor simulations take account of this. All the econometric equations were estimated on the assumption of exogenous fertility. With the exception of Greenhalgh's estimates, all the foregoing are based on data from the 1980 Women and Employment Survey. Some evidence was collected from the 1958 National Child Development Study (NCDS). This has not been used to generate parameters, but to compare the outcome of simulations with the data it provides at one particular age.

The individuals

The model (Davies and Joshi, 1992) allows for three occupational levels determined by educational attainment variables. Couples in the same skill band are compared, as well as the case of a man in a high-level occupation married to a woman in a low-level occupation, a combination which is becoming less common as women's skill levels increase in successive cohorts. These men are given 12.5 per cent more earnings than those who have the same educational level as their wives. This is an assumed educational lead which brings them closer to average earnings and gives husbands a hitherto typical educational lead within marriage. Even in couples within the same skill band, men have a lead over their wives due to differences in hours worked, the premium on hourly wages from age differences and the educational lead, as well as sex discrimination (Wright and Ermisch, 1991).

In general it is assumed that there are no interruptions to earnings histories, apart from those due to childcare responsibilities. Random employment interruptions across the board might alter the magnitudes involved in pension comparisons, but would be unlikely to change the ranking of the individual cases. Older married women are simulated to switch into part-time employment, but there is no allowance for sickness or unemployment. The illustrative people are not statistical averages, rather they are 'typical' individuals in a world where uninterrupted male careers are the norm.

There are four types of married women in the simulations: a woman without children, women with two or four children, and a 'career housewife' who has two children and does not take any paid work after her marriage. A woman marries at age 20, 22 or 24, depending (positively) on her occupational level. If she has two children these are born three years and six years after marriage. If she has four children, the first arrives two years after the marriage, and the others at two-year intervals. In each case the men are assumed to be two years older than the women. This assumption is taken from the average ages of the husbands of 33-year-old women in the NCDS. The marriages studied here are lifelong partnerships: even today, 63 per cent of marriages in Britain are not expected to end in divorce. Men are assumed to live to age 78, and women to age 81.

These examples show a restricted range of inequality in underlying earning power between spouses. For example, this study does not include any wife earning more than her husband, though such a situation occurs in about 12 per cent of the cases in the NCDS sample where both partners are working. One test of the realism of these simulated couples is offered in Table 14.1. For the NCDS women who were part of a couple with good income data, the share of the wife's income in the couple's joint net income was analysed according to the presence or absence of children and the size of the wife's contribution. A summary of the distributions is shown in the top panel. Among both groups of wives, only a minority contributed more than their husbands. Women with children clustered in the range below 30 per cent, and childless wives around 40 per cent.

Within these broad ranges are the net income shares of most of the simulated wives at age 33, shown in the lower half of Table 14.1. The shares of childless wives employed full-time range from 32 per cent to 44 per cent. Mothers' shares range around ten per cent, apart from highly-qualified women employed full-time. The others draw their income almost entirely from child benefit, supplemented in a few cases by very low part-time earnings. It is plausible that these few cases in the lower panel on Table 14.1 have been drawn from the empirical distributions reported in

Table 14.1 Wife's contribution to joint net income among 33-year-olds

Empirical data for 1991 (National Child Development Survey)

Share of wife in couple's joint net income	Percentage of childless couples	couples with children
0 per cent	2	1
0–15 per cent	4	34
15–30 per cent	9	27
30–50 per cent	52	26
50–100 per cent	30	11
100 per cent	3	2
N	544	2490

Wife's percentage contribution to joint net income as simulated at age 33

Skill levels of partners	None	Two	Four
Both low	39	13	18
Both mid	39	13	11
Both high	44	42	10
His high, hers low	32	5	10

Source: Authors' calculations: upper section based on female cohort members in NCDS; lower section derived from simulation model described in text

its upper panel. When further analysis of the NCDS data has been completed, it will be possible to compare the simulated histories with the employment trajectories of the cohort up to age 33. This comparison validates the simulations, which demonstrate how the cohort's life cycle would look if it were projected on to an unchanging economic environment.

Institutional features

This study uses a range of institutional features: income tax, child benefit, National Insurance contributions, National Insurance pension age, National Insurance basic pension, earnings-related pension and widowhood payments.

The income tax system provides personal and married couple's allowances, both of which are increased for people aged 65 or over (and increased again at 75). Under 'independent' taxation, a couple can choose to split the married couple's allowance (except for the age addition) between them to minimise their joint tax liability. Partial optimisation is assumed: the couple splits the married couple's allowance equally, unless assigning the entire allowance to one partner would result in a lower joint tax liability. Tax rates, bands and allowances are fixed at their April 1994 values, with one exception. The rate of relief for some allowances (principally the married couple's allowance) will be further restricted to a rate of 15 per cent (down from the April 1994 level of 20 per cent) from April 1995, and this change (and the consequent increase in the age addition for the married couple's allowance) has been incorporated into the simulations. The basic rate of income tax is 25 per cent.

In these hypothetical families, child benefit is paid to mothers of dependent children under 16. It is not taxable and is paid at a higher rate for the first child. For a woman with two children it amounts to £18.45 per week.

National Insurance contributions are paid only on earnings and only by people under National Insurance pension age. They are levied on the band of earnings between the lower earnings limit (LEL) and the upper earnings limit (UEL). In April 1994, the LEL was £57 per week and the UEL was £430 per week. For someone earning above the LEL, the rates in April 1994 were two per cent on the LEL and 8.2 per cent on the rest up to the UEL.[3]

National Insurance pension age is currently 65 for men and 60 for women. Under present rules, a person over this age can elect to defer receipt of their pension and earn increments of 7.5 per cent per annum on their entitlement. Under the proposals in the White Paper *Equality in State Pension Age* (DSS, 1993) the pension age for women would be raised to 65 in 2030. Simulations are made under the current and proposed pension ages,[4] and the latter incorporate other consequential changes specified in the White Paper.

National Insurance basic pension is a taxable benefit paid to men aged 65 or over and women aged either 60 or 65 and over. It is not earnings-related, but entitlement depends on the number of years that earnings have been above the LEL. A married woman who has low entitlement on the basis of her own earnings history (such as the career housewife), has the right to a category B pension based on her husband's earnings history. The category B pension is 60 per cent of the full pension. When widowed, a category B pensioner receives a full basic pension. Basic pension is counted as a state benefit. The full basic pension assumed is £57.60 per week.

There is a state earnings-related pension scheme (SERPS), but it is possible to 'contract out' of this into a private pension scheme. Most of those who are contracted-out are in final salary pension schemes. Contributions to these schemes are deductible from taxable income. Each person in the simulations has been assigned a default pension type. For men the default is a final salary scheme, although low-skilled men are assumed to be in SERPS. By default, women are assumed to be in SERPS except for the highly-skilled, who are in a final salary scheme. Even for

---

[3] The extra amount paid by employees not contracted out of SERPS has been counted as a pension contribution.

[4] No attempt is made to simulate the details of the transition period.

highly-skilled women, however, periods of part-time work are covered by SERPS rather than the final salary scheme. Those who contract out of SERPS pay a lower rate of National Insurance contributions. The benefits payable under SERPS are related to (lifetime) earnings between the LEL and the UEL. In this study the contributions payable in respect of SERPS are counted as pension contributions rather than as taxes, and SERPS benefits as pensions rather than state benefits. Current primary legislation provides for 'home responsibilities protection' under SERPS. Although the secondary legislation necessary to activate this provision has not yet been implemented, it is included in all the simulations.

Under both SERPS and final salary schemes a survivor's benefit of half the primary beneficiary's annual pension is paid to a surviving spouse. The National Insurance widow's pension does not enter into the picture.

Timing

The simulations reported here take place in a time warp. There is no inflation or economic growth: earnings levels are calibrated to 1994 levels. All relevant tax and benefit rates are fixed at their April 1994 levels, except as noted earlier.[5] Rules for tax, benefit and pension schemes are fixed as those faced by someone entering the labour force in 1994, except for the simulations involving the proposed changes in pension age.

Income components, sharing and equivalence scales

Income is classified as follows:

E = gross earnings
L = labour market income
U = earnings-related pension contributions (including SERPS)
P = earnings-related pension payments
W = survivor's pension
S = net state benefits
   = child benefit + basic pension – income tax – National Insurance contributions excluding SERPS contributions
F = family transfer
N = 'own' net income of each partner from external sources
R = equivalent net income
A = average net income of couple.

The annual relationship between these quantities for one of the partners is

$$L_{it}^k = E_{it}^k - U_{it}^k + P_{it}^k$$

$$N_{it}^k = L_{it}^k + S_{it}^k + W_{it}^k$$

where

k = number of children born to the family

---

[5] See Joshi and Davies (1994) for a discussion of indexation.

i   = h (husband), w (wife)

t   = year, running from date of marriage until death of longer-living partner.

Income components of a deceased spouse are defined to be zero.

Where income-pooling takes place, couples are assumed to share their annual net incomes equally. This *inter vivos* family transfer is defined as

$$F_t^k = \frac{(N_{wt}^k + N_{ht}^k)}{S_t} - N_{wt}^k$$

where S_t is the number of surviving members of the partnership.

Thus, the woman gets the benefit of the average net income of the couple:

$$A_{wt}^k = N_{wt}^k + F_t^k$$

To allow for possible expenditure costs of sharing, and the expenditure costs of children, the total net income of the couple is divided by the appropriate value of the equivalence scale to obtain R_{wt}^k, equivalent net income ('pooled income'). Hence, the 'consumption economies' term is defined as

$$\varepsilon_t^k = R_{wt}^k - A_{wt}^k$$

The consumption economies term thus depends on both the average income of the couple and the equivalence scale. It will be positive for a couple without dependent children, but may be negative for a couple with children if the expenditure costs of children exceed the economies of sharing. Both the average and the equivalent net income are the same for each partner while both survive.

No attempt is made to estimate equivalence scales, but administratively-determined ones are used. The equivalent income scales used are based on those implicit in supplementary benefit, the safety net that applied up to 1988. The first adult in a family counts as one, any second adult counts 0.59. Children under five count 0.22; those older but less than 11 count 0.27; those aged 11 and 12 count 0.35; those aged 13, 14 or 15 count 0.41; and those over 15 count 0.49. These scales are assumed to apply at all levels of income and thus the consumption economies will, given number and age of children, be proportionately the same at all levels of net income.

Undiscounted sums of these quantities will be used frequently over parts of the life cycle. This is not to imply that for particular purposes a zero discount should always be used. As implied earlier, the 'lifetime' runs from marriage until the death of the second partner.

Simulated lifetime incomes of illustrative individuals

An overview of lifetime incomes

Figure 14.2 shows the lifetime-income profile for two-child model couples in the cases where both partners have the same skill level. The figures show the net 'own' income for both husband and wife: the incomes each would have under the 'no sharing' assumption. Also shown are the average and pooled incomes per adult. In all cases, the shape of the average income profile is dominated by the shape of the woman's own income profile, which is dictated by variations in her labour force

Figure 14.2 Income profiles for couples with two children

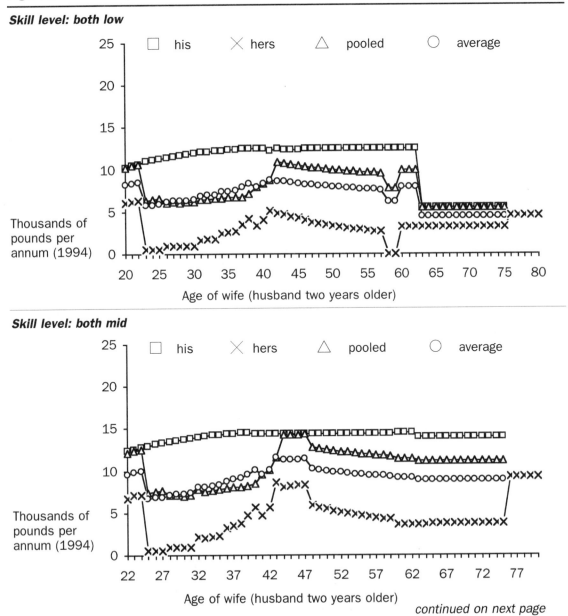

continued on next page

Figure 14.2 (continued)

Skill level: both high

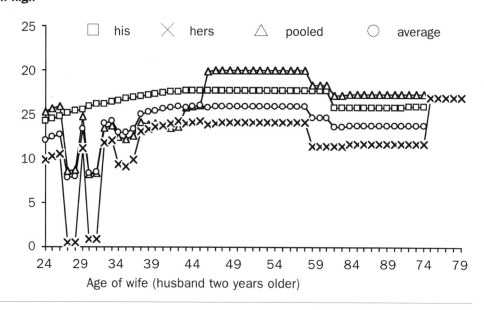

Skill level: his high, hers low

participation and hours. These variations, in turn, are driven mainly by the number and age of her children. The difference between the own and average lines represents the family transfer assumed to be paid under the pooling assumption. The difference between the average and pooled lines represents the consumption economies. For the highly-skilled couple, the economies of sharing and the woman's income are sufficiently large that the pooled (equivalent) income exceeds the man's at times when both are in full-time employment and they do not have dependent children.

For a number of reasons the man's income shows a very high replacement rate in retirement, especially in the mid-skilled case. At age 65, National Insurance contributions are no longer payable, tax allowances increase, and basic state pension is received. The simulated men's earning histories have no interruptions or job changes, thus producing the maximum possible earnings-linked pension: a level which few currently-retired men have achieved. In this time warp pension indexation policies are irrelevant, though their importance is demonstrated elsewhere (Joshi and Davies, 1994). Proportionately, these effects have their maximum impact on the mid-skilled man, largely because of the ceiling on National Insurance contributions and the flat rate character of the basic pension.

Widowed women's own income shows a sharp increase, particularly in mid- and highly-skilled cases. This is due to survivor's pensions received under late partners' occupational pension schemes. For the mid- and highly-skilled widows, over half the income arises from this source. While husbands are alive, women's standards of living depend on whether income is pooled, but after their partners are dead women have legal rights to survivor's pensions. Unlike *inter vivos* family transfers, a widow's pension is subject to income tax. Figure 14.2 illustrates the importance of widows' derived rights, the continuation of which have been questioned in a draft EC directive (Lister, 1992).

Table 14.3 shows undiscounted lifetime totals of the income measures given in Figure 14.2 (and for net state benefits) for the range of families studied. The differences between men and women for the pooled and average measures reflect differences in their lifespan and the age gap between them. The difference between the average and own net income for an individual is the spousal transfer *inter vivos*. Not surprisingly, the spousal transfer (if it is made) is highest in the cases where there is a large difference in the skill level of the two partners (he with high skills, she with low). Even absolutely, the spousal transfer between highly-skilled couples is smaller than that of the mid-skilled couples (except in the case of the career housewife). Generally speaking, mothers receive positive transfers from the state over their lifetime: the exception is the highly-skilled mothers, whose earnings attract enough tax to outweigh their child benefit.

While both partners survive, under the pooling assumption both enjoy the same standard of living. For each partner, however, the source of this income appears differently. This study concentrates on the point of view of wives, partly for economy of presentation, but also to highlight the effect of children on income and its composition. As Figure 14.2 illustrates, this is more transparent if women's income is highlighted. To put it another way, under the 'no sharing' assumption the men's incomes show relatively little variation over the life cycle, but the women's vary considerably. Although detailed tables from the point of view of the men are not shown in these simulations, it should be remembered that there is a corresponding negative flow wherever positive spousal transfers are received by wives while their husbands are alive.

Table 14.3 Lifetime income totals (thousands of pounds, 1994)

Retirement at 60

	Couples with							
	No children		Two children		Two children (housewife)		Four children	
	Woman	Man	Woman	Man	Woman	Man	Woman	Man
Skill level: both low								
Pooled	578	553	463	441	386	365	424	402
Average	465	440	405	382	340	318	396	373
Own net	312	592	192	594	63	596	174	595
State	19	- 137	72	- 134	54	- 133	80	- 134
Skill level: both middle								
Pooled	757	709	620	574	510	466	570	525
Average	612	563	540	494	447	403	526	481
Own net	418	757	275	760	88	762	247	760
State	- 23	- 208	46	- 206	50	- 203	74	- 206
Skill level: both high								
Pooled	1093	998	938	853	585	533	847	766
Average	889	793	824	739	515	463	785	704
Own net	812	871	691	871	101	877	618	872
State	- 201	- 264	- 124	- 263	45	- 257	- 76	- 262
Skill level: his high, hers low								
Pooled	796	744	666	615	614	564	622	572
Average	644	592	580	529	536	486	573	523
Own net	307	928	178	931	91	931	165	931
State	15	- 279	52	- 276	46	- 275	61	- 276
With retirement at 65								
Skill level: both low								
Pooled	567	543	454	432	386	364	419	397
Average	456	432	397	375	340	318	392	370
Own net	292	595	175	598	58	599	163	598
State	4	- 134	57	- 131	50	- 130	70	- 130
Skill level: both middle								
Pooled	758	710	621	575	507	463	571	525
Average	613	565	541	495	445	401	526	481
Own net	420	757	277	759	81	765	248	760
State	- 40	- 208	30	- 207	44	- 201	58	- 206
Skill level: both high								
Pooled	1099	1003	959	869	583	531	871	785
Average	894	797	842	752	513	461	805	719
Own net	820	871	723	871	95	880	653	872
State	- 230	- 264	- 163	- 263	41	- 255	- 114	- 262
Skill level: his high, hers low								
Pooled	786	734	660	610	612	562	618	568
Average	635	584	575	525	535	485	570	520
Own net	289	930	167	933	86	934	157	933
State	1	- 277	43	- 274	42	- 273	55	- 273

Source: Authors' calculations

Notes 1 Lifetime: years from marriage while either survive.   2 Pooled: net equivalised income.

3 Average: net income averaged over surviving members.

4 Own net: net income of this partner, including widow's pension and net state benefits.   5 State: net state benefits.

The effect of raising state pension age for women to 65

The White Paper *Equality in State Pension Age* (DSS, 1993) proposes to phase in the raising of women's state pension age to 65: women born after 1950 should have the state pension age raised in steps, to 65 for those born in and after 1955. Thus, if this becomes law, the women in the NCDS cohort could not expect their pension until age 65. Some simulations are therefore based on the alternative assumption of pension age at 65. The raised age has various possible effects on lifetime net income: the loss of five years' basic pension and SERPS and the possible liability to pay NI contributions for an extra five years; and possibilities that pension income after 65 would be enhanced if extra contributions were paid into SERPS or an occupational pension. For some with a deficient contribution record for basic pension, auto-credits after age 60 might boost basic pension. If the change in rules induced a change in earning, this extra earning would also offset the losses mentioned earlier. The whole list of items would be subject to income tax.

Crude allowances have been made for the effect of a different pension age on earning and income profiles, but they cannot be too well informed by any existing evidence. The participation propensities simulated for age 59 over the next five years are extrapolated. Cases simulated to be in full-time employment at age 59 are given another five years' full-time employment, those simulated as part-timers at 59 have this employment similarly prolonged for five years, and those already out of work at 59 do not have any further employment. The level of annual earnings is not in practice affected, as wages have already reached a fixed top level.

Thus all the graduates (other than housewives) remain in full-time employment and increase net lifetime income by between £8,000 and £35,000; women of middle earning capacity (other than housewives) stay in part-time jobs and earn just £1,000 or £2,000 more than the five years' worth of pension forgone and extra taxes paid; women of low earning power and all housewives gain no increase in earnings to offset a net loss of income from state transfers. Their net losses range from £5,000 (housewives) to £18,000 (low-skilled women with highly-skilled husbands and no children), which represents at most six per cent of lifetime own net income. The impact of state pension age is somewhat moderated for earning mothers compared to childless women, but on balance the effects on lifetime cash are not great. Any gain to be made depends on high earning. This is not to deny an impact on leisure and cash flow during the relevant years, but merely to say that, taking a long view over the whole lifetime, five years here or there on the pension age does not make much difference.

Addressing the questions

The family as source of income

How much of a married woman's lifetime income is derived from her partnership rather than the labour market and the state? The importance of the family as a source of women's income was apparent for some in Figure 14.2 and Table 14.3. It is shown in a different way in Table 14.4,

Table 14.4 Income sources as percentages of woman's pooled lifetime income

| | Number of children | | | |
	None	Two	Two (housewife)	Four
Skill level: both low				
Lifetime labour market	50	25	1	21
State	3	15	14	19
Consumption economies	20	13	12	7
Family transfer	27	47	73	54
Skill level: both middle				
Lifetime labour market	54	31	1	24
State	- 3	7	10	13
Consumption economies	19	13	12	8
Family transfer	30	48	77	55
Skill level: both high				
Lifetime labour market	89	82	2	77
State	- 18	- 13	8	-9
Consumption economies	19	12	12	7
Family transfer	11	19	78	25
Skill level: his high, hers low				
Lifetime labour market	31	13	0	10
State	2	8	7	10
Consumption economies	19	13	13	8
Family transfer	48	67	80	72

Source: Authors' calculations

Notes 1 Lifetime: years from marriage while either survive.   2 Pooled: net equivalised income.

3 Lifetime labour market: gross earnings plus earnings-linked pensions, minus contributions on those pensions.

4 Consumption economies: net equivalised income minus average net income.

5 Family transfer: includes widow's pension.   6 State: net state benefits.

which expresses various sources of gain, transfer and earnings as a percentage of a woman's lifetime income if she pools with her husband throughout. The contribution of a married woman's lifetime labour market income (which includes earnings-linked pensions) to her overall standard of living shows clear gradients by skill level and number of children, in the expected directions. Most of the simulated women are net beneficiaries from state transfers, except for the highly skilled. Only for the housewives, however, is the state a more important source of income than the labour market. The other two components relate to partnership. The consumption economies reflect the operation of the equivalence scale: these are always positive over the lifetime, gains from sharing with a partner more than offsetting the expenditure costs of children (where present). The uniformity of the consumption economies across occupational groups is merely a reflection of the assumed proportionality of the equivalence scales.[6]

The family transfer entries include the widow's pension as well as *inter vivos* pooling (if it occurs). The family transfer is the largest single component of pooled lifetime income for all the simulated mothers, except for the non-housewife graduates. It is around half of lifetime pooled income for employed mothers of middle skill, and around three-quarters for the housewives. Even for the childless non-graduate wives, the family transfer contribution to lifetime pooled income is much larger than that of the state.[7]

Thus the simulations suggest that the rise in the labour market participation of married women, and the increase in labour market equality, have not yet wholly (or nearly) brought about the demise of intra-family transfers as a potential major source of economic welfare for married women, except in the case of graduate women. Qualitatively at least, this impression is confirmed by other evidence. Using cross-section data from the Family Expenditure Survey (FES), Davies and Joshi (1994) found that the average family transfer component of married women's net pooled equivalent income was 32 per cent in 1986, having declined substantially from 56 per cent in 1968.[8] The similarities between the simulation results and the NCDS cohort have already been highlighted.

Revenue and expenditure costs of children

Joshi (1990) and, among others, Joshi and Davies (1992c) presented estimates of a woman's gross earnings cost of children. Table 14.5 shows comparable estimates, in this case using a retirement age of 60. The absolute amount in pounds varies with the year's currency used and the evolving details of the model; in Table 14.5 it is £204,000 for a mid-skilled mother of two married to a man in the same skill band.

Table 14.5 also breaks down the gross earnings cost into components due to lost years, lost hours and lost pay, showing a roughly equal three-way splitting of these costs. In this case, lost earnings are 57 per cent of potential earnings after motherhood; the forgone total splits 31 per cent

---

[6] They are not completely uniform because of differences in the assumed ages at marriage and childbirth.

[7] Similar calculations with retirement for women at 65 show that the effects of changing retirement age on the composition of lifetime pooled income are small. Generally speaking, state transfers contribute a somewhat lower fraction, and the labour market a somewhat higher one. The family transfer continues to be a potentially major contributor to married women's economic well-being.

[8] These figures are not strictly comparable with the simulation results: apart from the obvious difficulties of weighting and the differences between a cross-section and a lifetime perspective, the FES analysis used a somewhat different definition of the family transfer. It made separate allowance for housing costs, in a way which would reduce the size of the family transfer as compared to the method employed here.

Table 14.5 Gross earnings cost of motherhood

Totals and decomposition

Gross earnings loss	Number of children		
	Two	Two (housewife)	Four
Thousands of pounds (1994)			
Skill level			
Both low	165	252	190
Both middle	204	357	255
Both high	136	667	231
His high, hers low	160	216	181
As percentage of childless earnings after age of first birth			
Skill level			
Both low	66	100	73
Both middle	57	100	70
Both high	20	100	34
His high, hers low	74	100	81
Source of earnings loss (as percentage of total)			
Skill level: both low			
Lost years	36	68	41
Lost hours	41	0	33
Lost experience	23	32	26
Part-time penalty	0	0	0
Skill level: both middle			
Lost years	31	64	37
Lost hours	38	0	30
Lost experience	26	36	29
Part-time penalty	5	0	4
Skill level: both high			
Lost years	45	54	51
Lost hours	10	0	4
Lost experience	43	46	4
Part-time penalty	2	0	0
Skill level: his high, hers low			
Lost years	51	69	52
Lost hours	25	0	23
Lost experience	24	31	25
Part-time penalty	0	0	0

Source: Authors' calculations

lost years and 38 per cent lost hours, while the two components of lost pay, lost experience and the negative part-time premium account for 26 per cent and five per cent respectively. In the original estimates (Joshi, 1990), earnings lost amounted to 50 per cent of potential after age 25, and the corresponding decomposition was 38 per cent, 29 per cent, 30 per cent and three per cent. The model, though elaborated, has not come too far adrift from its origins. What the present calculations are able to illustrate is that the three-fold decomposition does not apply generally across all types of woman. For the more qualified, and for the unqualified married to a highly-skilled husband, lost years are proportionally more important than lost hours, though the total loss is smaller for the former and larger for the latter. Lost years have greater salience for mothers of four than for those of two. The hypothetical career housewives have the largest forgone earnings compared to a childless wife who remains in the labour market. Changing retirement age to 65 makes only minimal difference (not shown) to these figures.

The gross earnings cost of children measures the output lost to the economy, approximately,[9] but does not measure the income loss to the parents. The costs of children can be further studied to take account of the effects of pensions, state taxes and benefits, and expenditure costs.[10]

With these assumptions, the revenue costs of children can be shown entirely on the woman's account, for neither the man's earnings nor his net state benefits depend on the number of children.[11] These costs are independent of the amount of income-pooling practised by the couple (on the improbable assumption that labour force participation is independent of pooling). To what extent do the state tax and benefit systems, and the internal spousal transfer presumed to be paid under pooling, compensate a woman for these revenue losses?

Whether or not there is sharing *inter vivos*, the loss in labour market income due to children can be expressed as

$$\Delta L_{wt}^k = L_{wt}^0 - L_{wt}^k = \Delta N_{wt}^k - \Delta S_{wt}^k - \Delta W_{wt}^k$$

where the last term on the right-hand side (the difference in widows' pensions) is identically zero in these cases, and the second term is the compensation which the state tax/benefit system makes to the gross income loss. For illustrative cases of mid-skilled couples, Table 14.6 shows the steps involved in moving from the gross earnings cost of

---

[9] The lost output is actually greater than the earnings loss, since it includes employers' National Insurance contributions.

[10] Joshi and Davies (1991, 1992b) considered pensions, while Joshi and Davies (1993) considered the effect of taxes and benefits. The assumptions used in those papers, however, differ somewhat from each other and from those used here. This study presents a unified set of estimates on a common set of assumptions.

[11] There is one caveat to this. Under the assumptions used here about how couples manage their tax affairs, there is a very small effect on the husband's net income. This arises because it is assumed that he will claim the entire married couple's allowance in years when his wife is not earning (or earning below the tax threshold). In most cases a father will therefore have a slightly smaller tax liability than a childless man, due to differences in the labour force participation of their wives.

children to the net income cost; in other words, the quantities in this equation, together with the prior steps to get from earnings to gross labour market income. Net losses amount to about two-thirds of the gross for both family sizes and both pension ages.

Table 14.6 Gross and net revenue costs of children

Thousands of pounds (1994)

	Woman with	
	Two children	Four children
Gross earnings	204	255
Subtract		
Pension contributions	3	4
To get		
Earnings net of pension contributions	201	251
Add		
Earnings-linked pension	11	17
To get		
Lifetime labour market income	212	268
Add		
Net state benefits	- 69	- 97
To get		
Net income of woman	143	171

Source: Authors' calculations

Notes

1 Elements in table are values for woman with no children, less those for women with two and four children respectively.

2 Both partners have middle-level skills

Under the pooling assumption, the revenue costs of children can be set alongside the expenditure costs. No account is taken of any utility which parents may gain from having children, nor is the utility of the children themselves considered. Under the conventional income-pooling assumption, the costs of children may be measured by the equivalent net income enjoyed by a couple without children minus that enjoyed by a couple with children. This cost may be broken down into two components, the revenue cost and the expenditure cost, and may be expressed in terms of equivalent net income (for wives, similar for husbands) as

$$\Delta R_{wt}^k = R_{wt}^0 - R_{wt}^k = \left\{ A_{wt}^0 - A_{wt}^k \right\} + \left\{ \varepsilon_t^0 - \varepsilon_t^k \right\}$$

where the first term in braces is the revenue cost and the second term in braces is the expenditure cost. Figure 14.7 presents lifetime estimates of these costs for the illustrative couples (husbands plus wives, excluding

Figure 14.7 Revenue and expenditure costs of children

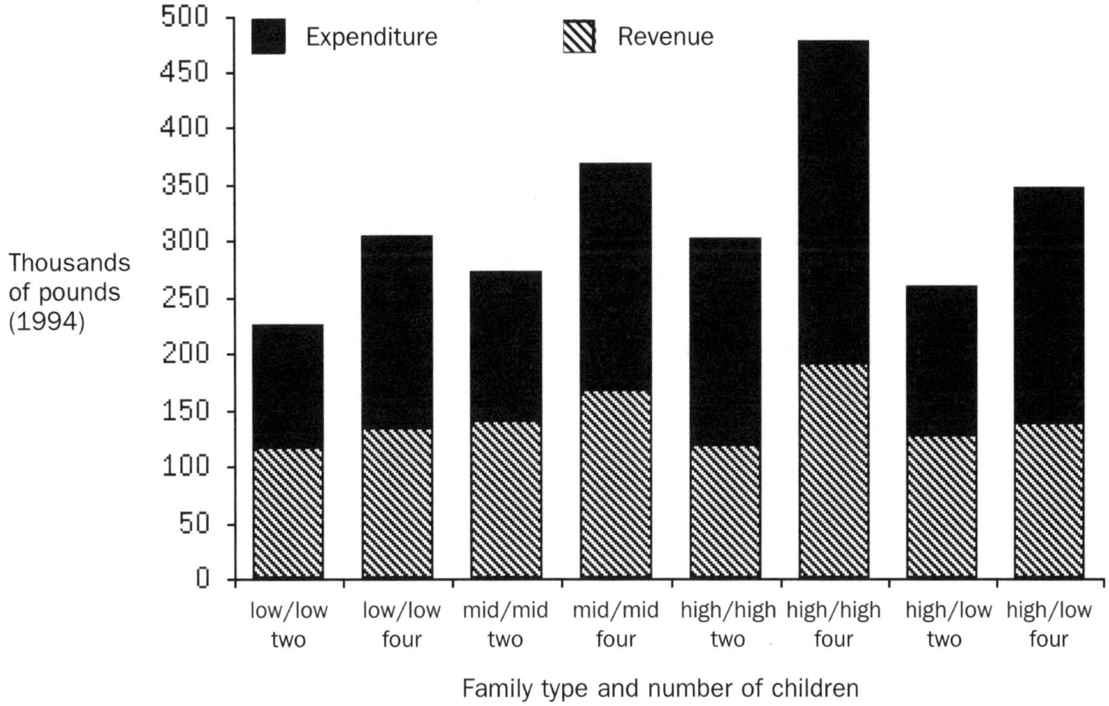

Source: Authors' calculations

career housewives). Generally speaking, these estimates suggest that the revenue and expenditure costs of children are about equal, though for the highly-skilled couples the revenue costs are only about 40 per cent of the total costs.[12] Even under the conventional assumption where period-by-period income is pooled, the lifetime costs are not split equally between the two parents: this would only be the case if they died at the same time. For these illustrative couples the expenditure costs are borne equally under pooling, as they are all incurred while the husbands are alive.

The expenditure costs of children if couples do not pool their income are not considered here. Instead, details of the revenue costs are explored.

Who bears the earnings opportunity cost of children?

No attempt has been made before now to estimate who forgoes the income which would have resulted from mothers' forgone earnings. To investigate the incidence of the cost involved, forgone labour market income is decomposed into that forgone by the state in reduced taxes and increased (child) benefit on the one hand, and by the family on the other. Thus

$$\Delta L_{wt}^k = L_{wt}^0 - L_{wt}^k = \Delta A_{wt}^k - \Delta S_{wt}^k - \Delta F_t^k - \Delta W_{wt}^k$$

[12] This contrasts with an earlier estimate (Joshi, 1990) that the (gross) earnings costs of two children are about double the direct (expenditure) costs (based on scales recommended for foster care), but it still gives a greater relative weight to forgone income than the US estimates by Espenshade and Calhoun (1986), whose direct cost per child came out more than three times greater than the 'indirect cost'.

where, again, the last term will be zero on the assumptions listed earlier. The net income loss would all be borne by the women if the couples did not pool resources. If they do, it is assumed they pool completely, so half the gap between the husbands' net income and that of the wives is said to be transferred. If these transfers occur in marriages which stay intact, the annual income costs (net of taxes and benefits) would be spread equally between wives and husbands (while they survived).

On this sharing assumption, Table 14.8 and Figure 14.9 decompose the lost labour market income of Table 14.6 into the portions borne by the state, the husbands and the wives. Generally speaking the division is into three roughly equal parts. Once the state's share is determined, men and women almost split the difference. The state's share is dominated by tax and National Insurance revenues forgone. For years when both the

Table 14.8 Who pays the revenue cost of children?

Percentage of labour market income loss

	Woman	Man	State
Skill level: both low			
Two children	35	35	30
Two children (housewife)	44	44	12
Four children	35	35	31
Skill level: both middle			
Two children	34	34	33
Two children (housewife)	41	41	18
Four children	32	32	36
Skill level: both high			
Two children	33	28	39
Two children (housewife)	39	35	26
Four children	33	28	39
Skill level: his high, hers low			
Two children	38	39	22
Two children (housewife)	44	44	12
Four children	37	38	25

Source: Authors' calculations

Note

1 Labour market income is wages plus earnings-linked pensions minus contributions on these pensions.

mothers and their childless counterparts are paying tax, this element of the state's share reflects the marginal rate of taxation in the system, set for most at 33 per cent, so this accounts for the order of magnitude in most of the state entries (the costs of child benefit offsetting years of lower tax loss). The split between men and women is not completely equal, although pooling is assumed and the shares are therefore equal in years when they are both alive. The extra costs borne by the women occur when the husbands are dead. If pooling husbands died earlier or divorced their wives, the sharing of the earnings cost would be less complete.

The general principle of roughly equal tripartite division of the cost does not apply across the social spectrum. A greater share of the (lower) forgone earnings of highly-qualified mothers is borne by the state. The state forgoes more tax revenue because the childless counterpart does not work part-time. Career housewives shift less to the state, because the untaxed tranche of their counterparts' earnings is forgone as well.

Figure 14.9 Who pays the revenue costs of two children?

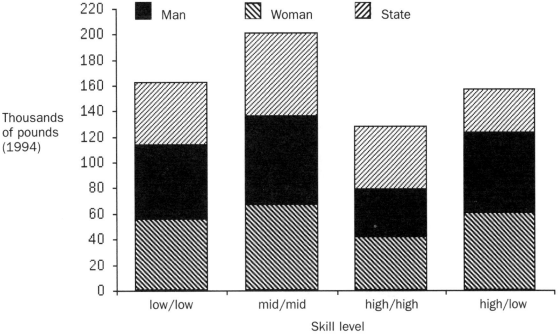

Even with no help from their partners, mothers do not personally lose the full amount of their forgone earnings: up to 41 per cent is shifted on to the Exchequer at current tax and benefit rates. Whether or not they bear the rest of the cost depends upon whether the couple pool their income and for how long. On the assumption of full pooling until his death, nearly half the net revenue cost is borne by the man.

Do the costs of children account for the gap in spouses' incomes?

This question relates to the proportion of the gap between spouses' incomes that could be directly attributed to women forgoing earnings through motherhood. Table 14.10 shows the lifetime transfer from men to women in 12 hypothetical, income-pooling couples: half the gap between their net incomes plus widow's pension. The income forgone by mothers because of child-rearing is the difference between their income and that of their childless counterparts. Therefore the part of the family transfer which arises out of mothers' reduced earnings can be read as the difference between the two right-hand columns of Table 14.10 and the column for the childless couples. The results are shown in the lower panel of Table 14.10. Mothers' forgone earnings account for a minor part of the total family transfer, ranging from one-seventh to three-sevenths of the total. Those which occur even without childbearing are shown in the first column of the top panel. Their relative magnitude reflects the size of the gender gap in pay, hours and years of participation in generating income differences.

Compared to the combined effects of these factors, differences between women's earnings are somewhat dwarfed.[13] Although the presence of children intensifies the need for family transfer, any source of inequality between partners' net earnings would indicate transfers to be made.

Table 14.10 Transfer from husband over lifetime

Thousands of pounds (1994)

	No children	Woman with	
		Two children	Four children
Total transfer			
Skill level			
Both low	159	219	228
Both middle	229	300	314
Both high	120	175	210
His high, hers low	379	444	451
Amount attributable to revenue cost of children			
Skill level			
Both low		60	70
Both middle		72	85
Both high		55	90
His high, hers low		65	72

Source: Authors' calculations

Note

1 Transfer includes widow's pension.

Gender discrimination as a source of income gap

Not all the difference between the lifetime incomes of spouses is attributable directly to discrimination or unequal treatment in the labour

---

[13] Joshi (1991) suggested that the effects of sex and motherhood on hourly pay were roughly equal.

market. The differences between the incomes of the simulated partners are partly due to assumptions built into the model, and employed to obtain simulated outcomes which mimic salient characteristics of the population. Table 14.11 displays the total gap between childless married men and their wives for various income sources, and decomposes these totals into various components, shown as percentages of the total. The entries in the table have positive signs where the difference between men and women is positive, and negative where women's incomes exceed those of men. The components of the differences shown in the columns are hours and years, life expectancy, gender, marriage and men.

It is assumed that, even when employed full-time, women work shorter weekly hours than men. For simulations under existing pension rules, it is assumed that women retire at 60 and men at 65. It is also assumed that women live three years longer than men and part of the difference in total income is due to this fact.

The gender effect, as measured here, has three components. The first is the difference in the hourly pay of men and women of the same age and skill level. Secondly, under the assumption about current pension rules and retirement behaviour, women would receive a pension for five years more than men, even if their life expectancies were equal. This component disappears in the simulations with equal pension ages. The third component reflects the default assumption about pension scheme membership. For the mid-skilled couples, men belong to a final salary pension scheme while women belong to SERPS. This component disappears in the simulations where both are assigned to the same pension scheme.

There are a number of differences between married and unmarried women, and the 'marriage' component picks these up. The estimated participation equation implies that there are participation differences between married and unmarried childless women, reflecting the division of labour within couples. The marriage assumptions are that women marry men who are two years older than them and that, even within the same skill level, men enjoy an educational advantage giving them an extra (12.5 per cent) wage premium. On the other hand, married women can avail themselves of part or all of the married couple's tax allowance.

All these differences appear on the women's accounts. Although it is assumed that the gross earnings of men are unaffected by their marital status, there are differences between married and unmarried men in some other income components. The married couple's tax allowance (or some part of it) will be available to married men. Furthermore, under the proposed equal pension age arrangements married men will sometimes be entitled to a dependency addition to basic pension for wives who would receive category B pensions under the existing rules, namely those aged 60 to 64 not themselves earning more than a certain amount.

Gross earnings are considered first. Table 14.11 reveals that only a modest proportion of the difference in gross earnings between these simulated married couples is due to the gender effect on hourly pay. The highest fraction attributable to gender is in the case of mid-skilled couples, where it accounts for 27 per cent of the lifetime gap, which in this case is itself 54 per cent of the women's lifetime earnings. Where both partners are highly skilled, the gender gap accounts for only 12 per cent of the gap in gross earnings. The value of the gross earnings gap itself is also highest for mid-skilled couples and lowest for graduates. The marriage component of the gross earnings gap is much larger than the gender component in the case of both the low- and highly-skilled couples, and the same size as the gender component for mid-skilled couples.

These results suggest that, even if there were equal pay, there might still be a substantial gap between the earnings of husbands and wives, especially among couples with low levels of labour market skills. Many of these wives might still be economically dependent on their husbands. A caveat is in order here, however: these calculations assumed that hours of work, participation and everything else remain unchanged, but the more equal the labour market opportunities for partners, the more equal one would expect the division of labour between them to be. Thus in a world of more equal opportunity, the labour market participation behaviour assumed (for men) and estimated (for women) here might not hold up.

The gap in net incomes follows the same ordering as that for gross earnings. Again, the gender component is largest in the case of middle-skilled couples. The gender component of the net income difference is negative for graduate couples – a reflection of the relatively high final salary pension earned by the women and assumption that they start drawing their pensions (and are excused from NI contributions) at 60 rather than 65.

Under existing pension rules, the simulated women get higher lifetime totals of basic pension than men, due to their longer life expectancy and earlier pension age, in the proportions shown in the life expectancy and gender columns respectively. For earnings-linked pensions the position is more complicated, as the effect of women's lower lifetime gross earnings works in the opposite direction. In the case of low-skilled couples, the net effect is to leave the women with lower earnings-linked (SERPS) pensions than their husbands, whereas graduate women still end up with higher total lifetime (final salary) pensions than their husbands. The outcome is complicated for mid-skilled couples by the assumption (reflecting the gendered pattern of pension provision in Britain) that the men are in final salary pension schemes whereas the women are in SERPS. The consequences of this assumption are included in the gender part of the gap.

The lower panel in the top section of Table 14.11 shows the results of the calculations for mid- and highly-skilled couples on the assumption that both partners are in SERPS. Both the size of the occupational pension gap and its gender component are much smaller than under the default pension assumptions. The gender component of the earnings-linked pension gap always runs in women's favour if both partners are in

Table 14.11 Decomposition of man–woman income gap for childless couples

With retirement at 60

	Gap	Component percentages of gap				
	(thousands of pounds)	Hours and years	Length of life	Gender	Marriage	Men
With default pension types						
Skill level: both low						
Gross earnings	433	41	0	20	40	0
Net income	280	45	- 5	13	43	4
Basic pension	- 24	0	- 37	- 63	0	0
Earnings-linked pension	17	62	- 32	- 27	96	0
Skill level: both middle						
Gross earnings	444	47	0	27	27	0
Net income	340	46	- 11	46	16	3
Basic pension	- 24	0	- 37	- 63	0	0
Earnings-linked pension	152	22	- 22	93	8	0
Skill level: both high						
Gross earnings	251	53	0	12	35	0
Net income	59	171	- 75	- 96	84	16
Basic pension	- 24	0	- 37	- 63	0	0
Earnings-linked pension	- 73	22	- 65	- 108	50	0
If both in SERPS						
Skill level: both middle						
Net income	276	54	- 5	21	27	4
Earnings-linked pension	13	94	- 50	- 32	87	0
Skill level: both high						
Net income	133	74	- 13	- 8	39	7
Earnings-linked pension	- 16	35	- 54	- 113	32	0

With retirement at 65

	Gap	Component percentages of gap				
	(thousands of pounds)	Hours and years	Length of life	Gender	Marriage	Men
With default pension types						
Skill level: both low						
Gross earnings	433	25	0	22	54	0
Net income	303	24	- 5	22	54	5
Basic pension	- 5	0	- 167	0	0	67
Earnings-linked pension	22	34	- 27	30	64	0
Skill level: both middle						
Gross earnings	417	29	0	32	39	0
Net income	337	28	- 11	55	24	3
Basic pension	- 9	0	- 100	0	0	0
Earnings-linked pension	160	20	- 21	94	7	0
Skill level: both high						
Gross earnings	142	7	0	21	72	0
Net income	50	28	- 90	38	105	18
Basic pension	- 9	0	- 100	0	0	0
Earnings-linked pension	- 9	127	- 558	0	330	0
If both in SERPS						
Skill level: both middle						
Net income	274	31	- 6	34	37	4
Earnings-linked pension	21	42	- 35	43	51	0
Skill level: both high						
Net income	83	10	- 22	26	74	11
Earnings-linked pension	- 3	19	- 296	65	112	0

Source: Authors' calculations

SERPS. The net income gap for mid-skilled couples is lower if both partners are in SERPS than if the men are in final salary pension schemes, but is higher for highly-skilled couples under SERPS than under default assumptions. The operation of the UEL under SERPS reduces the dispersion of the lifetime net income gap across social classes.

The lower section of Table 14.11 repeats these calculations for equal pension ages. The effect of assuming that women who were employed at age 59 continue in employment until age 64 is to narrow the gross earnings gap for the mid- and (especially) highly-skilled couples. The loss of five years' pension for the woman (and the extra NI contributions she must pay if employed) attenuates the effect on the net income gap. Indeed, the net income gap for the low-skilled couple (where the woman is not employed for extra years) is increased by about eight per cent. The same factors cause an increase in the gender component of the gross earnings and net income gaps. In particular, the gender effect (favourable to women) for the net income of the highly-skilled couples changes sign. The occupational pension gaps are increased or, in the case of highly-skilled couples, the gap in the women's favour is decreased. Any favourable gender components of the occupational pension gap in the women's direction are eliminated.

These conclusions hold both under the default pension schemes and if both partners are in SERPS. With retirement at 60, a woman's extra pensionable years may currently serve as a partial offset against her lower earnings. With equal pension ages, inequalities in lifetime earnings are perpetuated into retirement to a greater extent than under present arrangements. Equalisation of state pension age would remove the gender component of the basic pension gap, and reduce the size of the gap which currently runs in favour of the woman.

The largest effect of basic pension age equalisation among these simulated cases occurs in the case of low-skilled couples. Here the women are not employed during the extra five years. Under current arrangements they would be entitled to category A pensions at age 60, and to category B top-ups when their husbands are 65 and they are 63. Under the White Paper proposals, they would not receive any state pension until the age of 65. During the period while their husbands are of state pension age but the women are not, the men would receive dependant's addition – reflected in the 'man' column of the table.

Family transfer over the life cycle

The fifth issue investigated here concerns the phasing of income from various sources over the life cycle. Given the assumption of greater female longevity and unequal partners' ages, women face a longer period in retirement than their husbands. With unequal pension ages these are 21 years for women and 13 for men, whereas with equal pension ages women have 13 years in retirement. With a given period of widowhood (five years in this case, two for the assumed age gap and three for greater longevity), it is possible to illustrate the type of family for whom a widow's pension is a particularly important source of income in old age. It is also necessary to investigate the relative importance of *inter vivos* transfers, if made, while children are dependent compared to other times before retirement.

Details of the family transfer under the pooling assumption, and of how it varies over the life cycle, are shown in Table 14.12. Under the 'no sharing' assumption, the woman does not benefit from these transfers (except in widowhood); instead, the amounts shown represent half the gap between the resources of the two partners. A woman's survivor's pension is treated here as a 'posthumous family transfer' and included as part of the family transfer. Table 14.12 confirms the impression given by Figure 14.2 that this is indeed an important part of the family transfer. During their retirement, the simulated married women spend about three times as long as part of a couple (16 years) as they do in widowhood (five years). Apart from the low-skilled couples, they receive more (often much more) from their widows' pension than a third of the amount which they would receive from the family transfer under the pooling assumption during their years as a retired couple. Graduates with no or two children, whose earnings and pensions are more symmetrical with those of their husbands, receive a higher fraction of their lifetime spousal transfer after bereavement than before.

For most couples with children and an occupational pension, the family transfer in old age is somewhat greater than that in the years while there are dependent children. The picture is very different for the low-skill couple, where only about one-sixth of the total family transfer is received in old age, as against four-tenths while there are dependent children. This is because the low-skilled man has a much lower pension than higher-skilled men, and leads to a study of the effect of the type of pension provision on the family transfer.

Earning power and fertility are not the only determinants of lifetime income; there is also the return on pension contributions. In the foregoing, default pension types have been assigned to the simulations depending on skill level and sex. In particular, low-skilled men were assigned to SERPS, while others were assumed to be in an optimistically generous private occupational scheme, of a type to which women have poorer access than men. To investigate the sensitivity of the results to the assumed pension type, it is assumed that everyone is in SERPS and the time pattern of the putative family transfer under this assumption is compared with that obtained under the default pension type assumptions.

The bottom panel of Table 14.12 shows the results: a dramatic change in the time pattern of the family transfer. The proportion of the transfer which accrues in old age for the highly-skilled couples is now quite close to that for the couple with low skills. This is partly because the private

Table 14.12 Family transfer by stage of life cycle as percentage of lifetime total

		No children	Two children	Two children (housewife)	Four children
			Woman with		
With default pension types					
Skill level: both low	While dependent children	0	43	37	46
	Rest of 'working life'	80	41	45	36
	While retired, both alive	16	13	15	15
	While widowed	4	3	2	3
Skill level: both middle	While dependent children	0	35	32	38
	Rest of 'working life'	51	26	34	24
	While retired, both alive	34	27	25	27
	While widowed	15	12	9	11
Skill level: both high	While dependent children	0	37	33	44
	Rest of 'working life'	48	18	32	14
	While retired, both alive	16	21	25	22
	While widowed	36	24	9	20
Skill level: his high, hers low	While dependent children	0	31	30	34
	Rest of 'working life'	62	34	37	31
	While retired, both alive	27	25	24	26
	While widowed	11	10	9	9
If in SERPS					
Skill level: both middle	While dependent children	0	47	40	51
	Rest of 'working life'	78	35	43	32
	While retired, both alive	18	14	15	14
	While widowed	5	3	2	3
Skill level: both high	While dependent children	0	50	42	59
	Rest of 'working life'	66	25	41	19
	While retired, both alive	25	19	15	16
	While widowed	9	6	2	5
Skill level: his high, hers low	While dependent children	0	40	38	44
	Rest of 'working life'	83	44	46	39
	While retired, both alive	14	14	14	15
	While widowed	3	2	2	2

Source: Authors' calculations

Notes

1 The family transfer is here defined to include its posthumous component (widow's pension).

2 Retirement is defined as the period during which the woman is above National Insurance pension age.

3 The low-skilled couple are both in SERPS under the default, and are therefore omitted from the lower part of this table.

pension scheme modelled here is more generous than SERPS, but also because the UEL on National Insurance is binding in the case of the more highly skilled, and does not permit them to defer as much of their labour market income into old age (and to their surviving spouses) as the private pensions system.[14] The mid- and highly-skilled men pay about three times more in pension contributions under the assumed final salary scheme than they would under SERPS.[15]

Conclusions

This chapter offers a synthesis of a number of themes worked on by the authors in the past and points out the direction of further development.

The six initial questions covered by the study can be restated here, with brief answers.

- How much of a married woman's lifetime income is derived from her partnership?

  This could easily be more than half unless she is committed to a full-time career.

- How does the 'revenue cost of children' compare with the 'expenditure costs' of their consumption?

  Generally, the two are roughly equal, although for the highly-skilled couple the revenue costs are only about 40 per cent of the total.

- Who loses how much when mothers forgo earnings, and how far is their 'sacrifice' shared with the state and their spouses?

  If couples pool incomes the costs are split in three roughly equal parts. The higher the woman's earnings, the greater is the share born by the public purse. Thus women are not the only beneficiaries of policies, such as subsidised childcare, which cut the earnings cost of children.

- How much of the gap in spouses' incomes is attributable to the revenue costs of children?

  Not a great deal for these cases.

- How much of the remaining gap between spouses' incomes arises because of unequal treatment in hourly earnings (gender discrimination), and how much from other sources of disparity? Between an eighth and a third of the earnings gap between this simulated childless woman and her husband is directly due to unequal wages. Most of the rest is due to other differences between partners.

---

[14] The lifetime net incomes (and the size of the total family transfer) will be much lower in the case of the higher-skilled couples if they are in SERPS than if they are in the assumed default pension schemes. For the couples of mid-level skills, the man's own lifetime net income is about £84,000 less if he is in SERPS than in a final salary scheme. His wife loses about £20,000 of her own net income, due to her lower widow's pension.

[15] Under the assumption of a pension age raised to 65 for women, the main difference that is made to these estimates is a shift of a fraction of the total 'transfer' from retirement years to rest of 'working life'.

- Is the intra-family transfer greater while children are dependent than in old age?

  Not with a generous pension system, but much greater with SERPS. The generosity of widows' pensions is particularly important to this conclusion.

For these questions, the raising of the state pension age made little difference to the answers. The simulated women only stand to gain cash from the change if they earn substantial sums while they are aged 60 to 64.

The simulation methodology used here is relatively primitive, and it is planned to improve upon its deficiencies. For example, all these calculations assume an uninterrupted work history for men; one of the next steps is to relax this assumption. The employment and participation equations are based on evidence collected around 1980, and could be re-examined with more recent data. Another line of development would be to model household production, and explicitly recognise the extent to which it provides a *quid pro quo* for the 'family transfer' (Apps and Rees, 1993). A further step would be to generate simulated populations rather than illustrative individuals.

Nevertheless, the couples modelled represent some relevant British types. From NCDS evidence at age 33, the relatively egalitarian partnerships of graduate women in continuous full-time employment are reasonably well represented in the simulated graduate couples with no or two children. There is also evidence of a much larger group of women with the sorts of employment gaps and part-time jobs simulated here for women of middle and lesser skills. Seventy-eight per cent of women in couples are dependent to a substantial degree on pooling at age 33. The simulations suggest that in an unchanging world the more highly qualified and those more continuously attached to the labour market (for example the 'maternity leavers' identified by Waldfogel, 1993) will forgo rather less earnings (and pension) over their lifetime than some of their contemporaries, and maintain the low dependence on spousal 'transfer' observed and simulated at age 33. For those staying out of paid work to bring up their children, at least, access to a partner's earnings will remain important, as will the existence of a derived right in their partner's pension.

As long as there is either unequal treatment in the labour market or inequality in the division of unpaid and paid work between spouses, the family will be needed to act as a source of income security. That it has become superfluous in this respect for a privileged vanguard does not mean that it is dispensable for all. This study shows how the family may redress the impact of unequal treatment in the labour market. As the family becomes less reliable, the need for better labour market opportunities is evident. So too should be the need to preserve as much of its functions as is possible and consistent with equality of opportunity.

Acknowledgements

This work is partly supported under the 'Livelihoods: dependence and independence in the 1958 cohort' grant from the Joseph Rowntree Foundation to the Social Statistics Research Unit, City University. The authors thank Jane Humphries and Holly Sutherland for comments on the version of this paper presented at the EOC Expert Seminar. Earlier versions were presented at the Seventh Annual Meeting of the European Society for Population Economics held in June 1993 in Budapest, and the ESF Conference, The Economics of Ageing, held in June 1994 in Sitges. Participants at those conferences are also thanked for comments.

References

Apps, P. F. and Rees, R. (1993). *Labor Supply, Household Production and Intra-family Welfare Distribution*. Paper presented at European Society for Population Economics Conference, Budapest.

Arber, S. and Ginn, J. (1991). *Gender and Later Life*. London: Sage.

Davies, H. and Joshi, H. (1992). 'Constructing pensions for model couples' in Hancock, R. and Sutherland, H. (eds.) *Microsimulation Models for Public Policy Analysis: New Frontiers*. STICERD Occasional Paper 17. London: London School of Economics and Political Science.

Davies, H. and Joshi, H. (1994). 'Sex, sharing and the distribution of income' in *Journal of Social Policy*, 23 (3).

DSS (1993). *Equality in State Pension Age*. Cm 2420. London: HMSO.

Ermisch, J. F. and Wright, R. E. (1991). 'Welfare benefits and lone parents' employment in Great Britain' in *Journal of Human Resources*, 26, Summer.

Espenshade, T. J. and Calhoun, C. A. (1986). 'The dollars and cents of parenthood' in *Journal of Policy Analysis and Management*, 5 (4).

Greenhalgh, C. (1980). 'Male–female wage differentials in Great Britain: is marriage an equal opportunity?' in *Economic Journal*, 90.

Joshi, H. E. (1990). 'The cash opportunity cost of childbearing: an approach to estimation using British evidence' in *Population Studies*, 44.

Joshi, H. E. (1991). 'Sex and motherhood as sources of women's economic disadvantage' in Groves, D. and Maclean, M. (eds.) *Women's Issues in Social Policy*. London: Routledge

Joshi, H. E. (1993). 'Work, life cycle and social protection' in European Demographic Conference, Paris, October 1991, vol II, *Invited Papers*. Paris: John Libbey Eurotext.

Joshi, H. E. and Davies, H. B. (1991). 'Pension splitting and divorce' in *Fiscal Studies*, 12 (4).

Joshi, H. E. and Davies, H. B. (1992a). *Childcare and Mothers' Lifetime Earnings: Some European Contrasts*. CEPR Discussion Paper 600. London: Centre for Economic Policy Research.

Joshi, H. E. and Davies, H. B. (1992b). 'Pensions, divorce, and wives' double burden' in *International Journal of Law and the Family*, 6.

Joshi, H. E. and Davies, H. B. (1992c). 'Daycare in Europe and mothers' forgone earnings' in *International Labour Review*, 131 (6).

Joshi, H. E. and Davies, H. B. (1993). 'Mothers' human capital and childcare in Britain' in *National Institute Economic Review*, November.

Joshi, H. E. and Davies, H. B. (1994). 'The paid and unpaid roles of women: how should social security adapt?' in Baldwin, S. and Falkingham, J. (eds.) *Social Security: New Challenges to the Beveridge Model*. Hemel Hempstead: Harvester Wheatsheaf.

Joshi, H. E., Davies, H. B. and Ward, C. (1994). *Financial Dependency Within Partnerships: Patterns and Pathways*. Paper presented at Eighth Annual Meeting of the European Society for Population Economics, Tilburg.

Lister, R. (1992). *Women's Economic Dependency and Social Security*. Manchester: Equal Opportunities Commission.

Sorenson, A. (1993). *Women's Economic Risk and the Economic Position of Single Mothers*. Typescript. Berlin: Max-Plank Institut für Bildungsforschung.

Waldfogel, J. (1993). *Women Working for Less: A Longitudinal Analysis of the Family Penalty*. Welfare State Working Paper 93, STICERD, London School of Economics and Political Science.

Ward, C., Joshi, H. E. and Dale, A. (1993). *Income Dependency Within Couples*. NCDS Discussion Paper 36, SSRU, City University.

Wright, R. E. and Ermisch, J. F. (1991). 'Gender discrimination in the British labour market: a reassessment' in *Economic Journal*, 101.

CHAPTER 15 # Gender, Households and Access to Employment

Paul Gregg and Jonathan Wadsworth

Over the past 20 years male and female employment rates have converged rapidly, the result of a simultaneous rise in female employment and a decline in the employment of men, leaving the aggregate rate little changed from that of the mid-1970s (see Figure 15.1). Economic recovery may well equalise gender employment rates at around 75 per cent. While these employment trends undoubtedly help equalise incomes between men and women, it does not necessarily follow that household income inequality will decline as a result of the same process, or that all women benefit equally from an improved likelihood of gaining work. For example, Machin and Waldfogel (1994) have demonstrated that rising female employment has reduced household income inequality among working married couples. Growth in female participation has been greatest where male earnings are lowest. Gregg and Wadsworth (1994b), however, find that employment opportunities across all households, not just those with an earner, have become increasingly unequal over the past 20 years.

Figure 15.1 Employment rates by gender, 1975–93

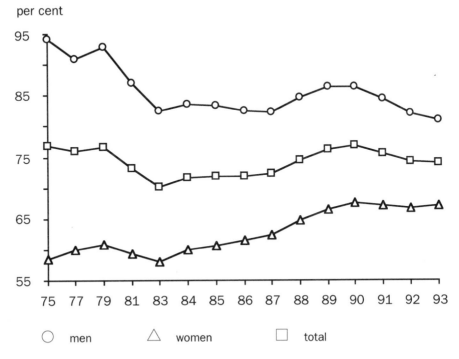

per cent

Source: The data used in all tables and figures in this chapter is calculated from data included in the Labour Force Survey, 1975–93

The proportion of the working-age population in households with no work rose from around five per cent in 1975 to nearly 15 per cent by 1993

Table 15.2 Non-employment rates by individual status

	1975	1979	1985	1990	1993
Total	.237	.234	.283	.232	.260
Men	.059	.071	.164	.137	.190
Women	.414	.391	.400	.324	.329
By education					
Degree		.084	.105	.095	.131
Intermediate		.159	.197	.162	.219
Low		.300	.348	.340	.393
By education and sex					
Men					
Degree		.021	.043	.057	.111
Intermediate		.044	.091	.104	.181
Low		.155	.228	.270	.337
Women					
Degree		.252	.266	.163	.164
Intermediate		.310	.322	.231	.262
Low		.406	.428	.366	.404

Note

1 Education information unavailable in 1975.

(Table 15.2). The difference in non-employment patterns for individuals and households is caused by a change in the distribution of work. Twenty years ago, many households contained a mixture of adults in and out of work. Since then, the proportion of partially-employed households has fallen by around one third. Thus the distribution of work has 'hollowed out', with a simultaneous rise in both the proportion of the population in fully-employed (work-rich) and non-employed (work-poor) households.

This chapter investigates the changing patterns of access to work implicit in these changes by gender across household types. The results indicate that women without a working partner, including those with no partner, irrespective of the presence of children, are increasingly losing out in the struggle to secure employment, despite being in the most obvious need of access to earned income.

It is well established (see, for example, Dilnot and Kell, 1989; Davies *et al.*, 1992) that women with unemployed partners have lower labour force participation rates than women with employed partners. However, these static models cannot determine whether this effect is caused by differences in the chances of gaining or losing work; nor can they assess whether these differences are changing over time. This chapter therefore also documents the relative contribution to the employment stock of changes in inflow and outflow rates over time. Employment entry rates of non-working women with working partners rose from 14 per cent in 1979 to 21 per cent in 1993; while entry rates for single female households and those with partners not in work fell (from 16 per cent to ten per cent and 15 per cent to nine per cent respectively). Significantly, these patterns also apply to men.

Finally, the study examines whether individual characteristics associated with a low transition probability increasingly occur in workless households, and the role of the changing nature of work on offer. Women in workless households may have characteristics which employers find unsuitable, and the jobs on offer may have attributes that these women find unsuitable. The observable characteristics of individuals in workless families, however, offer no further explanation of the changing fortunes of women across household types. The changing mix of full- and part-time employment engagements explains about one-third of the changing fortunes of women in workless households. Full-time employee engagements of women have fallen from half to one-third of all job openings. Full-time jobs are more likely to be taken by women in workless households, and part-time work by those in working households.

Yet even after controlling for this, women (and men) in workless families have increasingly lost out in the fight for full-time, and especially part-time, opportunities. This suggests that incentive problems created by the relationship between the benefit system and the wages attached to new jobs underpin the obstacles which women in workless households face in their attempts to gain access to employment.

The simultaneous rise of workless and two-income families

After nine years of continuous growth, the 1990 UK employment rate had recovered to the level prevailing in the mid-1970s. As Figure 15.1 demonstrates, the gender composition of employment moved sharply in favour of women between 1975 and 1993. Whilst the aggregate employment rate remained broadly constant, female employment rates rose by nine percentage points to 67 per cent, whilst male employment fell by nine points to 83 per cent. Even more than in the previous recession, the 1990–2 downturn was notable for the absence of a net decline in female employment, while male employment rates fell by some six points.

The changing composition of employment by gender and household type between 1975 and 1993 is given in Figures 15.3 and 15.4. Married women account for the entire rise in female employment over the past two decades. Almost the entire increase occurred in households with working partners. Table 15.5 also documents these changes; Table 15.6 gives the proportion of each household type in the working-age population over time. Employment rates of women with working partners rose by over 60 per cent, from 54 per cent in 1975 to 84 per cent in 1993. Employment

Figure 15.3 Employment rates by marital status, 1975–93

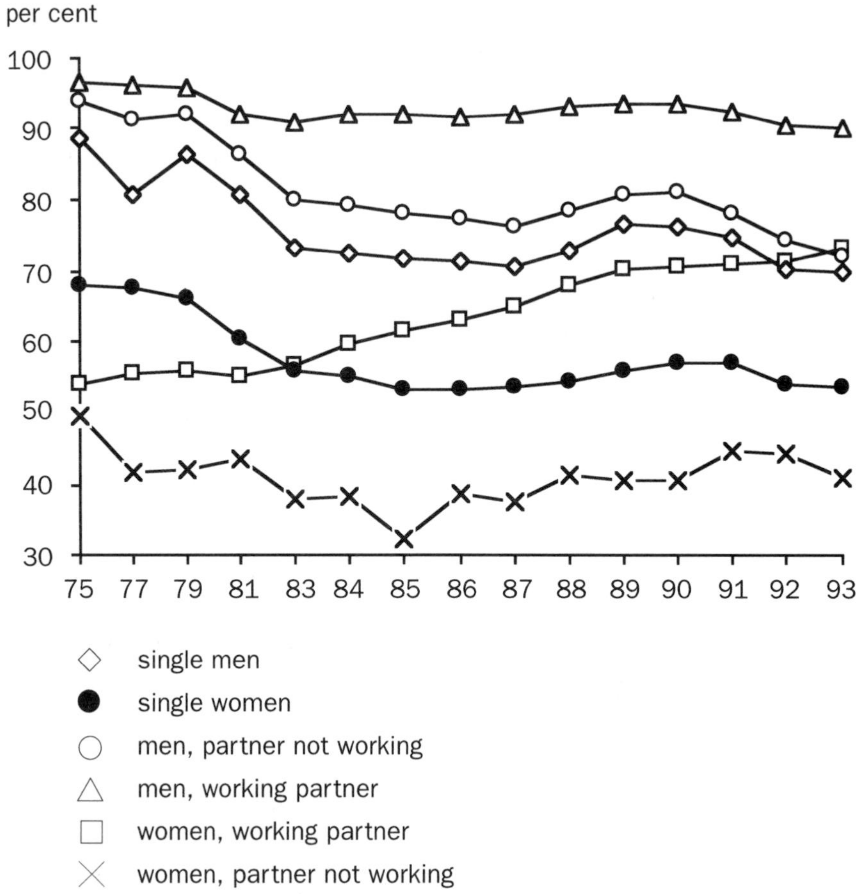

per cent

◇   single men

●   single women

○   men, partner not working

△   men, working partner

□   women, working partner

✕   women, partner not working

among single women fell, as it did among those with a non-working partner. The relative fortunes of men are delineated by the same household types. Employment of men with working partners has fallen by only five points, compared with falls of 19 and 24 points for single men and those with non-working partners.

The presence of dependent children does not appear to affect participation rates. Employment has risen most (from 45 per cent to 67 per cent) in dual-earning households with children (see Figure 15.4). Employment rates for single mothers have fallen by around six points to 35 per cent over the same period. Those for mothers with a non-working partner remained flat at around 33 per cent. Single men with dependent children have suffered the largest fall in employment. Thus the entire rise in female employment over the period has occurred in multi-adult households with working partners.

The net result of these changes is shown in the household distribution of work in the population aged 60 and under (Figure 15.7). There has been a dramatic shift away from a mixture of working and non-working members, and a corresponding polarisation of employment into fully-

Figure 15.4 Employment rates by presence of children, 1981–93

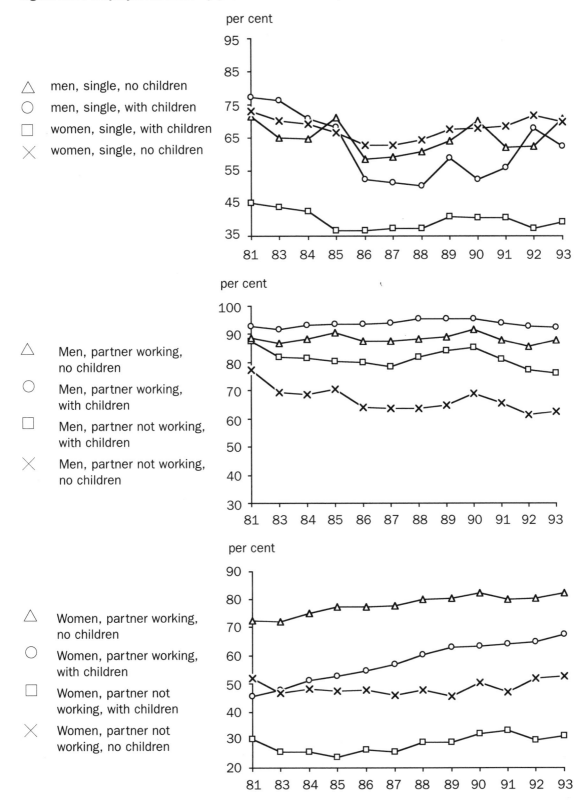

△ men, single, no children
○ men, single, with children
☐ women, single, with children
✕ women, single, no children

△ Men, partner working, no children
○ Men, partner working, with children
☐ Men, partner not working, with children
✕ Men, partner not working, no children

△ Women, partner working, no children
○ Women, partner working, with children
☐ Women, partner not working, with children
✕ Women, partner not working, no children

Table 15.5 Employment by household type

	1975	1979	1985	1990	1993
Single adult	.779	.752	.632	.656	.608
Men	.889	.864	.827	.762	.699
(with children)			(.670)	(.661)	(.538)
Women	.680	.660	.551	.573	.537
(with children)			(.408)	(.407)	(.377)
Two adult	.739	.743	.710	.777	.763
Men	.954	.942	.867	.892	.846
Partner works	.968	.965	.936	.940	.914
(Partner works, children)			(.942)	(.952)	(.931)
Partner not working	.938	.914	.782	.797	.699
(Partner not working, children)			(.797)	(.834)	(.736)
Women	.535	.553	.562	.667	.682
Partner works	.543	.567	.607	.808	.839
(Partner works, children)			(.518)	(.634)	(.675)
Partner not working	.496	.429	.424	.407	.411
(Partner not working, children)			(.313)	(.317)	(.305)
Household non-employment	.058	.062	.085	.104	.144

Note

1 Information on children unavailable before 1981.

employed (work-rich) and workless (work-poor) households (see Gregg and Wadsworth, 1994b, for more details). The proportion resident in jobless households tripled to 14 per cent over the sample period. This represents 19 per cent of all households, up from six per cent in 1975. This separation of work across households is likely to be an important factor in the growth of household poverty and income inequality in Britain.

Labour market flows by household types

An insight into the causes of these changes can be gained from the inflow and outflow rates associated with the changes in these stocks. Figure 15.8 gives outflow rates from non-employment into work (non-employment into employment – NE), and the inflow rate (employment into non-employment – EN), by household type.

In the 1970s, two-adult households with one working partner were less likely to gain additional work than single or jobless households.[1] Between

---

[1] The 1975 aggregate NE rates for two-adult working partner and non-working partner households were .156 and .184 respectively. By 1993 the corresponding figures were .247 and .144.

Table 15.6 Distribution of adult population aged 60 and under by household type

Household type	1981	1984	1990	1993
Single adult	.085	.100	.121	.140
of which:				
Men	.048	.057	.065	.063
(with children)	(.003)	(.007)	(.003)	(.004)
Women	.036	.043	.056	.077
(with children)	(.015)	(.019)	(.027)	(.038)
Two adult	.580	.575	.577	.616
(with children)	(.360)	(.350)	(.333)	(.363)
of which:				
Both working	.290	.297	.348	.382
(with children)	(.149)	(.159)	(.186)	(.210)
Man works, partner not working	.223	.191	.154	.136
(with children)	(.173)	(.143)	(.113)	(.101)
Woman works, partner not working	.026	.027	.028	.038
(with children)	(.010)	(.010)	(.010)	(.016)
No work	.041	.061	.047	.060
(with children)	(.027)	(.037)	(.025)	(.037)
Three adult	.335	.325	.303	.243

1979 and 1993, outflow rates into employment fell dramatically for jobless single adults and those in households with non-working partners, but rose for jobless adults with working partners. Figure 15.8 makes clear that the entire rise in employment was among women. The relative chance of successful entry for households with working, compared to non-working, partners rose by 22 percentage points in favour of the former.

The risk of becoming jobless, as measured by the inflow rate EN, also moved in favour of those with working partners. Women with working partners were again the sole beneficiaries of a reduced likelihood of experiencing joblessness. Inflow rates for all other groups rose over the same period.

Substantial changes in the relative fortunes of women across household type have emerged. The largest fall in outflow rates (NE) was experienced by single women, followed by those with non-working partners. In contrast, outflow rates for women with working partners rose by around 50 per cent. These swings occurred against an aggregate employment shift in favour of women. Male transitions into work have fallen for all groups,

Figure 15.7 Work-rich and work-poor households, 1975–93, proportion of working adults in households

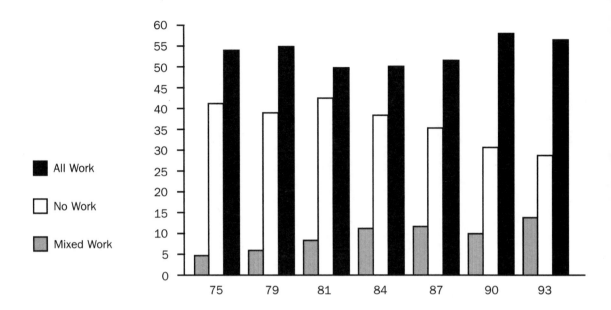

but most markedly for single men and those with a non-working partner. Women with a non-working partner are also more likely to leave employment than other women, and this effect has become stronger over time. This evidence points to the existence of a discouraged rather than an added worker effect present in non-employed households. The next section concentrates on access to work as captured by differences in the NE outflow rate.[2]

Competing explanations and evidence

There are three contending explanations for the growing divergence in transition rates for women across household types. Each must explain why members of workless families are less likely to enter work, and the relative swings over time. Traditional labour supply theory assumes individual utility maximisation across income and non-work time, taking the partner's employment status as given, thus ignoring the fact that labour supply is potentially a joint household decision (but see Ashworth and Ulph, 1981, for an exception using family utility with a specific function form). The literature places differing emphasis on three main factors.

Within-family considerations

Women married to unemployed men have lower employment rates than those married to men in work. After the addition of extra controls, many

---

[2] Given the non-employment rate, N/P = (s/P) x 1/NE, where 's' is the number of workers flowing from E to N, and P = N+E, the changing outflow rate accounts for 67 per cent, 27 per cent, 52 per cent, 73 per cent, 76 per cent and 90 per cent of the change in non-employment rates for single men, men with working partners, men with non-working partners, single women, women with working partners and women with non-working partners respectively.

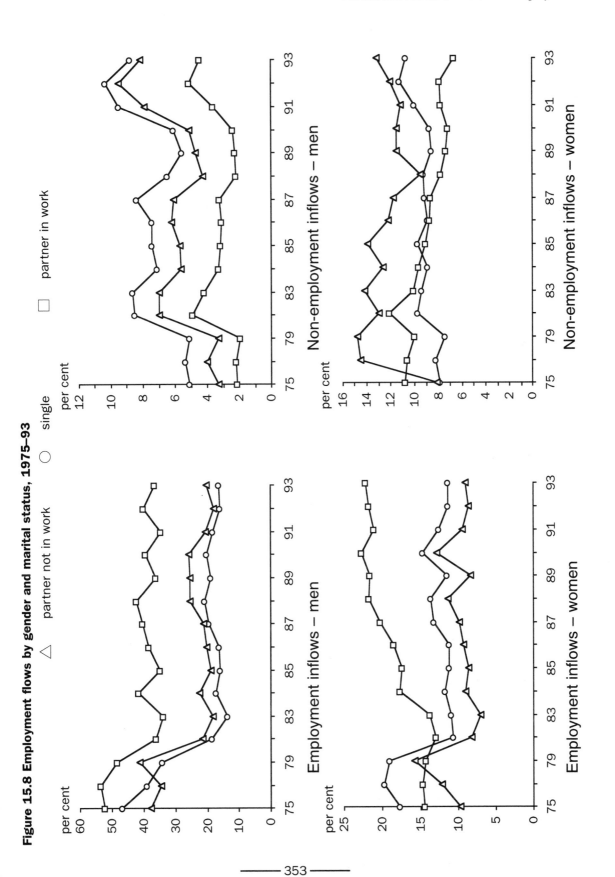

Figure 15.8 Employment flows by gender and marital status, 1975–93

△ partner not in work ○ single □ partner in work

Employment inflows – men

Employment inflows – women

Non-employment inflows – men

Non-employment inflows – women

studies find an unexplained residual, described by Pudney and Thomas (1992) as 'complementary leisure time'. Couples enjoy being out of work together more than when one individual is unemployed. McKee and Bell (1985) stress the role of male status within the family, suggesting that men lose self-esteem if women enter work. This explanation only applies to women and implies an asymmetry across men and women not apparent in other explanations. Both 'macho male' and complementary leisure predict differences between workless couples and single workless adults, not apparent in the other explanations. Variations across men and women and between couples and single adults can be studied to assess this reasoning.

Table 15.9 Job search activity of non-employed by household status, 1979–93

Own status	Single adult			Two adult Working partner			Two adult Non-working partner		
	All	Men	Women	All	Men	Women	All	Men	Women
1975									
Actively seeking work	.209	.445	.128	.083	.478	.065	.307	.590	.071
Looking after home	.420	.009	.563	.863	.003	.901	.444	.002	.812
Other inactive	.371	.546	.309	.054	.519	.034	.249	.408	.117
1985									
Actively seeking work	.311	.506	.202	.203	.613	.156	.390	.687	.140
Looking after home	.320	.042	.475	.609	.021	.677	.340	.016	.614
Other inactive	.369	.452	.324	.187	.366	.166	.270	.298	.246
1993									
Actively seeking work	.272	.450	.174	.206	.517	.122	.348	.558	.139
Looking after home	.340	.054	.497	.499	.031	.626	.283	.030	.534
Other inactive	.388	.495	.330	.295	.452	.253	.369	.412	.327

Table 15.9 outlines the degree of labour market attachment of the non-employed, disaggregated by household status over time. The proportion actively seeking work is always higher among single and non-working two-adult households than those with working partners, though the gap has narrowed over time. Active job search for non-employed men is higher in two-adult households with non-working partners. Single women are more likely to seek work. There is little evidence that workless households search less than others, which goes against the complementary leisure hypothesis. There remains a strong gender demarcation of family roles favouring men in seeking access to employment. In two-adult households, men are around five times more likely to assume the role of active job search.

The common experience of men and women with working partners relative to those without (shown in Table 15.5), if not explained by other factors, would tend to go against the importance of male status within the family (the 'macho male' argument). The framework also does not explain why single people should have lower exit rates than those with working partners. Furthermore, complementary leisure would have difficulty in explaining the change over the period. Falling entry rates into work for men and women in workless couples implies the desire for complementary leisure time is rising over the period. This seems implausible, especially as benefit levels relative to average earnings have simultaneously declined. While this argument might explain some of the cross-section evidence of lower participation of women married to non-working men, it can explain little of the emerging pattern of access to work across households.

Common characteristics

Between 1979 and 1990 the decline in employment rates for least-educated men was twice that for intermediate-qualified and four times that for graduates. The largest rise in female employment was among the most highly educated. If rising female employment and falling male employment do not occur in the same households, it may be because family members have similar education levels. The rise in household non-employment is then a coincidence of members experiencing common adverse trends in the labour market.

Table 15.10 gives predicted differences in NE transitions between household types over the sample period for each sex. The first panel reports unadjusted differentials between individuals with working partners and single adults (row one) or those with a jobless partner (row two). The second panel controls for attachment to the labour market. The latter variables are self-assessed statements on the degree of active job search shown in Table 15.10,[3] and capture any added worker effect.[4]

A large deficit has emerged in the relative likelihood of entering work for those without working partners (including single people). This deficit is larger for women, and rises when labour market attachment controls are included. Those with working partners are less likely to search, and should thus be less likely to enter work than the raw household differentials suggest. Correcting for lower search effort widens the differential in favour of working partners (compared with those with non-working partners from zero to 8.5 per cent in 1979, for example). By 1993 this effect is still present and raises the predicted difference in female transition rates to over 20 per cent; but the relative swing from 1979 to 1993 is reduced by about one quarter for women. The added worker effect for women in workless households has thus diminished, as fewer of those in workless households are actively seeking jobs. For men, controlling for differential search activity across household types increases the relative change in transition rates by 60 per cent, and their added worker effect has risen.

---

[3] These categories are broadened in the regression to include active job search, sick, retired, looking after family or the home, students and a residual category.

[4] In practice, these categories are extended to differentiate between active job search, early retirement, household production, sickness and a residual category.

Table 15.10 Annual individual employment inflow differentials by household status, 1979–93

Status one year ago	1979	1985	1990	1993	△1993–79
Female					
Unadjusted					
Two adult, one working v. one adult, not working	- .048	.089	.108	.151	+ .201
Two adult, one working v. two adult, none working	.004	.146	.135	.210	+ .194
With added worker controls					
Two adult, one working v. one adult, not working	.027	.151	.143	.204	+ .177
Two adult, one working v. two adult, none working	.085	.206	.170	.243	+ .158
With all controls					
Two adult, one working v. one adult, not working	.007	.121	.112	.177	+ .188
Two adult, one working v. two adult, none working	.037	.165	.127	.202	+ .165
Male					
Unadjusted					
Two adult, one working v. one adult, not working	.106	.287	.205	.270	+ .164
Two adult, one working v. two adult, none working	.058	.150	.133	.164	+ .106
With added worker controls					
Two adult, one working v. one adult, not working	.145	.214	.243	.227	+ .072
Two adult, one working v. two adult, none working	.082	.184	.169	.206	+ .164
With all controls					
Two adult, one working v. one adult, not working	.168	.167	.194	.224	+ .056
Two adult, one working v. two adult, none working	.066	.126	.107	.173	+ .097

The third panel shows the impact of individual characteristics. Added controls include education, age and region.[5] The net effect of the introduction of these controls does not change the relative swing between the transition rates for women with working partners and those with non-working partners or no partner, though it does capture around 40 per cent of the change for men. Moreover, the controls do not help explain differential household transition rates in any one year, particularly after 1985. The 'common characteristics' hypothesis cannot therefore account for the majority of the differential in access to work across households.

Employment trends and the social security system

The third explanation is that viable labour market opportunities differ according to the employment status of other household members. The presence of a wage-earner in the household changes the financial incentives facing the jobseeker, and can also act as a mechanism for

---

5 Information on children in the household is not available until 1981, and therefore not included in any of the regressions. The home production variable in the added worker controls will capture some of this effect. The explanatory variables should also refer to the individual's circumstances one year prior to interview. This restricts the range of included variables somewhat.

Table 15.11 Employment by type of work, within gender

| | Share of total employment | | | |
	1979	1985	1990	1993
Women				
Stock				
Self-employment	.033	.066	.043	.037
Full-time employees	.576	.539	.545	.538
Part-time	.391	.394	.412	.425
Inflow				
Full-time self-employment	.023	.071	.035	.025
Full-time employees	.524	.427	.363	.354
Part-time	.454	.502	.603	.621
Men				
Stock				
Self-employment	.100	.117	.177	.163
Full-time employees	.896	.839	.802	.803
Part-time	.004	.013	.031	.032
Inflow				
Full-time self-employment	.043	.101	.106	.153
Full-time employees	.937	.811	.791	.686
Part-time	.016	.088	.103	.161

Note

1 Flows calculated from annual inflows into respective states of individuals not in employment one year prior to sampling.

identifying vacancies.[6] Additional earned income will preclude access to means-tested benefits in almost all cases. Incentives to take certain forms of work are therefore likely to vary according to whether there is an income in the household, especially where weekly wages are low. Low weekly incomes, above a minimum disregard, face punitive rates of benefit withdrawal and taxation. The welfare state was designed around the premise that the family required one full-time job to lift them off benefit, and to provide positive incentives to move into work. As the variation in hourly wages was low and part-time working rare, nearly all vacancies fulfilled these requirements.

Earnings uncertainty may also prove problematic. The process of assessing claims when moves into and out of work are made is very slow

---

[6] Friends and relatives are a frequent source of information in job search and often one of the most successful: see Gregg and Wadsworth (1994a).

Table 15.12 Employment taken by household type and gender, 1979–93

| | Proportion of total jobs filled within each household type | | | | | | | |
| | Part-time | | | | Self-employment | | | |
	1979	1985	1990	1993	1979	1985	1990	1993
Total								
All persons	.307	.361	.429	.434	.033	.053	.059	.078
Single person household	.232	.381	.465	.445	.056	.077	.072	.091
Partner in work	.610	.636	.647	.567	.038	.051	.045	.062
Partner not working	.146	.222	.287	.304	.069	.136	.124	.164
Men								
All	.018	.098	.103	.161	.049	.091	.106	.153
Single person household	.041	.120	.122	.192	.092	.126	.115	.171
Partner in work	.018	.092	.131	.138	.082	.149	.138	.177
Partner not working	.015	.111	.132	.187	.091	.178	.163	.233
Women								
All	.482	.546	.603	.622	.023	.027	.035	.025
Single person household	.338	.571	.637	.613	.036	.041	.051	.038
Partner in work	.704	.764	.741	.720	.031	.028	.029	.021
Partner not working	.458	.450	.527	.523	.016	.051	.064	.034

(Family Credit normally takes around three months). Variable income from self-employment, temporary jobs or other uncertain forms of payment may make transitions into these employment forms more risky or financially difficult when there is no second income in the household to cover basic needs (see Jenkins and Millar, 1989).[7]

Table 15.11 outlines the evolving pattern of employment in the UK. The proportion of full-time employees in the employment stock fell from around 77 per cent to 67 per cent between 1979 and 1993. Self-employment grew strongly up to 1990 and then fell back, whilst part-time employment has increased by around six percentage points over the period.[8] Temporary work consistently accounted for only around four to five per cent of all employment. These trends do not appear to represent a major transformation of opportunities available to the non-employed. However, temporary jobs, part-time work and self-employment opportunities have shorter durations than full-time permanent jobs, and will therefore constitute a larger proportion of the stock of vacancies at any one time.[9]

---

[7] Dilnot and Kell (1989) provide a more detailed discussion of the disincentive effects of the benefits system for women married to unemployed men, although a similar picture emerges for anyone trying to enter part-time work when in receipt of means-tested benefits.

[8] Part-time self-employment is included as part-time working in this Table, as part-time status is felt to be crucial for income determination.

[9] Gregg and Wadsworth (1995) estimate job durations of nine months, three years and seven years for temporary, part-time and full-time jobs respectively, using Labour Force Survey quarterly flows, and the wage associated with new jobs using General Household Survey evidence.

Table 15.11 gives the proportion of each job type in the stock of new employment hires using annual flow data. Annual transitions miss short duration jobs, but the point is still clear. The effect of differential turnover and any growth in the importance of these untypical forms of employment has a magnified impact on new engagements relative to changes in the stock. Hence the share of full-time permanent jobs in new engagements has fallen by 16 per cent since 1979. Part-time engagements represent over 60 per cent of new jobs filled by women in 1993, up from 49 per cent in 1979.

Table 15.12 and Figure 15.13 confirm that part-time jobs are taken primarily by those with a working partner, though the relative ranking has fallen over time. Accession rates into full-time work declined during the 1980–1 recession, and never recovered subsequently. Groups most dependent on this form of employment (single men and women and those with non-working partners) were thus likely to suffer lower transition rates back into work than others. Likewise, the increasing number of part-time opportunities would suit households best placed to take such work: primarily those with working partners.

Transition rates into full-time jobs by women have fallen by around one-third (by around three percentage points) relative to 1979. If this decline was evenly distributed across household groups (if they all declined by one-third), it would have reduced exit rates for women with non-working partners by three points and those with working partners by just over one point. Similarly, transition rates into part-time work have risen by around one-fifth in 1990 and 1993 relative to 1979. Such a rise would produce increases in the exit rates for single women and those with non-working households of less than one point, whereas for those with working partners it is nearly two points.

Changing employment composition can on the face of it explain around 4.5 points of a 13-point swing away from women in non-earning households towards those with working partners, and four points of the 12-point swing away from single-person households. Although there is a marked gender difference between those taking full- and part-time work, the changing patterns of access to employment are common to both male and female workforces. The switch from full- to part-time job opportunities for women out of work explains roughly one-third of the changing fortunes of women across household type. Women in workless households in 1993 were only marginally more likely to take part-time work than men.

This explanation alone therefore appears incomplete. The declining flow into full-time work is much more pronounced for those with non-working partners. Further, among women the increase in part-time work is greatest for those with working partners. Individual characteristics are the obvious possibility. However, controlling for characteristics (as in

Figure 15.13 Employment flows by job type, 1977–93

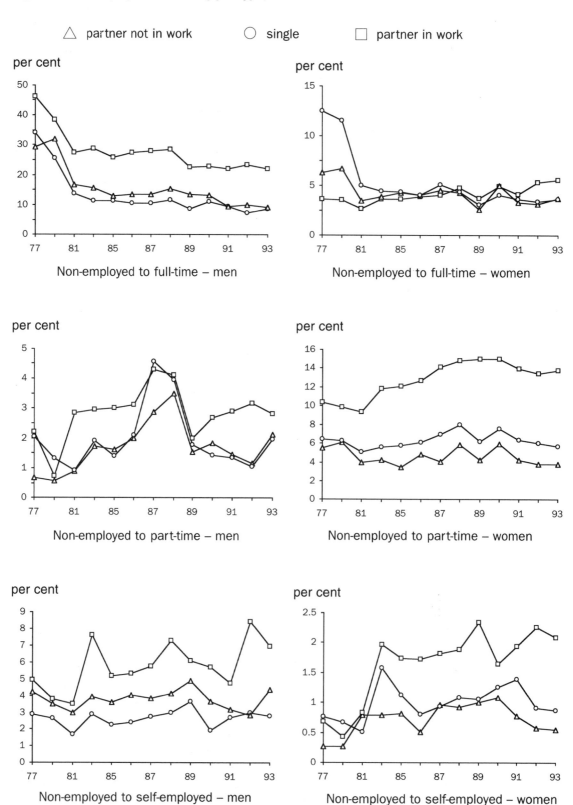

Table 15.10, but for full- and part-time jobs separately) helps explain none of this decline in fortunes of those with non-working partners. The exception is that women with working partners increasingly do not indicate that they are not in work because they are looking after the family or home (Table 15.9). This decline explains about half the increased likelihood of entry into full-time work.

To summarise, the substantial shift toward part-time work, now representing over 40 per cent of vacancies, can explain around one-third of the adverse relative deterioration of transition rates into employment of women with no working partner. The bulk of the emerging differential occurs within full- or part-time working, and remains unexplained.

Conclusions

There has been a profound change in the distribution of work across households and gender in Britain over the past 20 years. The number of households without a working member rose sharply in the recession of the early 1980s, but nearly all the subsequent recovery in employment occurred in households with one person already in work. This trend has occurred against a backdrop of rising female employment and falling male employment. Increased female participation has not replaced men as household breadwinners, but instead supplements existing household earned incomes. Where households lack work, there has been no increase in female employment. The net result is that there are many more multi-income households and three times as many workless households. This has been a significant factor in widening household income inequality. By 1993, 14 per cent of households had no work. Britain has become characterised by work-rich and work-poor families.

Much of the change in the relative fortunes of work-rich and work-poor households is caused by differential chances of moving into employment. The trend is so acute that women with no partner or non-working partners have seen their transition rates into work fall by 30 to 40 per cent, whereas rates for those with a working partner have risen by about a half. The change is not gender specific: similar declines are observed for men without working partners.

Explanations which centre on the characteristics of household members associated with lower transition rates, and on changing composition of employment toward more part-time jobs, offer fruitful avenues for exploration. However, while individual characteristics can explain some of the observed difference in transition rates across household types at any one time, they cannot explain the widening gap over the last 15 years. Full-time engagements were disproportionately taken by women in workless families, and part-time jobs by those with a working partner. The collapse in the number of full-time vacancies, by around a third, and the rise in part-time jobs explains around one-third of the relative deterioration in the position of women in workless families.

Even after allowing for this, women in workless families have increasingly been losing out in the fight for the full- or part-time opportunities available. Unobserved characteristics of the jobs and individuals involved, or changes in the benefit system, can probably explain the remaining elements but it is unclear as yet in what proportions. Changes in the benefit system (including rising housing benefit payments, more means-tested benefits and steeper tapers) can effectively shut out women from workless families from taking the available (largely part-time) work. This constraint on their employment appears to have become increasingly severe.

Differences in employment entry rates of women according to the presence of a working householder suggest that any employment growth during the current recovery will have a muted impact on the numbers of work-poor households and thus on benefits dependency. New jobs will be disproportionately taken by households where someone is already working. Furthermore, this effect is likely to be stronger than during the 1980s' recovery, as the employment differential in favour of women with working partners has substantially increased.

The feminisation of work has received considerable media attention and has been a strong force of equality in access to employment between the sexes, but not across households. Women have not lost out because of their observable characteristics (education, children, and so on); rather, feminisation appears to be driven by the impact of the changing nature of the work on offer, combined with the different incentives provided by the presence of a working partner (including the absence of benefit withdrawal in these circumstances). The task for the future is to ensure that all women benefit from improved employment opportunities, so gender equality does not conflict with reducing the number of work-poor families.

Acknowledgements

The Labour Force Survey data is used with permission of the OPCS, and supplied by the ESRC Data Archive at the University of Essex.

References

Ashworth, J. and Ulph, D. (1981). 'Household models' in Brown, C. (ed.) *Taxation and Labour Supply*. London: George Allen.

Davies, R., Elias, P. and Penn, R. (1992). 'The relationship between a husband's unemployment and his wife's participation in the labour force' in *Oxford Bulletin of Economic and Statistics*, 54 (2).

Dilnot, A. and Kell, M. (1989). 'Male unemployment and women's work' in Dilnot, A. and Walker, I. (eds.) *The Economics of Social Security*. Oxford University Press.

Gregg, P. and Wadsworth, J. (1994a). *How Effective are State Employment Agencies? Job Centre Use and Job Matching in Britain.* NIESR Discussion Paper.

Gregg, P. and Wadsworth, J. (1994b). *More Work in Fewer Households?* NIESR Discussion Paper.

Gregg, P. and Wadsworth, J. (1995). 'A short history of labour turnover, job tenure and job security' in *Oxford Review of Economic Policy*, 11.

Jenkins, S. and Millar, J. (1989). 'Income risk and income maintenance: implications for incentives to work' in Dilnot, A. and Walker, I. (eds.) *The Economics of Social Security*. (*Op. cit.*)

Machin, S. and Waldfogel, J. (1994). *The Decline of the Male Breadwinner*. Centre for Economic Performance, Working Paper 601.

McKee, L. and Bell, C. (1985). 'Marital and family relations in times of male unemployment' in Roberts, B., Finnegan, R. and Gallie, D. (eds.) *New Approaches to Economic Life*. Manchester: Manchester University Press.

Pudney, S. and Thomas, J. (1992). *Unemployment Benefit, Incentives and the Supply of Wives of Unemployed Men*. Mimeo, Department of Applied Economics, Cambridge.

Schmitt, J. and Wadsworth, J. (1994). *Why are Two Million Men Inactive? The Decline in Male Labour Force Participation in Britain*. Centre for Economic Performance, Working Paper 338.

Part VI
Implications for Policy

CHAPTER 16

Equal Opportunities Policies and Women's Labour Market Status in Industrialised Countries

Shirley Dex and Roger Sewell [1]

Equal opportunities policies have been adopted in nearly all industrialised countries over the past two decades, and in some cases at an earlier date. It is important and opportune to ask how far they have improved the labour market status and position of women in these countries. However, the question is not so easily answered.

One way of tackling the issue is to conduct before and after studies within one country to evaluate the effects of new policies. Studies of this kind have been carried out to some extent in certain countries, but are not free of problems. Often a range of policies will vary simultaneously; and the institutional setting may have an important influence on the way policies affect behaviour, but will be invisible within one country.

An alternative approach is to carry out cross-national comparisons between countries where policy regimes vary, in an attempt to identify the effects of policy differences between countries. A number of two-country studies have been carried out; for example, Dex and Shaw (1986); Dex *et al.* (1993); Rubery (1988); Hunter and Rimmer (this volume, Chapter 11). Extending this sort of approach to more countries brings considerably more problems and is not easily managed. Whitehouse (1992) considered the extent to which women's relative pay can be explained within a cross-national framework. Siaroff (1994) examined the relationships between women's relative status and the family welfare orientations of OECD countries' welfare state regimes.

This chapter takes the cross-national approach in tackling the question of how far equal opportunities policies have influenced women's status, and analyses a range of industrialised countries where appropriate data could be found. Every step of this analysis raised a number of issues, making it a difficult exercise. Comparing countries on a number of dimensions should ideally be done within a multi-variate framework. Enormous strides have been taken, especially in EC and OECD countries, in providing approximately harmonised data on a country level; but this still leaves only a small number of countries on which to carry out multi-variate analyses. Innovative methods have been used to solve some of the problems which arose, and for this reason the results should be viewed with interest but regarded as preliminary. Improving this approach would only be possible if substantially more data was available, however, and there is a limit to its availability if analysis is restricted to industrialised countries.

---

[1] Other authors of this paper include Hedwig Vermeulen, Siv Gustafsson, Tim Callan, Nina Smith, Jan Dirk Vasblom and Gunther Schmaus. The multiple authors are part of the Female Labour Force Participation Network.

Women's labour market status in industrialised countries

Investigating whether women's status has been improving in different countries requires some measures of their status. OECD and EC sources provide a number of measures of women's status: women's labour force participation rates, the ratio of women's to men's earnings, the extent to which women are in top occupational groups, and the percentages of women in low-paid jobs. Siaroff (1994) also generated some further unique status measures for women. Enormous advances have taken place in data collection across countries, but caution should always be exercised when drawing conclusions since it is still relatively rare for measures to be defined in the same way across countries.

Women's labour force participation rates for OECD countries vary considerably. Most countries show a systematic increase in these rates since 1970, and the increase would date back much earlier for many countries were the data to be assembled. Japan and Turkey are exceptions where decreases in women's labour force participation are visible over the period in question. Germany has had a rather unchanging picture of participation for much of the period. The increase in women's labour force participation certainly pre-dates the adoption of equal opportunities policies, and is more likely to have been a contributor to the adoption of such policies than a consequence of them. Nonetheless, labour force participation is an important measure of women's status in the labour market, since that status has been found to have cumulative effects to some extent. For example, women's earnings are influenced by the extent of their work experience, and periods out of paid work have been found to have damaging effects on status and earnings (Joshi, 1984; Dex and Walters, 1992; Wright and Ermisch, 1991).

The ratio of female to male earnings is another measure of women's status in the labour market. Ideally this ratio should be calculated for groups of men and women with identical levels of human capital, to make it a more precise measure of discriminatory earnings differentials. But this is rarely possible in cross-national statistics; the best available is usually the gross hourly wage ratio, so at least differences in hours of work are controlled for and do not influence the ratio. OECD sources provide a set of ratios for manual workers (excluding the public sector) for different countries, although not a systematically-defined series going back in time.[2]

A set of hourly wage ratios for manual earnings in manufacturing in selected countries at the end of the 1980s is displayed in Table 16.1. It is more difficult to find the non-manual earnings ratios of a wide range of countries, or the ratio for sectors other than manufacturing. The manual earnings ratios cover a varying percentage of women,[3] but these figures

---

[2] The OECD (1988, 1991) publications on equal pay do contain a series of female-to-male wage ratios, but the notes clearly document that the definitions used vary widely and the figures are not therefore comparable. However, the series from the 1960s to 1986 shows that this ratio steadily increased over the period in most of the countries displayed. The UK stands out as the one country amongst the others (Australia, Canada, Finland, Japan, New Zealand, Portugal, Sweden and the USA) which was in a steady state for much of the decade 1976–86.

[3] For example, in the UK full-time manual may only refer to under ten per cent of the female workforce, although it is higher in some other countries.

may still be representative of each country as a whole since there are likely to be strong correlations between these and other gender pay ratios by country.[4] Thus, despite the limitations, these ratios are used in later analyses. The range is large: the highest, in Sweden, is 90 per cent, while the ratio is only 48.9 per cent in Japan. Britain's ratio is 68 per cent.

The extent to which women are in top occupations in different countries is also presented in Table 16.1, based on ISCO codes. Sweden and Denmark have the highest percentages of women in either professional or managerial occupations (41 and 37 per cent respectively). The lowest percentages are from Portugal (11.6 per cent), Japan (11.8 per cent) and Luxembourg (14.7 per cent). The UK lies between these extremes, with 22.3 per cent of employed women in top occupations. Unfortunately, this measure of women's status can be altered in a number of ways, so not all these figures represent an unequivocal improvement in women's status. For example, the percentage of women in top occupations would increase if fewer women were employed at the bottom end of the occupational spectrum. Nonetheless, this measure is worth considering since it helps to fill out the wider picture.

In 1988 the OECD also provided some calculations of the extent to which men and women were in separate occupational groups. Occupational segregation has often been cited as a reason why women do not do better in the labour market and work in low-wage, low-status segments to a far greater extent than men. There are several ways of measuring occupational segregation, and it has been the subject of dispute in recent literature (for a review see Rubery and Fagan, 1993; Blackburn *et al.*, 1990).

This study only had access to the calculations for OECD countries using one of the possible measures, and not the best one at that: the dissimilarity index.[5] The higher the index, the greater the amount of inequality in the occupational distributions. In this chapter no comparisons are made over time, where this index is seen to have most problems. However, comparisons across countries involve comparing dissimilarity indices based on different occupational structures and female participation rates. It is arguable, therefore, that comparisons of this index across countries will encounter the same problems. Caution should be used in drawing conclusions, and this measure is not analysed later when multi-variate analyses are reported.

The figures across the range of countries considered are also displayed in Table 16.1. On the whole, the figures refer to 1986 (mostly) or 1985. Countries with the least inequality in their gendered occupational distributions, according to this index, are Japan, Greece, Portugal and Italy; countries with the greatest amounts of inequality are Luxembourg, Australia, Norway and the UK.

---

[4] Pay levels in the public and private sectors tend to be linked to a large degree in most countries.

[5] The dissimilarity index is defined as half the sum of the differences between the share of the female labour force in the occupation and the share of the male labour force in the occupation (all differences being measured positively). Rubery and Fagan (1993) review the advantages and disadvantages of this and other measures, especially for making comparisons over time.

Table 16.1 Women's status indicators by country, 1988–90

Country	Female/male earnings ratio	Top occupations per cent	Dissimilarity index women	Low paid percentage women‡	Percentage women low paid*
Sweden	90.0	41.3	37.9	68.0	16.0
Netherlands	78.0	28.5	40.0	53.0	28.0
Beglium	74.5	30.8	39.2	62.0	10.0
Germany	73.0	20.2	37.8	82.0	33.0
Denmark	84.4	37.1	40.5	68.3	16.0
Luxembourg	58.4	14.7	48.9		
UK	68.0	22.3	44.4	63.0	41.0
Ireland	68.9	24.8	42.9	51.0	29.0
USA	70.3	27.6	37.4		
Canada	66.0	30.8	41.0		
Italy	79.3	33.0	24.6	62.0	23.0
Australia	79.6	22.0	47.8		
Finland	77.2	27.3	43.0		
France	79.5	18.2	38.3	51.0	20.0
Greece	78.0	16.1	24.4	55.0	26.0
Japan	48.9	11.8	23.1		
New Zealand	75.3	18.2	41.9		
Norway	85.5	30.3	46.6		
Switzerland	67.5	16.2	39.2		
Spain	72.2	15.7	36.9	70.0	29.0
Portugal	70.8	11.6	25.1	49.0	19.0

Sources: Female/male ratio – *Historical Statistics*, OECD (1992); top occupations – *ILO Statistical Yearbook* (1990); dissimilarity index – OECD (1988); low pay – Rubery and Fagan (1993)

* Percentages of full-time women workers who are low paid; that is receiving less than 66 per cent of the median weekly earnings.

‡ Percentage of women among low-paid full-time workers.

The last measures of women's labour force status considered are those related to the extent of low pay. Statistics for EC countries on this topic are again displayed in Table 16.1. Two measures of the incidence of low pay amongst women are presented; the percentage of the low paid who are women (column four); and the percentage of women who could be classed as having low-paid earnings (column five). As with the other measures of women's labour market position, there are alternative definitions of low pay, and the definition adopted can affect the number of women classified as low paid. The figures cited all use a similar definition, although arguably not the best one.[6]

The figures on women's incidence of low pay amongst full-time workers rank countries according to the measure used. When the percentage of low paid who are women is examined, women's status is worst in Germany (82 per cent) followed by Spain (70 per cent), and best in Portugal (49 per cent) and France (51 per cent). The UK is in the intermediate range with 63 per cent of the low paid being women. Examining the percentages of women who are low paid the UK has the worst statistic (41 per cent) followed by Germany (33 per cent), Spain and Ireland (29 per cent). Belgium (10 per cent) and Denmark (16 per cent) have the best positions.

This review shows that women's status in the labour market varies considerably across industrialised countries. Apparently, women who have the best status according to one measure are not always ranked in that top position when alternative measures of status are compared. Women are ranked at the top of the hierarchy of earnings ratios and labour force participation rates in Scandinavian countries, but these countries do not necessarily occupy top places in the ranking of degrees of occupational segregation or, where data is available, in the extent of low pay. However, it is important to remember the caveats about the various measures and definitions used. What is more, the wage implications of segregation may vary according to the wage structure in each country. Being segregated in Sweden may be better than being desegregated in the UK, for example.

Equal opportunities policies in industrialised countries

Equal opportunities policies operating in industrialised countries have been reviewed in order to devise a set of measures of their strength which can be used in multi-variate analyses. Deriving such measures was not a trivial task: the measures constructed, although the best currently attainable, are not ideal.

Policies aimed at affecting gender inequalities in the labour market take a number of forms. On the whole, equal opportunities policies are those which tackle two issues: discrimination against women in the process of recruitment, promotion and opportunities for training; and the equal payment of women and men for the same (or similar) work. It can be argued that the concept of equal opportunities policies should be widened to include other policies which clearly affect women's ability to participate in the labour market, but this chapter adopts a narrow definition (albeit including maternity leave provisions). Having identified the policies of interest, the aim is to compare the workings of these policies across countries.

The OECD has reviewed equal pay policy across countries in at least two publications (1988, 1991). By the late 1970s, legislation on equal pay for

---

[6] For a review of the alternative definitions of 'low pay' and their implications, see Dex *et al.* (1994), who argue that an hourly and not a weekly definition of low pay is best.

equal work had been enacted in all industrialised nations.[7] In some countries, even Japan, such legislation has existed for considerably longer. Pay equity has been addressed by collective agreements and industrial tribunals in some countries; in others which have more decentralised wage-fixing institutions, legislation has been used. There is therefore little variation in the legislative position of different industrialised countries on the subject of equal pay, but variation exists in the lengths of time such policies have been in operation, and in the extent and range of possible comparators for women's pay. It would be possible to take the period since equal pay legislation was enacted at a national level as one measure of equal opportunities policy. However, in some cases this would overlook the fact that many sub-national agreements were in place before national legislation was passed.

On the issue of pay comparators for women, differences exist between countries on what is allowed. Equal pay for men and women is clearly easiest to apply when they are doing the same job. But the existence of gendered occupational segregation means this situation is relatively rare, and restricting the legislation solely to these comparisons would severely limits its applicability. Countries have recognised that comparisons between women's pay and jobs of equal value must be allowed. In 1975, the EC adopted a directive on equal pay for work of equal value which must be applied in member states. The OECD (1991) report suggests three dimensions of variation in the national legislation on this issue:

- the extent to which comparisons extend beyond identical or similar work to dissimilar work of equal value, and the measures which countries put into place for establishing the equal value of dissimilar work;
- the extent to which the law must be triggered by a complainant, or alternatively incorporates proactive measures such as inspectorates or mandatory reporting requirements;
- the extent to which it covers non-wage remuneration such as allowances and pensions.

It is clear that most countries and the EC have stopped short of allowing 'comparable worth' comparisons between women's and men's jobs. The principle of comparable worth has been seen as allowing a much wider range of comparisons to be made between quite different jobs. Comparable worth comparisons are allowed in public sector employment in some countries or regions (for example, states in the USA).

However, ways of distinguishing between countries on the basis of these variations in policy are hard to devise. There are considerable complexities in the wording of legislation, and differences in how far the principles are implemented and cases are pursued. In addition, data on all of the relevant issues is difficult to obtain.

Two duration measures of the effects of equal opportunities pay policies have been adopted. First is the length of time in years, up to 1990, since

---

[7] The OECD (1988) sets out the legislation and the dates it was enacted in 19 different countries.

equal pay legislation was enacted. The range on this measure varies from Japan (47 years), the USA (27 years), Italy (26 years) and Sweden (25 years) at the upper end, to Greece (six years), Spain and Germany (both ten years) at the lower end. The second measure is the length of time in years, up to 1990, since equal pay for equal value legislation was enacted. Japan and Germany have the minimum possible value of zero, since they have not enacted this legislation or its equivalent. At the other end of the spectrum, Australia and New Zealand have had the longest exposure to these provisions; 18 and 21 years respectively. These time-scales have been used as measures of the strength of equal opportunities policies because the longer legislation has been in operation, the more effect (in terms of improvement) it can be expected to have had on women's status within a country. They have defects for this purpose, but so do other measures considered.

A further measure has been adopted for policies concerned with discrimination in employment. Some anti-discriminatory policies have incorporated affirmative action proposals, thought to strengthen anti-discrimination legislation, so the existence of commitments to affirmative action could be expected to improve women's status. In some countries the affirmative action element is voluntary; in others it is the subject of legislation; and in some it applies only to the public sector. A three-point scale was devised to measure the element:

0   a lack of affirmative action commitments;

1   affirmative action in the public sector only, or where affirmative action is voluntary;

2   legislation on affirmative action across public and private sectors.

These three measures of equal opportunities policies were used in later analyses, alongside a range of other potential determinants of women's labour market status, to see how far they had a positive effect on that status.

Within-country studies of the effects of equal opportunities policies

It is worth briefly reviewing the studies carried out within some countries to evaluate how effective equal opportunities policies have been in improving women's status. On the whole, these studies have focused on the extent to which women's wages are significantly different to those of men after controlling for differences in human capital. They have been the subject of some controversy, in part because of the difficulties of carrying out such evaluations.[8]

---

[8] The OECD (1988) sets out some of the problems of conducting these sorts of evaluation studies under the heading of 'Policy impact'. The difficulties are listed as:
- legislation often follows behind societal changes that have already occurred and which may be primarily responsible for any observed changes in women's status;
- the near-universal coverage of most legislation makes it impossible to find 'control' groups who have not been exposed to the legislation;
- the general trend towards increased participation in the labour force by woman can hide the impact of anti-discriminatory programmes.

Studies in the UK have found some support for the view that the Equal Pay Act, 1970 (enforced by 1975), did improve women's pay. A study of organisations by Snell *et al.* (1981) found that little use was made of the five-year period for implementing the legislation, but some effective changes took place after 1973. Other studies found support for the idea that equal pay legislation improved women's pay, but that it was in conjunction with incomes policies operating at the same time to control inflation (Zabalza and Tzannatos, 1985; Wright and Ermisch, 1991; Paci *et al.*, 1994; Joshi and Newell, 1989). These incomes policies restricted pay rises to a flat rate and benefited the low paid disproportionately. That the legislation has improved the pay ratio is disputed by Chiplin and Sloane (1988) and Sloane and Theodissiou (1994). Borooah and Lee (1988) found that the changing industrial structure, as opposed to institutions or legislation, was mainly responsible for relative pay improvements.

In reviewing the Australian evidence on the effects of equal pay, the OECD suggests that the cumulative effect of the 1969 and 1972 pay ratios 'seems to have been substantial' (1988, 166). However, the extension of the minimum wage to women in 1974 is also thought to have contributed to significant improvements in their pay (Korosi *et al.*, 1993; Rimmer, 1991, 1994). The Canadian rise in the female-to-male pay ratio preceded as well as superceded legislation on pay equity, which suggests that effects of the legislation are not clearly evident.

A study of women's wages in Sweden (Gustafsson and Lofstrom, 1991) found evidence that 50 per cent of the increase in the relative wages of female blue-collar workers from 1960 to 1985 could be attributed to institutional changes – the agreement on equal pay for work of equal value, and the right of women to work nights in industry. The authors were unable to confirm that beneficial effects resulted from the 1977 agreement on equal opportunities for women and men.

Beller (1980) suggested that the US Equal Pay Act, 1963, had little discernible effect on the earnings ratio. Since the late 1970s, however, there has been a rise in female relative earnings arguably attributable to a mixture of causes: women's rising educational attainment, an increase in pay equity as a bargaining issue, comparable worth acts passed in a number of states, and a decline in occupational segregation (see OECD, 1988, for a review). Other studies of US legislation have also found support for women's employment share and occupational advancement being related to affirmative action policy (Leonard, 1984, 1985; Beller, 1982).

The OECD (1988) review of the effects of equal opportunities policies concludes that the evidence is mixed and not yet substantial enough to be sure that women's earnings and occupational advancement have been improved by such policies.

The determinants of women's labour market status across countries

A wide range of potential contributory factors affect women's labour market status and position within a country. The measures examined here are those for which sufficient data was available: the female-to-male hourly earnings ratios of manual workers, the percentages of employed women in the top two occupational groups, the percentage of the low paid who are women, and the percentage of employed women who are low paid.

Studying the range of explanatory variables likely to affect women's status in the labour market allows a consideration of the effects of equal opportunities policies within a multi-variate framework. Maurice states that understanding behaviour within a society involves knowing about that society in some considerable depth, and knowing about its history and institutions (Maurice, 1977; Maurice *et al.*, 1982). However, as argued elsewhere (Dex *et al.*, 1993), more limited questions can be tackled without necessarily knowing all historic or institutional details. Nevertheless, the range of countries considered placed some constraints on the depth to which any society can be represented in this analysis.

As well as equal opportunities policies, economic climate and structure, policy incentives and disincentives, institutional elements of wage fixing, and elements of the system of social reproduction and attitudes may all affect the position of women within a country's labour markets. The analyses in this chapter cover factors that could be described as general policies which operate and were introduced for all employees, as opposed to gendered policies introduced specifically to help women. Equal opportunities policies would be classed as gendered; minimum wage legislation would be a general policy. This distinction is often made in discussion of which gendered or general policies are likely to have had, or will be likely to have, the most significant improvement on women's labour market status (Rubery, 1988; Dex *et al.*, 1993; Hunter and Rimmer, this volume, Chapter 11).

It is also likely that women's position will be influenced by demographic factors: fertility rates, percentage of lone parents, percentage of three-children families, the size of young people's population relative to that of married women, and so on. These factors are not taken into consideration in this chapter.

Economic climate

There is relatively little discussion of how the economic climate and state of an economy affect women's position in the labour market. There is a common conception that women are more likely to improve their status during upswings. Rubery's (1988) consideration of women during recessions provides some support for the converse of this relationship, although it is yet to be systematically tested. Beller (1980) also investigated the effects of the business cycle on the female-to-male earnings ratio, concluding that it deteriorated for women during recessions.

Two measures of the state of the economy were used in this analysis: average growth rates over the two decades up to 1990; and average unemployment rate (all workers) over the decade 1980–90.

Structure of the economy

In late 20th century industrialised economies, women are often located disproportionately within the service sector. Women's labour force participation has clearly grown alongside the shift in industrial structure away from manufacturing and towards services. Borooah and Lee (1988) stressed the importance of this shift in explaining changes in women's relative pay in Britain. Much service sector employment, particularly women's work, is low paid. On the other hand, professional women have been able to improve their status in feminised niches in this sector. In the same way, public sector employment has had two-fold effects: Esping-Anderson (1990) described the important role of the public sector in improving Swedish women's labour market status. It is thus difficult to anticipate whether the extent of service sector or public sector employment in an economy will have a positive or negative effect on women's status.

This study uses the percentage of service sector to all employment in each economy and the percentage of public sector employment as two variables in the multi-variate analysis, partly to test whether these elements of economic structure can be seen to be affecting women's status. Unfortunately, since the OECD relative earnings measure does not cover the public sector, it was impossible to test the effect of public sector employment on the relative earnings measure.[9]

In addition, the extent to which marginal or non-standard jobs exist in an economy may influence women's status. Temporary contracts would on the whole probably be less well paid than permanent contracts.[10] On the other hand, the amount of temporary work in an economy may be related to the extent of labour market regulation. Economies with more regulation might expect to see higher percentages of non-standard forms of work which are not covered by the regulations, in comparison with economies with few regulations. In this case, the amount of women in temporary or low-hours work might reflect (negatively) the level of regulation.

A number of measures were used to capture the effects of the economic structure: the percentage of service sector in total employment; the percentage of public sector in total employment; government spending as a percentage of GDP; the percentage of temporary employment in all employment; and the percentage of low-hours work in all employment.

Policy incentives and disincentives

The most obvious policies creating incentives and disincentives for women to participate in the labour market derive from the tax and social security

---

[9] Whitehouse's (1992) claim to have examined this relationship using the ILO relative earnings data for manufacturing industries must be regarded with some scepticism.

[10] An argument put forward by some economists is that jobs with temporary contracts might expect to pay higher wages than those with permanent contracts, to compensate for the insecurity. However, efficiency wage theories imply that the premium on wages would be the other way around.

contribution systems. These financial considerations are likely to operate on women's decision to work, thus having an indirect effect on their status by increasing their employment continuity which, in turn, improves earnings and status. Whether these incentives and disincentives have a more direct effect on women's status is harder to determine.

It might be expected that the higher the tax rate faced by women the lower the likelihood of their participation in the labour force, although an examination of a set of tax rates against a set of participation rates shows that such a simple relationship does not apply in all cases (Vermeulen *et al.*, 1994).

Zero-rated thresholds in the tax system, if not transferable between spouses, and zero-rated thresholds before which social security contributions need not be paid, provide some incentives for women to restrict their hours of work. Since working part-time means that women do not accumulate the same work experience, their status could again be expected to suffer from these financial incentives. Part-time work in Britain is known to be associated with low pay, low status and often occupational downgrading (Dex, 1992). An earnings ceiling beyond which no further social security contributions need be paid could be argued to bias employers against part-time employment: non-wage costs per employee would be lower for one full-timer working the same hours as two part-timers. In this case full-time work may be encouraged and women's status might increase.[11]

The measures of policy incentives included in this analysis are the average tax rate faced by married women earning average manual earnings; the existence, as a dummy, of a zero-rated tax threshold; and the existence, as a dummy variable, of a social security threshold.

Institutional elements of wage-fixing

The within-country evaluations of the effects of equal opportunities policies drew attention to the importance of institutional aspects of wage fixing on women's labour market status; others have made similar points (Rubery, 1988; Dex *et al.*, 1993). If women tend to be amongst the lowest-paid groups in an economy, they will benefit from minimum wage legislation. Also, women's lack of unionisation and lack of coverage by collective bargaining are often cited as contributing to their low pay. Certainly, union membership does appear to have a mark-up on women's pay, just as it does for men (Main and Reilly, 1992; but see Millward and Woodland, this volume, Chapter 10, for new evidence on this issue).

A recent EC cross-country comparison of low pay provided some evidence that the form of wage-bargaining structures and unionisation were linked to percentages of low pay (CERC, 1992). Women tended to have the least amounts of low pay in countries with centralised systems of wage bargaining and strong collective bargaining; and the greatest amounts of

---

[11] This would only apply to reasonably highly-paid jobs, and would not be relevant for full-timers employed in the same types of jobs as most part-timers in the UK.

low pay where pay bargaining was decentralised and fragmented. Minimum wages, likewise, appeared to improve women's pay to some extent. These results are reviewed alongside other institutional details for EC countries in Rubery and Fagan (1994).

This analysis adopts two measures of these institutional elements. Firstly it includes a measure of women's union density. Arguably the coverage of women by collective bargaining might be an additional or even a superior measure, but data on female coverage was not so widely available for OECD countries. Secondly it uses a pay-bargaining scale based on the Rubery and Fagan (1994) and CERC (1992) categories:

0   weak and uneven collective bargaining, no minimum wage

1   weak collective agreements set rates below minimum wage

2   weak collective agreements set rates above minimum wage

3   strong collective bargaining without minimum wage

4   strong collective bargaining with minimum wage.

Systems of social reproduction

Systems of social reproduction are important elements of women's (and men's) labour force decision-making. Societies vary considerably in the extent to which mothers can support themselves and their families without working. Maternity leave provisions are one obvious element of this equation; childcare policies and provisions and the extent to which pre-school childcare is subsidised will also influence women's decisions to take paid employment, as do educational policies, the length of the school day and the duration of holidays. The greater the provision of childcare by society, especially if it is subsidised, the greater women's involvement in the labour market is expected to be. This greater involvement would also improve women's continuity of employment and thus their status.

This analysis restricts consideration of the social reproduction system to a few of its elements. Data has been drawn from several recent comparative sources of childcare provisions (for example, OECD, 1994; Moss, 1988), and includes measures of the percentage of babies to two-year-olds and three- to five-year-olds attending approximately full-time publicly-provided day-care provision. Some analyses incorporate social security transfers as a percentage of GDP, as a measure of the extent to which societies provide support for those who are not working. This study also includes a measure of total female participation in each country as an indicator of the extent to which mothers are providing childcare.

A further measure was used to indicate the broader aspects of equal opportunities policies; in particular, the duration in weeks of statutory paid maternity leave. The expectation is that the longer the paid leave, the more likely women are to be able to maintain employment continuity across childbirth; in due course this continuity will also help to maintain their labour market status. Again, the statutory amount of maternity leave will not accurately reflect the actual amounts of time individual women within each country spend on paid leave whilst giving birth.

However, statutory provisions are likely to set a benchmark to which other private and voluntary improvements are related. The data for this measure was largely obtained from the OECD (1994).

Attitudes

The attitudes of individuals are also expected to vary across countries and indicate reasons for differing behaviour. In particular, if women (and men) do not accept the role of a male breadwinner, it is expected that women would be more likely to be in paid employment and concerned about careers and labour market status than women who accept the male breadwinner role. Similarly, variations in attitudes towards non-maternal childcare are expected to lead to similar differences in behaviour.

Cross-country data on attitudes to these topics is difficult to find, with only one source for the EC which investigates the male breadwinner notion to any extent. Individuals' scores have been averaged per country in response to the question: 'Do men have a prior right to work in periods of high unemployment?' (Eurobarometer, 1984). This early date for the attitude data eliminates any worries about the endogeneity of attitudes. The inclusion of female participation rates acts as another proxy indicator of attitudes, since women in paid jobs are known to have different attitudes to those not in paid work (Dex, 1988).

A rather long list of explanatory variables helps to explain women's labour market status in industrialised countries. The precise definitions and data sources for these variables are described in Table 16.2. The means and standard deviations are displayed in Table 16.3. In some ways the list is still too short, but the limited number of countries which can be analysed and the lack of data prevent its extension at present. Despite its limitations, this analysis is a considerable advance on others with much more limited aims.

Multi-variate models of women's labour market status across countries

The previous section described the explanatory variables to be considered in this analysis of women's labour market status in industrialised countries. Although a large amount of comparative data has been amassed, it is still a relatively small sample of countries on which to carry out multi-variate analysis. In addition, values for some countries on some items are missing. Specially-devised routines were used to carry out this analysis using Bayesian statistics, allowing tests to see if expectations about the effects of the various explanatory variables were upheld.

The use of Bayesian statistics allowed the estimation of models which try to explain the various dimensions of women's status, despite limitations in the data. These techniques are described in Skilling (1993). A summary of the main components of the Bayesian approach and how it differs from non-Bayesian methods is provided in the Appendix. An *a priori* distribution must be derived from theory or guess for each of the slope

Table 16.2 Description of variables

Variable	Source	Transformation
Dependent variable		
Ratio of female-to-male hourly earnings	*	LN(v)
Percentage of women in professional and managerial occupations	•	LN(v/(100-v))
Index of dissimilarity of women's occupations	¤	LN(v/(100-v))
Percentage of low paid who are female	†	LN(v/(100-v))
Percentage of women who are low paid	†	LN(v/(100-v))
Independent variable		
Percentage change in gross domestic product, 1979–90 average	°	LN((v+100)/100)
Percentage change in gross domestic product per capita, 1979–90	°	LN((v+100)/100)
Percentage of employment in services, 1990	°	LN(v/(100-v))
Average unemployment rate, 1980–90	°	LN(v/(100-v))
Whether or not has social security threshold	§	none
Whether has social security ceiling	§	none
Collective bargaining/minimum wage scale	†	none
Social security transfers as percentage of gross domestic product, 1980–90 average	°	LN(v/(100-v))
Government spending as percentage of gross domestic product, 1980–90 average	°	LN(v/(100-v))
Government employment as percentage of gross domestic product, 1980–90 average	°	LN(v/(100-v))
Paid maternity leave, duration in months	◊	none
Average tax rate of second earner, average hours, average female earnings	§	LN((100-v)/100)
Childcare provision for age up to two years	¶	LN((100-v)/100)
Childcare percentage full-time provision for age three to five	¶	LN(v/(100-v))
Percentage female unionisation density	◊	LN(v/(100-v))
Equal opportunities (EO) policies: positive action scale	@	LN(v/(100-v))
EO policies: comparable worth duration since enacted (years)	@	none
EO policies: duration since equal pay law (years)	@	none
Percentage of low-hours work, one to ten hours per week	Δ	none
Percentage of employment in temporary jobs, 1989–90	*	LN(v/(100-v))
Percentage of women in part-time work, 1990	°	LN(v/(100-v))
Female participation rates, 1990	°	LN(v/(100-v))
Women's attitudes to male breadwinner	#	none
Whether tax system has non-transferable zero-rated allowance for married women	§	none

Sources
*OECD (1990)
•ILO (1990)
¤ OECD (1988)

† Rubery and Fagan (1993)
° OECD (1992)
§ Vermeulen *et al.* (1994)
◊ OECD (1994)

¶ Moss (1988)
@ OECD (1988, 1991)
Δ Female Labour Force Network
Eurobarometer (1984)

coefficients. Normal *a priori* distributions have been chosen, with means and standard deviations reflecting uncertain prior beliefs; had absolutely nothing been known *a priori* about these coefficients, a zero mean and very large standard deviation could have been chosen. A Bayesian model calculates an updated set of coefficients from the data, allowing comparison of *a posteriori* with *a priori* coefficients.

Similarly, missing values can be handled by providing a distribution of the likely values of the missing items. These distributions are based on the information already collected. When it is not clear what the range might be, an appropriately wide range is used. In addition, the programmes require some estimate of the 'noise' or measurement errors in the data. This is a comforting element in an analysis where one suspects that variations have occurred in the way variables are measured across countries.[12]

The results can exemplify various possibilities:
- no new information is gained about the effects of a particular variable;[13]
- the *a priori* hypothesis is confirmed;
- the *a priori* hypothesis is rejected but the new coefficient is not significantly different from zero;
- the *a priori* hypothesis is rejected and a new alternative coefficient confirmed which is significantly different from zero.

Having discussed earlier the general expectations about the variables included in the models, the more precise means and standard deviations of the *a priori* coefficients are listed in Table 16.4. These prior values are listed once only, since identical priors were used in each model. Their signs were reversed when necessary to take account of the direction in which the dependent variable improved women's status.

In some cases, several models were estimated on each of the status indicators to explore the effects of alternative highly-correlated variables. The results are all for a ten per cent noise level. Two standard deviations have been used as the criteria for judging the significance of the results.[14]

---

[12] A ten per cent error rate was chosen as the likely noise level in the first round of these analyses. Noise was assumed to be normally distributed and usually additional to the logarithm (or log odds) of the measured values. The standard deviation of the noise was chosen to be log (1.1).

[13] It is important to recognise that this result is not equivalent to a coefficient which is insignificant in multiple regression analysis. It cannot be said that these independent variables do not have any effect on the dependent variable. There is no new information to use as a basis for either accepting or rejecting the *a priori* hypothesis; the *a posteriori* distribution of the coefficient is essentially the same as the *a priori* distribution.

[14] A prior mean estimate is taken as confirmed when that estimate is within two posterior standard deviations of the posterior beta estimate, and the posterior standard deviation is less than one half of the prior standard deviation. A prior mean estimate is taken as rejected when it lies outside two posterior standard deviations of the posterior beta estimate. A result is described as positive or negative when the posterior beta estimate is more than two posterior standard deviations greater or less than zero.

Table 16.3 Means and standard deviations of transformed variables

Variable	Mean	Standard deviation	Number of cases
Female/male earnings ratio	4.29	0.13	21
Top occupations	- 1.26	0.49	21
Low paid, percentage women	0.42	0.48	12
Precentage women in low pay	- 1.20	0.48	12
Growth in gross domestic product	0.02	0.01	21
Growth in gross domestic product per capita	0.02	0.01	21
Average unemployment rate	- 2.67	0.68	21
Percentage services employment	0.53	0.30	21
Percentage public sector	- 1.56	0.46	20
Percentage temporary jobs	- 2.92	0.37	12
Percentage low-hours jobs	- 3.07	0.73	13
Percentage part-time jobs	- 0.98	0.82	20
Percentage government spending	- 0.04	0.37	20
Average tax rate	- 0.41	0.16	8
Social security threshold	0.30	0.48	10
Social security ceiling	0.67	0.50	9
Zero-rated tax allowance	0.30	0.48	10
Female union density	- 0.47	1.34	14
Wage bargaining scale	2.06	1.43	18
Childcare up to age two	- 2.74	1.55	13
Childcare age three to five	0.65	1.63	13
Percentage social security spending	- 1.72	0.38	20
Female participation rate	0.36	0.59	21
Maternity leave duration	17.63	9.91	20
Breadwinner score	2.56	0.32	11
Affirmative action score	1.00	0.82	10
Duration of equal pay legislation	17.33	9.12	18
Duration of equal value legislation	8.86	6.83	14

Table 16.4 Summary results of Bayesian analysis on female/male hourly earnings ratio

	Prior values on all variables		Female/male hourly manual earnings	
	Prior mean	Prior standard deviation	Post beta	Post standard deviation
Economic climate				
Growth in gross domestic product	2.00	2.00	2.391	1.985
Per capita growth in gross domestic product	2.00	2.00		
Average unemployment rates	0.00	0.26	0.035*	0.095
Structure of economy				
Percentage services employment	0.00	0.30	- 0.025	0.214
Percentage public sector employment	0.41	0.30		
Percentage temporary jobs	- 0.10	0.16	- 0.065	0.106
Percentage jobs under ten hours	- 0.10	0.21	- 0.043*	0.096
Percentage part-time employment	- 0.01	0.16		
Percentage government spending	0.41	0.30		
Policy incentives				
Average tax rate	0.00	1.00	- 0.359*	0.292
Social security threshold	- 0.02	0.02	- 0.019	0.020
Social security ceiling	0.00	0.02		
Zero-rated allowance	- 0.01	0.04		
Institutions				
Female union density	0.21	0.21	- 0.027†	0.079
Wage bargaining scale	0.02	0.02	0.021	0.015
Social reproduction				
Childcare up to age two	0.10	0.21	- 0.083*	0.092
Childcare age three to five	0.21	0.16	0.085*	0.068
Percentage social security transfers	0.00	0.25		
Female participation rate	0.21	0.21	0.160	0.124
Maternity leave duration	0.003	0.003	0.0005	0.003
Attitudes				
Breadwinner score	0.04	0.04	0.032	0.039
EO policies				
Positive action scale	0.02	0.03	0.016	0.023
Duration equal pay	0.01	0.02	0.011*	0.009
Duration equal value	0.01	0.01	0.013	0.009

* confirm *a priori* value of coefficient.   † reject *a priori* value of coefficient.

Female/male manual hourly earnings ratios

The summary conclusions for the two models which examined female/male hourly earnings ratios are given in Table 16.4. In the case of the majority of variables, no new information was learnt from estimating the models. However, there are a few results of interest. The effect of average unemployment rates on the ratio was confirmed as zero, which may show the importance of sex-segregated supplies of labour. The total average unemployment rates, the measure used to indicate economic conditions, may be failing to reflect fully conditions in the sectors of the labour market occupied by most women.

Average tax rates for married women were also confirmed as having a weak negative or zero effect – some small support for the hypothesis that increases in the tax rate will dissuade married women from working, which may lead to lower relative earnings in due course.

The expectation on the variable for female union density was rejected by the analysis in preference for one with zero effect. Rather than increases in female union density leading to improvements in the female/male earnings ratio, they had no effect on the manual private sector female/male hourly earnings ratio. This is rather surprising. If data were available, it would be interesting to substitute union coverage to see if a different conclusion emerged.

The extent of publicly-provided childcare for babies to two-year-olds was confirmed as having zero effect, but childcare for three- to five-year-olds had a weak positive or zero effect. Childcare provision for older pre-school children may be helping manual women workers to improve their earnings ratio relative to men. The extent of low-hours work was also confirmed as having zero effect.

Lastly, the period since equal pay legislation was enacted does not appear to have an impact on the female/male earnings ratio. This result differs from that obtained by Whitehouse (1992) in a time-series study, which found that equal pay legislation improved the ratio for women, although only a few explanatory variables could be included.

Percentage of women in top occupations

The results for two estimations attempting to explain the percentage of women in the top occupational groups are displayed in Table 16.5. As before, there is no new information about the majority of variables. The zero *a priori* for average unemployment rates was rejected in favour of a positive effect. Women's status may have been higher in some countries as a result of higher unemployment. This result may reflect that in times of high unemployment, low-level jobs are cut to a greater extent, with a consequent increase in the percentage of women in top occupations.

The percentage of government spending was found to have a positive effect on the percentage of women in higher occupations. The result here,

Table 16.5 Summary results of Bayesian analysis on percentage of women in top two occupational groups

	Model 1		Model 2	
	Post beta	Post standard deviation	Post beta	Post standard deviation
Economic climate				
Growth in gross domestic product	2.057	1.989		
Per capita growth in gross domestic product			1.825	1.985
Average unemployment rates	0.155*	0.100	0.177†P	0.089
Structure of economy				
Percentage services employment	0.185	0.225	0.155	0.234
Percentage public sector employment	0.172	0.188	0.129	0.182
Percentage temporary jobs	- 0.076	0.106	0.007	0.099
Percentage jobs under ten hours	0.062*	0.100		
Percentage part-time employment			0.018	0.102
Percentage government spending			0.458P	0.211
Policy incentives				
Average tax rate	- 0.718†N	0.299	- 0.525*	0.328
Social security threshold	- 0.023	0.020	- 0.021	0.020
Social security ceiling			- 0.003	0.024
Zero-rated allowance				
Institutions				
Female union density	0.140*	0.080	0.060*	0.076
Wage bargaining scale	0.022	0.015	0.022	0.015
Social reproduction				
Childcare up to age two	- 0.050*	0.097	- 0.017*	0.089
Childcare age three to five	0.079*	0.074	0.036†	0.067
Percentage social security transfers	0.191	0.163		
Female participation rate	0.147	0.138	0.174	0.135
Maternity leave duration	0.003	0.003	0.003	0.003
Attitudes				
Breadwinner score	0.033	0.039	0.033	0.039
EO policies				
Positive action scale	0.018	0.024	0.020	0.024
Duration of equal pay legislation	0.026P	0.009	0.023P	0.008
Duration of equal value legislation	0.007	0.009	0.008	0.008

* confirm *a priori* coefficient. N coefficient has significant negative value.

† reject *a priori* coefficient. P coefficient has significant positive value.

linking government spending with this aspect of women's status, leaves open the question of whether there are two effects of such spending: a stimulus to create more top occupations for women, but lots of low-wage jobs also being generated.

Average tax rates for married women were found to have a significant negative effect on the percentage of women in top occupations. In the case of the female unionisation density, the weak positive or zero *a priori* effect was confirmed as being a zero effect. In this case there is perhaps more justification for the result, since top occupations may be less likely to be unionised than lower-level jobs. Similarly, the extent of low-hours jobs was confirmed as having a zero effect.

Childcare provisions are confirmed as having little or no effect in the case of babies to two-year-olds. In the case of three- to five-year-olds, the *a priori* hypothesis that childcare provision has a positive effect on women's chances of reaching top jobs can be rejected. Women in top occupations may be better placed to solve childcare problems, since they can afford personal nannies; women lower down the occupational hierarchy may be those who rely most on publicly-provided childcare.

Equal opportunities policies appear to have a significant positive effect on the percentage of women in top occupations. The most significant measure is the period since equal pay legislation was passed.

Women in low pay

The results for the two estimations focusing on women in low pay are displayed in Table 16.6. These estimations were carried out on a much smaller set of data. In one case, the percentage of the low paid who were women, average unemployment rates were found to be negatively associated with women's share of low pay; higher average unemployment rates were associated with lower percentages of low-paid women. Possibly it is unemployed women on the margins of the labour force who are drawn into low-paid jobs when the economy is stronger.

The *a priori* expectation that increases in public sector employment would be associated with lower amounts of low-paid women is rejected. Average tax rates were found to have a zero effect on women's low pay. It is interesting to see that, as expected, higher levels of female unionisation rates are confirmed as being associated with lower levels of women's incidence of low pay and women's share of low pay.

Childcare provision for three- to five-year-olds is found to have conflicting effects. In the case of the percentage of the low paid who are women, the *a priori* expectation of a negative effect is rejected and a positive effect is supported. In this case, a higher proportion of publicly-provided childcare for three- to five-year-olds would be associated with higher proportions of the low paid who were women. This is not such a surprising finding, since it is likely to be women who are desperate to earn money who would benefit most from publicly-provided childcare. These would

Table 16.6 Summary results of Bayesian analysis on extent of women's low pay

	Percentage of low paid who are women		Percentage of women who are low paid	
	Post beta	Post standard deviation	Post beta	Post standard deviation
Economic climate				
Growth in gross domestic product	- 2.592	1.990	- 2.381	1.994
Average unemployment rates	- 0.266‡N	0.130	- 0.014*	0.130
Structure of economy				
Percentage services employment	- 0.308	0.234	0.059	0.226
Percentage public sector employment	- 0.233	0.205	0.043‡	0.202
Percentage temporary jobs	- 0.018	0.118	0.001	0.117
Percentage jobs under ten hours	- 0.046	0.124	- 0.027	0.178
Policy incentives				
Average tax rate	- 0.551*	0.345	0.248*	0.311
Social security threshold	0.033	0.020	0.027	0.020
Social security ceiling	0.002	0.024	0.002	0.024
Zero-rated allowance	0.012	0.015	0.012	0.015
Institutions				
Female union density	- 0.032*	0.091	- 0.153*N	0.066
Wage bargaining scale	- 0.020	0.015	- 0.023	0.015
Social reproduction				
Childcare up to age two	- 0.044	0.112	- 0.131	0.108
Childcare age three to five	0.175‡P	0.082	- 0.111*	0.077
Percentage social security transfers	- 0.542‡N	0.183	- 0.425‡N	0.167
Female participation rate	0.153‡	0.151	0.113‡	0.145
Maternity leave duration	- 0.003	0.003	- 0.003	0.003
Attitudes				
Breadwinner score	- 0.015	0.039	- 0.017	0.039
EO policies				
Positive action scale	- 0.006	0.024	- 0.017	0.024
Duration equal pay	- 0.038N	0.012	- 0.012	0.010
Duration equal value	- 0.011	0.010	- 0.014	0.010

* confirm *a priori* coefficient.   N coefficient has significant negative value.

‡ reject *a priori* coefficient.   P coefficient has significant positive value.

equally be the women most likely to take low-paid jobs. In fact, this may be a case of publicly-provided childcare drawing women into the labour force by making them more able to take low-paid jobs than if they had to find alternative and possibly more expensive childcare.

On the other hand, higher proportions of childcare provisions for three- to five-year-olds is associated weakly with a decreasing percentage of women with low pay, implying that more extensive childcare provision may make it less likely that employed women will be low paid. These results are not obviously consistent. The expectation that higher participation rates might be associated with lower levels of women's low pay was rejected in favour of participation rates having a zero effect.

The percentage of social security spending was found to have a negative effect on the percentage of the low paid who are women. Countries which spend more on social security transfers, which support women (and children and men) to a greater extent without working, may be those with lower percentages of the low paid who are women.

Equal opportunities policies, in particular the period since equal pay legislation was passed, were also found to reduce the percentage of low paid who were women.

Conclusions

This chapter begins to examine the factors which have affected women's labour market status within a cross-country framework. A main aim was to see whether equal opportunities policies designed to improve women's status have actually achieved their objectives, and this necessitated the use of the comparative framework to examine country-specific variations.

However, the task was fraught with problems. Comparative data is sometimes defined in country-specific ways, and it is often difficult to find the same information for a wide enough range of countries to carry out a multi-variate analysis. It was also difficult to create measures of some key effects: those of the strength of equal opportunities policies. Bayesian analysis was a useful framework to adopt to resolve some of these problems. Nevertheless, these results should be regarded as preliminary. In due course it may be possible to offer better measures of equal opportunities policies for a wider range of countries.

Given these provisos, several interesting results emerged from the analysis. In some cases these were the reverse of expectations, but in ways which often made a lot of sense. Having adopted relatively strong conditions for judging significance with high levels of noise, the findings can confidently be described as robust.

On the central issue of whether equal opportunities policies have affected women's status, the measure of the period since equal pay legislation was enacted was fairly consistently associated with improvements in women's occupational status and the extent of women's low pay. The findings support the view that such policies have improved women's status. However, this measure did not appear to be related to the female-to-male earnings ratio, where it might be expected to have had the most effect. There are a number of potential reasons for this. As mentioned at the outset, in some countries legislation on equal pay came after equality policies were starting to be pursued. Also, better measures of the strength of equal opportunities policies might produce better tests of the effects on women's status, if and when they become available.

It is worth noting that this analysis has tended to treat equal opportunities policies as separate from other sorts of policies. In practice, equal opportunities policies can also be enacted through union bargaining and attitude change. The policies can, in principle, create an environment in which gender equality is taken more seriously by everyone. That these results show improvements in women's status at both the bottom and top ends of the labour hierarchy is some support for this more general environmental effect. No provisions were made in the analysis for interactions of this kind, but better data would be required to treat them seriously within a modelling framework.

The relationship shown in this analysis is in some ways capturing a trend in these societies. But the trend towards improvements in women's status is correlated with the enactment of equality legislation, and thus equal opportunities policies can confidently be said to have helped to promote these changes. It may be too early to see similar effects from the adoption of equal pay for equal value principles, which, on the whole, are more recent.

Some other interesting results emerged. Government spending has led to improvements in women's occupational status, but has not had much effect on low pay. These results offer some support for the view that the Swedish model of improving women's occupational status, by boosting the public sector, has worked more widely. However, women at the bottom end have probably benefited from more extensive childcare provisions and greater unionisation. That policies and provisions act differently at different ends of the labour market is perhaps not surprising.

Acknowledgements

This research has been supported by the ESRC as part of the scientific programme of the ESRC Research Centre on Micro-Social Change in Britain, the EC Human Capital and Mobility Programme, and the Sanger Centre (University of Cambridge) which is in turn supported by the MRC and the Wellcome Foundation.

The Network on Female Labour Force Participation is funded by the EC Human Capital and Mobility Programme.

References

Beller, A. H. (1980). 'The effect of economic conditions on the success of equal employment opportunity laws: an application to the sex differentials in earnings' in *Review of Economics and Statistics*, August.

Beller, A. H. (1982). 'Occupational segregation by sex: determinants and changes' in *Journal of Human Resources*, XVII (3).

Blackburn, R., Jarman, J. and Siltanen, J. (1990). *Measuring Occupational Gender Segregation*. Working Paper 3, Sociological Research Group, Social and Political Sciences, University of Cambridge.

Borooah, V. K. and Lee, K. C. (1988). 'The effect of changes in Britain's industrial structure on female relative pay and employment' in *Economic Journal*, 98.

CERC (1992). *Low Pay in the European Community*. V/20024/91-EN, Centre d'Etudes des Revenus et des Couts, Paris, Report to the European Communities.

Chiplin, B. and Sloane, P. (1988). 'The effects of Britain's anti-discrimination legislation on relative pay and employment: a comment' in *Economic Journal*, 98.

Dex, S. (1988). *Women's Attitudes Towards Work*. Macmillan.

Dex, S. (1992). 'Labour force participation of women in Britain during the 1990s: occupational mobility and part-time employment' in Lindley, R. M. (ed.) *Women's Employment: Britain and the Single European Market*. London: HMSO.

Dex, S. and Shaw, L. B. (1986). *British and American Women at Work: Do Equal Opportunities Policies Matter?* Macmillan.

Dex, S. and Walters, P. (1992). 'Franco-British comparisons of women's labour supply and the effects of social policies' in *Oxford Economic Papers*, 44.

Dex, S., Walters, P. and Alden, D. M. (1993). *French and British Mothers at Work*. Macmillan.

Dex, S., Lissenburgh, S. and Taylor, M. (1994). *Women and Low Pay*. Manchester: Equal Opportunities Commission, Research Paper series.

Esping-Anderson, G. (1990). *The Three Worlds of Welfare Capitalism*. Princeton University Press.

Eurobarometer (1984). *European Women and Men*. European Community.

Gustafsson, S. and Lofstrom, A. (1991). 'Policy changes and women's wages in Sweden' in *International Review of Comparative Public Policy*, 3.

Hunter, L. and Rimmer, S. (1995). 'An economic exploration of the UK and Australian experiences' in this volume.

ILO (1990). *Statistics Yearbook 1990*. Geneva: International Labour Organisation.

Joshi, H. E. (1984). *Women's Participation in Paid Work: Further Analysis of the Women and Employment Survey*. Research Paper 45. London: Department of Employment.

Joshi, H. E. and Newell, M.-L. (1989). *Pay Differentials and Parenthood: Analysis of Men and Women Born in 1946*. Institute for Employment Research. Coventry: University of Warwick.

Korosi, G., Rimmer, R. and Rimmer, S. (1993). 'Contributions from gender and unions to earnings differences among young Australians: the analysis of a panel' in *Proceedings of the Conference on Contemporary Issues in Income Distribution*. Sydney: University of New South Wales.

Leonard, J. S. (1984). 'Employment and occupational advance under affirmative action' in *Review of Economics and Statistics*, August.

Leonard, J. S. (1985). 'What promises are worth: the impact of affirmative action goals' in *Journal of Human Resources*, Winter.

Main, B. and Reilly, B. (1992). 'Women and the union wage gap' in *Economic Journal*, 102.

Maurice, M. (1977). 'Theoretical and ideological aspects of universalism in the study of work organisations' in Haug, M. R. (ed.) *Work and Technology*. London: Sage.

Maurice, M., Sellier, F. and Silvestre, J. (1982). *The Social Foundations of Industrial Power*. Cambridge, Mass: MIT Press.

Meulders, D. and Plasman, R. (1989). *Women in Atypical Employment*. Women in the Labour Force Network Phase 5, V/146/89-EN, Report to the Commission of the European Communities.

Millward, N. and Woodland, S. (1995). 'Gender segregation and male/female wage differences' in this volume.

Moss, P. (1988). *Childcare and Equality of Opportunity*. V/746/88/-EN, Report to the Commission of the European Communities.

OECD (1988). *Employment Outlook*. Paris: Organisation for Economic Co-operation and Development.

OECD (1990). *Employment Outlook*. Paris: Organisation for Economic Co-operation and Development.

OECD (1991). *Equal Pay for Work of Comparable Worth: The Experience of Industrialised Countries*. Labour Market and Social Policy Occasional Paper 6. Paris: Organisation for Economic Co-operation and Development.

OECD (1992). *Historical Statistics 1960–1990*. Paris: Organisation for Economic Co-operation and Development.

OECD (1994). *Employment Outlook*. Paris: Organisation for Economic Co-operation and Development.

Paci, P., Makepeace, G., Joshi, H. and Dolton, P. (1994). *Is Pay Discrimination Against Young Women a Thing of the Past? A Tale of Two Cohorts*. Paper presented to EMRU Workshop.

Rimmer, S. (1991). 'Occupational segregation, earnings differentials and status among Australian workers' in *Economic Record*, 67.

Rimmer, S. (1994). *Australian Labour Market and Microeconomic Reform*. Victoria: La Trobe University Press.

Rubery, J. (ed.) (1988). *Women and Recession*. Routledge and Kegan Paul.

Rubery, J. and Fagan, C. (1993). *Occupational Segregation of Women and Men in the European Community, Network of Experts on the Situation of Women in the Labour Market*. Synthesis Report to the Commission of the European Communities.

Rubery, J. and Fagan, C. (1994). *Wage Determination and Sex Segregation in Employment in the European Community*. Report for the Equal Opportunities Unit DG V, Commission of the European Communities.

Siaroff, A. (1994). 'Work, welfare and gender equality: a new typology' in Sainsbury, D. (ed.) *Gendering Welfare States*. Sage Modern Politics Series, 35. London: Sage.

Skilling, J. (1993). 'Bayesian numerical analysis' in Grandy, W. T. Jr. and Milonni, P. (eds.) *Bayesian Numerical Analysis*. Cambridge University Press.

Sloane, P. and Theodissiou, I. (1994). 'A generalised Lorenz curve approach to explaining the upward movement in women's relative earnings in Britain during the 1970s' in *Scottish Journal of Political Economy*, 41

Snell, M. W., Glucklich, P. and Povall, M. (1981). *Equal Pay and Opportunities*. Research Paper 20. London: Department of Employment.

Vermeulen, H., Dex, S., Gustafsson, S., Smith, N., Callan, T., Schmauss, G., Vlasblom, J., Dankmeyer, B. and Warren, T. (1994). *Tax Incentives and Disincentives on Married Women's Labour Force Participation and Hours of Work in European Countries*. ESRC Centre for Research on Micro-Social Change, Working Paper No 95-98.

Whitehouse, G. (1992). 'Legislation and labour market gender inequality: an analysis of OECD countries' in *Work, Employment and Society*, 6 (1).

Wright, R. and Ermisch, J. (1991). 'Gender discrimination in the British labour market: a reassessment' in *Economic Journal*, 101 (406).

Zabalza, A. and Tzannatos, Z. (1985). *Women and Equal Pay: The Effects of Legislation on Female Employment and Wages in Britain*. Cambridge University Press.

CHAPTER 17   **Some Lessons for Policy**

Jane Humphries and Jill Rubery

Examining the economic issues associated with equal opportunities necessarily raises important questions, both of principle and practice, for policy-makers and lobbyists. Four major issues can be identified.

- To what extent does economic theory question or support the notion that policy intervention is necessary to achieve the principle of equal opportunities?

- Can an equal opportunities perspective be used to query the language and calculus of traditional economic cost-benefit analysis? And can an alternative calculus be put in its place?

- Should emphasis be placed on developing targeted equal opportunities policies and programmes, or should the stress be on the integration or 'mainstreaming' of equal opportunities issues within all policy areas?

- While recognising that the case for equal opportunities policy is primarily an ethical and not a contingent economic issue, is it possible to identify social and economic benefits that accrue both to women and to other major interest groups? Can the pursuit of equal opportunities policies be linked to other major policy objectives and concerns?

New theoretical developments and the case for intervention

Economists place obstacles in the way of policy intervention in the area of equal opportunities by giving the benefit of the doubt to market outcomes, unless these can be proven to be discriminatory. Economics thus adopts a similar stance to the law in the area of discrimination by placing the burden of proof on the complainant to show discrimination has occurred, instead of on the employer or society at large to show that discrimination has not occurred. This position of economists is summarised by Main:

> ...economists are quite prepared to accept the notion of sex discrimination in the labour market but owing to the importance they place on market prices they exhibit a certain caution in promoting solutions that involve interventions in the market process... the question that is first asked is, 'Where is the market failure?' (Main, 1993: 26.)

As if this approach did not provide enough of a barrier to policy intervention in the labour market, economists over recent years have also devoted effort to developing the argument that even where market failure and thus a *prime-facie* case for intervention can be identified, it does not automatically follow that intervention is better than the market solution. The intervention may create new problems and imperfections or have unintended consequences, and the agents of the state may have objectives which do not fully coincide with those of the state (Tulloch, 1965, 1988). The long-term costs of intervention may even outweigh the benefits.

Thus the economic framework used for most policy debates makes two assumptions:

- market outcomes are correct unless proven otherwise;
- the dangers of misdirected policy interventions and a self-seeking bureaucracy are as great if not greater than those of inefficient markets.

The unreconstructed position of economists that the market, left to itself, will produce the appropriate outcomes is still alive and well in the 1990s. A recent text on economics and earnings concluded:

> As for occupational choice, much of the differences between men and women can be explained as a rational response to differences in labour force intermittency, in mathematical abilities and in tastes. The alternative explanation is discrimination, but... such an explanation needs to rely on a motive for discrimination – and no strong motive has been found. Labour mobility and competition among firms will eradicate discrimination, and allocate labour to its most productive uses so minimising costs. (Polachek and Siebert, 1993: 208.)

These assumptions appear to create an almost insurmountable barrier to the development of a case for policy intervention on other than social, equity and ethical grounds.

However, the maintenance of this sceptical approach to the economic case for policy intervention stands in sharp contrast to the actual thrust of recent trends in economic theory. The dominant work in mainstream theoretical economics over the past two decades has emphasised the likely pervasiveness of imperfections and inertia, the persistence of non-optimal systems of organisation, and the possibility that a variety of institutional arrangements are consistent with efficient outcomes. Thus the same authors who are so confident about the effectiveness of market processes for removing discrimination conclude in a separate chapter on information and wages:

> Simple economic theory predicts a unique equilibrium in competitive markets. However, in the real world such equilibria are elusive. Labour markets typically contain considerable wage variation even when controlling for worker human capital differences. This chapter argues that incomplete information explains at least part of these wage variations. (Polachek and Siebert, 1993: 247.)

The market apparently works with incomplete information but can still be trusted to eliminate discrimination.

The case for intervention is rejected in standard theory, as Main (1993) correctly identifies, on the grounds that welfare maximisation is best achieved through adjustment to changing price and income constraints. Yet this proposition requires first that the price mechanism functions according to spot market rules, reflecting changes in economic conditions, and second that these price signals are sufficient to induce behaviour which maximises welfare and efficiency. These assumptions are difficult to justify in an environment where there are:

• costs of acquiring information, and thus information gaps;

• transactions costs to be weighed against the benefits of change;

• idiosyncratic skills and specific human capital which reduce the possibilities for lifelong welfare maximisation.

Within the new institutional approach markets do fail, and much of the effort of economists has been devoted to 'explaining' obvious failures, as for example in the development of efficiency wage theories to 'explain' unemployment. Moreover, within this new theoretical approach employers and employees are often locked into long-term employment policies, which reduce the possibilities of the economy adjusting smoothly and quickly to changing signals through the price mechanism. Adjustment processes are also impeded by the specificity of investments, both economic and familial. This specificity reduces the scope for individuals to adjust to new or unforeseen conditions to maximise their lifetime welfare. The relationship between actual outcomes and welfare will depend upon the ability of individuals to predict and know their future needs and opportunities.

At the theoretical level there are thus indications of a convergence between mainstream and non-mainstream thinking concerning the need for policy intervention. The new institutionalism appears to provide more scope at a theoretical level for a positive role for policy intervention. Three main areas for policy intervention can be identified.

First, the greater scope for discretion accorded to employers in the shaping of pay and employment practices by the new institutionalist approach provides opportunities for discriminatory policies and practices. The 'discipline' of the market is no longer expected to bring about uniformity of outcomes, and employment policies which develop high-trust relations and increase commitment involve a degree of managerial choice in the design of employment practices not found in firms organised around simple rules such as wage minimisation. The pursuit of greater competitiveness motivates the development of firm-specific personnel policy, and thus the 'market' cannot be invoked as the appropriate means of ensuring fair play within internal labour markets. Policy intervention is thereby required to ensure discrimination is not embedded in these sophisticated employment practices. The areas of discretion identified in the contributions to this volume include, among others, the decision over whom to recruit, train and promote (Felstead, Chapter 8), the shaping of pay structures and internal labour markets (Grimshaw and Rubery, Chapter 5; Bruegel and Perrons, Chapter 7) and working time and family policies (Holtermann, Chapter 6; Plantenga, Chapter 12).

Second, significant incentives may need to be given to employers to induce a move from one employment system to another – or more specifically to change their employment practices to fit with a new gender order – even if in the longer term such a move may enhance their productivity and flexibility (Bruegel and Perrons, Chapter 7). This conclusion follows from a recognition of costs related to transactions – where change requires investment in the development of new institutional arrangements – and of the advantages which may accrue from co-operative and co-ordinated strategies. Such policies may need to be fostered among the various actors in order to move towards more socially and economically desirable solutions.

The case for concerted and co-ordinated action was highlighted in the discussion of the links between the welfare state and the labour market by McLaughlin (Chapter 13) and Gregg and Wadsworth (Chapter 15). Unless these linkages are recognised, policies to increase labour market flexibility may decrease rather than increase access to employment. Plantenga's discussion of part-time work in the Netherlands (Chapter 12) also suggests that co-ordinated policy intervention is required if part-time work is to achieve the objectives of a more family-friendly working environment without reinforcing women's disadvantage in the economic and social system. Maier (Chapter 9) also outlines how initiatives in the training and skills area must be co-ordinated with general labour market policies towards training, career and pay structures. Implementation of an equal opportunities training policy without reference to how it fits with current labour market practices is likely to be counter-productive. Without co-ordinated intervention individual agents will find it costly, perhaps prohibitively costly, to break out from the prevailing gender order or will adopt piecemeal strategies that may have perverse and negative effects on equal opportunities.

Third, if investments are specific, and thus not flexible and transferable, policy intervention is necessary to mitigate the effects of decisions on lifetime equity and employment chances. This approach emphasises the bounded rationality of economic agents and does not assume, as in much economic literature, that individuals are able to make decisions in the knowledge of their implications for the rest of their lifetimes. Much of the work on women's labour market participation and family formation has stressed that women are freely entering into decisions to quit the labour market or work part-time. However, not only are these decisions not necessarily made with full information relating to future costs, but some future costs (such as marital breakdown) are possibly excluded from calculations because of the nature of the contract involved (the marriage service still makes explicit that marriage is a lifelong commitment, despite the high divorce rate).

Clearly it is important to maintain the principle of freedom of choice over how to organise child-rearing and labour market participation, and not to assume that all women, or indeed all men, will wish to participate on a continuous and full-time basis. But equally it cannot be assumed that current choices have taken into account all the negative consequences of leaving the labour market or participating in part-time work. The consequences of marital breakdown and the dependence of women on inter-family transfers are identified in Davies and Joshi (Chapter 14), while the costs of quitting the labour market and taking part-time work have been well researched in the past by the same authors and by Dex amongst others (Dex and Walters, 1989; Dex and Shaw, 1986).

Joshi and Davies (1992) have estimated that following a discontinuous participation pattern may cost women around 50 per cent of their expected lifetime earnings as a result of three factors (loss of years in work, reduced hours of work and lower hourly pay), each of which contributes fairly evenly to the lower total income. In Chapter 14 in this volume the same authors show how women are 'compensated' for this loss through state and family transfers, but this system of compensation also demonstrates women's vulnerability to marital dissolution.

Attention thus needs to be paid first to whether participation decisions are made within a set of external opportunities (specifically low wages and poor childcare) which constrain women's choices. Under these circumstances there is a need for policy changes to ensure women's choices are being exercised with respect to their preferences for child-rearing and are not being dictated by their low market power. Secondly, policy intervention is necessary to offset the negative lifetime effects of a decision to interrupt or reduce participation, through improving opportunities for re-entry and retraining and providing better individual lifetime income protection, particularly in old age. Similar principles apply in decisions to intervene to provide pension and health insurance, on the grounds that it is not reasonable to expect individuals to know what level of provision they need to make for old age or ill health. A woman or indeed a couple coping with the incessant demands of a new-born baby cannot be expected to take full account of the effects of the decisions they make to deal with the immediate and non-postponable childcare requirements on their future life course.

Given the wealth of literature on sub-optimality, information gaps and bounded rationality, the question remains as to why economists have retained their predilection for placing their faith in market outcomes unless proven otherwise. This gap between theoretical developments and economic policy analysis can perhaps be explained by the problems which much of the new institutional literature pose for empirical analyses of economic phenomena. Thus although some externalities are recognised (such as marriage dissolution in Main, 1993), the general preference is still to treat the labour market as functioning according to similar principles and rules across all organisations. For example, wage differentials between men and women are explored with respect to differences in work experience and not employer-based pay policies, possibly because the former allows for a general measurement of rewards for human capital and thus a measurement of discrimination. When the scope for employer-based employment practices is recognised, economists become uncertain as to whether to treat these as 'market imperfections' but independent of gender discrimination (Paci *et al.*, Chapter 4), or as one of the ways in which gender discrimination becomes embedded in the economic and social structure (Millward and Woodland, Chapter 10).

However, perhaps a more fundamental reason for this gap is not the problems of empirical research *per se* but the problems for the economic profession posed by the new institutional approach. As Maurice *et al.* (1986) have commented, economists have searched to make their theories more realistic, but at the cost of precision, prediction and measurement. Thus most of the energy of economists has continued to be devoted to showing that, however much it may appear to the contrary, current policies and practices are consistent with welfare- and efficiency-maximising behaviour (Osterman, 1984). The new developments do provide scope for eclecticism, as Sawyer describes (Chapter 2), but eclecticism is not a satisfactory alternative paradigm and economists still therefore tend to cling to their belief in the price mechanism even in the face of market failure.

Perhaps the problem lies in economists desire to find a universalist model of economic life unhampered by the influence of historical and institutional influences, and thus one in which gender differentiation is at most an imperfection and not an historically-embedded characteristic of the economy. However, the legacy of the new institutional economics is to open up the area of choice in economic and social organisation and to allow for more than one form of 'best practice' organisation. As gender discrimination has been an important feature of all societies it is at least plausible to suggest that these choices have been influenced, in the past and in the present, by gender discrimination. Thus the *a priori* assumption that market outcomes are gender neutral unless prove otherwise should be rejected.

Economic calculus and the case for equal opportunities

As with economic theory, economic costings are often used to provide an argument against the pursuit of equal opportunities policies. However, just as it has been noted that economic theory provides a range of perspectives on the appropriate scope for policy intervention, so it is also found that calculations of economic costs depend upon the approach adopted. This will shape the definition of costs and benefits, and determine the extent to which non-monetary costs and benefits are identified and 'quantified' and also the time-scale and population over which the calculation is carried out.

The engagement with economic calculus by the advocates of equal opportunities policy has become that much more imperative as the language of economics, and of cost-based decision-making, has spread outside the traditional private sector to all areas of economic, social and public life. The notion of the 'bottom line' has been applied to areas where ethical and social criteria were previously held to be the relevant framework for decision-making. The development of the internal market in the health service is but one, if the most obvious, example of the use of cost-based rationales as the basis of decision-making in the public sector.

The first lesson policy advocates perhaps have to learn from this spread of economic language and reasoning is that to combat the logic of the economic case against equal opportunities it is first necessary to interrogate the costings that underpin the economic case; to investigate how decisions are made as to what to include as a cost and a benefit and how the costings are arrived at (see Holtermann, Chapter 6; Bruegel and Perrons, Chapter 7). The example of the training system in Britain is a case in point. As Felstead (Chapter 8) makes clear, if the system of performance criteria as currently specified in contracts between the government and the TECs is accepted then it follows, as a logical consequence, that the training system will tend to reinforce rather than modify the existing system of gender segregation. However, if the basis of performance indicators were weighted not only by level of qualification achieved and employment outcomes, as at present, but also by whether either 'hard to place' workers had received training and employment, or whether courses met equal opportunities objectives, then performance criteria could boost rather than dampen commitment to equal opportunities. Such a change in criteria has already been called for by the EOC (Felstead, Chapter 8).

Training is an example of a pseudo-market, where performance criteria substitute for market conditions but where ultimately decisions are based on political priorities. These issues are not confined to public sector organisations, as is demonstrated by accountancy research into the role of social choice in budgeting rules and the definition of costs (Burchell *et al.*, 1980). For example, even within the private sector performance criteria against which internal decisions are made cannot be assumed to provide a unique or even a close measure of productivity. This is illustrated in research on payment systems which in principle are linked to individual performance, and thus again are justified by economic calculus. Yet such research suggests there is high level of ambiguity in defining performance, with even different criteria being used to assess men and women in the same jobs (Bevan and Thompson, 1992).

The second, related, lesson is that economic calculus should not be allowed to play only a constraining role in equal opportunities policies. Instead the tools of economic analysis can and need to be used to strengthen the case for policy action. Many costs and benefits associated with economic well-being are not captured in the accounting framework adopted by single organisations; even at the national level the tendency has been to sum up the estimated costs to individual employers without reference to the effects on other areas of economic and social life. It is widely recognised that the costs of pollution, for example, cannot be captured within market-based costings, but the recognition of the possibility of externalities, or market interdependencies, associated with employment issues is generally not conceded in costings of employment policy initiatives.

The externalities that could derive from equal opportunities policies range from long-term improvements in childcare, and associated decreases in costs to tax-payers of coping with disadvantaged children, to a decrease in urban deprivation as more families may be released from the poverty trap of low wages and household means-tested benefits. Economists pride themselves on looking beyond the obvious first round to the second- and third-round effects of policy initiatives, but government condemnations of employment policies based on the supposed costs to the country are based only on employer costs, with no feedback effects and recognition of market interdependencies. The work in both identifying and estimating these second-round or longer-term costs and benefits has hardly begun, but the lesson for policy is the need to make such costs and benefits visible.

Alternative approaches and costings are necessary to demystify economics and thereby make clear that there is no one solution, and that current arrangements are not necessarily optimal. It is also essential to demonstrate that current economic calculations are not 'gender neutral', only 'gender blind'. Thus the outcome of policy changes are analysed either with respect to the whole population or to an 'average household', and issues of distribution within the household are not usually addressed. The claim to gender neutrality in economic calculus needs to be challenged by separate analyses of the impact of policies on men, women and children. Economic theories of welfare have long cast doubt upon the justification of policy outcomes by reference to average changes; it is not necessarily possible or ethically acceptable to argue for policies which harm one group or individuals simply because the monetary gains to other groups or individuals outweigh the losses.

Similar problems arise when making welfare assessments based upon the overall impact on the household. Such assessments ignore the problems of intra-household distribution and issues of the long-term welfare of individuals if households dissolve. Analysis of the impact on men and women separately should clearly not ignore the fact that individuals live in households, and there will thus be positive and negative feedback effects from one group to the other. The recognition that men live with women may in fact lead to a more positive view of some policies which are often regarded as not very useful for men because they mainly help women. For example, if women were able to secure more stable and better-paid employment, and allowed by the benefit system to keep their jobs when their partners become unemployed (see McLaughlin, Chapter 13), there may be major benefits to a significant section of the male population.

Targeted gender policies or 'mainstreaming'? Towards a two-pronged approach

There are two overriding reasons why considerable effort needs to be devoted to the 'mainstreaming' of equal opportunities issues. First and foremost, policy debates and initiatives are unlikely, even under the most optimistic scenario, to be driven by equal opportunities issues; but all policies are still likely to have equal opportunities consequences. These consequences need to be identified before and not after the decision is taken.

Such thinking lay behind a recent agreement in Vienna between member states of the United Nations European region, including the UK, to incorporate in the platform of action which will be put forward to the 1995 UN World Conference on Women, Equality and Peace a statement that:

> Rethinking employment policies is necessary to integrate the gender perspective and to draw attention to a wider range of opportunities as well as to address any negative gender implications of current patterns of work and employment. Major shifts in employment policies need... to ensure *all macro and micro economic policies are subjected to a gender impact analysis and that results of the analysis are recognised and acted upon.* (UN E/ECE/RW/HLM/L.3/ Rev 2, para 81; emphasis added.)

If this commitment was actually implemented and the results publicised there could well be a major change in political decision-making. At present no such gender analyses of major employment policy changes are presented. The new jobseeker's allowance is a case in point. The White Paper on the Jobseeker's Allowance does not identify how many women as opposed to men will be affected by the restrictions of non-means-tested benefits to six months, but women are less likely than men to be eligible for means-tested benefits. Moreover, the requirement to be available for 40 hours' work a week does not seem compatible with a gender neutral policy, and the statement that those with caring responsibilities will be able to agree different hours' availability only provides a discretionary right to seek less than 40 hours' work a week. If the government had to publish the gender implications of its policy changes, these effects would be more visible and thus more subject to public scrutiny. The need for mainstreaming relates to defensive as much as to positive policy initiatives, to ensure gains are not eroded through new policy interventions and to develop policies from the start which may at least mitigate if not eliminate negative equal opportunity impacts.

The second reason for mainstreaming is that a piecemeal, incremental approach to equal opportunities is unlikely to be completely successful. Programmes may need co-ordinated and concerted action across a range of policy areas, an agenda which is unlikely to be achieved through a targeted gender equality approach developed outside the main policy arenas.

However, a delicate balance needs to be maintained between the promotion of mainstream and targeted equal opportunities polices. It is the existence of specific laws and policies providing for equal treatment by gender both in Britain and the European Community which keeps the issue of gender equality in the public eye. Research also suggests that equal opportunities programmes have had a positive impact on women's economic position (Dex and Sewell, Chapter 16) and thus the impact of targeted policies should not be discounted. Moreover, gender-specific policies are much more likely to be enshrined in statutes and laws than any new commitment, as under the Vienna platform for action, to consider gender issues in all employment policies. Compliance with such commitments is thus more likely to be subject to the political complexion and attitudes of the incumbent administration.

An appropriate approach is thus likely to be two-pronged, where gender-specific policies are developed and maintained in part to keep up the momentum and pressure for mainstreaming. These issues are perhaps well demonstrated by the two chapters in this volume which look at policies and systems of pay regulation. Millward and Woodland (Chapter 10) show how the current trend towards decentralisation of pay determination may have negative consequences for gender pay equity, as it will allow the premium associated with working in male-dominated establishments to be maintained or even increased. Thus future progress towards equal pay requires either amendment of equal value laws to allow cross-establishment comparisons, or a general change in the direction of pay policy. Initiatives around equal value have, however, undoubtedly contributed to the development of research on the gender pay gap and the identification of problems with the current legislation.

The comparison between Australia and the UK (Hunter and Rimmer, Chapter 11) demonstrates further the significance of the overall pay determination system in determining the level of gender inequality, with the move to decentralisation in both instances associated with actual or potential deterioration in conditions for significant parts of the female workforce. However, the Australian case also indicates the potential to build in measures which promote some aspects of gender equality, even in policies that in general may be less favourable for women. One example was the Australian Accord in the early 1980s, which moved away from the full wage indexation which had benefited women in the past, but introduced scope for extending the coverage of non-wage benefits which proved highly favourable to women.

As a general principle it may be necessary for equal opportunities policy-makers to take whatever opportunities are available to intervene in the widest possible range of policy debates. It is particularly important to establish the principle that all policies have potential gender impacts that need to be identified and, where potentially large, should be monitored. Monitoring of the gender impact may also, as suggested earlier, have an important effect in the long term on policy decisions. However, a corollary of the need for monitoring is the requirement to promote policies which increase or at least maintain the transparency of the labour market.

Social justice versus efficiency: a false dichotomy?

Ultimately, the case for equal opportunities must rest on ethical arguments. It has been argued in this volume that economic theory and calculus can be used to defend and not only to constrain the adoption of equal opportunities policies. In particular it has been argued that it is necessary to 'demystify' economics; to understand how markets are constructed and the basis for the calculations of economic costs and benefits; to identify what is missed out as well as what is included; and to look for externalities as well as direct costs borne by companies. Furthermore, it must be remembered that organisations are not necessarily currently operating at maximum efficiency: there is often organisational slack and wastage which could be eliminated to generate resources to pay for equal opportunities, and firms constantly do adjust to changing costs.

Nevertheless, it remains the case that some economic calculations of costs and benefits, particularly where firms' interests are given priority over those of workers, may suggest that equal opportunities policies are costly. Such findings are not in themselves sufficient reason for not pursuing a policy. To take that approach would imply that women's claim on national resources should be treated as a residual, and that the costs borne by women under unequal opportunity should not be recognised and measured. Policy measures which redistribute costs from women to other agents should not be discounted on those grounds, and policies must therefore firstly be promoted on the grounds that they promote the ethical principle of gender equality.

However, the assertion of the ethical principle does not mean that there should not be a search for policies which can be seen either to enhance the efficiency of the economy in the narrow sense and/or lead to significant complementary benefits for groups other than women in the economy. The more gender equality interests complement rather than contradict the interests of other groups, the greater the chances of developing the political will to introduce the major and co-ordinated changes necessary to make more than incremental progress towards greater equality. The benefits to the economy may stem from the better utilisation of resources within the employment system, which would enhance the competitive edge of the economy.

Holtermann (Chapter 6) points to short-term immediate benefits which firms may derive from family-friendly policies; Bruegel and Perrons (Chapter 7) develop that approach into a more dynamic even if necessarily more speculative perspective, where moves to reduce gender segregation in the economy also help the economy to move out of the so-called 'low-skill equilibrium trap' and develop multi-skilled and functionally flexible workforces. This extends the argument beyond the opportunities to retain skilled workers in their current work positions, and implies freeing up the economy to move away from a gendered hierarchy of narrowly-defined jobs and skills towards a more positive, flexible and highly-skilled system of work organisation.

A positive scenario should not, however, be regarded as inevitable. Some firms may espouse equal opportunities policies in the hope of avoiding the need to adopt more modern and competitive production systems. For example, it has been argued that in the USA (Reskin and Roos, 1990) desegregation has occurred in circumstances where employers are no longer able to attract male applicants because of unfavourable terms and conditions. In these circumstances inefficient employers may disguise a switch to cheaper female labour from a weak competitive position as an equal opportunities policy. These employers are taking advantage of women's continued unequal position in the labour force to enhance their relative competitiveness. Thus equal opportunities policies pursued at a piecemeal level by individual organisations do not always move the economy towards a higher-skilled and more productive system of organisation. Again the debate comes back to the need for co-ordinated and concerted action if the economic benefits of equal opportunities policies are to be fully realised.

One potential important spin-off from equal opportunities policies, however, is improvements to the family economy. Much can and should be made of the possible coincidence of interests between other groups in the economy and the interests of women; the joint interests of children and women are served by better policies to facilitate the reconciliation of work and home life, and policies which enable women to provide a better standard of living and more stable environment for children. Another constituency which may gain from equal opportunities includes the partners of women who achieve better employment opportunities. Escaping from the poverty trap associated with unemployment is probably only possible if female partners as well as male partners have good employment prospects and opportunities.

The competition of interests between men and women in the lower segments of the labour market has probably been much exaggerated. As Gregg and Wadsworth (Chapter 15) show, many of the new flexible jobs are not effectively available to the male unemployed, particularly if they have children. The perpetuation of the influence of the male-breadwinner system in both the wage structure and the benefit system leads to the creation of jobs which can only be taken by individuals with alternative sources of income. Thus flexibility without equal opportunities policies may increase the rigidity of the labour market and contribute to social exclusion. On this basis the way forward for equal opportunities policy-makers may be to identify the joint interests of men and children in the development of greater gender equality in the labour market.

References

Bevan, S. and Thompson, M. (1992). *Merit Pay, Performance Appraisal and Attitudes to Women's Work*. IMS Report 234. Equal Opportunities Commission and Institute of Manpower Studies.

Burchell, S., Clubb, C., Hopwood, A. G. and Hughes, T. (1980). 'The role of accounting in organisations and society' in *Accounting, Organizations and Society*, 5 (1).

Dex, S. and Shaw, L. (1986). *British and American Women at Work*. London: Macmillan.

Dex, S. and Walters, P. (1989). 'Women's occupational status in Britain, France and the USA: explaining the difference' in *Industrial Relations Journal*, 20 (3).

Joshi, H. and Davies, H. (1992). 'Day care in Europe and mothers' foregone earnings' in *International Labour Review*, 132 (6).

Main, B. (1993). 'Where "equal" equals "not equal": women in the labour market' in *Sex Equality: Law and Economics*. Hume Papers on Public Policy, 1 (1). Edinburgh University Press.

Maurice, M., Sellier, F. and Silvestre, J.-J. (1986). *The Social Foundations of Industrial Power*. Cambridge, Mass: MIT Press.

Osterman, P. (1984). *Internal Labour Markets*. Cambridge, Mass: MIT Press.

Polachek, S. W. and Siebert, W. S. (1993). *The Economics of Earnings*. Cambridge: Cambridge University Press.

Reskin, B. and Roos, P. (1990). *Job Queues and Lender Queues*. Philadelphia: Temple University Press.

Tulloch, G. (1965). *The Politics of Bureaucracy*. Washington, DC: Public Affairs Press.

Tulloch, G. (1987). 'Public choice' in Eatwell, J., Milgate, M. and Newman, P. (eds.) *The New Palgrave: A Dictionary of Economics*. London: Macmillan.

UN E/ECE/RW/HLM/L.3/Rev. 2 (1994). *Regional Platform for Action-Women in a Changing World – Call for Action from an ECE Perspective*. High-level regional preparatory meeting for the Fourth World Conference on Women, Vienna.

APPENDIX # Bayesian inference

Some background to Bayesian inference and Bayesian statistics is provided in this appendix, since they are less well known than other methods, although Bayesian inference is often applied generally in science and economics. Koop (1994) has provided a survey of the range of applications of Bayesian methods in econometrics (for a useful summary and formal presentation of the issues, see *The New Palgrave: A Dictionary of Economics*, items on 'Bayes' and 'Bayesian inference'). This appendix is a very brief précis of the main points of the Bayesian approach, as described in *The New Palgrave*.

A paper by Thomas Bayes was published posthumously in 1763, in which two original ideas were put forward to solve a problem in probability. One was Bayes's Theorem. The other idea, which is more controversial, has been acclaimed as the only coherent form of inference (de Finetti, 1974–5). This second idea provides a solution to the central problem of induction, enabling one to pass from a particular experience to a general statement. A probability can be assigned to the general proposition before the particular is observed. Acceptance of this step rests on the assumption that all probabilities are subjective. Cox (1961), amongst others, provided a justification for using Bayes's Theorem as a central tool of inductive reasoning.

Conventional statistics calculates the direct probability, for example, of observing six heads in ten tosses of an unbiased coin. Bayes is considered to have solved 'the inverse probability problem'. In this case, six heads in ten tosses are observed, and what must be inferred is the chance that the probability of a head on a single toss lies in a given interval of, say, 0.5 to 0.75. The probability of a head on a single toss is unknown, and must be inferred from the outcomes. The inverse probability is typical of scientific problems where outcomes are observed and the probabilistic model that probably produced them must be inferred.

Chapter 16 employs Bayesian methods for the analysis of hypotheses about parameter values. This involves choosing prior probabilities – in fact, prior probability distributions – which reflect the degree of confidence associated with them. Bayes's Theorem is employed to calculate posterior probabilities which reflect the information in the sample data. Where cases have missing data on a particular variable, the authors enter an unknown distribution which spans the possible range of the variable in question.

This approach differs from non-Bayesian testing procedures, in which one hypothesis, the null hypothesis, is assumed to be 'true' and a test statistic's distribution, calculated assuming the null hypothesis is true, is used to 'accept' or 'reject' the assumed true null hypothesis. In the Bayesian approach, the null hypothesis is not assumed to be true, but is assigned a probability between zero and one. This assignment represents a formal representation about the researcher's opinions about the inductive (not deductive) validity of the null hypothesis. This subjective element has been the source of some debate, but advocates of Bayesian methods have pointed out that those who use non-Bayesian approaches frequently have to use subjective beliefs in order to get sensible results (Lehmann, 1959; Zellner, 1971, 1984). The difference is that non-Bayesian methods do not use subjective beliefs formally or consistently.

Bayesian methods involve a statement of uncertainty in the form of the prior probabilities and prior distributions for parameters. The calculation of the posterior distribution provides a representation of views about alternative hypotheses as reflected by the information in the data.

References

Cox, R. T. (1961). *The Algebra of Probable Inference*. Baltimore: John Hopkins University Press.

de Finetti, B. (1970). *The Theory of Probability, vol. 2*. English translation. New York: John Wiley, 1974.

Eatwell, J., Milgate, M. and Newman, P. (eds.) (1987). *The New Palgrave: A Dictionary of Economics*. London: Macmillan.

Koop, G. (1994). 'Recent progress in applied Bayesian econometrics' in *Journal of Economic Surveys*, 8 (1).

Lehmann, E. (1959). *Testing Statistical Hypotheses*. New York: John Wiley.

Zellner, A. (1971). *An Introduction to Bayesian Inference in Econometrics*. New York: John Wiley.

Zellner, A. (1984). *Basic Issues in Econometrics*. Chicago: University of Chicago.

Index to Subjects

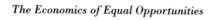

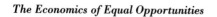

Index to Names

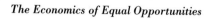

The Economics of Equal Opportunities